The UK Economy
A Manual of Applied Economics

The UK Economy
A Manual of
Applied Economics

Sixth Edition

Edited by

A. R. Prest M.A. Ph.D
Professor of Economics, London School of Economics

and

D. J. Coppock (B.A. Econ.)
Professor of Economics, University of Manchester

Weidenfeld and Nicolson

London

First published 1966
Second impression 1967
Third impression 1968
Second edition 1968
Second impression 1969
Third edition 1970
Second impression 1971
Fourth edition 1972
Fifth edition 1974
Sixth edition 1976

Weidenfeld and Nicolson
11 St. John's Hill, London SW11

ISBN 0 297 77230 9 cased
ISBN 0 297 77231 7 paperback

Text set in 10/11 pt. IBM Press Roman, printed by photolithography
and bound in Great Britain at The Pitman Press, Bath

CONTRIBUTORS

Chapter 1
> M. C. Kennedy *B.Sc. (Econ.) (London)*
> *Lecturer in Economics, University of Manchester*

Chapter 2
> N. J. Gibson *B.Sc. (Econ.), Ph.D. (Belfast)*
> *Professor of Economics, The New University of Ulster*

Chapter 3
> J. S. Metcalfe *B.A. (Econ.), M.Sc. (Manchester)*
> *Lecturer in Economics, University of Liverpool*

Chapter 4
> J. R. Cable *B.A. (Nottingham), M.A. (Econ.) (Manchester)*
> *Senior Lecturer in Economics, University of Warwick (on leave*
> *at International Institute of Management, Berlin);* assisted by
> M. Waterson *B.A. (Warwick) M.Sc. (London), Lecturer in Economics,*
> *University of Newcastle upon Tyne*

Chapter 5
> David Metcalf *M.A. (Econ.) (Manchester), Ph.D. (London)*
> *Reader in Economics, University of Reading*
> and
> Ray Richardson *B.Sc. (Econ.) (London), Ph.D. (Columbia)*
> *Lecturer in Economics, London School of Economics*

Contents

TABLES

FIGURES

STATISTICAL APPENDIX

ABBREVIATIONS

(1) Economic Terms

CAP	Common Agricultural Policy
c.i.f.	Cost including Insurance and Freight
FIS	Family Income Supplement
f.o.b.	Free on Board
GDP	Gross Domestic Product
GNP	Gross National Product
MLH	Minimum List Headings
PAYE	Pay as you Earn
PDI	Personal Disposable Income
R and D	Research and Development
REP	Regional Employment Premium
RPM	Resale Price Maintenance
SDRs	Special Drawing Rights
SIC	Standard Industrial Classification
SITC	Standard Industrial Trade Classification
TCF	Total Currency Flow
TFE	Total Final Expenditure at Market Prices

(2) Organizations, etc.

CBI	Confederation of British Industry
CIR	Commission on Industrial Relations
CSO	Central Statistical Office (UK)
DE	Department of Employment
DTI	Department of Trade and Industry
ECE	Economic Commission for Europe
ECSC	European Coal and Steel Community
EEA	Exchange Equalization Account
EEC	European Economic Community
EFTA	European Free Trade Area
FAO	Food and Agriculture Organization
GATT	General Agreement on Tariffs and Trade
IBRD	International Bank for Reconstruction and Development
IFC	International Finance Corporation
IMF	International Monetary Fund
IRC	Industrial Reorganization Corporation
MC	Monopolies Commission
NBPI	National Board for Prices and Incomes
NEB	National Enterprise Board
NEDC(O)	National Economic Development Council (Office)
NIESR	National Institute of Economic and Social Research

NRDC	National Research Development Corporation
OECD	Organization for Economic Cooperation and Development
OPCS	Office of Population Census and Surveys
PB	Pay Board
PC	Price Commission
TUC	Trades Union Congress
UN	United Nations
UNCTAD	United Nations Commission for Trade and Development

(3) Journals, etc.

AAS	*Annual Abstract of Statistics* (HMSO)
AER	*American Economic Review*
BEQB	*Bank of England Quarterly Bulletin*
BJIR	*British Journal of Industrial Relations*
BLS	*British Labour Statistics, Historical Abstract* (HMSO)
BTJ	*Board of Trade Journal* (HMSO)
DEG	*Department of Employment Gazette* (HMSO)
EC	*Economica*
EJ	*Economic Journal*
ET(AS)	*Economic Trends (Annual Supplement)* (HMSO)
FES	*Family Expenditure Survey* (HMSO)
FS	*Financial Statistics* (HMSO)
IFS	*International Financial Statistics*
JIE	*Journal of Industrial Economics*
JRSS	*Journal of Royal Statistical Society*
LBR	*Lloyds Bank Review*
LCES	*London and Cambridge Economic Service*
MBR	*Midland Bank Review*
MDS	*Monthly Digest of Statistics* (HMSO)
MS	*The Manchester School of Economic and Social Studies*
NIBB	*National Income Blue Book* (HMSO)
NIER	*National Institute Economic Review*
NWBR	*National Westminster Bank Review*
OEP	*Oxford Economic Papers*
PE	*Preliminary Estimates of National Income* (HMSO)
RES	*Review of Economic Studies*
ROT	*Report on Overseas Trade* (HMSO)
SIPEP	*Statistics of Income, Prices, Employment and Production* (HMSO)
SJPE	*Scottish Journal of Political Economy*
ST	*Social Trends* (HMSO)
TBR	*Three Banks Review*
TER	*Treasury Economic Report* (HMSO)
TI	*Trade and Industry* (HMSO)

Foreword to the Sixth Edition

In 1966, when the first edition of this book was published, the foreword began as follows:

> The central idea behind this book is to give an account of the main features and problems of the UK economy today. The hope is that it will fulfil two functions simultaneously, in that it will be as up to date as possible and yet will not be simply a bare catalogue of facts and figures. There are many sources of information, official and otherwise, about the structure and progress of the UK economy. There are also many authors to whom one can turn for subtle analyses of the problems before us. Our effort here is based on the belief that there is both room and need for an attempt to combine the functions of chronicler and analyst in the confines of a single book.
>
> The contributors to these pages subscribe rather firmly to the belief that economists should practise, as well as preach, the principle of the division of labour. The complexity of a modern economy is such that, whether one likes it or not, it is no longer possible for any individual to be authoritative on all its aspects; so it is inevitable that the burden of producing work of this kind should be spread among a number of people, each specialist in his or her particular field. Such a division carries with it obvious dangers of overlap and inconsistency. It is hoped that some of the worst pitfalls of this kind have been avoided and there is reasonable unity of purpose, treatment and layout. At the same time, it is wholly undesirable to impose a monolithic structure and it is just as apparent to the authors that there are differences in outlook and emphasis among them as it will be to the readers.
>
> The general intention was to base exposition on the assumption that the reader would have some elementary knowledge of economics — say a student in the latter part of a typical first year course in economics in a British university. At the same time, it is hoped that most of the text will be intelligible to those without this degree of expertise. We may not have succeeded in this; if not, we shall try to do better in the future.

Despite the usual extensive re-writing, we should still regard this an accurate description of our intentions.

Chapter 1, 'The Economy as a Whole', is primarily concerned with recent movements of total output and total demand in the economy. A good deal of time is spent on the short-term movements in demand and output of the last few years and the measures for dealing with them. Various problems of inflation and growth are also discussed. The chapter ends with a section on the economic prospects in the near future. Chapter 2, 'Monetary, Credit and Fiscal Policies', starts with a brief discussion of the general theoretical background and then analyzes in detail the theory and practices of monetary, credit and fiscal policies in the UK in recent years. The final section discusses the policy record and some policy implications of membership of the EEC. Chapter 3, 'Foreign Trade and the Balance of Payments', now written exclusively by Mr. J. S. Metcalfe, deals with the importance of foreign trade and payments to the UK economy and assesses UK balance of payments performance over the last two decades. It then looks at current problems and policies in this field and ends with a discussion of the reform of the international monetary system. Chapter 4, 'Industry and Commerce', has again had the assistance of Mr. M. Waterson in its preparation. It starts with a brief summary of various theories of the behaviour of firms and the structural characteristics of UK industry. Various aspects of public policy towards nationalized industries, competition policy and consumer protection, regional problems and so on are then discussed, all with due regard to the implications of EEC membership. A final section deals with industrial efficiency, including such issues as planning agreements and price control. The last chapter 'Labour', sets out the main characteristics of the UK labour force, and then discusses problems of wealth, income distribution, pay and incomes policy. The final section is concerned with trade unions and industrial relations.

Whilst we try to minimize unnecessary overlapping between chapters, we quite deliberately aim at complementary treatment of some topics. Thus different aspects of EEC membership are discussed in the relevant chapters; similarly, wages-inflation relationships appear in both Chapter 1 and Chapter 5. To minimize the use of space, factual material or definitions appearing in one chapter but relevant to another are not always duplicated and so it must be understood that to this extent any one chapter may not be self-contained.

Each chapter is accompanied by a list of references and further reading. The Statistical Appendix has twelve tables dealing with different aspects of the UK economy. There is an index as well as the detailed list of headings and sub-headings given in the Contents pages.

We acknowledge the great help given to us by Mr. J. Hassid in preparing the Statistical Appendix and by all those who have rendered secretarial or computing assistance.

London School of Economics
University of Manchester

A. R. PREST
D. J. COPPOCK

April 1976

1

The economy as a whole

M. C. Kennedy

I   INTRODUCTION
I.1   Methodological Approach

This chapter is intended as an introduction to applied macroeconomics. It begins
with a brief description of the national income accounts and goes on to discuss the
multiplier, the determination of national expenditure and output in the short run,
the policy problems of maintaining full employment, the causes of inflation and of
economic growth. It cannot claim to give all the answers to the questions raised,
but aims, in the space available, to provide the reader with a basis for further and
deeper study.

In principle there is no essential difference between applied economics and what
has come to be called economic theory. The object of applied economics is to
explain the way in which economic units work. It is just as much concerned with
questions of causation (such as what determines total consumption or the level of
prices) as the theory which is found in most elementary textbooks. The difference
between theoretical and applied economics is largely one of emphasis, with theory
tending to stress logical connections between assumptions and conclusions and
applied economics the connections between theories and evidence. Applied
economics does not seek description for its own sake, but it needs facts for the
bearing they have on the applicability of economic theory.

At one time it used to be thought that scientific theories were derived from
factual information by a method of inference known as *induction.*[1] Thus it was
supposed that general laws about nature could be deduced from knowledge of a
limited number of facts. From the logical point of view, however, induction is an
invalid procedure. For example, the fact that ten men have been observed to save
one-tenth of their income does not entail the conclusion that all men do so. The
conclusion may be true or false, but it does not rest validly on the assumptions.
Such conclusions have the status of conjectures and require further empirical
investigation.

More recently it has come to be understood that scientific method is not
inductive but *hypothetico-deductive.* This means that a hypothesis is proposed to
explain certain events, and from the hypothesis it is possible to deduce various
other factual consequences or predictions. If these predictions coincide with
observations of the factual evidence the hypothesis is said to be confirmed; but if
they are contradicted by the facts the hypothesis is said to be refuted or falsified.

It will be clear that this concept of scientific method places the role of factual

---

1 For a highly readable introduction to the problems of scientific method the reader is referred
   to P. B. Medawar, *Induction and Intuition in Scientific Thought,* Methuen, 1969, and the
   more serious student to K. R. Popper, *The Poverty of Historicism,* Routledge and Kegan
   Paul, 1961, and *Conjectures and Refutations,* Routledge and Kegan Paul, 1963. The
   distinction between 'normative' and 'positive' is set out in M. Friedman, *Essays in Positive
   Economics,* University of Chicago Press, 1953.

information in a rather different light from the inductive approach. Facts, instead of being the basis on which to build economic or scientific theories, become the basis for testing theories once they have been propounded. If a theory is able to survive a determined but unsuccessful attempt to refute it by factual evidence, it is regarded as well tested. But the discovery of evidence which is inconsistent with the theory will stimulate its modification or the development of a new theory altogether. One of the purposes of studying applied economics is to acquaint the theoretically equipped economist with the limitations of the theory he has studied. Applied economics is not an attempt to bolster up existing theory or, as its name might seem to imply, to demonstrate dogmatically that all the factual evidence is a neat application of textbook theory. Its aim is to understand the workings of the economy, and this means that it will sometimes expose the shortcomings of existing theory and go on to suggest improvements.

The discovery that a theory is falsified by some factual observation does not mean that it must be rejected out of hand or relegated to total oblivion. Economists, as well as natural scientists, frequently have to work with theories that are inadequate in one way or another. Theories that explain part but not all of the evidence are often retained until some new theory is found which fits a wider range of evidence. Frequently the theory will turn out to have been incomplete rather than just wrong, and when modified by the addition of some new variable (or a more careful specification of the *ceteris paribus* clause), the theory may regain its status. The reader who notices inconsistencies between theory and facts need not take the line that the theory is total nonsense, for it may still hold enough grains of truth to become the basis for something better.

It is often argued that our ability to test economic theories by reference to factual observations is sufficient to liberate economics from value judgements, i.e. to turn it into a *positive* subject. This position probably has more than an element of truth in it: when there is clear evidence against a theory it stands a fair chance of being dropped even by its most bigoted adherents. Nevertheless, it would be wrong to forget that a great deal of what passes for factual evidence in economics is somewhat infirm in character (e.g. the statistics of gross domestic product or personal saving) so that it is often possible for evidence to be viewed more sceptically by some than by others.

The discussion of economic policy which also figures in this chapter is partly normative in scope, and partly positive. The normative content of policy discussion consists in the evaluation of goals and priorities. But the means for attaining such goals derive from the positive hypotheses of economics. They involve questions of cause and effect, the hypothetical answers to which are appraisable by reference to evidence. In making recommendations for the achievement of policy goals, however, the economist treads on thin ice. This is partly because his positive knowledge is not inevitably correct, but also because it is seldom possible for him to foresee and properly appraise all the side-effects of his recommendations, some of which have implications for other policy goals. When economists differ in their advice on policy questions it is not always clear how much the difference is due on the one hand to diagnostic disagreements, and, on the other, to differences in value judgements. Indeed it is seldom possible for an economic adviser to reveal all the normative preferences which lie behind a policy recommendation. Thus policy judgements have to be scrutinized rather carefully for hidden normative assumptions. The reader of this chapter must be on his guard against the author's personal value judgements and he must remain critical of the hypotheses adopted. Economics is a young subject with uncertain answers even to some of the most pressing problems of our time.[1]

I.2   Gross Domestic Product

Most of the topics discussed in this chapter make some use of the national accounts statistics. A full explanation of what these are and of how they are put together would occupy more space than can be afforded and is, in any case, available elsewhere.[2] It will be useful, however, in the next few pages to remind the reader of the main national accounting categories in so far as they affect this chapter.

The most important concept of all is gross domestic product (GDP). This is the value of the total output of the whole economy. Its significance can be most readily appreciated by imagining that the economy is like some simple productive enterprise, such as a farm. Suppose that a farm produces only wheat, the total production during a single year being 100 bushels and the price £1. The value of total production is therefore £100. This is the sum which is divided as income between the various factors of production. It is distributed in the form of rent to the landowners, wages to the labour force and profit to the farmer. Thus total output is equal to total income. Furthermore, total output will also equal total expenditure on the output under the accounting convention that any output which is not sold for immediate consumption will be recorded as an addition to stocks, and as such regarded as investment expenditure by the farmer. Thus the income and output of the farm and the expenditure on its output are evaluated so as to make them identically equal to each other.

The GDP of the UK, by analogy with the simple production unit, can also be added up in three different ways: from the sides of income, output and expenditure. The first of these, total *income,* measures the sum of all incomes of the residents of the UK earned in the production of goods and services in the UK during a stated period. It divides into income from employment, income from self-employment and profit, and income from rent. These are factor incomes earned in the process of production and are to be distinguished from *transfer incomes,* such as pensions and sickness benefits, which are not earned from production and which, therefore, are excluded from the total. The breakdown of factor incomes for 1974 is illustrated in table 1.1 on page 4.

As with the simple production unit the value of output accruing in the form of unsold stocks is included in total factor output. But a problem arises when the prices at which stocks are valued in the national accounts vary during the course of the accounting period. When this happens the value of stocks held at the beginning and end of the period will have been reported at two different prices, and it is then necessary to make a special valuation adjustment known as the adjustment for *stock appreciation.* A firm holding stocks of wood, for example, may increase its holding

---

1   See E. H. Phelps Brown, 'The Underdevelopment of Economics', and G. D. N. Worswick, 'Is Progress in Economic Science Possible?', both published in *EJ,* March 1972.

2   See, for example, S. Hays, *National Income and Expenditure in Britain and the OECD Countries,* Heinemann, 1971; R. and G. Stone, *National Income and Expenditure,* Bowes and Bowes, 9th edition, 1972; H. C. Edey and others, *National Income and Social Accounting,* 3rd edition, Hutchinson, 1967; or the official handbook, *National Accounts Statistics, Sources and Methods,* HMSO, 1968.

TABLE 1.1

GDP and GNP at Current Prices, UK, 1974

FROM INCOME

	£m	% of domestic income
Income from employment	52,001	66.8
Income from self-employment	7,895	10.1
Income from rent	5,706	7.3
Gross trading profits of companies	9,706	12.5
Gross trading surplus of public corporations and other public enterprises	2,545	3.3
Total domestic income (before providing for stock appreciation)	77,853	100.0
less Stock appreciation	−5,964	
Residual error	736	
Gross domestic product at factor cost	72,625	

FROM OUTPUT

	£m	% of domestic output
Agriculture, forestry and fishing	2,116	2.8
Mining and quarrying	1,021	1.4
Manufacturing	20,645	27.4
Construction	5,645	7.5
Services and distribution	45,867	60.9
Total domestic income (after providing for stock appreciation)	75,294	100.0
Adjustment for financial services[1]	−3,405	
Residual error	736	
Gross domestic product at factor cost	72,625	

FROM EXPENDITURE

	£m	% of TFE
Consumers' expenditure	51,670	47.9
Public authorities' current expenditure	16,641	15.4
Gross domestic fixed investment	16,247	15.1
Investment in stocks	1,082	1.0
Exports of goods and services	22,205	20.6
Total final expenditure at market prices	107,845	100.0
less Imports of goods and services	−26,813	
less Adjustment to factor cost	−8,407	
Gross domestic product at factor cost	72,625	
Net property income from abroad	1,352	
Gross national product at factor cost	73,977	

Source: NIBB 1964-74, tables 1, 11, 51, 12. *ET,* October, 1975.

1 Deduction of net receipts of interest by financial companies.

from 100 tons on 1 January to 200 tons on 31 December. If the price of wood was £1.00 per ton at the beginning of the year and £1.10 at the end of the year the increase in the monetary value of stocks will show up as (£1.10 x 200) − (£1.00 x 100), which equals £120. This figure is inflated by the amount of the price increase and fails, therefore, to give an adequate record of what the Central Statistical Office (CSO) calls 'the value of the physical increase in stocks'. In order to rectify this the CSO attempts to value the physical change in stocks at the average price level prevailing during the period. If, in the example, the price averaged £1.05 over the period then the value of the physical increase in stocks would be shown as £1.05 (200−100) which equals £105. The difference of £15 between this and the increase in monetary value is the adjustment for stock appreciation. It must be deducted from the reported value of factor incomes in order to reach an estimate of gross domestic income.

GDP is measured from the *production* side by adding up the value of production of the various firms and public enterprises in the country. This procedure presents two types of problems. First, the goods and services produced by one firm may also form part of the output of some other firm. Wheat produced on a farm, for example, is entered as farm output. But it may also be used by a bakery as an input in the production of bread. If so its value will enter into the value of bread output as well as farm output. To eliminate double-counting of this kind a distinction must be drawn in the production accounts between, on the one hand, output sold to final buyers as total final output and, on the other hand, intermediate output sold to other productive units. Intermediate output must be excluded before arriving at a firm's contribution to gross domestic product.

A second problem arises in the case of imports which often form part of a firm's production (e.g. imported wheat in bread output), but which are produced by enterprises outside the UK. To arrive at UK domestic output, the value of imports must be deducted from the value of total final output. In table 1.1 the various categories in the output column are all evaluated net of intermediate output.

GDP can also be measured from the side of *expenditure*. Conceptually this total is identical to the income and output totals; but in practice the expenditure statistics are collected from independent sources and do not lead to exactly the same figure. The difference between the two estimates is known as the residual error and is sometimes quite large. In 1974 it was £736m, or about 1.0% of GDP.

The breakdown of the expenditure total is especially important in the analysis of aggregate demand. Expenditures are undertaken by four types of spending unit: persons, public authorities, firms and foreign residents.[1] Purchases by persons are described as consumers' expenditure, or, more loosely, as consumption. The latter description, however, may be slightly misleading when applied to expenditure on durable goods such as motor cars and refrigerators, the services of which are consumed over several years and not solely in the year in which they are purchased. One form of personal expenditure which is not classed as such is the purchase of new houses. These are deemed to have been sold initially to 'firms' and included under the broad heading of domestic capital formation or gross investment. Fixed investment, other than housing, represents the purchases by firms of physical assets that are not completely used up in current production, but which accrue as

---

1   The distinctions between types of spending units are not always clear-cut, e.g. expenditure by self-employed persons is partly consumers' expenditure and partly investment.

additions or replacements to the nation's capital stock. The preface 'gross' warns us that a year's gross investment does not measure the change in the size of the capital stock during the year because it does not allow for withdrawals from the capital stock due to scrapping, or for wear and tear. The concept of gross capital formation is also carried through into the definition of domestic product itself. Net domestic product is not easily measured but attempts to include only that investment which adds to the total stock of capital. It is less relevant to the level of employment than gross output.

The sum of exports, consumers' expenditure, government current consumption and gross investment is known as total final expenditure at market prices, or TFE for short. Each of the four components contains two elements which must be deducted before arriving at GDP at factor cost. The first is the import content of the expenditure which must, of course, be classified as foreign rather than domestically-produced output. The simplest way of removing imports is to take the global import total as given by the balance of payment accounts and subtract it from TFE, and this is the usual method. Estimates do exist, however, for the import content of the separate components of final expenditure in the input-output tables, but they are drawn up much less frequently than the national accounts. The second element of total final expenditure which must be deducted to obtain the factor cost value of GDP is the indirect tax content (net of subsidies) of the various expenditures. This is present for the simple reason that the most readily available valuation of any commodity is the price at which it sells in the market. This price, however, will overstate the factor incomes earned from producing the commodity if it contains an element of indirect tax; and it will understate factor income if the price is subsidized. The deduction of indirect taxes (less subsidies) is known as the *factor cost adjustment,* and is most conveniently made globally since it can be found from the government's records of tax proceeds and subsidy payments. Estimates of its incidence on the individual components of TFE are available annually in the National Income *Blue Book.*[1]

Gross domestic product from the expenditure side is thus reached by adding up the components of TFE at market prices, and by subtracting imports of goods and services together with the factor cost adjustment. It relates to expenditure on the total production in the UK of the residents of the United Kingdom. It differs from the other aggregate concept, gross national product (GNP), in that it does not include receipts of interest, profits and dividends by UK residents from productive activity carried out overseas; nor does it exclude the profits of foreign-owned enterprises producing in the UK. The balance of these two amounts is known as net property income from abroad and must be added to GDP in order to obtain GNP. It is a small total representing about 2% of GDP in 1974.

I.3   Gross Domestic Product at Constant Prices

Table 1.1 summarizes the national accounts for 1974 at the prices obtaining in 1974. As such it is a useful source of information as to the way in which domestic income, output and expenditure were divided in a particular year. If, however, we

---

1   *NIBB,* 1964-74, Table 12.

wish to compare the *volume* of goods produced in different periods we must use a different set of figures. These are the estimates of GDP at constant prices, the expenditure side of which is presented in the Statistical Appendix, table A-2. They show the value of GDP for each year in terms of the prices ruling in 1970. Similar estimates are available in index number form for the income total of GDP and for the output total together with its main industrial components. These totals are derived almost entirely from movements in quantities, the various quantities for each year being added together by means of the value weights obtaining for 1970. The result is three conceptually equal but independently derived estimates of real domestic output, and, as with the current price series, there are often large differences between them.[1] The existence of these differences means that there is normally some element of ambiguity as regards both the level of GDP in a particular year and changes between years. Thus the increase in real GDP between 1973 and 1974 was put at 1.0% by the expenditure estimate and at 0.6% by the output and income estimates. Since most macroeconomic discussion is concerned with expenditure relationships it is usual to put the main emphasis on this aspect of GDP.

Gross domestic product is an important entity in its own right and changes in its real amount are the best estimates available of changes in UK production. Even so, it must be remembered that it leaves a good deal out of the picture by excluding practically all productive work which is not sold for money. The national income statistics neglect, for example, the activities of the housewife and amateur gardener even though they must add millions of hours to UK production of goods and services. It is also important to recognize that GDP stands for the production of UK residents, not their expenditure. As an expenditure total it measures the spending of all persons, resident or foreign, on the goods and services produced by the residents of the UK. Thus if national welfare is equated to the expenditure of UK residents it is incorrect to represent it by GDP. The total appropriate for this purpose is GDP *plus* imports *minus* exports. This total is sometimes referred to as 'domestic absorption', and is equal to the UK's total use of resources, which is the sum of consumption, government expenditure and gross investment. It is an amount which can diminish quite substantially when there is a sharp correction to the balance of payments, such as might be expected from a devaluation of the currency.

I.4   Personal Income and Personal Disposable Income

Two further concepts, personal income and disposable income, are of importance in the analysis of consumption and the multiplier. Personal income is not directly obtainable from the income breakdown shown in table 1.1, although two of the categories there, employment income and the income of the self-employed, form part of it. The remainder consists of that part of total rent, dividends and profits which is actually paid to persons (a part of the total shown in table 1.1) and also transfer incomes received by persons from the central government and from charitable institutions. A full breakdown of personal income and personal disposable income is shown in tables 1.2 and A-3 (in the Statistical Appendix). It should be noted that the difference between personal disposable income (derived

---

1   These differences are usually referred to as 'the statistical discrepancies' so as to
    distinguish them from the residual error in the estimates at current prices.

TABLE 1.2

Personal Income, UK, 1974

	£m
Income from employment	52,001
Income from self-employment	7,895
Rent, dividends and interest	7,053
Current transfers to charities from companies	42
National Insurance benefits and other current grants from public authorities	7,850
Personal Income before tax	74,841
less	
National Insurance, etc, contributions	4,986
UK taxes on income	10,533
Transfers and taxes paid abroad	121
equals	
Total personal disposable income	59,201
of which	
Consumers' expenditure	51,670
Personal Saving (before provision for depreciation, stock appreciation and addition to tax reserves)	7,531

Source: NIBB, 1964-74, table 2 and *ET,* October 1975, table 5.

from the income side of the national accounts) and consumers' expenditure (derived from the expenditure side) is the most frequently quoted estimate of personal saving.

II   FLUCTUATIONS IN TOTAL OUTPUT AND EXPENDITURE
II.1   Fluctuations in Output and Employment

The British economy has experienced cyclical fluctuations since the time of the industrial revolution. During the nineteenth century these appear to have followed a fairly uniform pattern with a peak-to-peak duration of seven to ten years and a tendency for 'full employment' (roughly defined) to reappear at each cyclical peak. After the first world war this pattern ceased, and for nearly twenty years there were well over one million unemployed. Unemployment reached $12\frac{1}{2}$% of the work force in the recession of 1926 and 22% in 1932.

Since the second world war the business cycle has been much milder than before and unemployment has been relatively low. Nevertheless the cycle has not been without interest. Involuntary unemployment is wasteful and demoralizing even when it comes in small doses. And, whilst the national rate of unemployment has been low, rates in some of the regions (notably Northern Ireland, Scotland and the north of England) have been more disturbing. Again, the assumption by the state of responsibility for the level of employment, along with an improved understanding of how it may be regulated, has focussed political attention on each phase of the business cycle. Finally, there has probably been some connection between political popularity and the state of the economy.

The history of the postwar business cycle can be illustrated most directly by movements in the rates of unemployment or unfilled vacancies (figure 1.1). Movements in GDP have not displayed a typical cyclical pattern. The upturn of the cycle has always been reflected in a sharp increase in GDP, but GDP has seldom declined sharply in the recession phase of the cycle. In 1963, 1967 and 1971, for example, the annual increase in GDP was not sufficient to absorb the increase in potential output arising from the uptrend in output-per-man and/or employment. Thus unemployment increased without a corresponding drop in GDP. In two earlier recessions, 1952 and 1958, there were very slight declines in GDP (less than 0.5%), but the one outstanding exception to the postwar pattern was the most recent recession of all (1975) when the year-to-year decline in GDP was 1.8%.

The figures of unemployment and unfilled vacancies, both expressed as percentages of the labour force, indicate peak levels of economic activity in 1960-61, 1965 and 1973-74 whilst the main periods of recession are shown as 1963, 1971-72 and 1975. There is also a hint in the vacancy series of a minor peak in 1969 following a trough in 1967, although the unemployment figures suggest a prolonged period of stagnation between 1965 and 1973. In general the two sets of figures are in agreement about the *phases* of the cycle but in conflict as to its *intensity* (see p. 10).

The annual movements in employment shown in figure 1.1 tend to follow the same pattern as those of unemployment and vacancies. But they also reflect demographic factors such as movements in the total population of working age and its composition by age and sex, as well as social or institutional changes in the propensity to seek work. During the early 1960s there was still some upward trend in employment due to demographic factors with the result, in particular, that there was no decline in its level in the recession of 1963. In the later 1960s, however, the employment figures were affected by a levelling off in the population of working age, by a large increase in student numbers, and by the raising of the school-leaving age in 1973. The level of employment was almost exactly the same in 1974 as it had been ten years earlier.

Whilst employment and unemployment move together over the business cycle they seldom display the same relative variations from year to year. In most cycles the proportionate variation in employment exceeds the change in the unemployment percentage. This is probably explained by the presence of 'hidden unemployment', i.e. various groups of workers, such as married women, who do not register as unemployed when they are dismissed. A second common characteristic of cyclical movements in the economy is for the change in total output to be proportionately greater than the change in employment. This implies that productivity will tend to rise faster on the upturn of the cycle than on the downturn. It is explained partly by the presence of 'overhead labour', such as managerial and supervisory staff who remain on the payroll despite changes in turnover, and partly by a tendency for firms to 'hoard' labour, particularly those with scarce skills, during the recession so as to be sure of having it to hand when demand recovers.

Some of these characteristics are illustrated by the upturn of 1972-73 (see table 1.3).

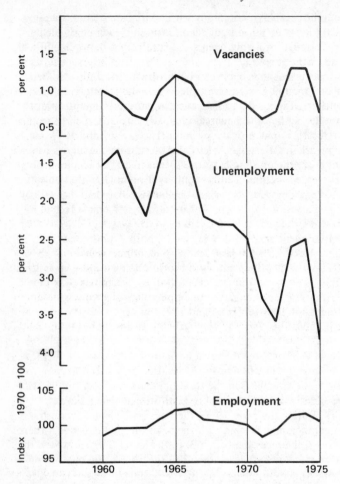

Figure 1.1   Vacancies, unemployment and employment, 1960-75.

TABLE 1.3

Changes in Output, Employment and Unemployment, UK, 1972-3 and 1974-5

Percentage change in:

	1972-3	1974-5
GDP	+5.3	−1.8
Employment	+2.0	−0.9
Unemployment	−1.2	+1.4

Sources: ET, October 1975 (average estimate of GDP and employed labour force), *NIER,* February 1976 (provisional employment estimate for 1976), *PE,* 1976, *DEG* (wholly unemployed excluding school-leavers and adult students as percentage of total employees).

The intensity of peaks and troughs: An accurate measure of the intensity of peaks and recessions is needed for policy purposes. It is important to have complete, sensitive and consistent indicators of inflationary pressure and of the degree of underutilization of resources. On two of these grounds the unemployment series is almost certainly superior. Most involuntary unemployment tends to be recorded because those involved are qualified to receive unemployment benefit and thus have a direct financial incentive to register. Unfilled vacancies, however, are recorded only in so far as employees believe it to be worth their while to report them to the employment offices. It is often argued that an employer who has notified vacancies for a particular type of worker will not bother to notify additional openings when they arise, since the original notice will itself be sufficient to attract job applicants. Thus the vacancy figures are incomplete, and it is officially estimated that only about one-half of all new vacancies are notified to the Department of Employment.[1] The vacancy figures also have a smaller cyclical amplitude (see figure 1.1) than the unemployment series, which suggests that they are not so sensitive to the varying intensity of the business cycle.

In the last ten years, however, both sets of statistics have been called in question by a sharp break in the relationship between them. Unemployment now tends to be higher for given levels of the vacancy rate than it used to be. This suggests that one or other of the two series, or possibly both, is not registering the intensity of labour shortage in the same way as before.

The actual measure of this shift in the unemployment-vacancy relationship can be assessed by comparing the two sets of figures at the peaks of 1965 and 1973-4 (figure 1.1). Vacancies were about the same in 1973-4 as in 1965 whereas the unemployment rate was higher by about 1.2%. A similar comparison may be made for the recessions of 1963 and 1971, where the recorded vacancies were the same but the unemployment rate was up by 1.5% in the second of the two recessions. Various explanations have been given for the shift in the relationship of unemployment to vacancies. One suggestion was that vacancies have been more effectively recorded than in the past as the result of active steps taken to improve the employment service.[2] This would imply that we should continue to prefer the unemployment series as our measure of cyclical intensity. Most of the argument, however, has gone the other way. Thus a second hypothesis is that the shift can be explained by an increase in 'structural' unemployment, i.e. by a tendency for the unemployed to be less well-matched in terms of skill, training and geographical location to the available vacancies.[3] If this explanation were true it would imply that unemployment was just as much involuntary now as in earlier periods. But it would also mean that greater difficulty than before would be encountered by attempts to reduce unemployment through increases in total demand. Bottlenecks and inflationary pressures would be likely to appear at higher rates of unemployment than previously. No evidence, however, has been found of any increase in the occupational mismatching of unemployment to vacancies, and there is only rather scant evidence of regional mismatching. Thus the case for a mismatching explanation of the shift, although it cannot be ruled out altogether, does not seem to be very solid.

---

1   See *BLS*, p. 18.

2   'Spare Capacity', *NIER*, November 1973.

3   J. K. Bowers, P. C. Cheshire, A. E. Webb and R. Weeden, 'Some Aspects of Unemployment and the Labour Market, 1966-71', *NIER*, November 1972, pp. 83-5.

Two explanations which seem to carry weight are the 'shake-out' theory and the argument that unemployment has increased because of better compensation. The shake-out theory rests on the supposition that since about 1968 employers have become much more economical in their use of labour, and, in particular, that the practice of hoarding labour between cyclical peaks was greatly diminished at about this time. The stimulus to greater economy may well have been given by the jolt to expectations of recovery after devaluation and by the promise in the Budget speech of 1968 of 'two years' hard slog'. Thus hoarded labour was shaken out with the result that recorded unemployment increased relative to vacancies.[1] The fact that output per man rose dramatically in 1968 (by 4.6%) is a point in favour of this hypothesis. But a weakness of the hypothesis is that it seems to imply a change in the relationship of vacancies to unemployment only in the recession phase of the cycle. One would expect a recovery of demand to be accompanied by a shake-in—a decline in unemployment faster than the rise in vacancies. This, however, did not happen when the recovery came in 1973. Vacancies rose to their previous peak level whereas unemployment did not fall correspondingly.

It seems possible that the raising of the school-leaving age in 1973 may have been responsible for a further shift in the vacancy-unemployment relationship in that year. But the fact that there was no restoration of the earlier relationship suggests that the shake-out hypothesis cannot be a complete explanation.

The remaining possible explanation is that better financial compensation for unemployment in the form of the earnings-related supplement introduced in 1965 and more generous redundancy payments (1966) have persuaded people to remain unemployed for longer periods than previously.[2] Under this hypothesis unemployment is less 'involuntary' than it used to be. Although this does not mean that anyone has volunteered for unemployment it could mean that there has been less willingness to accept job offers when they have been made. This hypothesis, unlike the shake-out theory, implies a new relationship of unemployment to vacancies at both the trough and the peak of the cycle. For this reason it seems to have a slight edge over the shake-out theory, but the issue is far from settled and it would not be surprising if a complete explanation did not embody elements from each of them. The main weight of argument and evidence, however, is now against believing that the unemployment statistics have acted as consistent indicators of the degree of scarcity of labour during the last ten years. The vacancy figures, incomplete though they undoubtedly are, probably function better as a barometer of the cycle.[3]

II.2   Expenditures in the Cycle

Fluctuations in domestic output have their origins in movements in total spending and its components. Theoretical accounts of the business cycle tend to stress investment fluctuations as the principal source of movements in the total, and this emphasis is largely confirmed by the figures in table 1.4.

---

1 See J. Taylor, 'The Behaviour of Unemployment and Unfilled Vacancies: Great Britain, 1958-71. An alternative view', *EJ*, December 1972.
2 See, for example, D. Gujarati, 'The Behaviour of Unemployment and Unfilled Vacancies: Great Britain 1958-71', *EJ*, March 1972.
3 For an official view see 'The Unemployment Statistics and their Interpretation', *DEG*, March 1975.

TABLE 1.4

Growth Rates of Expenditure (at constant prices) during the Main Cyclical Phases, UK, 1955-75
(*Percentage increases per annum*)

	1955-9	1959-61	1961-3	1963-5	1965-72	1972-3	1973-5
Fixed investment	4.6	9.4	0.8	11.1	3.1	2.6	−1.0
Investment in stocks (expressed as % of TFE)	0.0	0.2	−0.2	0.4	−0.2	1.4	−2.0
Exports	2.0	4.4	2.9	4.5	5.7	11.4	1.3
Government expenditure on goods and services	−0.6	2.9	2.4	2.1	2.6	4.2	3.5
Consumers' expenditure on goods and services	2.5	3.2	3.3	2.3	2.4	4.8	−0.6
Indirect taxes net of subsidies	3.6	3.4	2.1	2.5	3.1	6.7	−1.4
Imports	2.6	5.4	2.8	5.0	5.8	13.6	−2.7
GDP (average estimate)	1.7	4.1	2.5	4.4	2.2	5.3	−0.5

Sources: NIBB, 1964-74, *ET*, October 1975, figures for 1975 from *NIER*, February 1976.

Fixed investment has tended to grow at a much faster rate of increase per annum in the upswings of the cycle than in the ensuing downswings. The same is true of investment in stocks which, despite their small size relative to TFE, can swing so violently as to have quite substantial effects upon the level of total demand. The turnround from stock accumulation in 1973 to destocking in 1975 for example, resulted in a reduction of about 1.5% in TFE.

Whilst the investment items tend to move in phase with the cycle they are by no means the only source of fluctuations. The UK is an open economy in which exports of goods and services account for nearly one-fifth of TFE. When there is a recession in overseas markets, whether in the industrial or primary producing regions, the effect is either to reduce UK exports (as happened in 1951-2) or more usually to slow down their rate of increase. Table 1.4 suggests that most of the main downswings in the UK economy were associated with a slackening of demand overseas. Since 1967, exports have also been affected by devaluation and by the downwards floating of the exchange rate.

There is no reason to expect government expenditure to move closely with the cycle or against it. In 1972-3, its increase contributed to the upturn and was part of the government's recovery programme. In the recession of 1955-9, however, the decline in government spending reflected a cutback in defence expenditure, and was not introduced with the express intention of reducing the pressure of demand. Government expenditure can be used for stabilization purposes, but its main movements have originated with changes in social policy or defence.

Whereas government expenditure, investment and exports can be regarded as the principal *autonomous* causes of demand fluctuations, consumption and imports (and also indirect taxes) are often thought to be *dependent* directly upon total income and indirectly upon the autonomous expenditures. This distinction between the autonomous and dependent items cannot be completely watertight since all of the latter are capable of moving autonomously for other reasons. But it is a useful first approximation.

The dependence of consumers' expenditure upon GDP is not as well confirmed in table 1.4 as might have been expected. The rate of increase has not been noticeably faster in the upturn of the cycle than in the downturns. This is partly because of variations in tax rates. Indirect taxes are levied mainly upon consumption so that it is hardly surprising that their proceeds (net of subsidies) have moved closely in line with consumption.

Finally, it is noticeable from table 1.4 that the rates of increase in imports have moved in phase with those of GDP, but that their fluctuations have shown a somewhat larger amplitude. This reflects the fact that imports are taken first into stock, and tend to fluctuate with stockbuilding as well as with GDP.[1]

In the next section we describe some of the main hypotheses which have been advanced to explain movements in the components of total demand.

III   THE DETERMINANTS OF DEMAND

The level of national output is determined in the short run by the level of total expenditure. This is the sum of all demands for domestic output, and thus comprises all the elements of TFE net of their import and indirect tax components. A large area of macroeconomics is devoted to the attempt to explain how these expenditures are determined. Such explanations are essential if we are to understand economic fluctuations and to be able to forecast and control them.

III.1   Consumers' Expenditure

Consumers' expenditure is the largest single element in aggregate demand. It accounts for half of TFE (see table 1.1) and, after the removal of its import and indirect tax content, for about the same proportion of GDP at factor cost. Consumption is one of the more stable elements of demand in the sense that its fluctuations are small when measured as percentages of its total. But its total amount is so large in relation to GDP that even quite small percentage variations in it can have important repercussions for output and employment. An understanding of consumption behaviour, therefore, as well as an ability to predict it, are important objectives for economic analysis. A great deal of attention has been given to consumption, both in theory and statistically, although this work has been more heavily concentrated upon consumption in the US where the relevant statistical data are available for a longer period than for the UK.

The starting point for most studies of consumer behaviour is the well-known statement by Keynes[2]: 'The fundamental psychological law upon which we are entitled to depend with great confidence both *a priori* from our knowledge of human nature and from the detailed facts of experience, is that men are disposed, as a rule and on the average, to increase their consumption as their income increases, but not by as much as the increase in their income.' Keynes was

---

1   For a further discussion of cyclical fluctuations see J. C. R. Dow, *The Management of the British Economy, 1945-60,* Cambridge University Press, 1964, ch. 4 and R. C. O. Matthews, 'Postwar Business Cycles in the United Kingdom', in M. Bronfenbrenner (ed.), *Is the Business Cycle Obsolete?,* Wiley, 1969.

2   J. M. Keynes, *General Theory,* p. 96.

suggesting that current income was the principal, although not the only, determinant of consumers' expenditure in the short run, and that the marginal propensity to consume (MPC), i.e. the ratio of additional consumption to additional income, was positive, fractional and reasonably stable. In point of fact the MPC, when measured as the ratio of changes in the annual value of consumers' expenditure to changes in annual income, has not been particularly stable, nor always fractional, or even always positive. Between 1952 and 1974 the value of the MPC varied between 0.7 and 1.2 with an average annual value of 0.9. It was not fractional (i.e. it exceeded unity) in six years.[1] Provisional estimates for 1975 suggest that it may have then been negative, consumers' expenditure having fallen despite a very large increase in the nominal value of personal disposable income.[2] There is very little evidence for the proposition that the annual value of the MPC is stable, and less than unity.

If we focus attention upon savings rather than consumption it can be seen (figure 1.2) that the ratio of personal savings to personal disposable income has shown a strong upward trend over the postwar period with sizeable deviations from trend which have the appearance of cyclical fluctuations. The savings ratio was above trend in the peak years of 1956, 1961 and 1965 and below trend in the intervening recessions. These movements will have meant increases in the marginal propensity to save (MPS) on the upturn of the cycle and decreases on the downturn. The MPC, inevitably, has tended to rise in the downturn and increase in the upturn.

Cyclical movements in the savings ratio can be accounted for in various ways. One possible explanation is that consumer behaviour is driven partly by habit and convention so that when income declines the individual attempts to maintain his expenditure at its previous level with the consequence that the APC rises and the savings ratio declines. A related explanation can be found in the ideas of the normal income theorists.[3] Their main proposition is that consumption does not depend upon current income but on normal income, a concept which can be defined either precisely as the expected lifetime income of the consumer or much more vaguely as his notion of average income over some ill-defined future period. Thus it is changes in the level of income expectations which are likely to change consumption. If current income increases then it will raise consumption only in so far as it raises normal income, and the amount by which it raises consumption will depend upon the expected persistence of the income change. Cyclical changes in income are (by definition) not persistent, and the likelihood is that some consumers, perhaps a majority, will recognise them as such. Thus the APC will tend to rise during depressions and fall on the upturn, whilst the savings ratio will do the reverse. It is not impossible that the normal income hypothesis can also explain the pronounced and steady rise in the savings ratio since 1971 if, as seems plausible, the higher

1 Measured at constant prices the MPC varied between − 0.5 and 2.6. It was not fractional in six years and negative twice.

2 *NIER*, February 1976, p. 10.

3 For an examination of these theories, see M. J. Farrell, 'The New Theories of the Consumption Function', *EJ*, December 1959 (reprinted in Klein and Gordon (eds.), *Readings in Business Cycles*, Allen and Unwin, 1966); M. Bruce Johnson, *Household Behaviour*, Penguin Books, 1971. The classic reference is F. Modigliani and R. Brumberg, 'Utility Analysis and the Consumption Function' in K. Kurihara, *Post-Keynesian Economics*, Allen and Unwin, 1966.

average level of unemployment, the slowing down of real income growth and, more recently, the threat of anti-inflationary policies, have led consumers to revise their long-term income expectations downwards. But a further factor in 1975 was the additional uncertainty of real income expectations due to the rapid inflation. The problem with all these explanations, however, is the extreme difficulty in finding objective evidence of income expectations and of the degree of certainty with which they are held.[1]

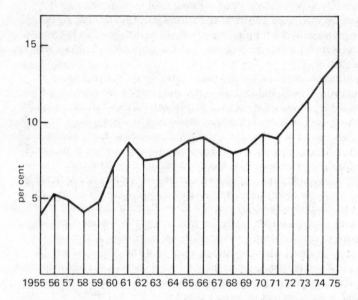

Figure 1.2   Personal savings as a percentage of personal disposable income, UK, 1955-75.

Whilst a change in the climate of expectations may have been partly responsible for the climb in the savings ratio between the 1960s and 1970s it is not clear why there should have been an uptrend in the 1950s. Postponed consumption after the second world war would explain a very low savings rate in the 1940s, but it is difficult to believe that it could have been responsible for the savings rate rising in the 1950s. Thus there may be something in the hypothesis that consumer wants tend, as Keynes once suggested, to become saturated as income increases, or at least that the income-elasticity of consumption in general is less than unity. If so then consumers would appear to have behaved differently in the UK from those in the United States, where the savings ratio has been roughly stable for a century despite enormous increases in personal income.

Besides current and normal income it is usual to recognize personal assets and

1   In periods when the APS is increasing there is generally an increase in the liquid assets of the personal sector. This is sometimes taken to be the *cause* of the higher savings ratio (see, for example, *BEQB*, March 1976) but in our view is more correctly considered as the *effect* of higher savings.

interest rates as two further influences upon consumption. Interest rates have not varied greatly from one year to another so that it is difficult to detect their effect on consumption. Keynes pointed out that this could be either positive or negative depending upon whether the income effects were sufficiently large to offset the substitution effects.[1] But in any case interest rates have probably not been sufficiently variable in the UK to have had much effect either way. Not much evidence is available on the role of personal assets, although they have been found to exert an influence upon consumer purchases of durable goods. These generally tend to vary inversely with the ratio of the durable goods stock to income.

A more important influence upon consumers' expenditure is the availability of credit, and particularly of credit for financing purchases of durable goods.[2] These goods, which constitute 7-9% of total consumption, are more of the nature of capital equipment than of consumption in that they yield a flow of utility over time. It is natural where income is generally rising that such goods should be bought extensively on credit, and something like one half of their total is financed by hire-purchase. The availability of this form of finance has been subject to government regulation in two main ways: by the stipulation of a minimum HP deposit and by the specification of a maximum period of repayment. The regulations have been varied extensively and have been associated with sharp but short-lived fluctuations in durable goods expenditure. The raising of the minimum down-payment, for example, means that an individual must wait a month or so longer in order to save the additional sum. Thus the effect of such restrictions is to postpone purchases rather than to alter their level in the longer run.

The explanation of aggregate consumption is usually regarded as one of the more satisfactory aspects of aggregate demand economics. In recent years, however, estimated consumption functions have furnished bad predictions of actual consumption,[3] and this has disturbed confidence in the economic theory of consumption. The uptrend in the savings ratio, moreover, and its contrast with US experience also leave room for further investigation.

III.2   Gross Fixed Investment

Fixed investment or gross domestic fixed capital formation is a heterogeneous total, comprising housing and business investment in both the public and the private sectors. Its breakdown by industry and sector in 1974 is shown in table 1.5. Of the three main components of total fixed investment it is manufacturing investment which is the most volatile. Investment in dwellings is the least volatile of three types of fixed investment. Nevertheless all three sectors vary enough from year to year to have important effects upon output and employment.

A hypothesis which goes some way towards explaining the behaviour of manufacturing investment is the capital stock adjustment principle. This states that the level of investment is related positively to the level of output and negatively

---

1   There is econometric evidence in favour of both cases – see R. Ferber, 'Consumer Economics, A Survey', *Journal of Economic Literature*, December 1973.

2   It should be noted that the *Blue Book* definition of durable goods includes cars, motor cycles, furniture, carpets and electrical goods, but, perhaps arbitrarily, does not include clothing, curtains, pots and pans or books.

3   See *NIER*, February 1976, p. 82.

TABLE 1.5

Gross Domestic Fixed Capital Formation, UK, 1974 (£m)

	Private sector	Public sector	Total
Dwellings	1,698	1,433	3,131
Manufacturing	2,982	278	3,260
Other fixed investment	4,649	5,207	9,856
Total	9,329	6,918	16,247

Source: NIBB, 1964-74, p. 122; current prices

to the existing capital stock (of land, buildings and machinery in productive use). The principle may be expressed as:

$$I_t = aY_{t-1} - bK_{t-1}$$

or, in ratio form, as

$$\frac{I_t}{Y_{t-1}} = a - b\frac{K_{t-1}}{Y_{t-1}}$$

Here I_t stands for gross investment in the current year, Y_{t-1} for last year's level of output, K_{t-1} for the capital stock at the end of the preceding year; and a and b are constant coefficients. The principle may be interpreted in various ways, one of which is to assume (not too implausibly) that technology dictates a fixed proportional relationship between the stock of capital equipment and the level of output. It follows, since net investment is an increase in the capital stock, that its amount will be planned in relation both to the expected volume of production and to the current size of the capital stock. If it is assumed as an approximation that the expected volume of output is equal to the level most recently experienced, then the expressions above may be seen to hold.[1]

---

1 The equations are derived by denoting K_t^* as the desired capital stock, Y_t^* as expected output, R_t^* as desired replacement investment, I_t^* as desired gross investment and I_t as actual gross investment. Then, by definition,

$$I_t^* = K_t^* - K_{t-1} + R_t^*$$

and, by assumption:

$$I_t = b I_t^* = b (K_t^* - K_{t-1} + R_t^*)$$
$$K_t^* = a_1 Y_t^*$$
$$R_t^* = a_2 Y_t^*$$
$$Y_t^* = Y_{t-1}$$

$$\therefore \quad I_t = b(a_1 Y_{t-1} - K_{t-1} + a_2 Y_{t-1})$$
$$= b(a_1 + a_2) Y_{t-1} - bK_{t-1}$$
$$= aY_{t-1} - bK_{t-1} \text{ where } a = b(a_1 + a_2)$$

Figure 1.3 illustrates the inverse relationship between the investment ratio and the capital-output ratio implied by the stock adjustment principle. It shows a fairly close correspondence between peaks in one ratio and troughs in the other. An estimate of the relationship by least-squares regression is as follows:

$$\frac{I_t}{Y_{t-1}} = .381 - .091 \frac{K_t}{Y_{t-1}}$$

where I_t, K_t and Y_{t-1} all refer to manufacturing industry. The equation fits the data moderately well. The residual errors between the estimated and actual data averaged out at the equivalent of 3½% of total manufacturing investment, and they exceeded 10% in four years out of the eighteen. The size of the residuals, however, must be judged in relation to an expenditure total which is highly volatile, and in

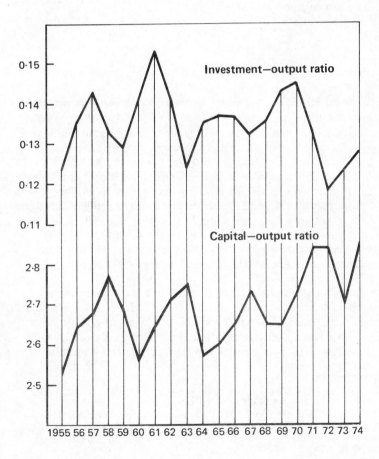

Figure 1.3   Manufacturing investment and capital stock as ratios of manufacturing output, UK, 1955-74.

which year-to-year changes exceed 10% in nine years out of eighteen.[1] It seems possible to conclude that there is at least an element of truth in the stock-adjustment principle, even though, it is difficult to regard its expectational and technological assumptions as more than approximately true.

Economic theory suggests that there are a number of relevant considerations ignored by the stock-adjustment principle. One of these is the expected profitability of the investment, which although related to the volume of expected sales and output is dependent on other factors too. Expected profitability is likely to be guided by actual profitability which, in recent years, has been exceptionally low. The ratio of profits to GDP has fallen very sharply and so too has the rate of return on capital employed:

	Averages		
	1964-9	1970-3	1974
Gross trading profits net of stock appreciation as percentage of GDP	13.2	10.4	6.6
Rate of return on capital employed (after providing for stock appreciation)	9.6	7.2	4.0

(*Source: NIER*, February 1976, pp. 83-4.)

There is not much doubt that these trends go a long way to explaining why investment in the 1970s fell so low relative to GDP.

A further factor is the rate of interest which, as the cost of borrowing, can never be completely ignored as an influence upon the level of investment. Interest must be paid on all funds that are borrowed from outside the firm and it must be forgone on internal funds which could have been lent at interest but which, instead, are used to finance the firm's own investment projects. If interest rates had fluctuated violently it would have been necessary to include them as an additional variable in the determination of investment in the UK. But they have shown only rather modest movements. Between 1958 and 1973 the largest annual rise in the debenture rate was 2% in 1968-9, and even this seems unlikely to have exerted any significant effect upon investment intentions. In 1973-4, however, the debenture rate rose from 11.4 to 16.4% and this almost certainly affected investment. But in general interest rates have been dormant rather than active determinants of fixed investment.

Another factor which must surely be taken into account in any general explanation of investment behaviour is the availability of funds for investment and the constraints that from time to time have been imposed by credit policy. Investment is financed predominantly from internal sources and only partly from outside credit institutions.[2] As far as internal sources are concerned it must be

1   The equation was estimated at 1970 prices for 1953-72. Its other statistical characteristics were r^2 = 0.57, t-statistics 7.50 and 4.84 respectively, Durbin-Watson statistic 1.42, standard error of the investment ratio 0.007. The mean prediction error for 1963-72 from a similar equation fitted to 1953-62 data was equivalent to 3.9% of the level of investment. The capital-stock data for 1955-63 were taken from *LCES* and converted into 1970 prices; otherwise *NIBB* 1964-74.

2   During 1954-63 some 70-90% of company investment was financed from internal sources. See 'Internal and external sources of company finance' reprinted from *ET*, February 1966, in CSO, *New Contributions to Economic Statistics*, Fourth Series, HMSO, 1967.

accepted that company profits, besides acting as a guide to future profitability, will also act as a financial constraint upon investment. As for external sources of credit, there seems little doubt that their availability or otherwise must be an influence of some importance, especially on the investment of small firms.

Other business fixed investment does not appear to conform with the capital stock adjustment principle anything like as readily as manufacturing investment. This may be because the assumption of a fixed relationship between capital and output does not hold well in non-manufacturing industries. It is less easy, therefore, to explain investment in these industries, although it must still be the case that expected sales, profits, interest rates and credit availability are relevant influences. Econometric studies have claimed a role for lagged changes in domestic output,[1] whilst short-term forecasts can be made on the basis of investment intentions surveys such as those carried out by the Department of Trade and Industry, the CBI and the *Financial Times.*

Housing investment needs to be divided between the public and private sectors and examined in relation to demand and supply influences in both sectors. The demand for public sector building comes indirectly from population trends and directly from the policies of the public authorities. The demand for private sector building depends upon both population characteristics (family formation and size) and also upon expected lifetime income, the cost of mortgage credit, the prices of new houses and of substitute accommodation. It is subject to the important and highly variable constraints set by the availability of mortgage credit which in turn are determined partly by general credit policy and partly by the policies of the building societies. Among the main influences on the side of supply are the size of the building industry and the number of building workers, the price and availability of building land, and stocks of bricks and other building materials. With such a variety of factors at work it is not easy to construct or present a satisfactory model of the determination of housing investment, and we do not attempt the task in this chapter. The problem of predicting housing investment is eased, however, by the statistics of new houses started, which, with an assumption about completion times, make it possible to forecast housing for at least a short period ahead.

III.3   Stocks and Stockbuilding

Stockbuilding or investment in stocks is the change in a level — the level of all stocks held at the beginning of the period. In any one year stock investment can be positive or negative, whilst the change in stock investment between successive years can exert an important influence upon GDP. The decline in stock investment in 1970-71, for example, was equivalent to 0.8 per cent of GDP whilst the increase in 1973-4 was equivalent to 1.5 per cent of GDP. At the end of 1974 the total value of stocks held in all industries was approximately £31,000m, or 43% of the value of GDP in a year. Stocks held by manufacturing industry amounted to £18,600m, or about 76% of the annual value of manufacturing output. Manufacturers' stocks

---

1 For example M. J. C. Surrey, *The Analysis and Forecasting of the British Economy*, NIESR and Cambridge University Press, 1971, p. 32, and HM Treasury, *Macroeconomic Model, Technical Manual*, February 1976.

divide into materials and fuel (£7,500m), work in progress (£6,500m) and stocks of finished products (£4,600m).[1]

Stocks of work in progress are held because they are a technical necessity of production, whilst stocks of materials and finished goods are held mainly out of a precautionary motive. They are required as a 'buffer' between deliveries and production; or, more precisely, because manufacturers are wise enough to know that they cannot expect an exact correspondence between the amount of materials delivered each day and the amount taken into production, or between completed production and deliveries to customers.

For these reasons it seems plausible to assume that manufacturers carry in their minds the notion of a certain optimum ratio between stocks on the one hand and output on the other. If stocks fall below the optimum ratio they will need to be replenished; if they rise above it they will be run down. The reasoning here is the same as that of the stock adjustment principle which we have already considered in connection with fixed investment. The principle holds moderately well for manufacturers' stockbuilding, which is by far the most volatile part of stock investment in the UK. Its application is illustrated in figure 1.4, where it can be seen, for example, that the stock investment peaks of 1956, 1960 and 1964 all coincided with low values of the stock-output ratio.

A regression estimate of manufacturers' stockbuilding using annual data is:

$$\frac{I_t}{Y_{t-1}} = 0.299 - 0.41 \frac{S_t}{Y_{t-1}}$$

where the terms all refer to manufacturing industry and S_t stands for the level of stocks held at the beginning of the year. The quality of this regression equation is less good than that for fixed investment. Its mean residual error (regardless of sign) is about 0.007 in units of stockbuilding-output ratio, and is equivalent to an average annual error of £80m at 1970 prices. This figure may be put in the perspective of a mean annual change in investment in stocks over the period of £150m.[2] It is probable that this equation would have performed better if we had estimated it for quarterly or semi-annual periods. This is because manufacturers are hardly likely to plan their stock changes for as long as a year ahead.

The stock adjustment principle is only the beginning of a complete explanation of planned investment in stocks. Other factors are likely to be the level of interest rates, the availability of credit, expected future prices and the degree of uncertainty. *Unplanned* movements in stocks, moreover, will occur whenever sales expectations are falsified. Thus there will be an involuntary accumulation of stocks if sales fall below expectation, and an involuntary run down of stocks if sales exceed their expected volume.

---

1 *NIBB*, 1964-74, table 76. The other main holders of stock are wholesale and retail businesses.

2 The estimation period was 1952-70, but excluded 1960 and 1964 which are both well above estimate: $r^2 = 0.40$, the t-ratios were 3.4 and 3.2 respectively, Durbin-Watson statistic 1.94, and the standard error of the equation was 0.009 in units of the stockbuilding-output ratio. A similar equation fitted for 1952-61 predicted the ratios for 1962-70 with a mean error (regardless of sign) of 0.013; the errors for 1971 and 1972 were large.

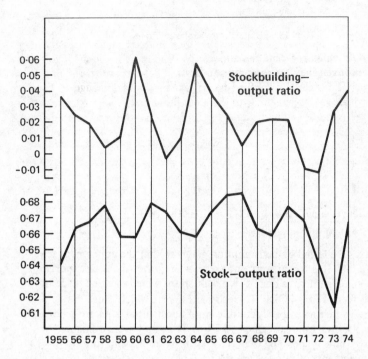

Figure 1.4   Manufacturers' stockbuilding and stock level as ratios of manufacturing output, UK, 1955-74.

III.4   Other Expenditures

It remains to discuss two further components of TFE — exports and public authorities' expenditure on goods and services — and two items which have to be deducted from TFE to obtain GDP — indirect taxes (net of subsidies) and imports of goods and services.

There is little to be said about public current expenditure since its amount is determined by the political aims and priorities of the central government and the local authorities. Exports of goods and services depend upon overseas demand which in turn is mainly influenced by the volume of overseas income (both in the industrial and primary producing areas), the sterling price of UK exports and the exchange rate.[1] These matters, however, are discussed more fully in chapter 3.

The components of TFE are normally evaluated at their market prices. If we are interested in UK production and factor incomes we must make the factor cost adjustment, i.e. deduct from these values the sum of indirect taxes net of subsidies. This is usually done for TFE as a whole, but estimates of the factor cost adjustment for its main components are given in table 1.6.

---

1 It can be shown that fluctuations in UK exports correlate fairly closely with the index of world industrial production, and that exports to particular countries are statistically linked to output in those areas.

TABLE 1.6

Domestic Output Content of Total Final Expenditure at Market Prices, 1971

Percentages of market price totals

	Consumers' expenditure	*Government current expenditure*	*Gross domestic fixed investment*	*Exports of goods and services*	*Total final expenditure*
Indirect taxes (less subsidies)	17	6	7	4	12
Imports of goods and services	18	9	22	20	17
Domestic output content	65	85	71	76	71

Source: 'Summary Input-Output Tables for 1971', *ET,* January 1975.

Most indirect taxes are levied on consumption goods so that the adjustment tends
to be higher here than it is for government expenditure, investment or exports.

The factor cost adjustment is one of two deductions which must be made in
order to progress from TFE to GDP. The other is imports which, since they are
produced by foreign factors of production, cannot constitute UK factor income. In
1971, as the table shows, imports came to 17% of TFE; they were a smaller
proportion of government spending than of other types of expenditure.

The main determinants of imports are the level of income, stocks of materials
and competitive factors. It is probably the latter which are responsible for the
sustained upward trend (see chapter 3) in the ratio of imports of goods and services
(at constant 1970 prices) to TFE:

1951-4	14.2%
1955-9	14.9%
1960-4	15.8%
1965-9	16.6%
1970-4	19.3%

It is possible that this trend can be broken down and explained in terms of price
competitiveness, trade policy and other variables, but many forecasting equations
for imports have simply extrapolated the trend at its average recent rate of
increase.

The influence of stocks upon the volume of imports has been recognized for
many years and at one time it was thought that every £100m of stockbuilding
would add about £50m to the import bill.[1] More recently, however, the influence of
stocks appears to have weakened. A recent estimate suggests an import content of
stockbuilding of 0.3 rather than 0.5.[2] The reason for the decline in the coefficients
is probably the increased weight of finished manufactures in the import total (see
chapter 3).

The underlying explanation of the import content of stockbuilding is to be
sought in terms of the stock-adjustment principle which, as suggested above, has a
useful part to play in determining stockbuilding and fixed investment. If imports

---

1 See 'Forecasting Imports' by W. A. H. Godley and J. R. Shepherd, *NIER,* August 1965.
2 M. J. C. Surrey, *Analysis and Forecasting of the British Economy, op. cit.*

are found to vary directly with stockbuilding, and if stockbuilding follows the stock-adjustment principle, then imports will vary with the level of income and the initial level of stocks. Thus equations in terms of income and stockbuilding can be recast in terms of income and initial stock levels.[1] The more general point is that approximately one-third of total imports of goods and services consist of items which are used as inputs in the process of production. These are classified in chapter 3 as imports of basic materials, mineral fuels and lubricants and semi-manufactures. They enter into stocks in the same way as domestically-produced iron ore or coal, and they are subject to similar laws of behaviour.

IV   THE MANAGEMENT OF DEMAND
IV.1   Objectives and Instruments

Since the end of the second world war successive governments have striven to influence the level of demand in the economy with the intention of maintaining or restoring acceptable levels of employment. This policy was originally advocated in the White Paper on *Employment Policy* (Cmd. 6527) issued in 1944 by the wartime coalition government. The White Paper stated that:

> The Government believe that, once the war has been won, we can make a fresh approach, with better chances of success than ever before, to the task of maintaining a high and stable level of employment without sacrificing the essential liberties of a free society.

It was recommended that there should be a permanent staff of statisticians and economists in the Civil Service with the responsibility of interpreting economic trends and advising on policy. It suggested that the execution of the policy should be examined annually by Parliament in the Debate on the Budget. Finally, the authors of the White Paper foresaw that high levels of employment were likely to endanger price stability and this pointed, therefore, to the need for 'moderation in wage matters by employers and employees' as the essential condition for the success of the policy.

The task of maintaining a high level of employment proved to be simpler than expected. The White Paper had not laid down any precise target for the level of employment. But it is generally agreed that the levels attained in nearly every postwar year (with exceptions in 1947, 1971 and 1975) were higher than the authors of the White Paper had hoped. It became apparent, moreover, that high levels of employment were compatible with a fairly moderate rate of inflation. The average rate of retail price inflation in the 1950s, for example, was about 4% per year whilst unemployment had averaged as little as $1\frac{1}{2}\%$ of the labour force.

As we observed in section II (above), however, the postwar economy passed through a series of fluctuations with the unemployment rate for annual periods varying between the limits of 1.0% and 3.9%. Part of the reason for these fluctuations lies in the different views taken by different governments (or sometimes by the same government at different times) as to the most desirable pressure of demand. The aim of high employment has been in some measure of

---

1   If M = mY + nI (where M, Y and I are imports, income and stockbuilding respectively, m, the marginal propensity to import and n, the import content of stockbuilding), and if I = aY - bK then M = (m + na)Y − nbK. The import ratio is now expressible in terms of the stock-output ratio.

conflict with the objectives of both balance of payments equilibrium and price stability. A conflict with the balance of payments has been present in so far as governments have been unwilling to make use of instruments of policy, such as exchange rate devaluation or import controls, for dealing with the external balance. Thus fiscal measures, which act upon the level of employment, have at times been used to attain the required balance of payments instead, with the consequence that the employment objective has taken second place. This conflict of objectives was particularly noticeable in two periods: from 1956 to early 1959 when the government was aiming at a long-term balance of payments surplus and preferred to deflate employment rather than depreciate sterling to achieve it; and also in the period of eighteen months preceding the devaluation of November 1967. It may be argued, however, that there is no conflict in principle between the balance of payments and employment objectives so long as exchange rate adjustments, or other instruments for dealing with the balance of payments, are effective and permissible.

The employment objective has also been in conflict with that of price stability. Here there is no independent instrument of control to parallel the variability of the exchange rate. Incomes policy, in the sense of voluntary or compulsory guidelines for the rate of increase in wages and prices, has not until recently been found to be particularly successful, and certainly not successful enough to permit nice percentage variations in the permitted rate of inflation. Thus the absence of an independent instrument for controlling inflation has implied a really genuine conflict of aims. It has necessitated a compromise between the two objectives, and the compromise has been struck at different target rates of unemployment by different governments. This, together with the balance of payments, helps to explain why the target level of employment has not been stable in the postwar period, but has tended to fluctuate according to the priorities of the government of the day.

Once it is assumed that the employment target is settled by political compromise, the problem of how to attain it becomes an essentially technical issue. It is a matter of how complete and precise is our knowledge of the workings of the economy.

One elementary point concerns the existence of appreciable time-lags between the detection of a policy problem and its remedy. This means that it is not sound strategy to wait until unemployment has reached some intolerably high figure before acting or thinking about action to correct it. The unemployment statistics are about a month behindhand; civil servants may take up to six months to advise the appropriate action; Parliament may take three months to enact it; and even after the policy is put into force the full economic effects may not appear for some months afterwards. Thus a strategy based merely upon the observation of past statistics can involve a time-lag of twelve months or more between the observed need for a change in policy and the effects of the change upon the level of employment.

It is partly for this reason that economic management in the UK is based upon a strategy of looking ahead rather than on response to observed behaviour. This means that the policy-maker relies very heavily upon the use of economic forecasts. If he can *correctly* foresee the emergence of a policy problem then the problem of the time-lag between the need for intervention and its effects is solved.

There is another reason, too, for relying upon forecasts. This is that the mere observation of some phenomenon such as intolerably high unemployment in no way justifies the belief that it will continue in the same degree of seriousness. It may get worse or it may get better. Quite clearly it is essential to form some view of what will happen in the future before deciding both the degree and the direction of policy intervention required. Failure to produce a correct forecast of the course of employment over the next twelve to eighteen months could result in an inadequate degree of corrective policy action. Or it could actually be destabilizing,[1] the effect of intervention being to remove the level of output still further from target than it would otherwise have been.

The last three decades have seen a very considerable advance in the various branches of knowledge which bear upon the problems of forecasting and managing the economy. The chief of these have comprised: (i) an enormous improvement, attributable to the CSO, in economic statistics, and particularly the development of quarterly, seasonally adjusted, constant price, national expenditure figures; (ii) the development of a conceptual framework and quantitative model for forecasting the levels of GDP and employment over a period of about eighteen months; (iii) the development of a framework and quantitative model for estimating the effects upon GDP of tax changes and other instruments of demand management.

IV.2   The Effects of Policy Instruments: Government Expenditure

If fiscal intervention is to be tailored to precise targets for employment and output it is necessary for the policy-maker to make a fairly precise quantitative assessment of the effects of their policy instruments upon the level of domestic output. In this section we shall concentrate upon the effects of three policy instruments: changes in government expenditure on goods and services, changes in indirect taxation and changes in personal income tax.

The effects of these changes divide into direct effects upon GDP and indirect effects such as the multiplier and accelerator consequences. In the case of an increase in government expenditure on goods and services the direct effects on GDP will be smaller in volume than the expenditure change itself. This is because there are always 'leakages' into imports and indirect taxes which do not influence domestic output. For government spending as a whole the indirect tax content averages 6% and the import content 9%,[2] so that £100m added to government expenditure will raise domestic output by £85m if the goods and services purchased are similar to government spending in general.[3] Similarly, if government expenditure is raised by £118m, GDP will rise by £100m.

The indirect effects of the additional expenditure cannot be evaluated without an estimate of the size and timing of the *multiplier*; they are common to all three types of policy change. If GDP is raised by £100m by some initial increase in government expenditure, the question to be asked is how much of this will be re-spent on new domestic output. The problem may be tackled by estimating how

---

1 A more accurate word would be 'perverse' since policy does not necessarily aim to stabilize anything.

2 See table 1.6.

3 If, however, the extra spending is all on the running of a new department in Whitehall the import content could be well below 9%; if it is all on military spending overseas it could be much higher.

much of the additional GDP will find its way into personal income, and by asking
how this income is distributed between income tax, saving and consumers'
expenditure. The addition to consumers' expenditure must be broken down into
its indirect tax, imported and domestically-produced components, and of these it is
of course the latter which constitutes the second addition to GDP.

The main quantities involved in this calculation are indicated in table 1.7. It can
be assumed that none of the additional GDP is distributed as rents, and if the
remainder is divided between profits and income from employment in the same
ratio as total incomes from profit and employment (see *NIBB*) then the addition to
personal income is likely to be about 82%. The increase in disposable income is
found by estimating the marginal tax rate for an average income recipient and the
increases in consumption by taking the marginal savings ratio. Next, the indirect tax
component of consumption is removed in order to obtain consumption at factor
cost. Finally, the import component must be subtracted so as to arrive at the
domestically-produced increase in consumption. On the basis of the assumptions
made this turns out to be quite a small increase — only 31% of the first addition to
GDP.

TABLE 1.7

Stages in the Multiplier Process

	£m	Assumed marginal relationships
1st round increase in GDP	100	
Increase in personal income	82	b_1 = .820
Increase in personal disposable income	56	b_2 = .683
Increase (after a time-lag) in consumers' expenditure at market prices	50	b_3 = .893
Increase in consumers' expenditure at factor cost	41	b_4 = .820
Increase in domestically-produced consumption at factor cost (equals 2nd round increase in GDP)	31	b_5 = .756

If the initial increase in GDP of £100m is not sustained, but is confined for
example to a single quarter's duration, then the indirect effects on GDP will be
£31m in the second quarter, 31% of £31m in the following quarter, and so on.
Under these circumstances the effects will tend to die out over time. The sequence
of quarterly deviations in GDP from the course it would otherwise have followed
would be:

£100, 31, 9.6, 3.0, 0.9, 0.3, 0.1 . . . million

If, however, the increment in GDP is a sustained increase (a continuous injection of
demand) then the same sequence is generated in each successive quarter so that the
series of quarterly deviations in GDP would be as follows:

£100, 131, 140.6, 143.6, 144.5, 144.8, 144.9 . . . million

Here the full multiplier effect on GDP is almost wholly realized in four quarters after the initial injection, and even by the third quarter the bulk of the multiplier effect has come through.[1]

The key to the timing of the multiplier process lies in the lag of one quarter which is taken to exist between the receipt of GDP in the form of income and the expenditure of this income on additional consumption goods. The analysis above also assumes that increased expenditure is matched instantaneously by additional production. This is rather an implausible assumption, and it is almost inevitable that the first impact of any increase in consumers' spending will be met out of stocks. So long as stocks behave passively and production responds to expenditure after a short time-lag the multiplier time path will be delayed but not altered in any fundamental sense. If, however, stocks are not passive but behave according to the stock-adjustment principle (or its offspring, the accelerator) then it is possible that the replenishment of stocks will cause the time path to wobble on its way to equilibrium.[2] The extent of these wobbles is not well established although our consideration of stock-building behaviour in section III.3 suggests that they must be present in some degree. Hopkin and Godley,[3] in their important discussion on the multiplier effects of policy changes, make small notional allowances for the accelerator both in stocks and in fixed investment. It is probably true to say, however, that these effects are not as well known as they ought to be.

IV.3 The Effects of Tax Changes and Other Instruments

The effects of changes in government expenditure have been discussed above mainly because an evaluation of them affords an easy introduction to the concept of the multiplier (which is common to all policy changes). In fact government expenditure has not been used extensively as part of short-term employment policy (1972 was an exception). This is chiefly because it is not easy to accomplish changes in this form of spending very quickly or with great precision. Clearly, however, changes in government spending are a potentially useful instrument at times when the economy is severely depressed and when the recovery is likely to take several years to accomplish. The more usual instruments of demand management, however, have been changes in direct and indirect taxes.

The estimation of the effect of a change in income tax may be illustrated by reference to the additional 3p on the basic and higher rates (and 8p on the top

---

1 The full multiplier value is 1.449 and is calculated from the marginal relationships set out in table 1.7 as follows:

$$\frac{1}{1 - b_1 b_2 b_3 b_4 b_5} = \frac{1}{1 - \dfrac{82}{100} \cdot \dfrac{56}{82} \cdot \dfrac{50}{56} \cdot \dfrac{41}{50} \cdot \dfrac{31}{41}} = \frac{1}{1 - 0.31} = 1.449$$

This is completely analogous with the simple textbook multiplier save that the marginal propensity to consume is replaced by a composite marginal propensity to re-spend domestic output.

2 In extreme cases there may be severe oscillations or even an explosive time path. On this the classic reference is L. A. Metzler, 'The Nature and Stability of Inventory Cycles' in R. A. Gordon and L. R. Klein (eds), *Reading in Business Cycles.*

3 W. A. B. Hopkin and W. A. H. Godley, 'An Analysis of Tax Changes', *NIER*, May 1963. This article is the basis of the discussion above.

rate) introduced in the Budget of March 1974. The effect of these changes on the income tax revenue was estimated by the Inland Revenue to be £942m, implying a reduction in personal disposable income of the same amount.[1] The direct effect of this upon the level of GDP may be found by applying the coefficients in table 1.7. Thus the change in consumers' expenditure at market prices is obtained by multiplying £942m by b_3 (b_3 being the marginal propensity to consume) and the additional consumption of domestic output is this amount multiplied by b_4 and b_5. Thus the initial effect upon GDP, measured at current prices, is £942m times $b_3 b_4 b_5$ = £521m. This is approximately 0.75% of GDP. The final effect may be found by multiplying this amount by the multiplier value of 1.449, and is almost exactly 1.0% of 1974 GDP.[2]

In estimating the effect of a change in indirect taxation it might be thought that the initial effect upon GDP could be found quite simply by taking the additional revenue (as estimated by the Board of Customs and Excise) and applying the coefficients b_4 and b_5.[3] But the problem is complicated by the fact that changes in indirect taxation invariably lead to differential changes in prices. The taxed goods go up in price whereas other prices are unchanged. Elementary economics suggests that there will then be substitution effects as well as income effects so that it is really quite a complicated task to work out the effects of the tax change upon consumers' spending on different articles and the revenue from the tax.[4] An indication of the magnitude involved may be taken from the estimate that a 10% increase in the rates of purchase tax (supplanted in 1973 by value added tax) and the excise taxes on betting, tobacco and petrol would have a direct effect upon GDP of 0.5% and a final effect (including the multiplier) of 0.7%. It can be assumed that the effect of raising VAT from 8% to say 9% would produce effects of the same order of magnitude.

One interesting and important feature of these estimates is that what are regarded as severe changes in taxation appear to have quite small effects upon the economy. If the Chancellor of the Exchequer decided, for example, to raise VAT by 1% in combination with a rise of 3p on the income tax rate, his action would reduce GDP by something less than 2%. There are circumstances, however, when the economic situation calls for a stronger package (in retrospect, 1962, 1971 and 1972 appear to be examples), and when it would be advisable to supplement tax changes by additional instruments of control.

One of the alternatives to tax measures is the control of hire purchase transactions. Alterations in the statutory minimum HP deposit and in the maximum repayment period are used frequently as policy instruments. The effect of raising the down payment is to choke off purchases until consumers have managed to save the increase in the deposit whilst a shortening of the repayment period will deter purchasers from buying until they are satisfied that their current income will cover the extra monthly payments. These restrictions cannot be expected to be effective if consumers have access to alternative sources of finance, but the presumption is that a good many of them have no such alternative. The chief objection to the use

---

1   *Financial Statement and Budget Report, 1974-75*, p. 28.
2   Strictly speaking the multiplier is different after the tax change because the coefficient b_2 is changed. But the effect of this is too small to be worth allowing for.
3   We are assuming no initial change in disposable income or the savings ratio.
4   For details see Hopkin and Godley, 'Analysis of Tax Changes', *op. cit.*

of HP controls is not that they are not effective but rather that their effects are disturbing to the industries affected and temporary in character. When the restrictions are tightened, they tend to postpone rather than to reduce personal spending, and the period of postponement may be fairly short-lived.

Monetary instruments of demand management are discussed more fully in chapter 2. Increases in interest rates may be expected (if they are sufficiently large) to affect fixed investment, stockbuilding and the purchase of consumer durable goods. These effects, however, are likely to be delayed for many months and their main impact will fall outside the normal policy (and forecasting) horizon of twelve to eighteen months. In this respect they are not as satisfactory as fiscal instruments of control. More rapid effects from monetary policy can, however, occur as a result of cutbacks in the money supply and in the availability of credit. But in this case, although the direction of effect is clear enough, the magnitude in terms of GDP is difficult to estimate. Thus monetary instruments are likely to take second place to fiscal instruments because their effects are either uncertain in magnitude or too long delayed. This need not mean that monetary policy has no role to play, but only that it is reserved for longer time horizons than those of fiscal policy.

IV.4   Economic Forecasts

It has been suggested above that it is not satisfactory to manage the economy simply by reacting to the current situation. If the government is to reduce the risk of unduly delayed, possibly destabilizing, actions it must attempt to forecast the course of output and employment. The difference between the prospective path of GDP and the path required by the employment target can then be used to determine the direction and extent of budgetary action.

National income forecasts are prepared in the Treasury three times a year. The timing of the three main forecasts is geared to the Budget, which is normally in the first half of April. A preliminary assessment of next year's prospects is generally made in late autumn, and this is brought up to date and extended a further six months in February and March. A third forecast is made in early summer.

From a policy point of view the most important forecast is the one made in February. This extends from the last known figures for GDP (which relate to the third quarter of the previous year) as far as the second quarter of the following year. It covers seven quarters altogether of which the last five quarters, from the second of this year to the third of next, are genuinely in the future. The first two quarters, from last October to March of the current year, represent a kind of no-man's land between an imperfectly known past and an unknown future. The problem for the forecaster is one of piecing together bits of statistical information such as the monthly figures of exports, imports, retail sales and industrial production into a reasonably coherent picture of the base period. This is always difficult because there is very little monthly information about investment or government expenditure, and the difficulties can be made worse by apparent contradictions between the various monthly figures of production, sales and employment.

Once the base period is established, the forecast proper (i.e. the part relating to the future) can be started. The methods by which this is done need not be described

•
in detail.[1] They have evolved steadily over a number of years and have made increasing use of econometric techniques as a result of the accumulation of economic statistics and their improvement. The forecasting model may best be thought of in terms of dependent expenditures, such as consumption, stockbuilding and imports, which are determined primarily by the current level of GDP, and autonomous expenditures, such as government purchases, fixed investment and exports which in the short run are largely independent of GDP. In forecasting the latter a good deal of use is made of direct information from business firms and government departments. Government current expenditure and the government component of fixed investment, for example, can be predicted from information provided by government departments and the nationalized industries. The forecast of business fixed investment is arrived at partly by reference to the sample enquiry into investment intentions conducted by the Department of Trade and Industry. The forecast of housing and investment may be derived largely from figures of housing starts and an assumption about the period of housing construction. The export forecast is made on the basis of expected trends in world trade, and will also be affected by sharp changes in the competitive position such as occurred after the devaluation of 1967. In forecasting the dependent expenditures it is possible to employ behavioural relationships of the type we have suggested in section III. There are many different ways, however, of formulating consumption and investment functions and it is not an easy matter to judge which of them is best. Thus although a very large econometric model is now used by the Treasury as part of its forecasting work it may be assumed that parts of the model will be disputed by those responsible for getting the forecast right and that the model, therefore, is not likely to dictate the forecast to the exclusion of all argument and discussion. Furthermore, as every forecaster knows, there are always events which the model is not able to handle (strikes and fuel shortages, for example) and which necessitate judgemental estimation of their effects upon economic activity.

The main upshot of the government forecasting work is a table in considerable detail of the course of GDP and its components, quarter-by-quarter, over a twelve to eighteen month period. In the case of the pre-Budget forecast it will extend to the middle of the calendar year after the Budget. Since 1968 these forecasts have been published with the *Financial Statement* at the time of the Budget.

IV.5　　Criticisms of Demand Management

It is not wholly surprising that the activity of demand management has come in for heavy criticism from journalists and economists. This is to be expected of any sphere of government policy, and especially one involving frequent changes in tax

---

1　The Treasury's forecasting methods are described in A. D. Roy, 'Short-term Forecasting for Central Economic Management', in K. Hilton and D. F. Heathfield (eds.), *The Econometric Study of the United Kingdom,* Macmillan, 1970, and J. R. Shepherd, 'Short-term Forecasting for the UK Economy', in Sir Alec Cairncross (ed.), *The Managed Economy,* Blackwell, 1970. Any *NIER* will give an impression of the methods used by the National Institute of Economic and Social Research, a full account of which is contained in M. J. C. Surrey, *The Analysis and Forecasting of the British Economy,* Cambridge University Press, 1971. More recent accounts are J. R. Shepherd, H. P. Evans and C. J. Riley, 'The Treasury Short-term Forecasting Model', Government Economic Service Occasional Papers (HMSO) and HM Treasury, *Macroeconomic Model, Technical Manual* (HMSO); February 1976.

rates. In assessing these criticisms it is not always easy to distinguish the positive from the normative.

The criticisms divide into four main groups: (i) that the economy has fluctuated considerably despite the advocacy of 'stable' employment in the 1944 White Paper; (ii) that the technical apparatus of demand management has been inadequate to its task; (iii) that economic policy has been in some sense destabilizing; (iv) that errors in demand management have been connected with the rapid inflation of the 1970s.

(i)   On the first of these points there is no doubt that the course of the economy has been something less than stable for most of the period since demand management was inaugurated. This phenomenon (which has sometimes been labelled the 'stop-go' cycle) has been described and charted in section II of this chapter. What is not so clear, however, is whether this instability implies criticism of the aims of policy (which is largely a subjective matter) or of the technical apparatus for achieving those aims. For even an unstable and highly cyclical time path for the economy cannot, in itself, imply that the technical aspects of demand management have been at fault. The conflicts or presumed conflicts between economic objectives are sufficiently critical to make it doubtful whether the target pressure of demand has always been the same. Indeed, in so far as the facts can be ascertained, the target appears to have fluctuated quite significantly.

Fluctuations in targets may be detected from the available information on Treasury forecasts. These forecasts, after allowance for the effects of tax changes introduced at the time, represent the increase in GDP which the government finds acceptable at the time they are made. As such they are tantamount to target increases in output. These targets can be related to the level of *potential output* (the level of GDP in a specific period which can be produced if employment is at some standard rate) so as to obtain an estimate of the intended utilisation of potential. A series of these targets running from 1955 to 1975 is shown in table 1.8. It shows intended GDP as a percentage of potential, and the movements in these percentages may be taken as indicating parallel movements in the intended rate of unemployment.

The table shows that the government's intended use of productive potential has undergone fairly large fluctuations in the period since 1955. It fell by about 4% in 1955-9, rose in 1960 and again in 1964, and was fairly stable from 1964 to 1970. The target appears to have dropped abruptly in 1971 and to have recovered equally sharply in 1972. There was another sharp decline in 1975. It can be shown that these fluctuations in the government's short-term objectives are very similar in magnitude (although not in timing) to fluctuations in actual GDP.[1] The amplitude of the intended and actual cycles in economic activity have unfortunately been very similar.[2]

Whilst these fluctuations in the target use of productive potential are regrettable in retrospect it must not be forgotten that the targets belong to a succession of Chancellors of the Exchequer and to widely differing economic circumstances. It is a fairly simple matter to point to some given utilization of resources as being the optimum level and to hold on to the hope that the economy might be stabilized at

---

1   See M. C. Kennedy, 'Employment Policy – What Went Wrong?', in Joan Robinson (ed.), *After Keynes,* Blackwell, 1973.

2   One measure of the amplitude of fluctuations is the mean deviation (regardless of sign) from the average utilization rate. This is 2.2% for the intended use of potential and 2.4% for the actual use over the periods shown in table 1.8.

TABLE 1.8

Short-term Targets and Forecasting Errors, UK, 1955-75

		Target Use of Potential Output (1) %	Forecast and Target Change in GDP from year earlier (2) %	Actual Change in GDP from year earlier (3) %	Error (forecast less actual) %
1955	(Year)	99	2.9	3.5	−0.6
1956	"	98	1.1	1.3	−0.2
1957	"	97	1.3	1.8	−0.5
1958	"	95	−0.4	−0.3	−0.1
1959	(4th qtr)	94	2.8	6.9	−4.1
1960	"	98	3.1	3.4	−0.3
1961	"	94	1.8	2.2	−0.4
1962	"	98	3.9	1.3	2.6
1963	"	97	4.6	6.2	−1.6
1964	"	101	5.4	4.1	1.3
1965	"	100	2.7	2.5	0.2
1966	"	98	2.0	1.3	0.7
1967	"	97	3.1	1.9	1.2
1968	(2nd half)	97	3.6	4.7	−1.1
1969	"	97	1.9	1.4	0.5
1970	"	97	3.6	1.9	1.7
1971	"	94	1.1	2.0	−0.9
1972	"	98	5.5	2.7	2.8
1973	"	99	6.0	3.6	2.4
1974	"	96	2.6	1.1	1.5
1975	"	92	0.0	−	−

Notes and Sources:

1 Potential output is GDP corresponding to 1.0 per cent unemployment: 1955-64 from M. C. Kennedy, 'Employment Policy – What Went Wrong?' in Joan Robinson (ed.), *After Keynes;* 1955-74 levels are derived from the trend of potential output in University of Cambridge, Department of Applied Economics, *Economic Policy Review No. 1,* February 1975.
2 Kennedy, *op. cit.* and *Financial Statements* (HMSO)
3 Average estimate of GDP, *ET(AS)* 1975.

the optimum for ever after. But circumstances can change from one year to another so that what once looked like an optimum utilization rate may later cease to be so because of a worsened balance of payments or serious inflation. It would be surprising indeed if a succession of Chancellors of the Exchequer, each of them representing different political parties or different shades of opinion within their parties, would somehow manage to arrive at a uniform target for the pressure of demand. Thus the fluctuating time-path of budgetary targets must probably be accepted as a fact of political and economic life.

(ii) As regards the technical apparatus of demand management the key question is whether, and by how much, it has failed to achieve the target levels of employment or of GDP. Since the target levels of GDP are equivalent to the government forecasts after allowance has been made for the effects of each Budget, this question is essentially a matter of forecasting accuracy.[1] If the government forecasts the increase in GDP incorrectly then it will be misled into taking the wrong measures. Given that its assessment of the measures is reasonably accurate the result will be that the target level of GDP will be missed by exactly the same amount as the forecast is in error.

The question of the accuracy of Treasury forecasts can only be answered satis-factorily for those forecasts which have been published or otherwise described with sufficient clarity to permit comparisons with the outcome. For 1968 and after the forecasts have been published as part of the *Financial Statement and Budget Report*. But before this date the information is not always as good, and it has to be assembled from official documents or even from forecasts made by other bodies at the same time. Nevertheless, the task is worth attempting even though the results (see table 1.8) cannot be sacrosanct.[2]

The main points to emerge from an assessment of Treasury forecasts is that, whilst they have not been as highly accurate as might have been hoped, they have led policy seriously astray on only four or five occasions. There is not much doubt that the 1959 forecast, when the error was 4%, was the worst forecast of all. It meant that an unforeseen recovery in total output was coupled with an expansionary Budget, and the result was a much higher level of employment at the end of the year than the government had actually intended. By contrast, the forecasting error in 1962 went the other way with the result that there was a recession despite the policy aim of a roughly 4% rise in output (implying high employment). The error was put right in 1963, although the recovery went further than intended. The worst forecasts in recent years appear to have been in 1972 and 1973.

Apart from those five bad years, in each of which the forecast was out by 2% or more, the record is not too discouraging. The average error (regardless of sign) for the remaining years was 0.9% of GDP.[3] This is roughly equivalent to the effect on GDP of 3p on the standard rate of income tax, and it also represents an error on the target rate of unemployment of about 0.3 percentage points. Clearly it would be desirable for the Treasury to do better than this, and it is to be hoped that further progress in the macroeconomics of demand management will have this result.

(iii)   A number of writers have sought to show or to deny that demand manage-ment has been destabilizing.[4] To do this it is necessary to make assumptions as to the target level of output and the level which output would have attained in the absence of discretionary intervention. Most writers in this field have made some-what questionable assumptions about the targets and the instruments of interven-tion. Thus one has claimed that policy was destabilizing because it was demonstrable that 'policy-off' changes in GDP (i.e. after deducting the effects of changes in taxation and government spending) were less widely scattered round the average

---

1   Forecasting accuracy is not always simple to interpret: there may be strikes or other events of an unforeseeable nature which disturb the accuracy of the forecasts without necessarily impairing the methods by which they are derived.

2   The same qualifications apply to the series for the Target Use of Potential Output. For a fuller discussion see my paper to Section F of the British Association, 'Employment Policy – What Went Wrong?', which is published in Joan Robinson, *op. cit.*

3   The average error for 1955-72, inclusive of the few bad forecasts, was 1.4%.

4   For reviews of these and other studies of short-term policies see G. D. N. Worswick, 'Fiscal Policy and Stabilization in Britain' in A. K. Cairncross (ed.), *Britain's Economic Prospects Reconsidered* and M. C. Kennedy, 'Employment Policy: What Went Wrong? in Joan Robinson, *op. cit.*

annual increase in GDP than policy-on (i.e. actual) changes in GDP.[1] It is arbitrary, however, to measure failures of policy in terms of dispersion around an average annual increase in GDP. For there is, first, no presumption that governments were aiming each year at a constant rise in GDP, and, secondly, there is every reason (in times of depression or boom) to suppose that they would aim at increases above or below the average.

The stabilizing effectiveness of short-term policy has also been investigated in terms of the stability of GDP around its trend. It has been shown by Artis[2] that for the 1958-70 period the dispersion of quarterly levels of GDP from their time-trend was smaller for 'policy-off' output (i.e. GDP after deducting the cumulative effects of tax changes) than for actual output, and this result may be taken to imply that policy was 'destabilizing'.

(iv)   During the period of fast inflation in the 1970s demand management came in for some further criticisms. One popular source of complaint was that the very fast expansion of demand in 1973 and 1974 was responsible for the acceleration in the rate of inflation. This criticism greatly overstates the case since by far the most important factor (see section V below) in the acceleration of inflation over the 1972-4 period was the massive increase in import prices (almost 100% in two years). This, however, is not to deny that the higher pressure of demand in 1973 and 1974 would have added something to the rate of inflation, or, in particular, that the very fast pace at which the expansion proceeded did not create its own special pressures. (The annual rate of increase in GDP between the 1st quarters of 1972 and 1973 was 9.3%.) But the main factor responsible for the inflation in this period was almost certainly the rise in world commodity prices and its inevitable consequence for UK materials and food prices.

It has also been suggested[3] that 'the whole intellectual basis of postwar "demand management" by government is undermined if the natural unemployment rate hypothesis is true'. The hypothesis in question postulates that there is some level of the unemployment rate, the natural rate, which is compatible with a zero rate of price inflation provided that the expected rate of price inflation is also zero. If the unemployment target is set below the natural rate then inflation will accelerate. Wage increases will generate price increases which lead to expected price increases and hence to further and larger wage increases. Some of the assumptions behind this hypothesis are rather dubious when applied to the UK economy (see section V). But even if the assumptions were true (and variants of them in the shape of the wage-price spiral hypothesis have been accepted for many years) there is no reason why it should undermine the basis of demand management. Governments which sought to avoid accelerating inflation would simply set the target rate at or below the natural rate of unemployment,[4] and they would seek to achieve their target by

---

1   B. Hansen, *Fiscal Policy in Seven Countries, 1955-65,* OECD, Paris, 1969.

2   M. J. Artis, 'Fiscal Policy for Stabilization', in W. Beckerman (ed.), *The Labour Government's Economic Record, 1964-70,* Duckworth, 1972.

3   M. Friedman and D. Laidler, 'Unemployment *versus* Inflation', IEA, Occasional Paper 44, p. 4.

4   According to Professor Laidler (*op. cit.*) the natural rate is provisionally estimated at 'a little less than 2 per cent'. If this is correct it is difficult to see how recent inflation could have been due to running the economy below the natural rate given that the actual unemployment rate has been in excess of 2 per cent since 1966.

manipulating the instruments of policy in the manner we have described. The suggestion that the natural rate hypothesis 'destroys the intellectual basis' of demand management does not appear to be correct.

A more acceptable line of criticism is that the Treasury's economic forecasting framework fails to take sufficient note of monetary variables.[1] This omission reflects a deep-seated failure of economics, both monetarist and Keynesian, to provide acceptable estimates of the quantitative effects of changes in the supply of money. The omission is probably most serious in the evaluation of the effects of tax changes (IV.3 above) since any reduction in tax rates will imply an addition to the budget deficit which must be financed either by an expansion of the money supply or by borrowing. Expanding the money supply will cause an increase in GDP which is *additional* to the effects through the multiplier. Strictly speaking these effects should be evaluated by the Treasury. But the probability is that they are too delayed to affect greatly the twelve to eighteen month forecasts made for the purpose of determining budgetary policy. They are more likely to affect next year's GDP than the current year's, and if they are ignored this will lead to errors in the forecasts. It is possible that the Treasury's forecasts in 1959 and 1963 were too low because they omitted the effects of monetary expansion in the previous year. But it is also a fact that in the 1970s, when monetary expansion was so rapid, the economic forecasts were generally above, not below, the actual outturn for GDP. Finally, the fact that government forecasting has generally had a fairly good record suggests that the omission of monetary variables in the forecasts, whilst regrettable, may not be as serious as some economists and journalists have feared.

V   INFLATION
V.1   Inflation and its Causes

Inflation is defined variously as *any* increase in the general level of prices or as any *sustained* increase. In this chapter we shall use the wider of these two definitions since it enables us to include short-lived increases in the general price level such as those of 1920, 1940 and 1951-52, within the sphere of discussion without raising the further definitional question of whether they were sufficiently 'sustained' to be called inflations.

In measuring the rate of inflation we have a choice of index numbers. The appropriate index of the prices charged for all goods produced in the UK economy is the implied index number for GDP, so called because it is obtained by dividing the value of GDP at current prices by GDP at constant (1970) prices. The GDP index includes export prices. If an index is required to measure the prices of goods purchased by UK residents the best general measure is the implied deflator for total domestic expenditure, since this is an average of the prices paid for consumption and investment goods, both privately and publicly purchased. If we are chiefly interested in the prices paid for consumer goods and services we have a choice between the implied price index for consumers' expenditure and the index of retail prices. The former, like all implicit indices, is not compiled directly from price data but is found by dividing the current value of consumers' expenditure by

---

1   See for example D. Laidler, Minutes of Evidence, *Ninth Report from the Expenditure Committee* (1974) HC 328.

the volume estimate as measured at constant prices. By contrast the index of retail prices (the cost of living index) is compiled directly from price data. It registers the prices of a collection of goods and services entering a typical shopping basket. The composition of the basket has been altered from time to time (most recently in January 1975) so as to keep up with changes in the pattern of expenditure. Being a base-weighted index it tends to become outdated in coverage, and in periods of inflation it will tend to exaggerate the increase in the cost of the average shopping basket because consumers will tend to switch their expenditure patterns towards those goods which are rising less rapidly in price. Nevertheless, it can probably be relied upon to give a reasonably good impression of how rates of inflation have varied.

Various indicators of the extent of the rise in prices since 1970 are given in table 1.9 below.

TABLE 1.9

Increases in Prices, UK, 1970-4

	Increase %
Retail prices	41.6
Consumer goods and services	44.6
Government current expenditure	59.0
Investment goods	66.0
Total domestic expenditure	51.4
Exports of goods and services	51.5
TFE	51.5
Imports of goods and services	84.9
GDP	51.9

Source: NIBB 1964-74, DEG

As these figures suggest rates of inflation have been very rapid during the 1970s. In 1974, for example, the index of retail prices rose by 16% and in 1975 its increase was 24%. These increases are quite exceptional when judged against the record of historical experience. Much lower rates of increase were experienced not only in the depression years of the 1920s and 1930s but also in the years of relatively full employment in the 1950s and 1960s. These contrasts are illustrated by table 1.10.

TABLE 1.10

Inflation Rates in Selected Periods, UK, 1925-75

	Average of annual increases (%) in retail prices	Average unemployment rate (%)	Average of annual increases (%) in import prices
1925-33	−2.8	14.7	−6.5
1934-9	2.1	14.9	3.7
1953-69	3.3	1.6	1.1
1970-5	12.1	3.1	18.4

Source: BLS, DEG, AAS, LCES. Note that the unemployment rates are not precisely comparable between the prewar and postwar periods. Import prices are average values for 1925-39 and unit values for 1953-75.

To explain these contrasts it is necessary to allow for at least three independent sources of inflation in an open economy:

(i)   increases in import prices
(ii) excess demand in the home economy
(iii) wage push.

Any economy which is engaged in overseas trade is exposed to inflationary impulses from the world outside. In the UK, where such a large part of our food and raw materials are imported from overseas, the effects of world inflation are felt primarily through higher prices paid for imported primary commodities and consequential increases in production costs and food prices. Many of our most violent changes in prices, both up and down, can be traced to changes in the world prices of primary commodities.

The second main ingredient in our theory of inflation is the pressure of demand upon productive potential and productive resources. One measure of this pressure is the percentage unemployment rate, although, as we saw in section I, there are reasons for distrusting unemployment comparisons between the periods before and after 1966. Excess demand is a manifestation of market forces. We should expect wages and/or prices to increase whenever excess demand (i.e. demand less supply at going prices) is positive and to fall when it is negative. In the economy as a whole we can expect positive and negative excess demands to exist simultaneously in different markets so that there is bound to be a mixture of conflicting tendencies with some prices tending to decline as others are tending to rise. From a macroeconomic point of view we are interested in the balance of excess demands and excess supplies, and this for most periods can be measured by the rate of unemployment or the vacancy rate. These relate to the labour market, and there are unfortunately no general statistical indicators of excess demand in the market for goods.

The third main ingredient in our model of inflation is more controversial, and is the potentially independent force of wage-pushfulness. It is necessary to include this as a third factor because wages are widely fixed by bargaining between the representatives of powerful groups, the union and the firm or employers' federation, each of which has the ability to influence the bargain by threatening to interrupt production and employment. Whilst there is every reason to expect that the pressure of demand for labour will always be an influence in the bargaining process we cannot exclude the possibility that alterations from year to year in the strength of the union, in the loyalty of its members, and in its preparedness to strike, may act as an independent force (i.e. independent of market forces) in the determination of wage increases.

We can combine these three main initiating causes of inflation into a more complete model by relating them to wage increases, price increases and expected price increases in the manner illustrated in figure 1.5. The model assumes that the *process* by which excess demand leads to price inflation is through the rate of increase in wages. Higher wages mean higher average costs of production and these lead after a time-lag to higher prices. This will happen either because business firms tend to set prices by a constant markup over variable costs or because they seek to maximize profits. Higher prices lead, again after a time-lag, to higher wages since trade unions will tend to claim compensation for increases in the cost of living, or in other words to restore the real wages of their members. Thus the central ingredient of our model is a wage-price spiral which is superimposed upon the excess demand for labour. The spiral may, moreover, be set into operation by exogenous increases in wages coming from wage-push or by increases in import prices as a consequence of movements in world commodity prices.

A possible objection to this manner of presenting the inflationary process is that it does not appear to allow for a direct influence of excess demand upon the rate of price increase. This omission is forced upon us mainly by the dearth of statistical indicators of excess demand in the goods market and partly, too, by the fact that a number of studies have attempted to find evidence of this relationship and have not been successful.[1] However, we do not wish to pretend that there is no direct effect of excess demand upon prices — only that the main identified connection is through the medium of wages.

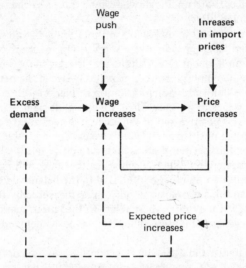

Figure 1.5 Inflationary Processes

A second objection might be that there is no reference to the quantity of money. This lack of an explicit reference, however, does not rule out monetary causation of inflation since additions to the quantity of money will raise prices through the medium of excess demand and excess demand has a prominent place in the model. This amounts to saying that monetary inflation is a branch of demand-pull inflation. An increase in the money supply will act via interest rate reductions or more directly through credit availability to increase the demand for goods and services, and hence excess demand. There is no place in our model, or in economic theory in general, for an influence of money upon prices which is not transmitted through the medium of excess demand.

Besides the wage-price spiral figure 1.5 allows for two other possible interactions between wages and prices, both of them operating through the effect of rising prices upon expected future prices. The first of these is the possibility that price expectations may be taken into account in wage bargaining. It has been suggested

---

1 For example L. A. Dicks-Mireaux, 'The Inter-Relationship between Cost and Price Changes, 1945-1959,' *OEP* (NS) Vol. 13(3). Reprinted in R. J. Ball and P. Doyle, *Inflation*, Penguin, 1969. The model of figure 1.5 is an extension of the relationships estimated by Dicks-Mireaux.

by some writers[1] that the expectation of a price increase of, say, 10% in the ensuing twelve months will induce trade unions and employees to settle for increases in nominal wages of as much as 10% more than would have occurred if prices had been expected to be stable. This hypothesis assumes a high degree of sophistication upon the part of bargaining groups and may not be of great relevance to the UK economy during much of its history. Few would deny, however, that really rapid inflation will force the realization that failure to allow for future price increases can lead to a painful erosion of purchasing power between one wage settlement and the next. Thus expectational wage bargaining is a form of behaviour which is likely to evolve as a consequence of rapid inflation. It is possible that this form of behaviour has emerged in the UK economy over the last year or two.

The second additional link between wages and prices runs from the expectation of higher prices to the level of excess demand. As consumers become aware that prices are going to rise rapidly in the future they protect themselves from an erosion of the value of their money by switching out of money into goods. The effects of this form of behaviour will be manifested in a tendency for the savings ratio to decline (which has not happened in the UK) and for the velocity of circulation of money to rise (which has also not happened). We have included it in the figure, along with the link between price expectations and wage bargaining, because it is a mode of behaviour which has been observed in other countries in periods of hyperinflation.[2] It is a form of economic behaviour which, along with expectational wage bargaining, is likely to develop as inflation gathers pace and as people learn from experience how money can lose its value. The fact that such behaviour can develop adds greatly to the danger of inflation getting out of hand and provides an extremely powerful case for stopping it as early as possible.

One further point which will not be clear from the scheme in figure 1.5 is that increases in the price level always tend to raise the demand for money. If the quantity of money is kept unchanged the effect will be to raise interest rates and thus to lower the levels of real output and employment. In an economy where the central bank is attempting to maintain interest rates so as to keep down the cost of the national debt the usual reaction will be to neutralize the excess demand for money by increasing the money supply. This tendency will be reinforced by the government's commitment to high employment. Thus although inflationary processes may be started by excess demand, wage push or increased import prices, they may continue only through permissive increases in the supply of money.

V.2   Imported Inflation

There is a very real sense in which the UK economy takes its price level from the world outside. It can be shown that nearly every annual increase or decrease in UK prices in the region of 9% or more has been associated with a rapid change in world

1   For example M. Friedman, 'The Role of Monetary Policy', *AER*, Vol. 58(1), pp. 1-17 and *Unemployment versus Inflation*, Institute of Economic Affairs, 1975.

2   See, for example, A. J. Brown, *The Great Inflation*, London, 1955 and P. Cagan, 'The Monetary Dynamics of Hyperinflation' in M. Friedman, *Studies in the Quantity Theory of Money*, Chicago, 1956.

commodity prices and in UK import prices.[1] There have in fact been ten such
increases since 1920 and with only one exception they have all been generated
by a rapid rise in import prices. These increases are shown in table 1.11 below.

TABLE 1.11

Selected Annual Price Changes, UK, 1920-75

	Change in retail prices (%)	Change in import prices (%)	Previous year's change in import prices (%)
1920	15.8	19.0	141.7
1921	−9.2	−33.3	19.0
1922	−19.0	−19.6	−33.3
1940	16.5	38.5	0.0
1951	9.1	33.0	14.9
1952	9.2	−1.8	33.0
1971	9.4	4.7	4.6
1973	9.2	27.3	4.8
1974	16.1	55.5	27.3
1975	24.2	13.5	55.5

Sources: retail prices *BLS, DEG;* import prices 1920-40 *LCES* (average value indices for
merchandise imports), 1951-75 *ETAS, AAS,* (unit value index for merchandise imports).

As the table shows there was only one year in which a dramatic change in retail
prices was not accompanied by a large change in import prices. This was 1971 when,
as we discuss below, there were exceptionally fast increases in wage rates (apparently
not attributable to excess demand) in the same year and the previous year. The
price increases that occured in 1951 and 1952 were associated with the boom in
world commodity prices that resulted from the Korean War, whilst the exceptionally
fast inflation from 1972 to 1975 was associated with another rapid boom in world
commodity prices, especially oil. During these three years the rise in UK import
prices was accentuated by a fall in the official exchange rate.[2]
    Changes in import prices also help to explain why in longer periods of years the
UK has experienced different rates of inflation at similar pressures of home demand.
They explain, for example, why prices were falling from 1925 to 1933 and rising
from 1933 to 1939 despite similar average unemployment rates in the two periods
(see table 1.10).
    Imported inflation is not readily curable because there is not much prospect of
offsetting the effect on final prices other than by inducing very large reductions in
total demand and employment. It is only when the balance of payments is in surplus
that a rise in import prices can be corrected by an appreciation of the exchange rate.

---

1 We have chosen 9% rather than the round number of 10% because of the rather higher
   incidence of 9% annual price increases.
2 The effective exchange rate fell by 11.1, 3.9 and 9.6% in 1973, 1974 and 1975
   respectively.

V.3   Demand-pull Inflation

Whilst external influences seem to have been responsible for nearly all the most dramatic periods of inflation in UK history, there is not much doubt that the internal pressure of excess demand exerts its own contribution to the domestic inflation rate. The evidence for such an influence can be found by examining rates of wage or price inflation at differing demand pressures. Numerous studies have shown a strong negative relationship between the level of unemployment (which is inversely related to excess demand) and the rate of change of money wage rates. One of the earlier studies of this kind, and certainly the most influential, was published in 1958 by Professor A. W. Phillips.[1] This examined the relationship between unemployment rates and the rate of increase in weekly wage rates for nearly a century, and on the basis of data for 1861-1913 suggested that the relationship was negative, as expected, and also non-linear.[2] The wage increases to be associated with different rates of unemployment were as follows:

Unemployment rate	1.0	2.0	3.0	4.0	5.0
% change in wage rates	8.7	2.8	1.2	0.5	0.1

The relationship has become known as the *Phillips Curve* and it implies a changing marginal 'trade-off' between the rate of wage increase and unemployment. Thus the rate of wage increase declines by nearly 6% if the unemployment rate goes up from 1.0% to 2.0% but by only 1.6% if it goes up from 2.0% to 3.0%. Indeed, the trade-off suggested by the Phillips Curve is a modest one at all but the highest pressures of demand for labour.

One of the more remarkable features of the Phillips Curve, and one which distinguishes it from most similar studies, was that it was found to be highly reliable in predicting increases in wages during much later periods of time than the years 1861-1913 which had been used to derive the equation. Thus Phillips was able to show a very close correspondence for 1948-57 between the wage changes implied by his relationship and those that actually took place (the largest error occurred in 1951 when prices had increased exceptionally fast). It can be seen from the series in table 1.12 that the predictive claims of the Phillips Curve were

---

1   A. W. Phillips, 'The Relation between Unemployment and the Rate of Change of Money Wage Rates, 1861-1957', *Economica,* November 1958; reprinted in R. J. Ball and P. Doyle, *Inflation,* Penguin Books, 1969.

2   The equation for the schedule was:

$$\frac{\Delta W}{W} = -0.900 + 9.638U^{-1.394}$$

It can also be expressed in logarithmic terms as

$$\log\left(\frac{\Delta W}{W} + 0.9\right) = 0.984 - 1.394 \log U$$

where $\frac{\Delta W}{W}$ is the percentage rate of wage change and U is the unemployment rate,

(Phillips, *op. cit.*).

sustained for a good many years after the publication of Phillips' article. During the period 1958-66, for example, there was not a single error in excess of 2.5%, and the mean error (regardless of sign) was only 1.1%; furthermore, the positive and negative errors tended to offset each other so that the mean algebraic error was only 0.1% over this period.[1]

TABLE 1.12

Annual Indicators of Inflation, UK, 1953-75

	Change in Retail Prices[1] (%)	Change in Wage Rates[2] (%)	Displacement of Phillips Curve[3] (%)	Unemployment Percentage[4]
1953	3.1	3.0	−1.1	1.5
1954	1.8	4.4	−1.6	1.2
1955	4.5	6.9	−0.6	1.0
1956	2.0	7.9	+1.3	1.0
1957	3.7	5.4	+0.3	1.3
1958	3.0	3.6	+1.1	1.9
1959	0.6	1.1	−1.2	2.0
1960	1.0	4.1	0.0	1.5
1961	3.4	3.4	−1.2	1.3
1962	2.6	4.4	+1.6	1.8
1963	2.1	4.3	+2.5	2.2
1964	3.3	3.8	−0.3	1.6
1965	4.8	4.6	−0.6	1.3
1966	3.9	3.3	−1.3	1.4
1967	2.5	5.9	+4.0	2.2
1968	4.7	7.1	+5.2	2.3
1969	5.4	5.7	+3.8	2.3
1970	6.4	13.5	+11.9	2.5
1971	9.4	12.1	+11.4	3.3
1972	7.1	11.0	+10.4	3.6
1973	9.2	12.2	+10.7	2.6
1974	16.1	29.4	+28.9	2.5
1975	24.2	25.4	+25.4	3.9

Notes: (1) Change from annual level of previous year. (2) 12 monthly change in weekly rates from December of previous year. (3) + underprediction, − overprediction by Phillips equation, *op. cit.*, using unlagged unemployment data, GB, including temporarily stopped and school-leavers. (4) Wholly unemployed, GB, excluding school-leavers and adult students.

Sources: DEG, BLS.

Since 1966, however, the Phillips Curve has been quite unreliable as a guide to the rate of wage increase. The various reasons advanced for its breakdown include (i) the altered meaning of the unemployment figures, (ii) its omission of the rate of price change as a separate causal variable, (iii) its neglect of price expectations, (iv) the presence of wage push forces not previously encountered. Of these factors

---

1 An assessment of predictions from similar equations to the original Phillips Curve is given by J. G. Pencavel, 'A Note on the Comparative Predictive Performance of Wage Inflation Models of the British Economy', *EJ*, March 1971. The Phillips Curve appears to have done as well as any of the more complex equations that followed it.

it is probable that (i) and (ii) taken together are able to explain why the Phillips Curve was underpredicting wage increases by 4-5% over the years 1967-9. It has been shown by Artis[1] that wage equations which are estimated on the basis of the vacancy rate rather than the unemployment rate, and which allow for the influence of price changes, are capable of predicting wage increases in these years. The wage increase of 1970, however, was 6-7% higher than these relationships implied, and this suggests that there was a large residual element which was due neither to the changed meaning of the unemployment figures nor to the higher rate of price change.

This leaves explanations (iii) and (iv) as the two main possibilities. As regards (iii) it seems extremely doubtful, in the light of all the evidence, that price expectations have been a systematic element in wage bargaining. If they had been we should have expected outbreaks of fast inflation such as those which occurred in the Korean War period (1951-2) and in 1920 to have been followed by the continuation of fast inflation for several years afterwards. Furthermore, there is little, if any, direct evidence that the participants in wage bargaining have paid attention to price forecasts.[2] What does seem possible is that over the period 1970-5 wage bargaining in a small but growing number of sectors might have become sensitive to price expectations, whilst in a much larger number of sectors trade unions probably became more determined than hitherto to negotiate compensation for changes in the cost of living. This amounts to the conclusion that the response coefficients between the rise in average wages and the rate of increase in prices has probably increased during the 1970s as people have learned to live with inflation. This conclusion still leaves some room for a wage-push explanation of recent inflation, especially in the earlier years of the 1970s.

V.4 Wage-push Inflation[3]

The question of whether wages have increased as a result of unions pushing up wages independently of market forces is a controversial issue chiefly because of the very large volume of historical evidence in favour of a demand-pull explanation. This evidence, however, need not preclude the possibility of sporadic outbursts of wage-push inflation. Nor is there any case in principle why wage bargaining procedures should respond precisely to the pressure of demand in the labour market.

The main evidence in favour of a wage-push contribution to recent inflation concerns the 'pay explosion' of 1970 when the rate of wage increase rose abruptly (see table 1.12) even though there was no marked increase either in the pressure

---

1 M. J. Artis, 'Some Aspects of the Present Inflation', *NIER*, February 1971, reprinted in H. G. Johnson and A. R. Nobay (eds.), *The Current Inflation*, Macmillan, 1971.

2 Although it would not be surprising if such evidence were uncovered for 1974 and 1975.

3 See Aubrey Jones, *The New Inflation*, Penguin, 1973; D. Jackson, H. A. Turner and F. Wilkinson, *Do Trade Unions Cause Inflation?*, Cambridge University Press, 1972; P. Wiles, 'Cost Inflation and the State of Economic Theory', *EJ*, June 1973; E. H. Phelps Brown, 'The Analysis of Wage Movements under Full Employment', *SJPE*, November 1971; K. Coutts, R. Tarling and F. Wilkinson, 'Wage Bargaining and the inflation process', *Economic Policy Review*, No. 2, March 1976, Department of Applied Economics, University of Cambridge; M. C. Kennedy, 'Recent Inflation and the Monetarists', *Applied Economics*, June, 1976.

of demand for labour or in the rate at which prices were increasing. It is difficult
to see how price expectations could have been responsible when prices had been
rising quite moderately. And although in 1970 there was a marked relaxation (in
response to union pressure) of the government's incomes policy, this could not
have explained why in 1971 and 1972 the rate of wage increase continued to be
much higher than would have been expected on the basis of what was happening
to excess demand and prices.

There are a number of possible explanations for the abnormal wage increases in
these years. They include a growing frustration on the part of trade unionists with
the slow increase in real wages, both before and after tax, and resentment towards
the policies of high (or apparently high) unemployment after 1966. These feelings
of frustration may well have been intensified by the brave predictions set out in the
National Plan of 1965. In addition to these factors the succession of incomes policies
tried since 1965 was seen as interfering with the traditional freedom of collective
bargaining, whilst the proposals (in 1969) and legislation (in 1971) for the reform of
industrial relations were interpreted, rightly or wrongly, as a deliberate act on the
part of government to shift the balance of power from unions to employers.

Independent evidence for a greater militancy on the part of trade unions is to be
found in the very large increase in the incidence of strikes. It may be significant
for example that the number of days lost in industrial disputes more than doubled
between 1968 and 1970 and remained extremely high for some years. It is also the
case that the proportion of disputes over pay increased appreciably over the same
period.[1] These figures are certainly suggestive of a higher degree of militancy
within the trade unions than in earlier years.

In the years following 1972, when rising import prices became the main factor
in the exceptionally fast rate of inflation, it is difficult to distinguish the influence
of wage-push from the increased sensitivity of wages to past (and perhaps expected)
price increases.

V.5   Notes on Recent Controversies[2]

The rapid inflation of the 1970s gave rise to a sharp controversy as to its manner of
causation between two groups of economists, the monetarists and the 'Keynesians'.
The monetarists maintained that the rapidity of the inflation could be explained in
two ways: first, by the very large increases over the period in the supply of money

1   *DEG*, February 1976, p. 115, gives the proportion of stoppages caused by pay disputes as
    47% in 1966 and 1967, 54% in 1968, 59% in 1969 and 64% in 1970. See also Ch.5, N.2.
2   The various sides of the controversy can be found in Aubrey Jones, *The New Inflation*,
    Penguin, 1973; D. Jackson, H. A. Turner and F. Wilkinson, *Do Trade Unions Cause
    Inflation?*, Cambridge University Press, 1972; P. Wiles 'Cost Inflation and the State of
    Economic Theory', *EJ*, June 1973; E. H. Phelps Brown, 'The Analysis of Wage Movements
    under Full Employment', *SJPE*, November 1971; M. J. Artis, 'Some Aspects of the Present
    Inflation', *op. cit.*; M. Parkin, 'United Kingdom Inflation: the Policy Alternatives', *NWBR*,
    May 1974; M. Parkin, 'Where is Britain's Inflation Rate Going', *LBR*, July 1975; Sir John
    Hicks, 'What is Wrong with Monetarism?', *LBR*, October 1975; Lord Kahn, 'Thoughts on
    the Behaviour of Wages and Monetarism', *LBR*, January 1976; H. G. Johnson, 'What is
    Right with Monetarism', *LBR*, April 1976; E. H. Phelps Brown, 'A Non-Monetarist View of
    the Pay Explosion', *TBR*, March 1975; M. C. Kennedy, 'Recent Inflation and the
    Monetarists', *Applied Economics*, June 1976.

(see table 1.13); secondly, by the theory of the augmented Phillips Curve under which the rate of wage increase was taken to be determined by a constant and stable relationship with both the pressure of demand for labour and the expected rate of increase in prices.[1] It was maintained that the level of unemployment had been held at a lower rate than the natural rate with the certain consequence that price expectations would lead to accelerating inflation.

The evidence for the monetarist case lay in a series of attempts to identify and estimate the augmented Phillips Curve econometrically and also in one rather crude correlation between the rate of increase in the money supply (M1) and the rate of price inflation some two and a half to three years afterwards.

As against this position the 'Keynesians' have argued that the increase in the quantity of money was permissive rather than causal, and some of them were reluctant to accept the Phillips relationship between wage increases and the pressure of demand for labour.[2] They saw the inflation as having been caused predominantly by the rapid rise in import prices (which the monetarists had neglected) and also by some measure of wage-pushfulness. Their case would have been stronger if they had produced a more vigorous critique of the monetarist evidence or if they had provided better evidence for their own point of view.

It will be clear that the position adopted in this chapter lies very close to the 'Keynesian' view. It agrees that the increase in the quantity of money was permissive not causal; if money had caused the inflation it would have done so through the normal mechanisms of demand-pull, with the consequence that there would have been an observable increase in the pressure of demand. In point of fact the vacancy rate (see table 1.13) was no different in 1970-5 than in the previous six years. We also agree that the principal factor in the increased rate of inflation was the colossal rise in import prices (100% from 1972 to 1974), only a small part of which was attributable to exchange depreciation. Indeed the neglect of import prices by the monetarists (especially in attributing the rise in prices wholly to monetary expansion) appears to be a most serious omission.

We also agree that a secondary, but earlier, cause of the recent inflation was the more militant stance which was taken by the trade unions (see the disputes figures in table 1.13), but, contrary to some Keynesians, we accept the basic message of the Phillips relationship. Thus we are prepared to regard demand-pull in the labour market as having been the main determinant over long periods of history of the rate of wage increase, and regard the upwards shift in the Phillips Curve in 1970-2 as an exception to the historical record. We disagree with the monetarists in regarding this shift as due to price expectations on the grounds that there is no direct evidence that wage bargaining was influenced by such expectations and because the rate of inflation prior to the 1970 pay explosion was not sufficiently rapid to warrant the expectation of a high price increase. Indeed the lack of overt attention by the monetarists to the 1970 pay explosion seems to be an important omission from their case.

As regards the augmented Phillips Curve we take the view that it provides an

---

1 Symbolically as $\dot{W} = f(U) + a \dot{P}^e$ where $\dot{W}$ = annual percentage wage increase, U = unemployment, $f'(U) < o$, a = a constant coefficient, generally assumed to be unity, $\dot{P}^e$ expected rate of increase in prices. The natural unemployment rate is the rate where $\dot{P}^e$ and $\dot{W}$ are both zero.

2 By no means all Keynesians reject the Phillips Curve.

TABLE 1.13

UK Inflation, 1964-9 and 1970-5

	1964-9	*1970-5*
Average of annual increases in retail prices (%)	4.1	12.1
Average of annual increases in hourly wage rates (%)	6.0	16.9
Average unemployment percentage, GB, excluding school leavers and adult students seeking work	1.9	3.1
Average unfilled vacancies as percentage of labour force	1.0	0.9
Average of annual increases in import prices (unit values, %)	3.5	18.4
Average of annual changes in the effective exchange rate (%)	–	−4.7
Average number of days lost per year in industrial disputes	3.7m	12.8m
Average annual increase in money supply (M3, %)	5.5	14.5

Sources: ETAS, DEG, NIER, FS, AAS.

unrealistic account of wage bargaining behaviour during the period of moderate, creeping inflation. In our view wage bargaining was characterized by considerable money illusion and lack of foresight. Indeed, if expectational wage bargaining had been the normal form of behaviour we should expect the rate of inflation to have accelerated in the 1950s, when the economy was being run at much lower unemployment rates (and higher demand pressure) than in the late 1960s. Thus we do not believe that running the economy below the natural rate of unemployment was the initiating cause of the acceleration of inflation.

We agree with the monetarists in regarding the augmented Phillips relationship as an important hypothesis of great potential application. But we regard its expectational assumptions as standing for a mode of behaviour which will tend to emerge only as people learn to live with inflation, and not as true for all time. (These assumptions *may* have been partially true of UK behaviour in 1974 and 1975.) Inflation can accelerate both as people learn to live with it and, once the learning process is complete, because price expectations become fully matched by wage increases. This dual danger of acceleration means that a high priority has to be given to correcting it.

V.6   Inflation and Economic Policy

In the period when inflation was merely creeping it was possible to regard it as a small price to pay for the benefit of high employment. A gently sloping trade-off between inflation and unemployment made the problem of political compromise minimal compared with the recent situation. The advocacy of an incomes policy in the 1960s was associated either with those who hoped to be able to run the economy at a pressure of demand which now seems unthinkable, or else with those who sought to use it as an instrument of income re-distribution.

The arrival of fast inflation in the 1970s transformed the policy problem. It resulted in a rapid erosion of real incomes during the intervals between wage settlements, with effects that were socially divisive and disruptive. It also transformed economic behaviour. Economic units learned how to live with inflation and sought to defend their real wages either by insisting on a full compensation for past increases in the cost of living or possibly, in a few cases, by bargaining on the basis of price forecasts. This meant that by 1975, if not earlier, there were only two ways of bringing inflation under control. One was to deflate domestic demand to such a low pressure that the effect of unemployment upon the rate of wage increase was large enough to offset that of cost-of-living compensation and/or price expectations. Given that prices in 1975 were increasing by 24% a year this would have necessitated either an intolerably high unemployment figure or an impossibly long period of correction. The other alternative was to subject the rate of wage increase to firm, quasi-statutory control. In early 1975 the only form of wage control in existence was the so-called 'social contract' between the government and trade unions, under which wages were being driven upwards by compensation for price increases. In July 1975, however, the government was able to reach agreement with the trade unions upon a maximum wage increase of £6 a week, equivalent to about 10% of the average wage packet.[1] The winning of union agreement to this proposal was a singular act of diplomacy, although it must have owed a good deal to the growing realization by trade unionists that inflation was not in their interests. By March 1976 the rate of price increase over a six month period had fallen to about 7%, which suggested that the £6 a week policy might well have been the first form of incomes policy to have made a significant impact upon the inflation rate. But it also raised the question of whether the policy would continue to be acceptable for much longer and of whether a satisfactory replacement for it would be found late in 1976 without resort to full statutory control.

VI   ECONOMIC GROWTH
VI.1   The Growth of Productive Potential

In ordinary language it is usual enough to speak of any increase in GDP, however it comes about, as economic growth. In economic theory and applied economics it is best to reserve the term for increases in a country's productive potential. This means that demand-induced spurts of economic expansion, such as those occurring in cyclical recoveries, do not qualify as economic growth in the sense we have in mind.

The growth rate of productive potential can only be measured satisfactorily over very long intervals of time or between periods when the utilization of resources was closely similar. Thus the periods indicated in table 1.14, which presents estimates of the growth rate in the UK, have been chosen because they begin and end with similar rates of unemployment.

---

1   *The Attack on Inflation,* Cmnd. 6151, July 1975.

TABLE 1.14

Economic Growth, UK, 1900-74

	GDP	Percentage increase per annum in		
		GDP per Man	Employed Labour Force	Capital Stock excluding Dwellings
1900-13	1.0	0.0	1.0	1.9
1922-38	2.3	1.1	1.2	1.1
1950-7	2.5	1.7	0.8	2.6
1957-65	3.2	2.4	1.0	3.8
1965-74	2.3	2.4	−0.1	4.3

Sources: ET, October 1975, *NIBB 1964-74, ETAS,* London and Cambridge Economic Service, *The British Economy, Key Statistics, 1900-1970.*

The table shows that both the growth rates of productive potential and the underlying trend in productivity have increased since the beginning of this century.

The concept of the growth rate of productive potential is not without its limitations. In the first place it says little or nothing about the causes of growth but simply describes a time-trend. An extrapolation of the growth rate for any period into the future could easily turn out wrong if the forces that determine full employment output are going to be present in different amounts or combinations from those of the past.

A second reservation concerns the interpretation of growth *rates* generally and their relation to *levels.* In calculating growth from 1965 to 1974, for example, one takes the compound rate of increase which will transform the level of GDP in 1965 into that of 1974. This does not tell us anything about the intervening years, during which the level of GDP could have been above or below the suggested time path. Thus the average *rate* of growth is, in general, no guide to the average *level* of output over the period. An allied point is that the *level of potential output* is arbitrarily defined by the unemployment (or vacancy) rate at which it is measured. This does not necessarily represent the maximum attainable level.

One of the questions which the economics of growth must try to answer is why some countries have grown so much faster than others and why, in particular, the underlying growth rate of the UK economy has been slower in the postwar period than that of most other industrial countries (see table 1.15). The answer, if it is to be found at all, must be sought under the more general heading of the causes of economic growth.

The causes of economic growth have been debated by economists since the time of Adam Smith. Growth must depend, in the first instance, upon the increase in the quantity and quality of the factors of production and the efficiency with which they are combined. These increases may be influenced, however, by factors on the side of demand such as the pressure of demand on resources and the degree to which it fluctuates.

The supply of labour depends primarily on the evolution of the population of working age, including net migration, the secular decline in hours worked, and the increase in the length of annual and national holidays. Changes in the pressure of

TABLE 1.15

Rates of Growth, 1962-72

	Annual percentage rates	
	GDP	*GDP per capita*
Belgium	4.3	4.8
Denmark	3.9	4.6
France	4.7	5.7
Germany	3.6	4.5
Italy	3.9	4.6
Japan	9.2	10.4
Netherlands (1963-72)	4.4	5.6
Sweden	2.9	3.7
United Kingdom	2.2	2.7
Canada	3.8	5.5
United States	3.0	4.2

Source: National Accounts of OECD Countries, 1961-72.

demand, however, affect the size of the labour force and the number of hours worked, and, over the longer period, may influence migration.

The quality of labour must in large degree depend upon the facilities available for education and training, the opportunities taken of them, and the degree to which they match the changing demands for skills arising out of changes in technology and the structure of aggregate demand. Measurement of these influences, however, is difficult and there is little evidence to show which way, if at all, they have affected the international comparison in table 1.15. The mobility of labour from job to job and from area to area is probably an important factor in economic growth in so far as it reflects the degree to which the labour force can adjust to economic change. It has been argued, not without evidence, that much of the relatively fast growth of the German, Italian and French economies can be attributed to the movement of labour from the agricultural to the industrial sectors.[1] But it is still not clear how much of this mobility has been a cause and how much a consequence of the disparity in growth rates between the agricultural and industrial sectors.

One obvious influence on the growth of labour productivity is the rate of increase in the nation's stock of capital, both in quantity and in quality. Some indications of the growth of the UK capital stock are given in table 1.14, where it can be seen that the rate of increase, like that of productivity, has tended to rise during the course of this century. The stock of capital, however, is extremely difficult to measure. This is because the figures of depreciation in the national accounts are based on data collected for tax purposes and cannot serve as very precise indications of the rates of scrapping and deterioration of existing capital. Moreover, the economic value of a piece of capital equipment is an inherently subjective concept, depending on expectations of future returns and modified by problems of evaluating risk. Estimates of the capital stock, therefore, must be treated with a good deal of reserve.

---

1 A. Maddison, *Economic Growth in the West,* Allen and Unwin, 1964.

The quality of the capital stock is, perhaps, even more important and even more difficult to measure. According to one widely accepted view the quality of capital depends, by and large, upon its age structure. This view looks upon the capital stock as a series of vintages of gross investment, each new vintage containing machines of higher quality than the previous one. Scientific and technical progress are embodied in new machines, not old ones, so that the most recent capital equipment is likely to be the most efficient. This view is the basis of the 'catching-up hypothesis' which has been advanced to explain the faster growth of some countries in the early postwar period. The argument is that those countries in which the capital stock was seriously depleted by the war were in a position to replenish it with brand new equipment, and were thus enabled to grow faster than those countries where the bombing and destruction had been less severe. The embodied view of technical progress, together with the difficulties of measuring the quantity of capital, has led a number of economists[1] to emphasize gross rather than net capital formation as the better indicator of the extent to which capital resources have been enhanced. A high rate of gross investment, even if it is entirely for replacement purposes, will reduce the age of the capital stock and increase its quality.

Turning to influences on the side of demand, two aspects of the question need to be distinguished: the average pressure of demand and the size of fluctuations around the average. It can certainly be argued that a low average pressure of demand such as obtained (to choose an extreme example) in the 1930s is inimical to innovation and investment. It hinders investment because capital equipment is under-utilized and because its continuation for any length of time is likely to set an unfavourable climate for expectations. High demand, on the other hand, will generally have the opposite effect. It has also been argued that high demand encourages managers and workers to devise new and better ways of working with existing equipment, thereby making technical progress of a variety which is not embodied in new types of machine. This effect has sometimes been described as 'learning by doing', and it fits in with the view that the scale of productive problems that have to be solved is itself a stimulus to their solution. Evidence has been produced, for example, to show how the time taken to assemble a prototype airframe has progressively diminished as the work force has gained experience of repeating the same jobs over and over again. On the other hand, it has also to be borne in mind that high demand pressure may work the other way. The presence of a sellers' market with easy profits could also diminish the incentive to innovate and even lead to lazy attitudes to production. Again, extreme pressure can promote mental and physical exhaustion. Thus for any single firm there may be some optimum pressure of demand where technical progress is maximized and beyond which the rate of progress tends to fall. For the economy as a whole the optimum pressure of demand is likely to be a rather complex average of the individual production units, and not something about which it is easy to make generalizations.

Another question is whether the amplitude of fluctuations tends to impede economic growth. It seems probable that the expectation of fluctuations will retard capital formation because profitability will be held down in periods of recession. It may also be the case that expectations of cycles lead to the installation of machinery which can be adapted to use in periods of both high and low output,

---

1 For example, A. Maddison, *ibid.*

whereas the prospect of steady growth could enable the introduction of machinery which would be specially designed to produce at a steadier level of sales. In this case it is likely that the extra adaptability will be achieved at some cost to the efficiency of capital, and growth will be slowed down. It may be no coincidence, therefore, that three countries with some of the lowest growth rates in the 1950s — the UK, US and Belgium — suffered sharper fluctuations in unemployment than the others.[1] (Japan was the exception to this rule.)

VI.2   Economic Growth and Policy

Governments prefer a fast rate of growth to a slow rate because it results in greater tax revenues from a given structure of tax rates, and thus permits a larger provision of public services (hospitals, schools and so forth) than would otherwise be possible. Fast growth may also render a policy of income redistribution less painful to the better off than would be so if the growth of income was slow or non-existent. Thus it is not surprising that governments have often announced a faster growth rate as a goal of economic policy.

What is not so clear, however, is whether the means of attaining faster growth are sufficiently well known and understood. There is considerable controversy among economists as to the effects on economic growth to be had from, say, a faster growth of the capital stock and from technical progress. Many would argue that neither are quantifiable, and that the attempts which have been made to quantify them are suspect in a number of ways. Thus it does not seem that growth policy is in the same category as, for example, demand management policies, in which moderately fine calculations can be made as to the effects of changing the instruments of policy by known amounts. Probably all that can be hoped for from policy to promote growth is action, or a series of actions, designed to create a climate which is favourable to worthwhile investment and innovation. It seems doubtful, however, if even the most determined attempt to alter the environment in this way would show results within the lifetime of a single government. Nor does it seem likely, to judge from earlier experience, that dramatic effects can be expected from the mere announcement of a growth target. This was last done in 1965 when the government published a National Plan in which the rate of growth of GDP was to have been 4% per annum for 1964-70. In the event the growth rate turned out to be only 2.4%, and much of the public investment which had been based on the 4% growth assumption proved to be excessive. It is still debatable whether the growth rate would have been any higher if the balance of payments had been managed more adroitly than it was.[2]

VII   ECONOMIC PROBLEMS AND PROSPECTS 1975-80

1975 was a bleak year for the UK economy. Business and financial confidence at the beginning of the year had sunk very low. The *Financial Times* index of share

---

1   On these points see A. Maddison, *ibid,* pp. 43-56, and R. C. O. Matthews, 'The Role of Demand Management', in Sir Alec Cairncross (ed.), *Britain's Economic Prospects Reconsidered,* Allen and Unwin, 1970.
2   See, however, W. Beckerman *et al., The Labour Government's Economic Record 1964-70,* Duckworth, 1972.

prices had fallen below 160, compared with over 530 in May 1972. The industrial
countries of the world were in their worst recession of the postwar period and UK
exports, in consequence, fell by 5% in volume between the second half of 1974 and
the second half of 1975. Over the same period GDP declined by $3\frac{1}{2}$% and manufacturing production by 7%. By March 1976 there were 1.2 million unemployed
(5.2% of the labour force).

In spite of low economic activity 1975 was a year of exceptionally rapid
inflation. In June both hourly and weekly wage rates were 36% higher than they
had been 12 months earlier, whilst the rise in retail prices was 24%. There was a
real danger that inflation would get out of hand as both wage settlements and
consumers began to anticipate its course. It was an achievement, therefore, for the
government to win union acceptance in July for a £6 maximum for pay increases
(about 10% of average hourly earnings). This maximum was widely observed, and
by March 1976 the rate of inflation in retail prices had come down to about 7%
over a six month period.

The UK inflation rate in 1975 was roughly twice as fast as in other OECD
countries. It helped to explain why the exchange rate declined and the balance of
payments was in deficit. The current account deficit in 1975 as a whole was £1,700
million, or roughly 1.7% of the value of GDP. The deficit in 1974 was even larger,
at 5.0% of GDP. These deficits were financed by substantial overseas borrowings
and drawings on the IMF, the repayment of which will put a considerable burden
on the economy in the late 1970s and 1980s.[1] It meant that policy had to aim at a
current account surplus, with the consequence that much of the growth in GDP
has to be allocated to exports (net of imports) rather than to expenditure of UK
residents. Thus the Public Expenditure White Paper provided for a growth of GDP
for 1974-9 of 3.4% a year but a growth of personal consumption of only 1.8% a
year[2] (see table 1.16).

These prospects of slow expansion and even slower domestic absorption were
confirmed in the Budget speech of April 1976, when the Chancellor of Exchequer
announced a target rate of unemployment of 3% for 1979, with the clear
implication that unemployment would be above this figure in the intervening
years.[3] Thus the Treasury's short-term forecast[4] provided for a rise in GDP of 4%
between the first halves of 1976 and 1977 (implying a small reduction in
unemployment) whilst the Budget speech referred to $5\frac{1}{2}$% increases in 1977, 1978
and 1979.

The government's strategy of slow economic expansion was based upon the need,
at some point of time, for the expansion to come mainly from exports. The
alternative would have been to stimulate consumption sufficiently to achieve 3%
unemployment in 1977 or early 1978. But this would have meant cut-backs later
(via tax increases) in order to permit exports to rise sufficiently to attain the
balance of payments target. Another probable reason was that a very fast expansion
of demand, even at a high unemployment rate, would have added to inflation.

Whether the plan to restore balance of payments equilibrium would succeed was

1 For details see *Economic Policy Review No. 2*, March 1976, p. 44, University of Cambridge,
   Department of Applied Economics.
2 *Public Expenditure to 1979-80*, Cmnd. 6393, February 1976.
3 Hansard, 6 April 1976.
4 *Financial Statement and Economic Report 1976-77*, HC 306, 6 April 1976.

TABLE 1.16

Growth and Use of Resources, UK, 1974-9
At 1970 factor cost prices

	1974	1979	Growth (% per annum) 1974-9
GDP	47,200	55,800	3.4
Balance of trade in goods and services	−200	+2,600	
Available for domestic use, of which:	47,400	53,200	2.3
Investment	6,000	8,700	7.7
Public expenditure (direct)	11,800	12,100	0.5
Personal consumption	29,600	32,400	1.8

Source: Public Expenditure White Paper, op. cit.

a subject of some uncertainty. The government was evidently assuming that the sharp fall in the exchange rate combined with a recovery in world markets would be enough. But doubts about the elasticity of demand for exports, the extent to which wages and domestic prices could be insulated from the effects of higher import prices, together with the extreme difficulty of forecasting world commodity prices, mean that the economic strategy outlined in the Budget and Public Expenditure White Paper could easily need amendment. A much more pessimistic view of the prospects was taken by the Cambridge Economic Policy Group which would have preferred import restrictions to devaluation as the main instrument of balance of payments adjustment on the grounds, first, that they would have been less inflationary via import costs, and secondly, that the sacrifice of domestic expenditure would have been smaller.[1] Their case, however, has to be weighed against the economic inefficiencies of import restrictions, the breach of international agreements, and the possibility that other countries might retaliate.

The other great uncertainty was the prospect of bringing inflation under control. The government's target, announced in the Budget, was to bring the inflation rate down to 10% in the winter of 1976-7, and to halve this figure by the end of 1977. To achieve this result the Chancellor took the highly original and controversial step of announcing in the Budget speech income tax reductions of about £900 million which were to be *conditional* upon union acceptance of a 3% level for pay increases. This was to succeed the £6-a-week policy in August 1976. These tax reductions would increase domestic demand and employment whilst leaving real take-home pay at the average level it would have attained without tax reductions but with an earnings increase of 7.5%. In terms of employment prospects the economy would be slightly better off with the 3% pay increase.

Negotiations between the government and the TUC immediately after the Budget reached agreement on a limit for pay increases of a little over 4%. If individual settlements conform to this limit it seems probable that the inflation rate will not be very far from the Chancellor's target during 1977.

1 *Economic Policy Review No. 2, op. cit.*

In summary, the problems of the UK economy for the late 1970s are those of a slow growing economy with a strong trade union movement which failed in mid-decade to achieve balance of payments equilibrium or to contain inflationary forces as readily as its competitors. It must now restore a balance of payments surplus although this means that a large part of its economic growth must accrue to overseas buyers. The residual left for home buyers has to be divided between public consumption, private consumption and investment. Real disposable personal income cannot rise faster than scheduled unless public consumption or investment is reduced. But because the increase in real net income is bound to be slow there is a danger of wage inflation breaking out again before price stability is achieved. A simultaneous failure to achieve the three objectives of price stability, balance of payments equilibrium and high employment leaves the slow growing economy with little room for manoeuvre.

REFERENCES AND FURTHER READING

An elementary textbook which introduces most of the policy issues discussed in this chapter is A. K. Cairncross, *An Introduction to Economics,* 5th edition, Butterworth, 1973, whilst intermediate books are F. S. Brooman, *Macroeconomics,* 5th edition, Allen and Unwin, 1973, and D. C. Rowan, *Output, Inflation and Growth,* 2nd edition, Macmillan, 1974. A good short guide to the national accounts is S. Hays, *National Income and Expenditure in Britain and the OECD Countries,* Heinemann, 1971. Economic fluctuations in the UK are described by R. C. O. Matthews in 'Postwar Business Cycles in the UK', in M. Bronfenbrenner (ed.) *Is the Business Cycle Obsolete?,* Wiley 1969. An advanced treatment of aggregate demand theory is given in M. K. Evans, *Macroeconomic Activity,* Harper and Row, 1969, whilst M. J. C. Surrey, *The Analysis and Forecasting of the British Economy,* NIESR and Cambridge University Press, 1971, is useful on forecasting. On economic policy there is S. Brittan, *Steering the Economy,* Penguin Books, 1971, and W. Beckerman (ed.), *The Labour Government's Economic Record 1964-70,* Duckworth, 1972, together with the articles by R. C. O. Matthews, G. D. N. Worswick and E. H. Phelps Brown in Sir Alec Cairncross (ed.), *Britain's Economic Prospects Reconsidered,* Allen and Unwin, 1970. On inflation the reader may refer to the reading in R. J. Ball and P. Doyle (eds.), *Inflation,* Penguin Books, 1969, whilst a contemporary discussion is G. Maynard and W. van Ryckegham, *A World of Inflation,* Batsford, 1976. On the current state of the economy the best general guide is given quarterly in the *National Institute Economic Review* and this may be supplemented by the annual *Economic Policy Review,* Department of Applied Economics, University of Cambridge.

2

Monetary, credit and fiscal policies
N. J. Gibson

I   INTRODUCTION: THE POLICY DILEMMA

The previous chapter attempts to convey an overall picture of the operation of the UK economy, paying particular attention to fluctuations in economic activity, the behaviour of prices, and economic growth. This chapter concentrates on a narrower area, the monetary, credit and fiscal policies of the authorities, that is, the UK government and the Bank of England.

The term 'policy' implies the existence of goals and a strategy or instruments to achieve them. For the greater part of the period since the second world war the most frequently cited policy goals in the UK have been the maintenance of full employment, price stability and fixed exchange rates, the encouragement of economic growth and the achievement of a 'satisfactory' balance of payments.[1] However, since the late 1960s the emphasis on the maintenance of fixed exchange rates has largely disappeared and instead more flexible exchange rates have become the norm, though this does not mean that the balance of payments has become a matter of little concern. Furthermore, in the last few years a reduction in the rate of inflation, rather than the maintenance of price stability, has come to dominate the policy goals of the authorities.

The standard policy instruments at the disposal of the authorities are monetary, credit and fiscal. That is, by changing the money supply, interest rates, the availability of credit and by altering tax rates and government expenditure the authorities may hope to realize some or all of their policy goals. But in addition to the instruments mentioned the authorities may vary exchange rates, restrict imports and impose controls on prices and incomes. They may even go beyond this and introduce rationing and other measures.

Once a set of goals is chosen a host of questions arise. Can they be defined precisely? Are they mutually compatible within the particular economic system, given the policy instruments at the disposal of the authorities? If they are not, which goals should be sacrificed or modified? Are there alternative policy instruments that might be used to achieve one or more of the policy goals? Have the authorities, or for that matter has any one else, the necessary knowledge about the relationships between instruments and goals? Do they know exactly when and by how much to manipulate the policy instruments or even how many instruments they need?

These questions highlight what might be called the policy dilemma. It is, for instance, not at all certain that full employment and price stability can be attained simultaneously with the help of the policy instruments currently at the disposal of the authorities. The reason, at least in part, is that there is apparently no simple,

---

1   See Chapters 3 and 5 respectively for an extensive explanation and discussion of the balance of payments and incomes controls.

well-understood relationship between the policy actions of the authorities and such magnitudes as full employment and price stability. The effects of monetary and fiscal policy may be apparent only after some delay and the delay itself may be variable, depending on the initial economic and other circumstances when the policy actions were first taken, as well as the events that subsequently impinge on the system.

This type of uncertainty and lack of knowledge and information about the precise relationships between instruments and goals has encouraged the search for what are called 'target' and 'indicator' variables. Target and indicator variables are, as it were, intermediate between instruments and goals and may be simply explained by an example.

Suppose it is known in a qualitative if not a precise sense that there is an inverse relationship between the rate of interest and real income, then it may be reasonable for the policy-maker to aim at a particular interest rate or set of interest rates as a policy target though his ultimate goal is the level of real income. However, the target may be affected by other influences besides the actual policy being pursued and so it may be important to have another variable or set of variables which indicate the direction of policy or the policy stance. In the field of monetary policy it might be the reserve base of the monetary system, which in principle is under the direct control of the authorities, and where an expansion of the base would be considered as a policy of ease and a contraction the reverse. Thus on this approach a policy designed to expand real income might be one which had as targets a lower set of interest rates than those ruling at present and the cash base as an indicator. Now if the interest rates in these circumstances were to decline as a consequence of a fall in investment expenditures, which could not be observed at the time, the authorities might be inclined to feel that they had already achieved their target. But if at the same time the cash base was being used as an indicator it might be found that this is not expanding as contemplated, thus alerting the authorities that other forces are at work and affecting interest rates. But, of course, the reality is more complicated than envisaged here. This is especially true of an open economy like that of the UK which is heavily dependent on external trade and which may, for instance, find that its ability to affect interest rates or the reserve base is severely limited by conditions in money markets in the rest of the world. Optimal policy in a world of uncertainty and incomplete knowledge poses extremely difficult problems.[1]

Implicit in the foregoing discussion of goals, targets, indicators and instruments are questions concerning both value judgements and how an economic system works. Each of these questions is a recurring theme in this chapter. Section II looks briefly at the theoretical and empirical basis of monetary and fiscal policy. Section III discusses the structure of the banking and financial system and examines some money and credit theories. The taxation system is considered in section IV which also includes a brief discussion of taxation within the EEC. Finally, in section V policy since the early 1960s is briefly surveyed and a short discussion of the prospects and possible implications of economic and monetary union within the EEC is also included.

---

1 T. R. Saving, 'Monetary-Policy Targets and Indicators', *Journal of Political Economy,* vol. 75, supplement, August 1967, no. 4, part II, pp. 446-65, also in W. E. Gibson and G. G. Kaufman, *Monetary Economics: Readings on Current Issues,* McGraw-Hill, 1971.

II   SOME THEORETICAL AND EMPIRICAL BACKGROUND
II.1   Certain Keynesian and Monetarist Positions

As implied above the use of monetary and fiscal policy presupposes some knowledge about policy instruments and goals. One view is that monetary policy is by and large ineffective and that, say, increases in the money supply and reductions in interest rates will have little or no effect as an encouragement to expenditure and hence will have little or no impact on economic activity, whereas fiscal policy in the form of changes in taxation and government expenditure will have substantial effects. Another view, but this time applied to fiscal policy, is that an increase in government expenditure will not stimulate an expansion of output and employment but will only substitute government expenditure for private expenditure. And, similarly, that a reduction in taxation will have no net expansionary effect on expenditure and hence output and employment. In contrast, however, changes in the money supply are believed to have marked effects on an economy.

Implicit in these contrasting statements are different models of the economic system. The first, which completely discounts the importance of monetary policy, is generally associated with an extreme Keynesian viewpoint; and the second, which completely discounts the importance of fiscal policy, with an extreme monetarist position.

It has now been argued persuasively that the first viewpoint does far less than justice to Keynes himself and that it is a serious misinterpretation of his work to attribute to him the general view that 'money does not matter'.[1] On the contrary he was greatly impressed by the power of monetary policy for good or ill as regards the functioning of the economic system. In particular, and despite the experience of the great depression, he was not an adherent of what has come to be called the liquidity-trap hypothesis, that is, that the rate of interest might have a floor below which it would not fall and possibly prevent the achievement of full employment. However, he certainly envisaged this as an extreme possibility and wrote 'whilst this limiting case might become practically important in the future, I know of no example of it hitherto'.[2] At the same time, neither theoretical nor empirical work supports an extreme monetarist position, one which has perhaps been unkindly paraphrased as 'money is all that matters'.[3]

However, to contrast the Keynesian and monetarist positions in this stark way may be unnecessary and even misleading. Recent work on the US economy suggests that, 'In the "short run" both monetary and fiscal policies have powerful effects, first on real output and, more gradually, on prices, with the relative size of the two effects dependent on the degree of slack in the economy'.[4] The same study also states that, 'in the longest run the response of the economy to both monetary and fiscal policy is very much consistent with the views advanced by Friedman and the monetarists. In particular, the money supply does *not* affect real output, or real

---

1   Axel Leijonhufvud, *On Keynesian Economics and the Economics of Keynes: A study in Monetary Theory*, Oxford University Press, 1968.
2   J. M. Keynes, *The General Theory of Employment, Interest and Money*, Macmillan, 1936, p. 207.
3   James Tobin, 'The Monetary Interpretation of History: A Review Article', *AER*, June 1965.
4   F. Modigliani, 'The Channels of Monetary Policy in the Federal Reserve – MIT – University of Pennsylvania Econometric Model of the United States', in *Modelling the Economy*, edited by G. A. Renton, Heinemann Educational Books Limited, 1975, p. 241.

interest rates (money is neutral) but only the price level; and a change in real
government expenditure, money supply (and tax rates) constant, does *not* affect
real output but only its composition, as the expansion in government expenditure
tends to displace an equal amount of private demand'.[1]

Though there are dangers in applying uncritically to another economy findings
which relate to a particular economy the views expressed in the foregoing
quotation are, subject to important qualifications, similar to those which underly
this chapter. The qualifications concern the openness of the UK economy in the
sense of its large dependence on foreign trade, the ease with which funds can move
between UK and other monetary and financial markets and the existence of fixed
or floating exchange rates vis-à-vis the rest of the world.

In a regime of fixed exchange rates — or, indeed, floating rates if held within a
narrow range — and highly developed international capital markets, with freedom
of movement of funds between them, the ability of a single country such as the UK
to maintain interest rates at levels substantially different from those in the rest of
the world may be limited. This may clearly reduce the usefulness of monetary and
credit policy as an instrument of domestic economic policy. However, in the case
of fiscal policy and fixed exchange rates the conclusion is rather different; changes
in fiscal policy may still affect domestic output and employment. For instance, an
expansionary fiscal policy will in the short run generally tend to increase output and
employment.

With flexible exchange rates the conclusions are more or less reversed. An
expansionary monetary and credit policy will tend to depress the exchange rate and
thereby stimulate exports and discourage imports and so help to increase domestic
economic activity.[2] But an expansionary fiscal policy will tend to increase interest
rates and encourage a net inflow of capital, which will raise the exchange rate with
adverse effects on exports and hence output and employment. This in turn will
tend to offset the expansionary impact of the original fiscal policy. However, these
conclusions may of course require modification depending on how the rest of the
world responds to the particular policy changes.

For monetarists inflation is essentially a monetary phenomenon and in principle
can be controlled by restricting the rate of growth of the money stock to a rate
equal to the secular rate of growth of output, making if need be some allowance
for population growth. Monetarists go on to argue that once an inflationary process
is under way economic behaviour is strongly affected by expectations about the
future levels of prices and that attempts to reduce the pace of inflation by a more
restrictive monetary policy will generally bring about conditions in which output
and employment may be static or declining, whilst prices continue to rise. In other
words monetarists are not surprised by what has come to be called 'stagflation'.
Indeed monetarists tend to believe that inflation in market-based economies cannot
be cured without the cost of sluggish or even declining rates of growth of output
and rising unemployment in the short run.

---

1 *ibid.*

2 The term 'exchange rate', in conformity with British practice, refers to the price of one unit
   of the domestic currency in terms of a foreign currency. It is frequently much more
   convenient to follow the opposite practice and define an exchange rate – just like any
   other price – in terms of the number of units of domestic currency per unit of foreign
   currency.

Keynesians, and indeed others — with varying degrees of emphasis — are inclined to see inflation not primarily as a monetary phenomenon but as a consequence of a dynamic adjustment process whereby groups of workers and business interests struggle to preserve or improve, largely by wage and price fixing, their relative shares of the real national income.[1] This struggle is seen as often bringing both workers and business into conflict with government, upon which each of them may put such pressure that it feels obliged to pursue policies consistent with at least their short-term wishes. The apparent logic of this approach is *not* restrictive monetary and fiscal policies but rather a wages, prices and incomes policy; for whilst it is generally not denied that the former may succeed in reducing the growth of output and increasing the level of unemployment it will do little, on the basis of this argument, to come to grips with the fundamental causes of inflation.

Apart from the last paragraph the preceding brief exposition stresses the simple comparative statics of monetary and fiscal policy. This has its uses but is necessarily incomplete, particularly because of its neglect of the dynamics of adjustment processes, that is the ways in which the economic system acts and inter-acts through time. Such considerations are basic to an understanding of the on-going working of an economy and especially to the problems associated with inflation.

On the face of it the so-called Keynesian and monetarist approaches to the explanation of inflation are strongly opposed. It is doubtful, however, if this need be true. It is, for instance, possible to accept the importance of the rate of growth of the money stock to the inflationary process and yet allow for the possibility that a wages, prices and incomes policy may lead people to revise downwards their expectations about future price increases and hopefully avoid or lessen the phenomenon of 'stagflation'. At the same time, however, it must be conceded immediately that the success to date of so-called prices and incomes policies as a means of avoiding 'stagflation' would seem to have been limited.[2]

II.2   Views of the Bank of England

The Bank is necessarily committed to pursuing the major policy goals mentioned earlier in the introduction, though the relative emphasis placed on the individual goals may and does change through time. But, in addition, the Bank sees itself as having an overriding responsibility for the financing of the government and the management of the national debt and a general responsibility for the efficiency and stability of the whole financial system. These latter responsibilities, as interpreted by the authorities, are fundamental to an understanding of their approach to monetary and credit policy.

The Bank would argue that its approach to policy is pragmatic and necessarily conditioned by the economic and institutional circumstances existing at any point of time, as well as the general climate of professional opinion about the power of

---

1   This is not to deny that the behaviour of import prices, and capital flows and the like, over which a particular country may have little or no control, may be a further important factor influencing domestic prices.

2   For further discussion of inflation and prices and incomes policy see chapters 1 and 5.

monetary and other policies to influence the economic system. Just how important these considerations are is illustrated by the following excerpt from a lecture delivered by a governor and referring to the period immediately following the second world war. 'At the end of the war it was widely believed that interest rates should be kept low to finance reconstruction as well as to ease the servicing of a greatly increased national debt; and it was some while before it was universally accepted that a slump was not after all inevitable. A fairly comprehensive system of physical controls had been maintained to suppress inflation; and the doctrine of Keynes, at least as interpreted by his followers . . . had led to a totally new emphasis on fiscal policy. The active drive for cheap money was succeeded by a period in which monetary policy went into limbo. There was general scepticism about its relevance'.[1] There can be little doubt that the Bank shared this scepticism.

But towards the end of 1951 the authorities, largely in response to balance of payments problems, decided to reactivate monetary policy. This, however, did not in any sense imply that the authorities had become convinced that careful control of the money supply was the key to effective monetary policy. On the contrary, and with the possible exception of a period in the mid-1950s, monetary policy throughout the whole period up to the late 1960s placed major emphasis on influencing the cost and availability of credit to the various sectors of the economy. Much reliance was placed on hire purchase controls, the control of bank lending through quantitative and qualitative restraints, including ceilings on advances, liquid asset ratios and special deposits. Furthermore, through time the credit controls became more specific and direct with the authorities detailing the priorities that should be observed.

Since about 1969, however, the authorities have been more prepared to acknowledge the disadvantages of quantitative and qualitative controls and give more attention to the growth of monetary aggregates, including the money supply. This does not by any means imply that they have been converted to a monetarist approach to policy. Indeed a former governor has spoken of the 'emergence of a form of inflation markedly different from that of the immediate post-war period. Excess demand appears no longer to be the root cause . . . We have the unwelcome and unusual sight of rising unemployment and declining capital utilization coupled with rising prices'— circumstances which call into question the possibility of controlling inflation through measures of orthodox demand management'.[2] Nevertheless the Bank seems to have retreated from its extreme Keynesianism of earlier years. This viewpoint gets some reinforcement from the introduction in September 1971 of a uniform reserve ratio for the whole banking system, as a basis for monetary control, and a declared willingness to allow market competition to allocate credit and to determine interest rates, especially on longer dated government securities; and more recently the Bank has drawn forceful attention to the need to restrict the size of the public sector borrowing requirement if the growth of monetary aggregates is to be restrained to appropriate rates.

---

1   'Monetary Management in the United Kingdom', *BEQB.*, vol. 11, no. 1, March 1971, p. 41. See also, 'The Operation of Monetary Policy since the Radcliffe Report', *ibid.*, vol. 9, no. 4, December 1969, pp. 448-60.

2   *BEQB*, Vol. 12, no. 2, June 1972, p. 228.

II.3   Some Empirical Work

A great deal of the empirical work on the relative merits of monetary and fiscal policy as stabilization instruments has been carried out in relation to the US economy.[1] The evidence, as indicated above, suggests that monetary policy in terms of acceleration or deceleration of the rate of change in the money supply is important for the behaviour of both nominal and real income in the short-run and that fiscal policy may also have effects on output, employment and prices. Furthermore, some of the evidence also indicates that for stabilization purposes monetary policy is more powerful than fiscal policy. However, it should be stressed that these conclusions are provisional and should be treated as such. Nevertheless, there is no doubt that since the late 1960s there has been a major shift in professional opinion in the US on the importance of monetary policy as a stabilization instrument, which has frequently been coupled with a reduced emphasis on the significance of fiscal policy, which is not to say that the latter is unimportant.

Unfortunately, as far as the UK is concerned there is rather less empirical evidence available about the relative merits of monetary and fiscal policy as stabilization instruments. Moreover, the evidence that is available is to some extent conflicting.

One study, under the auspices of the National Institute of Economic and Social Research, tentatively suggested that fiscal policy might be more powerful and quicker-acting than monetary policy.[2] This conclusion is, of course, contrary to the analagous conclusions of studies for the US. However the authors of the National Institute study have major reservations about the econometric methods employed in these studies, including their own, and place little confidence in the conclusions of any of them.

Putting aside the fundamental questions relating to the methods used it would seem that the tentative conclusions of the National Institute study are extremely sensitive to the data employed, and perhaps to the time period used. For an alternative study, using different measures of economic activity and fiscal policy as well as a slightly different time period, produces conclusions about the relative effectiveness of monetary and fiscal policy that are consistent with studies for the US.[3]

There remains however some indirect evidence about the potential effectiveness of monetary policy which is worth mentioning. In a recent impressive study of the demand for money in the UK it has been shown that when proper allowance is made for major changes from late 1971 in emphasis and approach by the Bank of England towards the banking system — following the publication of their document on Competition and Credit Control (see below, p. 68) — there is reason to believe

---

1   The term 'stabilization' gives rise to problems of meaning and definition, particularly when a number of different policy goals are being pursued simultaneously. In the rest of this section it is assumed that the primary stabilization objective is the rate of growth of real and nominal gross domestic product.

2   M. J. Artis and A. R. Nobay, 'Two Aspects of the Monetary Debate', *NIER*, no. 49, August 1969.

3   M. W. Keran, 'Monetary and Fiscal Influences on Economic Activity: The Foreign Experience', Federal Reserve Bank of St. Louis, *Review*, vol. 52, no. 2, February 1970.

that the demand for money, variously defined, is stable and with income and interest rate elasticities which are, at least, suggestive of the potential effectiveness of monetary policy in terms of its power to influence income and prices through control of the rate of growth of monetary aggregates.[1]

Nevertheless, the absence of objectively convincing evidence about the merits of monetary and fiscal policy in the UK context makes it very difficult as will be seen to give a confident assessment of the policies pursued by successive governments. However, it seems fair to say that professional opinion in the UK, whilst it may not have moved as much as in the US, is less sceptical about the relevance of monetary policy, in terms of control of the money supply, as an instrument for economic management than it was a few years ago. This is not to say that professional opinion has seriously downgraded fiscal policy. Many British economists would still view it as the more important instrument. But there is perhaps one thing on which professional opinion is now generally agreed and that is that neither monetary nor fiscal policy can, in the present state of knowledge, be used for 'fine tuning' or, alternatively, sensitive, short-run control of the economic system. Furthermore there is growing conviction that the control of inflation must be a concern of monetary and fiscal policy which may perhaps be complemented by a prices and incomes policy.

➤ III THE BANKING AND FINANCIAL STRUCTURE AND MONEY AND CREDIT CONTROL
III.1 The UK Banking Sector

The UK banking sector consists of UK offices of all those banks which observe the uniform reserve ratio introduced in September 1971 and, in addition, the Banking Department of the Bank of England, the discount market and the National Giro. The banks which observe the uniform reserve ratio are classified into three main groups, UK, overseas and consortium banks. The UK banks include the London clearing banks, the Scottish clearing banks, the Northern Ireland banks, accepting houses and other UK banks. The overseas banks are made up of three main groups, American banks, Japanese banks and other overseas banks. Consortium banks are banks which are owned by other banks but in which no single bank has more than 50% of the capital and where at least one of the participating banks is an overseas bank.

Perhaps the most notable feature of the UK banking sector in recent years is its remarkable rate of expansion in terms of the number of banks involved and in the growth of deposits. The growth in numbers has been concentrated amongst other UK banks, overseas banks and consortium banks. At the end of 1975 almost 350 institutions were covered by the official UK banking sector tables published by the authorities. Ten years ago the figure was perhaps one-third of this number.

Because of the growing number of banks which get incorporated in the statistics there are difficulties in determining precisely the growth of deposit liabilities in the UK. However, bearing this in mind, at the end of 1970 total deposits of the UK

---

1 See, Graham Haache, 'The Demand for Money in the UK: Experience since 1971', *BEQB*, vol. 14, no. 3, September 1974, pp. 284-305. (It should be added that Mr Haache is more cautious in his inferences than is the statement of the author made above.)

banking sector were about £34,000m, whilst by the end of 1975 they had reached almost £108,000m, a compound rate of growth of nearly 26% p.a. Of these totals over £16,000m and £35,000m respectively were sterling deposits and the rest were denominated in other currencies. Thus sterling deposits grew at about 17% p.a. These developments have the most profound significance for the operation and control of the monetary and financial system of the UK. This point is returned to below in discussing the major categories of banks included in the UK banking sector.

III.2   The Bank of England

The Bank of England acts as banker to the government and plays a basic role in smoothing government cash transactions and in administering and managing the national debt — broadly speaking the debt liabilities of the state to its nationals, to its own agencies and to overseas holders. As agent of the government the Bank helps to regulate and control foreign exchange transactions and manages the Exchange Equalisation Account, which controls the official gold and foreign exchange reserves of the UK.[1]

The Bank is divided into two parts for accounting purposes; it produces two balance sheets, one for the Issue Department and one for the Banking Department. The origin of the double balance sheet system is to be found in monetary controversies during the first half of the nineteenth century. But the two balance sheets still retain a certain, if somewhat artificial, significance in that the Issue Department is classified in the national accounts of the UK as belonging to the public or government sector, whilst, as already mentioned, the Banking Department is classified for banking purposes with the banking and financial sector. The position of the Issue Department in December 1975 is shown in table 2.1.

TABLE 2.1

Issue Department (selected items), 10 December 1975 (£m)

Liabilities			*Assets*	
Notes:				
In circulation	6,138		Government securities	5,430
In Banking Dept.	12		Other	720
	6,150			6,150

Source: BEQB.

The notes in circulation are necessarily held by persons, companies and financial institutions. Notes in the Banking Department would, of course, disappear from the accounts if the two balance sheets were amalgamated. The assets of the Issue Department, except for some commercial bills, local authority debt and refinance credit for shipbuilding and refinance exports, under the heading of 'other assets',

---

1   See 'The Exchange Equalisation Account: Its Origins and Development', *BEQB*, vol. 8, no. 4, December 1968.

are almost entirely government securities and so any increase in the note issue generally implies an equal addition to holdings of government securities. In other words, when the Issue Department issues additional notes it obtains interest-earning government securities in exchange. Indeed the note issue may be looked upon as a means by which the government helps to finance its expenditure.

The assets of the Issue Department are a means of helping the government to organize its finances in another way. The government is continuously concerned with the issue and redemption of the national debt; it may need to borrow new funds or pay off maturing obligations. The government, and indeed the Bank of England also, is generally anxious to avoid large transactions, perhaps involving hundreds of millions of pounds, that might temporarily upset the securities market. They do this by arranging for the Issue Department to purchase new issues of securities that are not taken up by the public on the day of issue. Similarly, the Issue Department purchases stocks nearing redemption, avoiding large cash payments to the public when the actual redemption dates arrive. The Issue Department may in fact be in the market as a buyer or seller of government securities or both almost continuously. That is, it engages extensively in open market operations.

The balance sheet of the Banking Department is shown in table 2.2.

TABLE 2.2

Banking Department (selected items), 10 December 1975 (£m)

Liabilities		*Assets*	
Deposits:			
Public	21	Government securities	1,405
Bankers	322	Advances and other accounts	264
Reserves and other accounts	420	Premises, equipment and other securities	84
Special deposits	989	Notes and coins	13
	1,752		1,766

Source: BEQB
Note: The balance sheet does not exactly balance because certain subsidiary items have been omitted. This is also true of other balance sheets summarized in this chapter.

Public deposits are all government balances. They include those of the Exchequer, the National Loans Fund, HM Paymaster General, the National Debt Commissioners and Dividend Accounts. The total amount involved is relatively small by comparison with bankers' deposits despite the enormous scale of government transactions. The main reason for this is that government attempts to keep these balances as low as possible consistently with carrying out its operations. Any so-called surplus balances are used to retire government debt in an attempt to keep down costs. Net payments from the government to the community will have an immediate effect on bankers' deposits, increasing the cash holdings of the banking system. The reverse is, of course, also true and smoothing out movements of funds between public and bankers' deposits is a major pre-occupation of the Bank day by day.

Bankers' deposits belong to the London clearing banks, the Scottish clearing banks, the UK offices of other deposit banks, the accepting houses, a number of overseas and other banks and the discount houses. As bankers' deposits necessarily appear as assets in the balance sheets of these financial institutions and will therefore be discussed later, nothing more is said about them at this point.[1]

Reserves and other accounts include balances of overseas central banks, of the Crown Agents for overseas governments, certain dividend accounts, as well as unallocated profits of the Banking Department. The accounts of the bank's remaining private customers are also included here. These accounts are not without importance but they are not central to this chapter and so are not discussed further.

Special deposits were a new category of deposit, first introduced in April 1960, that the London clearing banks and Scottish clearing banks were from time to time obliged to transfer to the Bank in support of its monetary and credit policy. This scheme came to an end on 15 September 1971 when all outstanding special deposits were repaid. Since then two new deposit schemes have been introduced, the first on 16 September 1971 for interest-bearing special deposits and the second on 17 December 1973 for non-interest-bearing supplementary deposits. Both are discussed below.

Government securities introduce the assets of the Banking Department and include Treasury bills and longer-dated government securities and Ways and Means Advances to the Exchequer.[2] These advances occur if the Exchequer finds itself short of funds at the end of the day and wishes to make up its balance; the advances are generally only overnight loans, being repaid the following day.

The Banking Department, through sales and purchases of government securities, affects the volume of bankers' deposits and hence the cash holdings of the banking system. In general, government securities in the Banking Department can be used in much the same way as those in the Issue Department to facilitate debt management and monetary policy. However, the assets at the disposal of the Banking Department are much smaller than those available to the Issue Department.

Advances and other accounts are of two main types: discounts and advances to the discount houses and to the remaining private customers of the Bank. The first are by far the most important to the operation of the monetary and financial system and attention is concentrated entirely on them. They are discussed in the section dealing with the discount market.

Premises, equipment and other securities and notes and coins can be dealt with briefly. Other securities are non-government securities and include bills purchased by the Bank in order to keep a watch on the quality of the bills circulating in the London market. The Bank will not purchase bills of which they disapprove and this acts as a deterrent to their circulation. Other securities also include some holdings of equity share capital of other companies. Notes are the counterpart of the item in the Issue Department and some coin is held for ordinary business purposes.

---

1 See below, p. 76.

2 A 'bill' in the sense used here is a piece of paper which is evidence of indebtedness on the part of the person or body on whom it is drawn. The bill is said to be 'discounted' when it is purchased at a price below its value on maturity. Hence Treasury bills are evidence of indebtedness of the Treasury. These bills have usually ninety days to run to maturity and might be acquired by the discount houses at, say, £97.50 per £100, which would represent a discount of some 10% per annum on the value at maturity.

III.3   Money and Credit Control and the Bank of England

It was indicated above (p. 62) that in the late 1960s the Bank became increasingly
concerned that its use of quantitative and qualitative controls for the purposes of
monetary and credit policy adversely affected the efficiency and operation of the
banking and financial system. After very careful study it issued in May 1971 a
consultative document entitled 'Competition and Credit Control', setting out
proposals which purported to have 'the objective of combining an effective measure
of control over credit conditions with greater scope for competition and
innovation'.[1]

The main proposals in the document were:

(i)   to introduce right across the banking system a uniform minimum reserve
       assets ratio fixed at 12.5% of its sterling deposit liabilities,
(ii)   to extend the special deposits scheme to all banks, enabling the Bank to
       call for additional deposits to be made with it; and
(iii) that the London and Scottish clearing banks should abandon their cartel
       arrangements for the fixing of interest rates.

The foregoing proposals, after detailed discussions with the interested institutions,
became effective from 16 September 1971. Separate proposals were put before the
discount houses and finance houses; these are considered later.

The detailed definition of sterling deposit liabilities or what are now called
eligible liabilities of the banks gives rise in practice to certain difficulties. The
Bank has, for instance, excluded from the total, deposits, except certificates of
deposit, having an original maturity of over two years since it considers these to be
more akin to loan capital; and inter-bank transactions and transit items both
within individual banks and between banks are dealt with in special ways in order
to eliminate double counting.

From the point of view of monetary policy the most important question about
the eligible liabilities total is whether or not it is the appropriate aggregate for
stabilization purposes. In other words is there a reasonably stable and predictable
relationship between the chosen aggregate and some measure of economic activity
such as nominal income? A necessary condition for this to be true would seem to
be that the components of the chosen aggregate should be 'highly substitutable
one with another but largely complementary with other assets excluded from the
aggregate'.[2] In the present case this is unlikely as eligible liabilities vary from
demand deposits at one end to term deposits at the other, with, as mentioned
previously, a maximum life of two years. This has led to the surmise that the
Bank chose the eligible liabilities total not primarily for the reason indicated above
but because in the implementation of monetary policy it wished to treat all banks
more or less equally since, for many years, it has been arguable that the London
and Scottish clearing banks bore the brunt of restrictive monetary policies.[3]
However to impose *equal* reserve ratios on banks which would ordinarily operate
with very different asset and liability distributions is to affect their earnings very

---

1   *BEQB*, vol. 11, no. 2, June 1971, p. 189.
2   H. G. Johnson, 'Harking Back to Radcliffe', *The Bankers' Magazine*, September 1971, p. 117.
3   *Ibid.*

differently and in this respect is not equal treatment at all — the uniform reserve ratio may, in fact, be regarded as a form of discriminatory taxation. But it may be presumed that the authorities felt that in the interests of monetary and credit control over a greatly enlarged banking system these considerations had to be put aside.

The assets which are eligible for inclusion as reserve assets are very carefully defined. They 'comprise *balances with the Bank of England* (other than special and supplementary deposits); *money at call* (secured and immediately callable) with the listed discount market institutions . . . and with listed brokers: British government and Northern Ireland government *Treasury bills;* UK *local authority bills* eligible for rediscount at the Bank of England; commercial bills eligible for rediscount at the Bank of England — up to a maximum of 2% of eligible liabilities . . .; and *British government stocks* and stocks of nationalized industries guaranteed by the Government with one year or less to final maturity'.[1] In addition, the London clearing banks have to maintain as part of their minimum reserve ratio the equivalent of 1.5% of their eligible liabilities in balances at the head office of the Bank of England. Till-money is not eligible for inclusion as reserve assets. /

The most striking features of the reserve assets are their variety and their concentration directly and indirectly on government securities. As far as the first point is concerned, it is widely agreed that for the purpose of effective control of a monetary aggregate it is essential for the reserve base to be under the control of the authorities and that the demand for it 'from the banks and the rest of the economy [be] both highly stable and highly predictable'.[2] This is generally felt to be true of cash holdings and hence helps to explain the historical attachment to the cash base as a means of controlling the money supply. However, it did not seem likely that this would be true of the assets eligible for inclusion in the reserve assets ratio and the evidence so far would seem to bear this out. The banking sector would appear to have had little difficulty in satisfying its reserve asset requirements since the introduction of the new scheme and indeed has been able to support a massive increase in deposits.[3] In principle, however, the Bank could have prevented or at least slowed down this growth of deposits if it had been prepared to restrict the expansion of the cash base of the system — notwithstanding the existence of the reserve assets ratio — always assuming of course, a reasonably stable and predictable relationship, which is not to say a constant relationship, between the cash base and the volume of deposits. It seems highly plausible to suppose that whatever the authorities may have said from time to time about the growth of deposits they were not — perhaps for good economic, social and political reasons — prepared to take the kind of actions required to curtail their rapid expansion. This

1 Additional notes to Table 3, *BEQB*, vol. 16, no. 1, March 1976. The listed discount market institutions are the discount houses, discount brokers and the money trading departments of listed banks — there are six of the latter. Listed brokers comprise money brokers and jobbers on the stock exchange. Eligible commercial bills are bills which are payable in the UK and have been accepted by certain approved banks (*ibid.*).

2 M. J. Artis and J. M. Parkin, 'Competition and Credit Control: A General Appraisal', *The Bankers' Magazine,* September 1971, p. 113.

3 See below, p. 109. See also, E. V. Morgan and R. L. Harrington, 'Reserve Assets and the Supply of Money', *The Manchester School,* March 1973, no. 1, pp. 73-87 and Michael Parkin, 'The Discount Houses Role in the Money Supply Control Process under the Competition and Credit Control Regime', *ibid.,* pp. 89-105.

statement, however, needs some qualification as the authorities in the last couple of years have paid increasing attention to the rate of growth of deposits.

But to place excessive emphasis on the use of the reserve assets ratio as a means of controlling the supply of deposits is to misunderstand the intentions of the Bank. For spokesmen of the Bank made it abundantly clear at the time that they saw the new credit controls as an important means of retaining influence over *interest rates* in the short end of the market and not primarily as a means of controlling the volume of deposits. The then governor of the Bank stated that 'It is not expected that the mechanism of the minimum asset ratio and special deposits can be used to achieve some precise multiple contraction or expansion of bank assets. Rather the intention is to use our control over liquidity, which these instruments will reinforce, to influence the structure of interest rates'.[1] Nevertheless, it is doubtful if a spokesman of the Bank would be prepared to make this statement today.

At the same time as the authorities announced their minimum reserve assets ratio they amended and extended the coverage of their interest-bearing special deposits scheme.[2] The initial version of the scheme required that each bank should be prepared to deposit with the Bank of England a uniform percentage of its eligible liabilities, that is, its sterling deposits suitably defined. The Bank intimated, however, that in the future it might want to call for special deposits at different percentage rates on domestic and overseas deposits.[3] And subsequently the Bank announced a revised scheme.

Under the revised scheme the Bank may as before decide to operate a uniform rate of call for special deposits applied to *all* eligible liabilities or — and this is new — a variable rate of call. The variability may be achieved in a number of ways. First, eligible overseas liabilities may be subject to a lower rate of call or be exempted from a particular call. Alternatively, the Bank may call for special deposits in relation to the *increase,* if any, in eligible overseas liabilities over a specified time period. The call may be in addition to or separate from a call applied to the *total* of each bank's eligible liabilities. The revised scheme clearly gives the Bank considerable flexibility in differentiating between domestic and overseas deposits in making calls for special deposits.

In December 1973 the Bank announced a non-interest-bearing special deposits scheme as a supplement to the existing scheme. The supplementary deposits scheme is designed to curtail the growth of the banks' interest-bearing deposits and works as follows.

The Bank specifies a maximum or target rate of growth over a given time period for interest bearing eligible liabilities and any growth in excess of this is subject to progressively higher rates of call for supplementary deposits. The initial maximum rate of growth specified by the Bank was 8% for the six months from November 1973 to May 1974, the November figure being defined as the average amount of interest-bearing eligible liabilities outstanding on the make-up days for October,

---

1 'Key Issues in Monetary and Credit Policy', *BEQB,* vol. 11, no. 2, June 1971, p. 197.
2 The rate paid on interest-bearing special deposits is adjusted weekly to the nearest $\frac{1}{16}\%$ per annum to the average rate of discount for Treasury bills issued at the latest weekly tender.
3 *BEQB,* 'Competition and Credit Control: Further Developments', vol. 13, no. 1, March 1973, pp. 51-5.

November and December and likewise for the May figure. For rates of growth in excess of the 8% maximum the Bank announced calls for supplementary deposits at the following rates: for an excess of 1% or less the rate of call was 5%; for an excess of over 1% but not more than 3% the rate was 25%; thereafter the rate of call was 50%.

The Bank subsequently announced revised targets and arrangements for the supplementary deposits scheme. For August 1974 the reference level for calls and releases of supplementary deposits became 9.5% above the October-December 1973 average of interest-bearing eligible liabilities, rising to 17% for January 1975. The rates of call for a growth in eligible liabilities in excess of the permitted targets were changed to 5% for an excess of 3% or less, 25% for an excess over 3% but not more than 5%, and 50% thereafter. The scheme was temporarily suspended in February 1975.

Since the supplementary deposits scheme has been operative for such a short period it is difficult to assess its significance as a restraint on the growth of interest-bearing eligible liabilities. However, there can be little doubt that it was designed, in effect, as a form of incremental tax to make 'excess' growth highly expensive to the banks. But like all such schemes directed at a particular area of a complex and interdependent monetary and financial system it very likely encouraged institutions both subject to and outside the scheme (it also applies to finance houses) to provide alternative outlets for interest-seeking deposits. To the extent that that happens the scheme only succeeds in diverting money and credit flows away from the banks (and finance houses). And in so far as one of the proximate causes of the growth of interest-bearing deposits is the expansion or permitted expansion of the cash base of the system by the authorities themselves the scheme may in the longer term turn out to be relatively ineffective, at least as regards the overall problems of monetary and credit growth. In the short term, however, it may be somewhat more effective as it takes time for institutions, borrowers and lenders to find ways to circumvent such controls.

The foregoing discussion implies some scepticism about the effectiveness of the minimum reserve assets ratio and the special and supplementary deposits schemes as instruments of monetary and credit policy and hence as means of influencing the pace of economic activity, inflation and other economic magnitudes. The fundamental reason for this scepticism is the relative unwillingness – at least until recently – of the authorities to curtail the rate of growth of bank deposits. In other words the authorities have been prepared to provide the cash that enables the growth to take place. No doubt the reasons for this are complex and indeed the problems of controlling the cash base of the monetary system in an open economy subject to large capital flows should not be underestimated. Having said this, however, there remains the strong misgiving that the attention given to the minimum reserve assets ratios and the special deposits schemes is in part an evasion of the basic problem of the availability of cash to the system. Why this should be so raises many difficult problems including the scale and role of government financing and debt management and ultimately perhaps the functioning of our whole economic, political and social system.

III.4   The Discount Market

The discount market is officially described as being made up of eleven discount houses, two discount brokers and the money trading departments of six banks which all carry on essentially the same type of business.[1] The discount houses are a special type of financial institution which borrows a substantial proportion of its funds from the clearing banks and other institutional lenders such as accepting houses, overseas and other banks. Most of these funds are at call or short notice in the sense that these lenders may demand their repayment immediately or subject to very short notice. The discount houses use these borrowed funds to acquire both sterling and other currency assets. The assets include short-dated British government securities, Treasury bills, commercial bills, local authority bills and securities and certificates of deposit. Under the new credit control arrangements the discount houses were obliged to hold a minimum of 50% of their eligible borrowed funds in 'British government and Northern Ireland government Treasury bills, local bills and bonds and British government-guaranteed and local authority stocks with not more than five years to run to maturity'.[2]

In practice, however, the Bank found that the operation of the compulsory minimum public sector debt ratio had many disadvantages. In particular, it produced interest rate distortions in short-term money markets and complicated 'the Bank's task of securing adequate influence over credit extended by the discount market'.[3] The distortions arose primarily when a house or houses were operating near to the limit of their public sector debt ratio. In these circumstances if a house wished to acquire other assets it could only do so by simultaneously purchasing public sector assets. This had the effect of pushing rates on the latter to relatively low levels in comparison with rates on other assets. Similar problems arose when the Bank attempted to give help to the market through the purchase of public sector assets.

For reasons such as these the Bank abolished the public sector debt ratio and replaced it from 19 July 1973 with a new form of control. This limits for each member of the discount market its aggregate holdings of what are clumsily called 'undefined assets' — largely private sector assets — to a maximum of twenty times its capital and reserves.[4] The actual ratio these undefined assets bear to capital and reserves is known as the 'undefined assets multiple'. The new control should avoid at least some of the major distortions that arose from the use of the former public sector debt ratio. Nevertheless it still discriminates in favour of the public sector and could clearly give rise to difficulties for members experiencing a loss of reserves and thus inhibit their ability to expand. The capital resources base for the calculation of the multiple was £105m for 1976; it is calculated as a three year moving average of the end of December figure of the net worth of each member. If the clearing banks or other lenders demand repayment of their loans and the discount market cannot borrow elsewhere or otherwise obtain funds, the members

---

1   For a list of the names, see additional notes to tables 7, 8 and 10, *BEQB*, vol.15, no. 3, September 1975.
2   'Competition and Credit Control: the Discount Market', *BEQB*, vol. 11, no. 3, September 1971, p. 314. Company tax reserve certificates were also eligible for inclusion in the public sector lending ratio.
3   'Competition and Credit Control: Modified Arrangements for the Discount Market', *BEQB*, vol. 13, no. 3, September 1973, pp. 306-7.
4   Undefined assets are all assets other than the following: balances at the Bank of England; UK and NI Treasury bills, British government and local authority stocks with not more than five years to final maturity; local authority and other public boards' bills eligible at the Bank; local authority negotiable bonds; and bank bills drawn by nationalized industries under specific government guarantee. Source; *BEQB*, vol. 16, no. 1, March 1976.

TABLE 2.3

Discount Market (selected items) 10 December 1975 (£m)

Borrowed Funds		Assets	
Sterling: Bank of England	–	Sterling: UK and NI	
Other UK banking sector	2,262	Treasury bills	819
Other UK	200	Other Public	
Overseas	74	sector bills	197
Other currencies:		Other bills	783
UK banking sector	84	Certificates of	
Other UK	20	deposit	303
Overseas	39	Other funds lent	136
		British government	
		stocks	96
		Other investments	336
		Other currencies:	
		Certificates of deposit	129
		Other assets	15
	2,679		2,814

Source: BEQB
Note: Total undefined assets £1,441m; undefined assets multiple 15.3.

turn to the Bank of England which makes funds available to them against suitable collateral which, except for eligible bank bills, consists of the public sector assets formerly included in the public sector debt ratio. Furthermore, the collateral must include a minimum proportion of Treasury bills. The members of the discount market are the only financial institutions which have automatic access to the Bank in this way. This privilege was extended to the discount houses on the understanding that they apply each week for the full amount of the Treasury bill issue.

The traditional practice was that the bank acted as lender of last resort to the monetary and financial system, through the intermediation of the discount houses, by lending to them at or above a rate called Bank rate. But with the increased flexibility of short-term rates following the introduction of the new credit control arrangements in September 1971 the significance of Bank rate, which had formerly been a major reference point for other rates, declined. By September 1972 the rate on Treasury bills which historically had always been below Bank rate jumped to almost 1% above it. With the approval of the Chancellor of the Exchequer the Bank published 'new arrangements for determining and announcing their minimum rate for lending to the [discount] market. From 13 October 1972, the lending rate was to be ½% above the average rate of discount for Treasury bills at the most recent tender, rounded to the nearest ¼% above'.[1] The Bank, however, retained the right to depart from these arrangements and if need be announce independently of them a change in the *minimum lending rate* – the title which has superseded Bank rate.[2]

---

1 'Commentary', *BEQB*, vol. 12, no. 4, December 1972, p. 443.
2 The Bank did in fact depart from the minimum lending rate formula on 13 November 1973 when it raised the rate from 11¼% to 13%. The operation of the formula was restored when market rates adjusted to the new rate.

Traditionally, Bank rate was described as a penal rate as it was generally at a level in excess of what were called 'market rates' – the rates ruling in the market for Treasury bills and prime bank bills. The theory was that if the discount houses were borrowing at Bank rate they were therefore making losses and would hasten to pay off their debts to the Bank, with a consequential reduction in the cash base of the banking system. However, there were periods when public sector debt of the kind held by the discount houses yielded more than Bank rate. Thus the penal rate argument would not be valid for borrowings from the Bank against these securities and a similar argument holds as regards the minimum lending rate. Moreover, it is conceivable that if the discount houses were expecting a reduction in interest rates they might be prepared to borrow for a time at the so-called penal rates to take advantage of capital appreciation and high running yields on some or all of their asset holdings. The Bank, of course, has the option, which it may or may not use, to charge more than the minimum lending rate or to raise it. However, it is clear that the penal rate argument is not totally convincing, though the Bank is now in such a powerful position in relation to the very existence of the market that it is almost inconceivable that it would flout the wishes of the authorities.

For many years, however, the Bank has helped to relieve cash shortages in the money market by purchasing bills from the members at market rates, as well as providing funds at Bank rate (or, now, minimum lending rate) or above, depending on which the Bank felt more appropriate in the light of monetary and economic conditions. Furthermore, in June 1966 the Bank introduced an important modification in its method of lending. Previously *loans* to the discount houses had usually been for a minimum period of seven days and charged at Bank rate or occasionally above. But since then the Bank is prepared to lend overnight and generally at market rates.

Thus the Bank now exercises great flexibility in the supply of funds to the discount market. The Bank is also prepared to absorb by sales of bills to the discount houses surplus funds that they cannot otherwise conveniently employ. The Bank is therefore in a commanding position to influence day-to-day rates in this money market.

The discount houses occupy a very special position in the market for Treasury bills. Before the introduction of the new credit control arrangements the discount houses tendered as a syndicate at a single rate for the whole weekly issue of Treasury bills. Under the new arrangements and with the encouragement of the authorities they still tender for the whole issue but no longer at an agreed rate.

Covering the tender has the merit from the point of view of the Treasury that it 'guarantees' them the funds and probably helps the authorities to stabilize Treasury bill and other short-term rates. However, from another point of view the procedure is an odd one. For in the final analysis the discount houses are able to tender for the whole Treasury bill issue because, as already explained, the Bank stands ready to support them. Moreover, they would presumably become concerned if they could only cover the tender over a sustained period by borrowing at minimum lending rate. To avoid this the Bank may, as has been shown, supply the discount houses with funds at market rates. The discount houses then use the funds to acquire the new Treasury bills. But this is tantamount to the Bank lending directly to the Treasury and so increasing the cash base of the banking system, as the Treasury spends the funds, unless the whole process is offset in some other way, such as by the Bank selling securities to the non-bank public.

There is, in fact, an element of charade about the whole procedure of the discount houses tendering for the full Treasury bill issue. The danger is that the charade hides what is really happening — the financing of the Treasury by borrowing from the Central Bank. This may tend to subordinate monetary policy to the exigencies of government financial needs; and there is a lot of evidence to suggest that the consequences of this may be inflationary. Moreover, the procedure, and indeed the whole treatment of the discount market is fundamentally inconsistent with the competitive determination of interest rates by market processes, emphasized by the Bank in introducing the new credit control arrangements.

III.5   The London Clearing Banks[1]

The London clearing banks are so named because they are all members of the Committee of London Clearing Bankers. Up to 1968 there were eleven clearing banks, although not all of them were independent. But with the mergers of 1968 and 1970 only six clearing banks remain and these also are not all independent. The banks are dominated by the big four, Barclays, National Westminster, Lloyds and Midland, who between them control over 95% of total deposits and have a network of over 12,000 branches. The clearing banks' primary function is the management of the payments system in England and Wales, although they necessarily carry out all the usual commercial banking functions and, since the introduction of the new credit control arrangements and the greater freedom that has gone with them, have shown themselves increasingly willing to compete for time deposits, including negotiable certificates of deposit.

For many years the clearing banks acted as a cartel in fixing the interest rates they paid on deposits and charged on advances. These practices had come in for increasing criticism because of the encouragement they undoubtedly gave to uneconomic non-price competition, especially in the form of branch extension, and the general lack of dynamism they had imparted to the whole system. It would, however, be false to argue that the banks had totally stood aside from competing in terms of price for deposits and in granting credit. For many of them had done so through subsidiaries and associated companies such as finance houses (described below) and other financial institutions. To be unduly critical of the banks may be unjustified as it is highly likely that the authorities, with their predilection for short-run stability of nominal interest rates, condoned the existence of the cartel arrangements and would not have welcomed interest rate competition by the banks for deposits and advances.

Sight deposits and time deposits are the main liabilities of the London clearing banks. Sight deposits, which may or may not be interest-bearing, are withdrawable on demand and transferable by cheque; they are the most important means of payment in the economy. Until the introduction of the new credit control arrangements in September 1971 time deposits were interest bearing and subject to notice of withdrawal, generally seven days, and not ordinarily transferable by cheque. However, these conditions could be waived, though usually with some loss of interest. Since September 1971, however, the London clearing banks have in

---

1 Limitations on space do not permit discussion of the Scottish clearing banks and the Northern Ireland banks which carry on very similar activities in Scotland and Northern Ireland respectively.

Monetary, credit and fiscal policies

addition been prepared to take what are called fixed term deposits, that is, deposits for fixed periods which may be far in excess of seven days. Deposits and other items of the balance sheet of the London clearing banks for December 1975 may be seen in table 2.4.

TABLE 2.4

London Clearing Banks 10 December 1975 (£m)

(i) *Liabilities* Sight and time deposits:	Sterling[1]	Other Currencies[2]	Total
UK banking sector	695	824	1,519
Other UK	20,225	373	20,598
Overseas	1,015	2,453	3,468
Certificates of deposit	598	368	966
Capital and other liabilities	--	–	4,950
	22,533	4,018	31,501

(ii) *Assets*	Sterling	Other Currencies	Total
Notes and coin	798	–	798
Reserve assets: Balance with Bank of England	308	–	308
Money at call	681	–	681
UK and NI Treasury bills	912	–	912
Other bills	339	–	339
British government stocks up to 1 year	343	–	343
Special and supplementary deposits	564	–	564
Market loans and advances (other than reserve assets): Banks in UK and discount market[3]	(2,819) .... (2,566)	1,162	(3,981) .... (3,728)
Certificates of deposit	198	30	228
UK public sector	369	527	896
UK private sector	102	412	514
Overseas	1,869	1,863	3,732
Other advances[3]	(11,747) .... (12,000)	–	(11,747) .... (12,000)
British government stocks over 1 year and undated	1,370	–	1,370
Other investments	893	133	1,026
Bills	144	14	158
Sterling and other currencies miscellaneous assets	–	–	3,905
	(23,456) .... (23,456)	4,141	(31,502) .... (31,502)

Source: BEQB

Notes: Eligible liabilities £18,815m. Reserve assets £2,583m. Ratio 13.7%

1 Of total sterling deposits of £22,533m, sight deposits amounted to £9,724m.

2 The figures are affected by changes in exchange rates.

3 The second set of figures has been adjusted for the transfer of one of the former contributors to the banking statistics to other advances. The two sets of figures are provided to enable comparisons to be made with subsequent data.

Closely related to the fixed term deposits, though with at least one fundamental difference because of their negotiability, are negotiable certificates of deposit. These too have only appeared in the balance sheets of the London clearing banks since September 1971. The certificates are generally denominated in either sterling or US dollars. In the words of the Bank of England: 'A sterling certificate of deposit is a document, issued by a UK office of a British or foreign bank, certifying that a sterling deposit has been made with that bank which is repayable to the bearer upon the surrender of the certificate at maturity'.[1] The definition of a dollar certificate of deposit is analogous.

A sterling certificate of deposit is generally for a minimum amount of £50,000 and normally a maximum of £500,000 'with a term to maturity of not less than three months and not longer than five years'.[2] Certificates of deposit have advantages for both the issuers and the holders. Issuing banks have found them to be a useful means of raising large amounts for strictly fixed periods – unlike the so-called fixed term deposit where payment may be requested, and be hard to refuse, before maturity. And holders have found them highly convenient as they can sell them in the secondary market if they need liquid funds. The discount houses are the major operators in the secondary market. Certificates of deposit first made their appearance in the UK in May 1966 with the introduction of certificates denominated in dollars. Sterling certificates did not appear until October 1968.

Turning to the assets part of the balance sheet it may be seen that these consist of notes and coin, the various kinds of reserve assets, special and supplementary deposits, different types of market loans and advances, British government stocks of more than one year to maturity and certain miscellaneous assets. Some of these items require further discussion.

Notes and coin are used by the banks for their day-to-day business. The reserve assets include balances with the Bank of England which the banks use to settle their inter-bank indebtedness and to make payments to the authorities. If for some reason a bank, or the London clearing banks as a whole, find that their cash holdings are tending to fall below some desired ratio to deposits, they can rectify the position in a number of ways. It may be possible for them to sell or exchange some of their assets for cash, drawing on their balances with other UK banks, by selling stocks or negotiating repayment of advances or by recalling some of their money at call – another reserve asset – from the discount market. If the latter happens the discount market may, as already explained, have to turn for assistance to the Bank of England. This will generally happen if the banking system as a whole is short of cash. If the Bank does not wish to lend at its minimum lending rate, perhaps because it is anxious to keep interest rates from rising, then it will normally enter the open market and purchase securities at market rates, paying for them with cheques drawn on the Bank and so relieving the cash shortage. However, if the Bank wishes to see some upward pressure on interest rates it will wait for the discount houses to come to the Bank and only make cash available at the minimum lending rate or even possibly above.

---

1 'Sterling Certificates of Deposit', *BEQB*, vol. 12, no. 4, December 1972, p. 487. See also 'Sterling Certificates of Deposit and the Inter-Bank Market', *BEQB*, vol. 13, no. 3, September 1973, pp. 308-14; and the 'London Dollar Certificate of Deposit', *BEQB*, vol. 13, no. 4, December 1973, pp. 446-52.

2 *BEQB*, vol. 12, p. 487.

In so far as the Bank is not prepared to make a permanent net addition to the stock of cash available and ruling out a surplus of cash in the rest of the banking system then, unless there is an inflow of funds from abroad and which the authorities do not neutralize, some reduction in deposits of the London clearing banks or in the deposits of the banking sector as a whole may be expected. One of the consequences of this is likely to be upward pressure on interest rates.

Of the remaining reserve assets shown in table 2.4 money at call includes not only funds lent to the discount houses but also funds lent for periods not exceeding one month to money brokers on the stock exchange, discount brokers, jobbers and stockbrokers and bullion brokers. Treasury bills and other bills have been described previously. The London clearing banks, by an understanding with the discount houses and the Bank of England, do not generally bid for Treasury bills at the weekly tender, at least not for themselves, though they may do so on behalf of clients. Bills bought on their own account by the clearing banks are usually held to maturity, though they are, on occasion, sold to the Bank if the latter is looking for maturities that are no longer held by the discount houses. The purchase of bills by the Bank from the clearing banks is one of the ways by which the Bank may relieve pressure on the discount houses and obviate their need to borrow at Bank rate or above. This is described as 'indirect help' to the discount houses as opposed to 'direct help' by means of purchases from the houses themselves.

Special and supplementary deposits which have already been discussed need not be considered further. Market loans and advances includes a wide range of assets some of which are indicated in table 2.4. Loans to the discount market refers to funds which are not immediately callable and are unsecured in contrast with the money at call included in reserve assets. Advances, which are quantitatively of major importance, comprise not only other advances but also advances in other currencies under various headings and not individually specified. Advances are of two main types, loans and overdrafts. With the loan the customer's account is credited with the amount whereas the overdraft is literally an overdrawing of a current account which is debited accordingly. Advances are generally assumed to be the most lucrative of the banks' assets. Until the introduction of the new credit control arrangements by the London clearing banks, rates on advances were tied to Bank rate under their cartel agreements on interest rates. Each bank now fixes what it calls a *base* rate for advances. The base rate may differ between the banks but is generally close to the minimum lending rate of the Bank of England. The actual rates charged for advances varies with the nature and status of the customer but most rates are between 1% and 5% higher than the base rate. The London clearing banks do, however, have uniform rates for nationalized industries borrowing under Treasury guarantee and for certain other government supported borrowing.

The London clearing banks have responded to the increased flexibility provided by the new competition and credit control arrangements by competing more strongly amongst themselves and with other financial institutions. This is indicated by the marked change in their balance sheets over the last few years, both in terms of their rate of growth and of the structure of their liabilities and assets. They are now much more actively involved in what has been called the parallel money markets, such as the market for negotiable certificates of deposit, the inter-bank sterling deposits market – both as borrowers and lenders – and similarly in the euro-dollar market, that is the market or markets for US dollars held outside the US. In each of these ways the London clearing banks have in recent years diversified their activities and in so doing have narrowed some of the differences between themselves and other types of bank. However, the London clearing banks, like their Scottish and Northern Ireland counterparts, have a predominant proportion of their assets and liabilities in sterling and remain largely responsible for the day-to-day payments system; other types of bank, as will be seen in the next section, tend to concentrate their activities in other currencies.

III.6 Accepting Houses, Other UK Banks, Overseas Banks and Consortium Banks

The business of this group of banks varies substantially amongst themselves, although they have enough in common to allow them to be discussed together. Since about 1957-8, when exchange control restrictions were substantially relaxed and funds could begin to move more freely between international financial centres, the accepting houses, other UK banks, overseas banks and, more recently, consortium banks, have greatly expanded, and at a much more rapid rate than the clearing banks. Moreover, these banks have been active participants in the development of new and important money markets.

The term accepting house arose because of the important role the houses played and that many still play in 'accepting' bills of exchange, the commercial or financial bill already encountered in the discussion of the discount houses and the clearing banks. A bill is accepted by signing it and in so doing the acceptor becomes liable for payment of the bill on maturity. The accepting houses accept bills on behalf of clients and in this way earn commissions.

Accepting houses are also known as merchant banks since the banking side of their activities generally emerged as a consequence of their business as merchants, particularly in overseas trade. The activities of the accepting houses are excitingly diverse. The individual houses engage in one or more of the following activities: in the gold and silver bullion markets, the foreign exchange market, the foreign currency deposit business – including certificates of deposit – the making of new issues of both domestic and overseas securities, advising on mergers and takeovers, managing investments on behalf of clients, and acting as trustees.

Other UK banks refers to banks with majority UK ownership, leaving aside consortium banks which have foreign participation. The group also includes the offices in GB of the NI banks and also branches of their subsidiaries. The composition of the group is very diverse; it now consists of almost eighty members some of whom were formerly classified as finance houses as well as highly specialized banks in the fields of investment and international finance.

The overseas banks are banks which maintain branches or subsidiaries in London but whose main business is overseas. There are now almost one hundred and eighty of these compared with around eighty in the early 1960s; they play a major part in the movement of funds into and out of London and in the finance of international trade. Of the one hundred and eighty almost sixty are branches and subsidiaries of American banks and nearly twenty of Japanese banks.

Consortium banks are a recently introduced classification. There are nearly thirty of them and they are predominantly concerned with international finance and the management of foreign currency deposits.

In terms of total deposits this group of banks far exceeds in size the London clearing banks. In December 1975 the former had deposits totalling some £104,000m whilst the latter had some £27,000m. These are, however, gross

Monetary, credit and fiscal policies

TABLE 2.5

Accepting Houses, Other UK Banks, Overseas Banks and Consortium Banks 10 December
1975 (£m)

(i) Liabilities	Sterling[1]	Other Currencies[2]	Total
Deposits:			
UK banking sector	6,582	18,014	24,596
Other UK	7,139	2,273	9,412
Overseas	2,263	54,476	56,739
Certificates of deposit	2,329	5,984	8,313
Capital and other liabilities	–	–	4,741
	18,313	80,747	103,801

(ii) Assets	Sterling[1]	Other Currencies[2]	Total
Notes and coin	24	–	24
Reserve Assets: Balances with Bank of			
England	12	–	12
Money at call	951	–	951
UK and NI Treasury bills	783	–	783
Other bills	253	–	253
British government stocks up to 1 year	78	–	78
Special and supplementary deposits	361	–	361
Market loans and advances (other than reserve assets):			
Banks in UK and discount market	4,828	17,740	22,568
Certificates of deposit	1,444	1,729	3,173
UK public sector	1,947	2,041	3,988
UK private sector	774	4,923	5,697
Overseas	289	54,008	54,297
Other advances	8,376	–	8,376
British government stocks over 1 year and undated	377	–	377
Other investments	610	628	1,238
Bills	419	301	720
Sterling and other currencies miscellaneous assets	–	–	1,227
	21,526	81,370	104,123

Source: BEQB
Notes: Eligible liabilities £11,857m. Reserve Assets £2,077m. Ratio 17.5%.
  1 The figures are affected by changes in exchange rates.
  2 Of total sterling deposits of £18,313m sight deposits amounted to £3,209m.

figures and include inter-bank transactions as well as some internal accounts. This
element of double counting inflates the figures of the other types of bank to a
proportionately greater extent than it does those of the London clearing banks.
Nevertheless, in the last twenty years there has been a radical restructuring of the
banking system in the UK with the growth of these banks. The scale of the change
can perhaps be appreciated when it is recalled that their deposits totalled less than
£1,000m in the late 1950s.

It might, however, be argued that to contrast the total deposits of this group of banks with those of the London clearing banks is to exaggerate the significance of the growth of the former since so much of that growth has taken the form of foreign currency deposits or what is widely called euro-currency business, as may be seen in table 2.5. It should be noticed that the foreign currency deposits are roughly matched by foreign currency assets. To the extent that this is the case they do not directly affect the UK gold and foreign currency reserves. However, there may be indirect effects, both on the foreign currency reserves and on the management of monetary and credit policy generally, through the earnings of the banks and through effects on interest rates, which will necessarily have repercussions on the highly integrated London money markets.

But even in terms of sterling deposits this group of banks has come to rival the London clearing banks in terms of size with liabilities of some £18,000m and £22,500m respectively in December 1975. However, for the purposes of monetary and credit control the eligible liabilities of this group of banks of almost £12,000m in December 1975 remain somewhat less than the nearly £19,000m of the London clearing banks. But there can be no doubting the dramatic changes that have taken place in the UK banking system and there is good reason to believe that those changes accelerated in the past five years, in part under the influence of the new competition and credit control arrangements.

Furthermore, it seems doubtful that the reserve assets ratio introduced under those arrangements, as a means of influencing the activities of the banking sector, has been entirely successful. It would not be surprising if the authorities are at some stage forced to reconsider the introduction of cash ratios for the banking sector. This is not to suggest that cash ratios are necessarily a panacea for an effective monetary and credit policy but they just might make it rather more easy to implement one. Furthermore, the banking sector of the UK now operates on what would appear to be an extremely narrow cash base, with this group of banks in particular holding practically no coin, notes and balances with the Bank of England.

III.7 Finance Houses

A finance house is an institution which specializes in the financing of hire purchase, credit sales and other forms of instalment credit. There are hundreds of companies involved in this business but the bulk of it is carried on by a small number of large firms. Hire purchase and credit sale, though legally distinct, generally take the form of a down-payment by the purchaser with the rest of the debt being paid off by instalments over a specified period. The period varies with the type of product and may be as little as six months for some household goods or as much as five years for industrial machinery; the period for cars — the most important type of hire purchase debt — may be up to three years.[1] The finance houses attempt to organize their contracts so that the debt outstanding at any time on the transaction is less than the value of the product being acquired; this gives them some security and indicates why they concentrate on financing the purchase of durable or semi-durable goods rather than perishable goods. In practice hire purchase debt is frequently paid off well in advance of the terminal period. This is important in assessing the liquidity of finance houses' assets.

---

1 These periods are subject to controls by the authorities.

Deposits are the single most important liability of the finance houses and are of two main kinds: fixed term deposits, usually for three or six months, and deposits subject to notice of withdrawal, again normally for three to six months. Deposits may, however, be for as long as twelve months or even longer. The deposits earn interest at rates which are greatly influenced by those ruling in the money markets, especially the inter-bank deposits market and the market for sterling certificates of deposit. The chief depositors are industrial and commercial companies, banks, other financial institutions and other residents, as well as a small amount of funds from overseas residents. Current accounts are not unknown amongst the finance houses but do not appear to be a significant part of their business. Banks provide most of the remaining funds to the finance houses by means of discounting bills and by advances. Capital reserves are also important.

Hire purchase and instalment credit generally accounts for around 70% of their assets with most of the remainder made up of other advances and loans, leased assets and now reserve assets under the new credit control arrangements. Not all the hire purchase and instalment credit outstanding is owed directly to the finance houses; part of it arises from the purchase by the latter of debt from retailers and is known as 'block discounts'. Retailers do of course retain some hire purchase debt, but the finance houses own the bulk of it. Their next most important asset is advances and loans. These include loans to garages (to finance stocks of vehicles) and to property companies; and short-term loans to industrial and commercial companies. Until the introduction of the new credit control arrangements the finance houses held very few assets in liquid form, relying on their ability to attract additional deposits, on their borrowing powers and on the speedy repayment of their assets to meet any liquidity requirements.

The new credit control arrangements for those finance houses which come under the scheme are very similar to those applied to the banks. (Finance houses with eligible liabilities of less than £5m are exempt so long as they remain below this limit.) The minimum reserve assets ratio for those within the scheme is 10% compared with 12.5% for the banks. The main reason indicated by the Bank for the difference is that the imposition of the reserve assets ratio was more of a burden on the finance houses than on the banks since the former in the ordinary way did not hold any eligible reserve assets.

In December 1975 the eligible liabilities of the finance houses totalled only £250m and their holdings of reserve assets were £26m giving them a ratio of 10.5%. Like the banks, the finance houses are subject to calls for both special deposits and supplementary deposits. As regards calls for special deposits the Bank has stated that they 'will normally be at the same rate as calls on the banks, but the Bank will have the right in certain defined circumstances to call special deposits from the finance houses at a higher rate. In no circumstances, however, will the total of reserve assets and special deposits represent a higher proportion of eligible liabilities for the finance houses than for the banks'.[1] Only eight finance houses now come under the new credit control arrangements since a number of former finance houses have acquired the status of banks for purposes of the scheme.

It is clear that the introduction of a minimum reserve assets ratio for the finance houses imposes on them a significant burden, especially as the return on reserve assets tends to be below their cost of borrowing. Furthermore, the banking sector as

---

1 'Reserve Ratios and Special Deposits', *BEQB*, Supplement, vol. 11, no. 3, September 1971.

a whole now offers the finance houses much more competition than before the advent of the new competition and credit control arrangements. In terms of size the finance houses, excluding those which are now classified as banks, with total assets in September 1975 of around £1,200m are very small in relation to the banking sector.

To their cost, the finance houses have for many years – with some intermissions – been subject to the special attention of the authorities. From time to time they have stipulated some of the terms on which the finance houses could do business; in particular the minimum down-payments that must be made on different products by borrowers and the maximum repayment periods. These kinds of restrictions on the activities of the finance houses have come in for much criticism because of their arbitrariness and selectivity and the – at any rate short-run – disruptive effects they could have on the production and sales of certain consumer durable industries, especially the car industry. The Crowther Committee on consumer credit gave great impetus to criticisms such as these, recommending the abolition of terms control and credit ceilings and the encouragement generally of equal competition amongst credit institutions.[1] The new credit control arrangements as applied to the finance houses went some way in this direction, though they might legitimately claim that, as regards the problem of credit control, the authorities pay them more attention than the scale of their activities warrants.

III.8   Building Societies

Building societies are mutual or non-profit-making bodies which specialize in the provision of finance for the purchase of both new and secondhand houses. There are about four hundred building societies, about one-sixth of the number some seventy years ago. The individual societies differ greatly in size from some very large ones with a national network of branches to those with only one office.

About 90% of the liabilities of the building societies are shares and deposits. Both are essentially deposits, so that the term share is something of a misnomer. However, the shareholder is a member of the society whereas the depositor is not, and the latter has a prior right of liquidation over the shareholder. Deposits earn a slightly lower rate of interest than shares. Shares and deposits are subject to notice of withdrawal, though in practice both are paid on demand or on very short notice. The interest rate on shares and deposits are quoted *net* of income tax, which is paid by the societies at an average or composite rate and is less than the basic rate of tax. In early 1976 the interest rates recommended by the Building Societies Association were 7% on paid-up shares and 6¾% on deposits. These rates are net of tax and are equivalent approximately to 10.8% and 10.4% respectively before deduction of tax.

Mortgages usually account for over 80% of the assets of building societies and are predominantly for private house purchase. Most mortgages are for between twenty and thirty years with continuous repayment by instalments. The average life is about ten years, making the assets of building societies much shorter-lived than might appear. The recommended interest rate on new mortgages to owner occupiers was 11% in early 1976. But this is the gross rate as interest payments on a housing loan – up to £25,000 for a principal residence – are allowable against

---

1   *Report of the Committee on Consumer Credit*, Cmnd. 4596, HMSO, March 1971.

income tax assessments: if allowance is made for income tax relief at the basic
rate the interest rate is reduced to about 7.2% net. For those who pay less than the
standard rate of tax, or no tax at all, there is an option mortgage scheme, supported
by the government, which reduces the cost.

All other assets, except such things as office premises, are classified as liquid
assets by the societies. Liquid assets must be at least 7.5% of total assets and both
the type of asset and the maturity distribution are regulated by the Registrar of
Building Societies. At the end of 1975 the actual liquid assets ratio was 21.1% of
total assets. Two years previously it had been 16.3%. Cash holdings and balances
with banks are relatively small and vary a lot seasonally.

The building societies dominate the market providing finance for house purchase
and they are therefore relevant, directly and indirectly, to the activity of the housebuilding industry. The societies cannot for long expand the supply of finance to
borrowers unless there is a corresponding net inflow of funds from new shares and
deposits; otherwise they would deplete their liquid assets and in time risk upsetting
public confidence in their management. The interest rates the societies pay and the
relationship they bear to the competing rates would appear to be a major determinant
of the net inflow of funds to the societies.

In the twelve months between October 1972 and October 1973 the Building
Societies Association found it necessary to raise their recommended rates of interest
on shares and deposits five times, and on mortgages three times. This frequency of
change would seem to be almost unprecedented in the history of the building society
movement. The changes were felt to be necessary because of the competition for
funds offered by other financial institutions, particularly on fixed term bank
deposits, local authority deposits and even in the gilt-edged market. Since then their
rates of interest have been much more stable.

Despite the frequency of change in interest rates on shares and deposits the net
inflow of funds to the building societies remained highly irregular. For instance,
during 1973 they reached a peak of £315m for the month of June, fell to £59m for
September, rose to £142m for October and fell to £95m for November. These
fluctuations in inflows seriously affected the ability of the building societies to
make advances for house purchase. By 1974 the situation was so acute that the
government offered the building societies in early April loans of up to £100m and,
if the societies needed it, a further £400m at an average rate of £100m a month.
These funds, of which £483m was taken up by the societies, together with an
improvement in the inflow of funds from the public alleviated their liquidity
position and enabled them to expand their lending. As short-term interest rates
generally eased later in 1974 and early 1975 the net inflow of funds to the societies
accelerated and allowed them to pay off their government debt. Throughout 1975
and in the first quarter of 1976 their liquidity position remained strong. The lesson
to be learned from the experience of the last few years is, however, clear; it is
imperative to the liquidity and financial viability of the building societies that their
interest rates, especially their borrowing rates, should not get out of line with
those of their competitors.

III.9   Other Financial Institutions

The United Kingdom is particularly rich in the variety and number of its financial
institutions. The term 'rich' is used advisedly, for financial institutions that are able

to mediate freely between borrowers and lenders help to make the allocation of
scarce resources more efficient. 'Improvements in their efficiency and the
development of new financial intermediaries are analagous to productivity increases
and innovations in industry'.[1] However, limitations on space prevent more than a
brief mention of some of the remaining major financial institutions.

National Savings Bank and Trustee Savings Banks: The National Savings Bank,
formerly the Post Office Savings Bank, and Trustee Savings banks offer a range of
facilities, many of them similar, to depositors. Both of them accept ordinary savings
deposits which earn interest at 4% per year; the first £40 of interest is free of all
income tax. Both banks also allow depositors to hold deposits in investment-type
accounts on which higher rates of interest are paid. In 1965 the Trustee Savings
Banks were given power to provide current accounts with chequing facilities and
the Post Office in October 1968 introduced a new system for transmitting payments,
based on the continental giros and known as the National Giro. By December 1975
its gross deposits had reached £149m. From June 1975 the National Giro has been
able to offer loan and overdraft facilities to its customers.

The funds on deposit at 4% are paid directly to the National Debt Commissioners,
an official body with certain responsibilities for the national debt, who invest them
in government securities. Both the National Savings Bank and the Trustee Savings
banks have slightly more freedom in employing the funds obtained through their
investment accounts. As well as investing directly in government securities they lend
to local authorities. Thus the savings banks are channels by which funds flow directly
to central and local government.

For a considerable number of years there has been concern about the operations
of the National Savings Bank (and its predecessor the Post Office Savings Bank), and
the Trustee Savings Banks. Under the joint impact of rising interest rates and
inflation their deposits, especially their ordinary savings deposits, became much
less competitive with other forms of financial assets. In 1971 the government
appointed a committee under the chairmanship of Sir Harry Page to enquire into
the whole National Savings Movement.[2]

The chief recommendations of the Committee included a major restructuring of
the Trustee Savings banks in which they would be largely freed from specific
government controls and become a mutual banking organization able to offer a full
range of banking functions, including the making of personal loans and mortgages.
Some of these changes are already under way. The seventy-two Trustee Savings
banks in the UK are being reorganized into seventeen regional banks and it is
expected that by late 1976 they will be offering a comprehensive banking service
to their customers, including credit facilities.

The Page Committee felt that the National Savings Bank should 'remain under
Government control, channeling all its funds into public sector securities, and
without any material change in its services'[3] The government has accepted these
recommendations.

---

1 N. J. Gibson, *Financial Intermediaries and Monetary Policy*, Hobart Paper 39, 2nd edition,
   Institute of Economic Affairs, 1970, p. 20.
2 *Committee to Review National Savings*, (Page Report), Cmnd. 5273, HMSO, June 1973.
3 *Ibid.*, para. 806, p. 269.

Insurance Companies: There are some seven hundred insurance companies engaged in business in the UK, but by far the greater part of British business is carried on by the members of the British Insurance Association, which has less than three hundred members. The discussion below concentrates on these.

Insurance falls into two main categories, life assurance, and a catch-all, general insurance, which includes fire, marine, motor and other accident insurance. Life assurance for the most part gives rise to long-term liabilities which the companies must be in a position to meet. This gives them an interest in long-term investments and in assets that may be expected to increase in capital value over the years. General insurance, on the other hand, is carried on much more on a year-to-year basis, ideally with premiums for the year being sufficient to cover the risks underwritten and to allow for expenses and the accumulation of limited reserves. So the disposition of funds arising from general insurance is largely governed by short-term considerations; assets must be quickly realizable without undue fear of capital loss.

The insurance companies, with total investments at the end of 1975 of around £25,000m, are of great importance in the UK's capital markets. They are large holders of both government and company securities.

Investment Trusts: Investment trusts are limited companies which specialize in the investment of funds provided by their shareholders or borrowed from debenture holders or other lenders. Despite the term 'trust' they do not operate, as do the unit trusts, under trust deeds which specify the terms and conditions governing the management of investment funds. In addition to investment trusts there are private investment companies and investment holding companies which often perform similar functions. But these are not considered to be investment trusts in the sense used here and are not discussed in this chapter. Attention is concentrated on the group of about two hundred and sixty investment trusts that currently make returns to the Bank of England.

Investment trusts expand by raising funds from new capital issues and by retaining some of the income and capital profits from previous investments. But once again it is the asset side of the balance sheets that is of chief interest. At the end of 1975 the total market value of assets of investment trusts making returns to the Bank of England was almost £5,700m. Most of this was invested in company securities, practically all ordinary shares. Over one-third of the company securities were those of overseas companies.

This extremely heavy concentration of investment in ordinary shares is a postwar phenomenon. Before the war investment trusts had substantial holdings of fixed interest securities. But the fear of inflation eroding the real value of fixed interest investments has encouraged the investment trusts to rearrange drastically the distribution of their assets. The size of the investment trusts makes them important operators in the ordinary share market. They also fulfil a useful function in helping to finance small companies by holding their unquoted securities. Their ability to invest overseas has from time to time been seriously affected by government restrictions and tax measures.

Unit Trusts: Unit trusts perform a similar function to investment trusts. But unlike the latter they do operate under trust deeds and have trustees, often a bank or insurance company. The unit trusts are authorized by the Department of Trade and are run by managers who are quite distinct from the trustees. Three hundred and

fifty-nine unit trusts made returns to the Bank of England at the end of 1975 and
the number continues to grow; in 1960 the figure was fifty-one.

Unit trusts do not issue share capital and are not limited companies but they
issue units which give the owners the right to participate in the beneficial ownership
of the trusts' assets. The units are highly marketable as they can always be bought
from or sold to the managers at prices which reflect the market value of the
underlying assets. As more units are demanded the managers provide more; for this
reason they are sometimes called 'open-end' trusts, as opposed to 'closed-end' trusts,
such as the investment trusts which do not expand in this way.

Like the investment trusts the assets of the unit trusts are almost entirely
company securities, made up of ordinary shares. But in contrast to the investment
trusts, some 85% of the assets are domestic and about 15% overseas. At the end of
1975 the total assets of the unit trusts were £2,515m. Their rate of growth has been
rapid; in 1960 their total assets were only £190m. There is little doubt that the
rapidity of their growth is an attempt by small investors and others to protect
themselves against inflation by participating indirectly in ordinary share investment.

The Stock Exchange: The Stock Exchange provides a market for variable price
securities, both government and company securities. Without this market where
securities may readily be bought and sold the whole business of raising funds
through outside sources would tend to be more expensive and less efficient. Since
March 1973 the Stock Exchange comprises the Stock Exchange of the UK and the
Republic of Ireland. Before that date, though with close links, they were distinct
organizations.

A feature of the Stock Exchange is the jobbing system. Jobbers are traders in
securities; they act as principals, buying and selling on their own account and
making their profits on the difference between their buying and selling prices,
which they generally stand ready to quote for the securities in which they specialize.
This function can be extremely important in giving stability to the market which
might otherwise be much more volatile and possibly mislead investors.

Brokers generally act as agents for customers, buying and selling on their behalf,
usually but not always through jobbers.

Speculation is a term frequently associated with the Stock Exchange and nearly
always carries overtones of abuse and criticism. To some degree this may reflect
ignorance of the functions of the Stock Exchange, though this is not to imply that
speculation is always economically and socially beneficial. But the speculator at his
best, if he is doing his job properly, will be helping to keep the price of shares in
touch with economic realities, damping down the effects of irrelevant rumours and
false information; he will, in fact, be improving one part of the communication
network of the economic system. However, the economic, social and moral implications of speculation are much wider and more far reaching than can be dealt with
here.

Traditionally the terms 'bulls' and 'bears' have been applied to particular types
of speculation though they are now used more generally to refer respectively to
markets tending to rise and fall in price. But traditionally a 'bull' was someone
who bought securities on a rising market hoping he would be able to sell them at
a profit before he had to pay for his purchase. The 'bear' sold the shares that he had
not got, on a falling market, in the hope that he would be able subsequently to buy
and deliver them at a lower price.

An idea of the scale of Stock Exchange activities can be obtained from the figures on turnover, that is, sales and purchases. The total turnover during 1975 was about £94,000m, a relatively good year. Turnover of British government securities was some £67,000m. Clearly the Stock Exchange is of major importance to the financial activities of both the public and private sectors of the economy.[1]

IV   THE TAXATION SYSTEM
IV.1   Introduction

Taxation and the role of government in society are necessarily closely linked and discussion of the one involves some consideration of the other. It is often said that taxation in a market economy has broadly three main functions: (1) to provide or encourage the provision of goods and services that are not easily or adequately supplied by the market if left to itself and also to discourage the provision of those goods and services that are considered to have harmful effects on society – and perhaps the reverse for those goods and services which are considered beneficial to society: (2) to redistribute income and wealth; and (3) to facilitate the exercise of fiscal policy as a means of economic stabilization.

The first may be approached by making a distinction between so-called private and public goods and noting a possible discrepancy between private and public costs and benefits – what has come to be called the externalities problem. A private good refers to those goods where the utility a person gets from their consumption depends on how much of them he has and at the same time the more he has the less anyone else gets. Public goods on the other hand are such that once the goods are produced their consumption by one person does not diminish the amount available to others. Any kind of food is an example of a private good and some forms of national defence are an example of public goods. The market system can by and large handle the problem of producing and pricing private goods but not public goods since the price system cannot operate effectively to determine an appropriate amount to produce, nor determine its distribution. It needs to be stressed immediately that private goods and public goods are ideal cases and that in general elements of both may be combined in the same good.

Externalities are said to arise when the costs and benefits are not internalized to the individual producer or consumer. A typical example is what has been called the 'smoke nuisance', when a producer engages in a productive activity that gives off smoke and spreads grime and dirt in the immediate neighbourhood and possibly causes chemical erosion of buildings in the surrounding area. The costs of these nuisances are generally not voluntarily paid for by the producer and reflected in the quantity produced and price of his product. This kind of example could be greatly extended, as could similar examples on the benefits side. Indeed, in so far as a so-called public good was provided privately it would be an example of external benefits being conferred widely throughout a community. Clearly, externalities pose a fundamental problem for society, and in particular suggest that where they are present in a market based economy, the market if left to itself will produce too much of a good which imposes external costs on the society and too little of a good which confers external benefits on it. In such circumstances there seems to be no

---

1   The effects of taxation on the operation of the capital market are touched on below,
    pp. 97–8.

simple answer to the question, on the one hand of the appropriate domain of market processes and, on the other, of the role of government. These are difficult and far reaching issues in political economy.

The second function of taxation — the redistribution of income and wealth — is closely related to the matters just discussed. For there is no self-evident reason why a competitive market economy should lead to an optimum distribution of income and wealth — however difficult that may be to define — so governments have come to use taxation and the revenue raised thereby to bring about some redistribution. It should perhaps be said that there is also no obvious reason why government redistribution policies will be optimal since the distribution and exercise of political power in society also begs some fundamental and intractable questions.

The third function of taxation as an aspect of fiscal stabilization policy is already familiar from earlier discussion in this chapter and the preceding one.

IV.2   The Size of Government

It is well known that in this century governments have become, in terms of their own activities, far more important in relation to the economic life of the community. Nevertheless, it is by no means straightforward to measure the size of government economic activity relatively to the rest of the economic system. Perhaps the best that can be done is to take a number of different measures.[1]

One of these is the direct claims the government makes on the volume of goods and services available to the community in any time period. In this context 'government' includes central and local government, but excludes such things as the nationalized industries or, more generally, public corporations. Table 2.6 shows that government expenditure has claimed just over 20% of the gross national product for most of the 1960s but since then has gradually increased to around 25%.

TABLE 2.6

Central and Local Government (Including National Insurance Funds) Current and Gross Capital Expenditure on Goods and Services as a Percentage of GNP at Market Prices, 1961-74

Year	1961	1962	1963	1964	1965	1966	1967	1968
%	20.0	20.6	20.5	20.7	21.0	21.6	22.9	22.8

Year	1969	1970	1971	1972	1973	1974
%	22.3	22.8	22.9	23.2	23.2	25.4

Sources: NIBB, 1972, 1973 and 1964-74.

Note: The figures exclude capital formation by public corporations. Its inclusion in 1974 would have increased the figure from 25.4 to 29.1%.

It is arguable that the foregoing understates the 'size' of government. For instance, no account was taken of subsidies, grants and debt interest paid by the government and its net lending. The reason for this is that these are mainly classified as transfer

---

1   See A. R. Prest, *Public Finance in Theory and Practice,* 5th edition, Weidenfeld and Nicolson, 1975, for a discussion of some of the latest issues involved.

payments. That is, the government raises the necessary funds by taxation and borrowing and transfers them back to the community and overseas. Thus the government does not buy goods and services directly as far as this type of expenditure is concerned. But there is no doubt that these transfers are extremely important, both in relation to taxation and government borrowing, and do influence the economic system. When they are included in government expenditure then the previous percentages are greatly increased. Table 2.7 shows that the 1961 percentage is raised to around 36% of gross national product and that over the next thirteen years the trend has been upwards, with the 1974 figure some 47%. Clearly, grants, subsidies, debt interest and net lending have been increasingly important over the last ten years or so as a component of government expenditure.

TABLE 2.7

Central and Local Government Combined Current and Capital Expenditure as a Percentage of GNP at Market Prices 1961-74

Year	1961	1962	1963	1964	1965	1966	1967	1968
%	35.5	36.1	35.8	35.9	37.2	37.9	41.5	42.3

Year	1969	1970	1971	1972	1973	1974		
%	41.0	40.9	40.9	41.9	41.8	47.1		

Sources: NIBB, 1972, 1973 and 1964-74.

IV.3   The Budget

The Budget is traditionally the annual financial statement which the Chancellor of the Exchequer makes in the House of Commons either in late March or early April about the end of each financial year. The statement includes an account of the revenue and expenditure for the previous financial year and forecasts for the year ahead. In the ordinary way there is only one budget, but in times of crisis a supplementary budget may be introduced to give the Chancellor the opportunity to modify his earlier policies by altering taxation and expenditure. Tables 2.8, 2.9 and 2.10 bring together in an aggregated form the main features of the 1976-7 Budget accounts.

The receipts of the Consolidated Fund shown in table 2.8 fall under four main headings: inland revenue, customs and excise, vehicle excise duties and miscellaneous receipts. The first two refer to the great revenue-collecting departments of state and the major taxes and duties collected by these are discussed below. Vehicle excise duties are collected by the Department of the Environment. Miscellaneous receipts include interest and dividends, broadcast receiving licences and certain other receipts.

The two main categories of expenditure shown in table 2.9 are supply services and consolidated fund standing services. The first is voted annually by Parliament; the second is a standing charge against revenue.

The National Loans Fund was set up in April 1968. Broadly speaking it is intended to carry further the separation of current and capital items in the accounts. Most of the domestic lending of the government and all transactions relating to the National

TABLE 2.8

Central Government Revenue, 1976-7 (Forecast) (£m)

Inland revenue

Income tax	17,045	
Surtax	30	
Corporation tax	2,650	
Capital gains tax	400	
Estate duty	70	
Capital transfer tax	212	
Stamp duties	293	
Total Inland Revenue		20,700

Customs and excise

Value added tax	3,650	
Oil	2,025	
Tobacco	1,790	
Spirits, beer and wine	1,850	
Betting and gaming	295	
Car tax	190	
Other revenue duties	10	
Protective duties	555	
Agricultural levies	60	
Total Customs and Excise		10,425
Vehicle excise duties		835
Total Taxation		31,960
Miscellaneous receipts		1,237
Grand Total		33,197

Source: Financial Statement and Budget Report 1976-77.
Note: The forecast revenue was conditional on agreement being reached on a low pay limit.

Debt now appear in the National Loans Fund; they were formerly part of the Consolidated Fund. Table 2.10 clearly shows just how important the central government is as a source of capital funds for the nationalized industries and local authorities. The government must raise these funds either through taxation or by borrowing. In these accounts there is a substantial deficit forecast for the consolidated fund and a large net borrowing item of £10,750m.[1]

To explain adequately the financing of the borrowing requirement (whenever it is positive) would necessitate going far beyond the budget accounts and involve an extensive discussion of the financial transactions of the central government.

---

1   This item (see table 2.10) is not identical with what is known as the central government borrowing requirement since the latter also covers net transactions with official funds such as the national insurance funds, some departmental balances and certain Northern Ireland government debts.

TABLE 2.9

Central Government Supply Services and Consolidated Fund Standing Services, 1976-7
Forecast (£m)

Supply services

I	Defence	5,604
II	Overseas Aid and other Overseas Services	815
III	Agriculture, Fisheries and Forestry	856
IV	Trade, Industry and Employment	2,860
VI	Roads and Transport	1,247
VII	Housing	2,089
VIII	Other Environmental Services	337
IX	Law, Order and Protective Services	991
X	Education and Libraries, Science and Arts	1,406
XI	Health and Personal Social Services	4,907
XII	Social Security	4,001
XIII	Other Public Services	915
XIV	Common Services	890
XV	Northern Ireland	526
XVII	Rate Support Grant, Financial Transactions, etc.	7,124

Total Supply[1]	34,568
Allowance for price changes (rounded)	2,300
Supplementary provision	60
Total Supply Services	36,928

Consolidated Fund Standing Services

Payment to the National Loans Fund for service of the National Debt.	1,770
Northern Ireland – share of taxes, etc.	631
Payments to the European Community, etc.	568
Other Services	18
Total Consolidated Fund Standing Services	2,987
Total	39,915
Consolidated Fund Deficit	−6,718
Grand Total	33,197

Source: Financial Statement and Budget Report 1976-77.
Note: 1   At 1976-7 Estimate prices.

However, it may be useful to indicate a few of the factors involved. For instance, and as previously mentioned, an increase in the note issue will help to finance it, as will net purchases of government securities by the National Savings Bank and Trustee Savings banks and the non-bank private sector, including the non-bank financial institutions discussed previously. If these sources of funds are insufficient the government may have to borrow from the banking system, probably by issuing Treasury bills, unless the banks voluntarily make net purchases of gilt-edged securities. The amount that must be borrowed will rise in the first instance if there is an *increase* in the gold and foreign currency reserves. This is because the government must make sterling available to the Exchange Equalization account to enable it to purchase an inflow of gold and foreign currency. To the extent that the government has to finance its borrowing by expansion of the Treasury bill issue it is, of course, increasing the volume of reserve assets available, which may lead to an accelerated growth in the money supply and, on a monetarist interpretation, be inflationary. However, the money supply need not increase and indeed generally would not if the authorities sold securities to the non-bank public to the extent of the inflow of foreign funds. But clearly, the budgetary system and monetary and financial system are highly interdependent and hence so are monetary, fiscal and credit policy.

The annual budget as an instrument of fiscal policy has frequently been criticized because of its inflexibility. In the ordinary way the major taxes such as income tax and corporation tax cannot be varied between Finance Acts.[1] Thus though it might be thought desirable, because of changed economic conditions, to alter these taxes more frequently, this cannot be done without all the inconvenience of a supplementary budget. However, the authorities have more leeway over some other sources of revenue. From the point of view of flexibility one of the most important has been the power first granted in the Finance Act 1961, to vary the rates of nearly all customs and excise duties and purchase tax by at most 10% and known as the regulator.[2] Moreover, this kind of power was retained with the introduction of value added tax in 1973. Thus there are new substantial powers to vary taxes between budgets. This of course, leaves other crucially important problems, such as the timing and scale of tax changes, but these are taken up later.

Alterations in government expenditure are also, in principle, a possible manner of making fiscal policy more flexible. But government expenditure may be planned years in advance of its formal inclusion in the budget estimates and modifications of the plans may give rise to problems, since much of the expenditure is on a continuing basis and cannot be easily altered. Furthermore, it may be extremely costly to slow down or postpone some kinds of expenditure, particularly investment expenditure. Hence frequent variation of government expenditure is not an ideal instrument of fiscal policy.

The budget accounts, as already indicated, are incomplete in a number of ways. They deal, for example, only peripherally with local government finances and the national insurance funds.[3] Yet both of these 'tax' the community, the first mainly by levying rates and the second through insurance contributions. For the fiscal year 1975-6 rates were some £4,140m and national insurance contributions £7,154m. Together they amounted to the equivalent of almost 41% of the taxes on income and expenditure in the same period.[4] The scale of taxation in the UK may be better appreciated when it is realized that taxes on income, expenditure and

---

1 The Finance Act puts into law the budget proposals, subject to any amendments made by the House of Commons.
2 Thus if a current rate of duty were 20% it might be varied between 18% and 22% (with VAT between 16% and 25%).
3 National insurance is discussed further in chapter 5.
4 Figures from *Financial Statement and Budget Report*, 1976-7.

TABLE 2.10

National Loans Fund, 1976-7 (Forecast) (£m)

(i) *Payments*

Interest, management and expenses of national debt		4,900
Consolidated Fund Deficit		6,718
Loans (net)		
To nationalized industries	1,286	
Other public corporations	1,023	
Local and harbour authorities	1,566	
Private sector	6	
Within central government	151	
Total		4,032
Grand Total		15,650

(ii) *Receipts*

Interest on loans, profits of the Issue Department of the Bank of England, etc.	3,130	
Balance of interest service of the National Debt met from the Consolidated Fund	1,770	
Total		4,900
Net Borrowing		10,750
Grand Total		15,650

Source: Financial Statement and Budget Report 1976-77.

capital, and on rates and national insurance contributions totalled almost £40,000m in 1975-6 which would be about 42% of GNP at factor cost. This is a further indication of the scale of government in the UK economy.

IV.4   Income Taxation and Tax Credits

The taxation of income has recently undergone major changes. Up to April 1973 individuals were subject to income tax and surtax with the latter chargeable in addition to income tax on incomes in excess of £3,000. However when allowances and reliefs were taken into account, and if income was wholly earned, a single person could receive over £6,000 before surtax was payable.

Apart from certain residual matters the existing income tax and surtax were replaced by a single graduated personal tax, known as unified tax, from 6 April 1973. The main aims of unified tax were to simplify the tax structure, permit a smoother graduation in tax rates as income rises and simplify the administration of the whole system. The unified tax is constructed on the concept of earned income and so manages to dispense with the calculation of earned income relief, which was required under the previous system since it was constructed in terms of investment income. As well as earned income and investment income a further concept requires to be mentioned, that is taxable income. Taxable income is the income which remains from all sources after deduction of personal, family and certain other allowances.

For 1976-7 some of the personal allowances and some of the higher rate tax thresholds have been made conditional[1] on agreement with the TUC on a pay limit of about 3% for wages and salaries. The Chancellor of the Exchequer has stated that if the settlement is in excess of 3% then the conditional allowances will have to be reduced accordingly. This approach to budgetary policy is a complete departure from previous practice. For some observers it raises fundamental questions about the sovereignty of Parliament. However, putting these on one side, without in any way wishing to detract from their importance, it is arguable that the Chancellor is being economically realistic in that fiscal policy must take account of actual and anticipated economic conditions. In other words a further element of flexibility is being introduced into the budgetary process.

The main conditional allowances for 1976-7 are as follows: for single persons £735 and for married couples £1,085. The child allowances are unconditional in the sense that they do not depend on a low pay agreement with the TUC. For children under eleven years of age the allowance is £300, for eleven to sixteen £335 and for over sixteen £365. The age allowances for the elderly are also unconditional and for a single person is £1,010 and for a married couple £1,555.

Once taxable income has been determined the various tax rates come into operation. For 1976-7 the tax bands or ranges of income in relation to each tax rate are conditional on a low pay agreement. The basic rate is 35% on the first £5,000 of taxable income and thereafter the rates gradually increase in steps of 5% to 75% for taxable income between £15,000 and £20,000 and rises to a maximum of 83% for taxable income over £20,000.

The unified tax retains the former distinction between earned and investment income but has been modified in an important way. The first £1,000 or less of investment income is treated in exactly the same way as earned income but investment income between £1,000 and £2,000 (£1,500—£2,000 for pensioners) is subject to a 10% surcharge and in excess of £2,000 to a 15% surcharge.

It is evident from the foregoing discussion that one of the main features of income taxation is its progressiveness. This is, of course, by design. It can be traced to notions of ability to pay. It is assumed that those with larger incomes are or should be able to pay proportionately more of them in taxation. In addition, progressive taxation lends itself to income redistribution, to the extent that government expenditure benefits the less well-off in the community; and some would argue that greater equality of income is important to the maintenance of politically stable society. But progressive taxation also diminishes the direct reward for extra work as income increases and may act as a disincentive to more effort.

It has also been suggested that steeply progressive taxation is a disincentive to movement from one job to another; it may be difficult to get a sufficiently large income after tax to compensate for the costs of upheaval and change. If this is correct then the tax system may misallocate resources and be a drag on economic efficiency and growth. There is also no doubt that highly progressive taxation stimulates tax avoidance — the search for loopholes in the law permitting a reduced tax bill. If it is possible to spend less than a pound on advice to save a pound in tax then clearly this is a powerful incentive. The energies and resources of lawyers, accountants and tax experts generally may thus be diverted into socially costly tasks.

1 And subsequently made definite.

To the extent that some or all of these problems arise the community may have to make difficult choices between more redistribution, a smaller total income and less acute social and political conflict or somewhat less redistribution and a larger total income with rather more social and political conflict. Once more there would seem to be no escape from the difficult problems of political economy and the deep issues which arise in sustaining the on-going life of a complex and diverse society.

It has long been a goal of taxation policy that the system of taxation should be easy to understand, equitable and cheap to administer. One proposal which has been much discussed in the United States and more recently in the UK with these considerations in mind is the idea of a negative income tax which ideally would permit a single assessment of income and provide either for calculating the tax due if income is above a certain level or for the benefit to be paid — hence the term negative income tax — if it is below that level.

The particular scheme that has received most official attention is known as a tax-credit system. In October 1972 the government issued a Green Paper on the subject and later established a Select Committee on Tax-Credit, which reported in June 1973.[1]

The main provision of the tax-credit system as described in the Green Paper is that those who came within the scheme would receive an entirely new form of tax-credit for themselves and their families, which would take the place of the main income tax personal allowances and family allowances[2] where the latter includes family income supplement now paid as cash benefit as part of the social services. However, other means-tested benefits including rent and rates rebates, free school meals and free welfare milk would remain within the ambit of the social services. But under the scheme most national insurance benefits, such as retirement pensions, widows' pensions and sickness and unemployment benefit, as well as most occupational pensions, would be covered and be taxed as if they were income from employment, since they would give rise to a right to tax credits. A further feature of the scheme was that tax due and credit entitlement would normally be settled week by week or month by month, depending on the employment payment period. This form of tax system is described as non-cumulative in contrast with a cumulative system, such as the present pay-as-you-earn system, where personal allowances are spread over the tax year. This would be a radical change in UK income tax arrangements. The tax-credit scheme was intended to cover practically all those in employment, except those on very low incomes, but at least to begin with was to exclude the self-employed.

There seems to be little doubt that a tax-credit scheme such as that proposed could achieve some simplification and economies over present arrangements for taxation and in the administration of at least some social security benefits. However, the scheme has been criticized on the grounds that it lacks flexibility because of its use of a single rate of tax for the vast majority of taxpayers and because it does not do enough to redistribute income. It is far from conclusive that these criticisms are completely justified or that ways cannot be found to meet them within the broad framework of the scheme. However, the Labour Government has

---

1 *Proposals for a Tax-Credit System,* Cmnd. 5116; Select Committee on Tax-Credit, Session 1972-3, Vol. 1, Report and Proceedings of the Committee, Vol. II, Evidence and Vol. III, Appendices to Minutes of Evidence and Index, HC341.
2 Cmnd 5116, p. 3.

made it clear that it dislikes the details of the proposals, whilst not necessarily rejecting the principles. Whatever finally happens it is now clear that the previous government's aim to legislate in 1974, with a view to implementation by 1979, will not now be realized.

IV.5   Capital Gains Taxation

Until the Finance Act of 1971 there were two capital gains taxes, the short-term and the long-term tax, but under this Act the former was abolished, leaving what is called capital gains tax. Under this tax gains are taxable on the disposal of most assets. Important exemptions are principal private residence, private motor cars, National Savings securities, most life assurance policies and bettings winnings, gifts to charities and British government and government-guaranteed securities. In addition, the gains of individuals are exempt if the total proceeds from all disposals made in a year do not exceed £1,000, and since 1971 all gains at death are exempt. There are provisions generally allowing the offset of losses against gains on those assets that are subject to the tax. The gains are taxed at a rate of 30% except that an individual, if it is to his advantage, may have one-half of his net gains up to £5,000 ignored and the remainder taxed at the income tax rate applicable to investment income. Thus for an individual liable to begin with at the basic rate of income tax the initial rate chargeable would be 17.5%. The foregoing applies to individuals, as gains realized by companies are ordinarily chargeable to corporation tax, which for the year 1975-6 is at 52%. However, from 1973 the effective rate of tax on company gains has been only 30% − achieved by the expedient of leaving out of account a fraction of the gain. Special provisions apply to the taxing of unit trusts, investment trusts, superannuation funds and other bodies and, since the Finance Act 1974, to the taxation of capital gains from land. However, the latter is to be superseded by a separate development land tax. The basic proposal is that realizations of development value from land, including buildings, would be subject to development land tax at a rate of 80%.[1]

The major justification put forward for the introduction of capital gains taxation is on grounds of equity. The argument is roughly as follows. An individual may purchase £100 worth of securities in 1974 and − if he is lucky − find that in 1975 they were worth £200. If he sold the securities and if there were no capital gains tax he could maintain his capital intact and still have £100 to spend, therefore this £100 is essentially income and should be taxed as such. But is this really equitable with progressive income tax rates? It might be that if the £100 were spread over a number of years a lower tax charge would arise. Does this mean that gains should be averaged over a number of years or would a compromise solution be to charge rates somewhat less than income tax rates? The UK capital gains tax seems to favour the latter.

In discussing the £100 gain above nothing was said about prices. But if prices have risen by 20% over the period then £120 would be required to maintain real capital intact and the remaining £80 would be only worth some £64 in real terms. Is it llegitimate to tax nominal gains as opposed to real gains? The equity argument

---

1   See *Development Land Tax,* Cmnd. 6195, H.M.S.O., 1975.

is by no means as straightforward as it might seem; and a really comprehensive discussion of the matter would have to consider the wider issues of the distribution of income and wealth generally in relation to the operation of the social and political system.

Capital gains taxation is, of course, important for other reasons besides those of equity. It may affect investment and saving and the functioning of the capital markets, and pose difficult problems of administration. To the extent that the return on investment takes the form of capital gains – especially the return on risky investment – taxing them may discourage such investment. This discouragement may, however, be mitigated to some extent, since the tax is postponable and payable only on realized capital gains. The allowance of losses as an offset to taxable capital gains also works in the same direction. Nevertheless, the effect may well be to depress investment.

The effects on saving are perhaps even more problematic but may also be adverse, as may the effects on the operation of the capital markets. Since the tax is on realized gains this encourages the retention of the same securities as, of course, the holder has the income on the tax that would otherwise have to be paid if the securities were realized. There is therefore a discouragement to switching between securities which reduces the flexibility of the market and perhaps makes the raising of capital more costly. A possible offset to these effects is the realization of capital losses since these are allowable for tax purposes against corresponding capital gains.

The administrative problems are particularly great where problems of valuation arise. This is especially true of changes in the value of assets which do not ordinarily have a market value; an example is unquoted securities. The problem of valuation may become less acute as time proceeds and the community gets accustomed to the tax.[1]

IV.6   Corporation Tax, Depreciation and Other Allowances

Corporation tax draws a forceful distinction between the company and the shareholder, taxing each as separate entities. A basic argument used in favour of corporation tax is the opportunity it gives the authorities to distinguish between the personal and company sectors for policy purposes. They may wish, for instance, to curtail consumption expenditure with as little adverse effect as possible on investment expenditure. An increase in income tax, leaving corporation tax unchanged, may tend to have the desired effect and may even encourage smaller dividend distributions, leaving more funds available to companies for investment purposes.

The foregoing analysis begs, however, a number of important questions. Among these are the following. Should future consumption be preferred to present consumption, in so far as larger current investment makes possible a larger future income and so consumption? Are the companies with retained profits the ones which should grow? This is not at all self-evident. It means that companies avoid the discipline of having to raise funds in the market and probably favours the larger established company at the expense of the smaller or newer company. Furthermore,

---

1   These last few paragraphs and the next section rely heavily on Prest, *Public Finance in Theory and Practice, op. cit.*

greater encouragement of profit retention tends to reduce the flow of funds through the capital market to the detriment of companies dependent on it. The corporation tax also tends to distort the operation of the capital market by encouraging firms to rely more on loan or debenture capital at the expense of ordinary or other forms of share capital, since the interest on the former is allowed as a cost in the calculation of profits and hence liability for tax, whereas this is not true of the latter. It may, of course, be argued that the gains from introducing corporation tax outweigh the disadvantages.

From April 1973 the government introduced a new form of corporation tax known as the *imputation system*. Under this system all profits, whether distributed or not, are subject to the same corporation tax rate, but part of the tax is imputed to shareholders, and collected from the company at the time of payment of dividends. If, for instance the corporation tax rate is 52% and the basic income tax rate is 35% then a company whose activities are entirely within the UK and which had profits of 100 would have a corporation tax liability of 52. If during a year it paid a dividend of 19.5 to its shareholders it would be treated as a gross dividend of 30 from which income tax of 35% had been deducted. The company would pay the 10.5 to the Inland Revenue and this would be credited against the company's corporation tax liability of 52. Shareholders subject to basic rate income tax would be deemed to have discharged their tax liabilities; only in the case of those exempt or subject to higher rates would a refund or additional charge be necessary. Small companies whose annual profits do not exceed £30,000 are subject to a reduced rate of corporation tax with the scale of reduction tapering off for companies with profits up to £50,000.

The imputation form of corporation tax has certain advantages over the two-rate system when it comes to negotiating double-taxation agreements with other countries; it is favourable to the UK balance of payments and should facilitate the movement towards tax harmonization within the European Economic Community, as it puts Britain broadly in line with French and German company taxation and with recent proposals by the Commission.

In assessing liability to corporation tax allowance is made, broadly speaking, for all the costs incurred by the company, including the wear and tear of physical capital and, as mentioned above, interest on loans and debentures but not dividends paid on shares. However, depreciation is not allowed on all physical assets; there are no allowances on such things as retail shops, showrooms and offices.

In addition to depreciation allowances for wear and tear successive governments have attempted to stimulate investment by various kinds of incentive. Three main kinds are or have been operative in the UK: initial allowances, investment allowances and investment or cash grants. Initial allowances, introduced in 1945, are permitted in the first year in addition to the ordinary depreciation allowances and the two together are known as first-year allowances. In other words the rate at which depreciation may be written off is accelerated; the total amount of depreciation permitted remains 100%. Investment allowances on the other hand, introduced in 1954 and abolished in January 1966 with the advent of investment grants, did permit more than 100% of the cost of the asset to be written off over its life. Thus if the investment allowance was 20% – it was normally allowed in the year the investment took place – the total allowances would be 120%.

Investment or cash grants are now largely confined to what are called the assisted areas and are known generally as regional development grants. There are four main types of assisted areas: special development areas, development areas, intermediate areas and derelict land clearance areas. Altogether the areas comprise all of Scotland and Wales, the whole north of England roughly above the Wash, and south-western England. Special investment grants are also payable to the shipbuilding and computer industries.

The position since the 1972 Budget is that all capital expenditure throughout the UK on machinery and plant, excluding passenger cars, is subject to a first-year allowance of 100%, often called free depreciation; and the initial allowance on new industrial buildings is 50%. Thus as far as these allowances are concerned no distinction is made between the assisted areas and the rest of the country. However, as already indicated, the assisted areas do receive special treatment. In addition to the allowances mentioned the special development areas and the development areas receive regional development grants of 22% and 20% respectively of qualifying capital expenditure on new plant and machinery, mining works and buildings. Grants of 20% for buildings have also been available in the intermediate areas and the derelict land clearance areas.[1]

An important feature of the new system of regional development grants is that unlike previous grants they do not affect the recipient's entitlement to first-year or initial allowances on the *full* amount of the capital investment. This means that the new grant of 22% is the equivalent, for a company making profits, to one of over 30% on the previous basis when allowances were calculated on the *net* amount of the investment after deducting any grants.

With the rapid rise in prices in the last few years many companies found themselves subject to heavy taxation on the increase in the value of their stocks. In November 1974 the government introduced measures giving special tax relief on such increases and these have recently been extended in the 1976 budget. This is an important innovation as it is tantamount to an acceptance, at least in part, of inflation accounting.

The whole system of allowances and grants thus gives rise to many complicated issues, only a few of which can be touched on here. First, should depreciation allowances be on an original or a replacement-cost basis? This question would be of little or no significance if prices were generally stable. But in periods of rising prices it would seem that, if the community is to preserve intact its physical stock of capital, allowances should be made on a replacement-cost basis. However, if the problem is approached in a different way the argument may not be so clear-cut. Suppose a firm purchases a piece of equipment and thereafter prices rise, including the price of the equipment, then the capital value of the old equipment rises, giving a capital gain to the firm. If allowances are permitted on a replacement-cost basis the firm is, in fact, receiving untaxed capital gains. Is this equitable in relation to other sections of the community or is it a useful compromise to allow only original costs in calculating depreciation, so that the apparent capital gains are subject to corporation and income tax as, until the recent modification relating to the increase in the value of stocks, was the practice in the UK? The answer is far from obvious but clearly the issues become more acute in periods of rapid inflation.[2]

Initial allowances, investment allowances and, more recently, investment grants should all act as a stimulus to investment. The first two may be regarded as reducing

---

1 *Industrial and Regional Development,* Cmnd. 4942, 1972.
2 See Prest, *Public Finance in Theory and Practice,* for further discussion.

the amount of tax payable, and to that extent make investment more profitable. The third is, of course, a direct subsidy to investment and the benefits do not depend, as they do in the case of the first two, upon the availability of profits out of which to pay taxes. It is not at all self-evident that the subsidy is to be preferred as it may mean that investment takes place in forms of dubious profitability – there is therefore the likelihood of misallocation of resources, at least as determined in relation to market prices.

A major feature of investment grants and regional development grants is the extent to which they are discriminatory. They make investments in certain places more profitable than in others and some types of investment more profitable than other types. This, of course, is by design and is intended to stimulate investment in the places and in the forms the government desires. The basis for this intervention hinges on the conviction that the market, reflecting the interacting decisions of consumers, savers and investors, if left to itself will lead to misallocation of investment and to underinvestment, and to regional imbalance in the levels of employment and economic activity. However, as far as regional employment is concerned, it is not at all obvious that this form of capital subsidization, which cheapens capital relatively to labour, with the latter generally in excess supply, is the best way to proceed.[1] But the issues that regional development grants and investment incentives generally raise are extremely complex. Some of the issues, such as the distribution of income and wealth in society and stabilization policy, were referred to in the introduction of this section but cannot be explored further here, except to say that the empirical evidence, such as it is, suggests that investment incentives have not been very effective in stimulating capital growth in the country as a whole – though they certainly seem to have stimulated growth in the assisted areas – since the overall growth rate has lagged behind that of the US and most western European countries. Moreover, their use as stabilization instruments depends crucially on the timing and actual variation in the grants and allowances. It may be doubted that government or anyone else has the knowledge to manipulate these successfully. Indeed, as far as the management of the UK economy is concerned, their use may well have been destabilizing.[2]

IV.7   Value Added Tax

Value added tax, as its name implies, taxes value added at each stage of the productive process with the final selling price to the consumer being made up of the cost of production plus the rate of tax. An example may help to make the matter clearer. Suppose the value added tax rate is 10% – the standard rate for 1976-7 is 8%[3] – and that a manufacturer imports all his raw materials at a cost of 100. He is immediately liable for tax of 10. The manufacturer processes the raw materials and sells the final product to a retailer for 200, exclusive of tax. The tax due on value added by the manufacturer is 10, making a total of 20 altogether, so that the retailer pays 220, tax inclusive for the product. Thus whilst the manufacturer has had to pay 20 of tax he has passed it on or invoiced it to the retailer. The retailer

---

1   See Chapter 4, section VI. 3
2   See section V below.
3   There is also a higher rate of 12½% on a wide range of consumer durable goods and the like.

may be supposed to sell the product to the consumer for 300 plus tax of 30, making 330 in total. Thus the difference between the tax inclusive price paid by the retailer and his selling price is 110, 10 of which is the tax on his value added and which he pays to the authorities. Thus the tax, as it were, comes to rest with the consumer, and this is why value added tax is frequently described as an indirect tax on consumer expenditure.

It should be stressed, however, that the foregoing is intended only as a simple arithmetic explanation of the value added tax method and should not be interpreted as implying that the tax is necessarily wholly passed on to the final consumer. The problems of tax incidence are extremely complex and, in principle, require to be examined within the framework of a dynamically adjusting process. And even then most economists would be far from confident that they understood the intricacies of tax incidence. Notwithstanding the difficulties surrounding tax incidence, the matter is returned to briefly below in relation to the form of value added tax in the UK.

The government has given many reasons for substituting a value added tax for the previous purchase tax and selective employment tax.[1] The latter taxes were felt to be over-discriminatory in their effects on the prices of goods and services and they needed to be replaced by a more broadly based indirect tax, causing less distortion of consumer choice and so allowing a more efficient allocation of resources. It was also argued that value added tax would benefit the balance of payments as it is more easily remitted than purchase tax. Finally, value added tax has either been adopted or is in process of being adopted by actual and prospective members of the European Economic Community — as a step towards harmonization — and so the UK had little or no alternative but to move in the same direction.

There can be little doubt that the way purchase tax and selective employment tax were levied certainly distorted relative prices and that difficulties would arise in trying to levy them in a way that minimized this kind of distortion. Thus value added tax may well be superior on the basis of this criterion. However, in solving one problem another one may be created in that it can be argued persuasively that a general tax on consumer expenditure is regressive and discriminates against those on lower incomes. Successive governments have attempted, and it would seem with some success, at least as far as short-run consequences are concerned, to get round this criticism by what is called zero-rating most food, coal, gas, electricity, the construction of buildings, public transport fares, and drugs and medicines supplied on prescription. Zero-rating means that the trader does not have to charge tax on his sales and, in addition, he can claim a refund of any tax he may have paid to his suppliers.

The balance of payments argument in favour of value added tax is superficially persuasive in that imports bear the tax whereas exports are zero-rated. However, it is not at all clear that balance of payments considerations should be a criterion of the appropriateness of a particular tax as balance of payments adjustment is primarily a question of exchange rate policy and monetary and fiscal policy. This, of course, is not to imply that value added tax will not have at least short-run implications for the balance of payments.

---

1 See Green Paper, *Value Added Tax,* Cmnd. 4621, 1971; and *Value Added Tax,* Cmnd. 4929, 1972.

Certain other features of value added tax deserve to be mentioned. As well as a zero-rated category of goods there is also an exempted category. For exempted goods the trader does not have to charge tax on his sales but he cannot claim a refund for any tax included in the price of his purchases. Exempted goods and services include land, insurance, letter and parcel post, betting and gaming (which already carry excise duty), finance, education and health services. Small traders with a business turnover of less than £5,000 in taxable goods and services are exempt from the tax.

IV.8   Customs and Excise Duties

The term customs duties refers to duties imposed on imports, whereas excise duties, as already mentioned, are imposed on domestically produced goods. Customs duties may be primarily either for revenue-raising purposes, being levied on imported goods which are similar to the domestic goods that carry excise duties, or primarily for giving protection to British goods or preference to goods from specified countries. As may be seen from table 2.8 the large revenue yielders are tobacco, oil and alcohol with a total estimated yield of £5,665m in 1976-7 or almost 18% of total revenue from taxation. Moreover, this does not take account of VAT on these products.

An outstanding feature of the duties and taxes on tobacco, oil and alcohol is their scale, the large proportion that they represent of the purchase price. Ordinarily it might be expected that something which has the effect of substantially increasing the price of a product would lead to less of it, perhaps much less of it, being bought. By and large this does not seem to have happened with these three products — their demands are said to be inelastic with respect to price. However, some doubts are beginning to be expressed about the buoyancy of the revenue from tobacco, though this may be due to other causes besides the scale of taxation. The at-any rate apparent inelasticity of demand with respect to price implies that these duties and taxes may have little direct effect on the allocation of resources. But there will be an indirect effect because the funds withdrawn by taxes from consumers will scarcely be spent by the state in the same way as if they had been in the hands of the former.

It is often argued that indirect taxes are to be preferred because they are less of a disincentive to the supply of labour than direct taxes. This is an extremely difficult issue and depends on many factors, such as the scale of duties and taxes to be substituted, say, for a reduction in direct taxes or for foregoing an increase, and the type and the extent of the goods involved. For an individual, in choosing between additional work or leisure, may well consider not only the direct tax on extra earnings but also the real value of goods and services that can be bought with additional income.

It is also arguable that on equity grounds indirect taxes are regressive in that they fall more heavily on the relatively low income groups. There would seem to be some truth in this as far as tobacco and beer are concerned, but possibly to a lesser extent for petrol, though bus fares are obviously affected by oil duties. On the other hand the relatively less well off seem to obtain benefits from government welfare and other services. But if the community opts for extensive government expenditure on welfare services and education it seems unavoidable that one way or another a large proportion of the tax revenue must be raised from the mass of taxpayers. If at the same time the latter are important beneficiaries from government expenditure then they are indirectly paying for perhaps all of or a major part of these benefits. This is in no way to deny, however, the power of taxation, or at least certain forms of it, to redistribute income and wealth.

IV.9   Capital Transfer Tax and Wealth Tax

Capital transfer tax was introduced under the first Finance Act 1975 at the same time as estate duty was abolished. The tax, often called a gifts tax, applies, subject to certain exemptions, to gifts made during life and to transfers on death. Transfers of what is called settled property or property held in trust are also subject to the tax. The tax is chargeable as the gifts or transfers occur and is cumulative. That is, in calculating the tax due on successive gifts or transfers the previous ones are taken into account and progressively higher rates of tax apply. The rates of tax on what are known as lifetime transfers are lower than for transfers on death. The tax is in general payable by the donor but may be recovered from the beneficiary.

The main exemptions are transfers between husband and wife both in life and on death; transfers in any one year of up to £2,000 plus any unused part of the previous year's exemption; outright gifts to any one person during the tax year up to a value of £100; and transfers made out of income after tax as part of normal expenditure which leave the donor sufficient income to maintain his usual standard of living. Marriage gifts are given special treatment; transfers by a parent up to £5,000 are exempt and up to £2,500 by any other ancestor and £1,000 by anyone else. Business owners and working farmers also get special relief; for purposes of the tax, value transferred is reduced by 30% and 50% respectively. Transfers to charities or political parties are completely exempt if made more than a year before death. There are also special provisions relating to the exemption of gifts of works of art and historic buildings made during the individual's lifetime.

The first £15,000 of transfers, after taking into consideration all exemptions, is tax free whether made during lifetime or on death. The rates for lifetime transfers then rise from 5% on the next £5,000 by gradual steps to 75% on transfers of over £2m. Transfers made within three years of death become subject to the rates applicable on death.

The intention of the capital transfer tax (and indeed the wealth tax to be discussed below) is to reduce the inequality of wealth distribution. It should clearly be more effective in achieving this than the estate duty which it replaced, since the latter was avoidable if gifts were made during lifetime and outside the *inter-vivos* period. However, it is arguable that an accessions tax, that is a tax on recipients rather than on donors, would have been even more effective as a means of achieving greater wealth equality. For an accessions tax would encourage a spreading of gifts between recipients in a way that would reduce tax liability; this is not true of the capital transfer tax.

The precise form of the capital transfer tax and the exemptions it incorporates make it extremely important for individuals with even quite modest capital assets to plan their affairs carefully if they wish to minimize their tax liability. This too could be a source of inequity, depending on the foresight and luck of donors. Finally, like all such taxes it may encourage increased consumption expenditure and perhaps expenditure on education, travel and the like.

The Chancellor announced in his 1974 Budget that the government intended to introduce an annual wealth tax. Subsequently a Green Paper was published outlining the proposals the government had in mind.[1] In a foreword to the Green Paper the Chancellor states that 'income by itself is not an adequate measure of taxable capacity. The ownership of wealth, whether it produces income or not, adds to the economic resources of a taxpayer so that the person who has wealth as well as income of a given size necessarily has a greater taxable capacity than one who has only income of that size'.[2]

It is not clear what precise form the wealth tax will ultimately take as it has run into much criticism both in and outside Parliament. A Select Committee of the House of Commons established to examine a wealth tax has not found it possible to present an agreed report. However, the Green Paper suggests that the tax would cover individuals, trusts and estates in administration but charitable trusts and pension funds would be exempted, as would companies and unincorporated associations. The tax would be levied on the total value of an individual's chargeable assets, less liabilities, where these were in excess of probably £100,000. The rate of tax envisaged might be 1% on this amount with higher rates for larger sums.

Two important criticisms have been made against the wealth tax proposals. First, they do not distinguish the source of the wealth, whether it comes from inheritance, capital gains, gambling winnings or through saving and the creation of real assets. Yet many people might feel it is more equitable to tax some of these forms of wealth than others. Secondly, if a wealth tax is to have a substantial effect on inequality then it has to be relatively high and if so it is likely to require realization of assets in order to meet the payments. This could be a serious disincentive to capital accumulation and adversely affect economic growth. Indeed, like the capital transfer tax it could encourage consumption expenditure. However, the detailed form of the tax remains to be seen.

IV.10   Taxation and the EEC

It is evident from the preceding discussion that some of the recent tax reforms of the UK are designed to bring its taxes, or at any rate some of them, more closely into line with those of the EEC. Members of the Community are obliged under the Treaty of Rome and subsequent directives to harmonize their tax legislation as regards turnover taxes, excise duties and other forms of indirect taxation. In particular, the Community has adopted value added taxation as its main general indirect tax and this is binding on all members, though many of the details, including the actual tax rates, or range of rates, remain to be determined. Contributions to the Community budget are to be calculated on the basis of the harmonized value added tax. It is also the intention of the Community to harmonize the main excise duties on tobacco, oil and alcohol. As far as the UK is concerned this may mean a reduction in the duties on tobacco and alcohol since these are much higher than in most of the countries of the present Community. Corporation tax harmonization is still under consideration within the Community

---

1   *Wealth Tax*, Cmnd. 5704, 1974.
2   *Ibid.*, p. III.

but it seems likely that the credit or imputation system will be adopted and, as was seen earlier, the UK has anticipated this eventuality. The Community does not require harmonization of direct personal taxation.

The fundamental justification for tax harmonization within the Community stems from the very concept of the Community as, amongst other things, a common, unified competitive market. This requires, it is argued, the disappearance of all artificial barriers to trade and capital flows between the member countries, including those that might be created by different tax systems. On the basis of this approach the impetus towards uniformity or harmonization of taxation is immense. This is especially clear in the case of value added tax and excise duties and becoming more so, as far as corporation tax is concerned, with the increasing importance of international companies and the mobility of capital, which the Community is determined to foster among its members. The need to harmonize personal direct taxation is not felt to arise as it is believed that mobility of labour is not greatly affected by differences between member countries in this type of tax.[1]

The whole process of tax harmonization carries important consequences for both the Community and its member countries. By implication it places great stress on the efficient allocation of resources as indicated by the static competitive model. By the same token it neglects, or at least puts on one side, the fundamental question of externalities and of income and wealth distribution, except to the extent that these will be dealt with by harmonization of social security arrangements and with the help of the Community budget, and by regional policy measures. Up to the present none of these areas is well developed though some progress has been made in each of them. Finally, the harmonization is relevant to the whole issue of stabilization policy. It remains to be seen to what extent it will be possible for individual members to vary indirect taxes such as value added tax as an instrument of fiscal policy. This could obviously pose serious problems for member countries.

V POLICY IN RETROSPECT AND PROSPECT
V.1 The 1960s and early 1970s

In the brief review of policy below attention is concentrated on the record of the authorities in the pursuit of their major policy goals. For most of the 1960s the authorities were preoccupied with the achievement of full employment, price stability, economic growth, stability of exchange rates and a 'satisfactory' balance of payments. But in the late 1960s the commitment to fixed exchange rates became less strong and was abandoned in the early 1970s; and in the last couple of years a reduction in the rate of inflation rather than price stability has come to dominate the other policy goals, including full employment and economic growth. Indeed the authorities now see the curtailment of the pace of inflation as a necessary means to achieving more employment and faster economic growth.

During the 1960s unemployment in Great Britain averaged less than 2%, though from 1967 onwards it was in excess of this figure and in 1972 it averaged 3.9%. By late 1973 it had declined to 2.2%, though the average for the year as a whole was

---

1 However, the Community intends to harmonize such matters relating to direct taxation as tax deduction of dividends at source.

2.7%. This rate was maintained in 1974 but rose to 4.3% for 1975 and reached a peak of 6.1% in January 1976. Thus until the last five years or so the policy goal of full employment had been more or less achieved, at least if 2% is taken as the norm, though some might think that rate is too high. This is not to say that full employment was achieved continuously throughout the 1960s; unemployment did, of course, fluctuate, but within a relatively narrow range. However, the experience of the 1970s has so far been very different with the unemployment rate averaging well over 3%.

Retail prices rose over the 1960s at a compound rate of some 3.8% a year, with the rate of increase accelerating in the later years to around 5%. However, even this latter rate seems low in comparison with the rates experienced since then. Over the four years 1969 to 1973 the rate has been over 7%, almost twice the rate of the 1960s. But even 7% is moderate in comparison with rates of 16% between 1973 and 1974 and 24% between 1974 and 1975. Thus there has been a complete failure to achieve price stability, as measured by retail prices, and the degree of failure has increased dramatically over the last five years.

If economic growth is measured in terms of gross domestic product then this has grown at a compound rate of around 2.8% a year during the 1960s, though by no means regularly, and just over 2.6% a year between 1969 and 1973. In 1974 gross domestic product remained almost static or even declined slightly and in 1975 fell by almost 2%. However, this understates the fall in the standard of living as it makes no allowance for the adverse changes in the terms of trade in these years. The average rate of growth of about 1.5% for the early 1970s is just above half what it was in the 1960s. Moreover, most of the growth in the early 1970s took place between 1972 and 1973 when it reached some 5.5%. Thus whilst economic growth has indeed taken place it has been far from regular, has been low by international standards for developed countries and in 1974 and 1975 was actually negative, something which has not happened since 1952.

For the first half or more of the 1960s fixed exchange rates were a major goal of economic policy. But in the year or two leading up to the devaluation of sterling in November 1967 this policy came increasingly under question and by 1972 the Chancellor of the Exchequer was prepared to say in his budget speech that 'the lesson of the international balance of payments upsets of the last few years is that it is neither necessary nor desirable to distort domestic economies to an unacceptable extent in order to maintain unrealistic exchange rates, whether they were too high or too low.' In the light of the exchange rate fluctuations in the last few years and their repercussions on international monetary and economic cooperation it seems doubtful that this somewhat cavalier statement now represents official policy, though this is not to say that fixed exchange rates have once more become a policy goal.

Whatever may be true of the official attitude to exchange rates and whether it is to be regarded as a goal or an instrument of policy, there is no doubt about the authorities' concern over the balance of payments. For most of the 1960s and again since 1972 the balance of payments has been a matter of grave concern to the authorities and time and time again they have felt constrained to take drastic action to improve the position.

The 1960s began with the current account of the balance of payments in serious deficit. This culminated in a crisis in July 1961 when a whole new battery of restrictive monetary and fiscal measures was introduced in an attempt to rectify the situation. For the next couple of years the current balance ran a surplus but from time to time this was eroded by capital flows so that the overall position was precarious.

The period 1964-8 was one of sustained crisis for sterling and the balance of payments. In the five years ending in December 1968 the cumulative deficit on current account was £858m and the total currency flow, which includes the current account deficit, investment and other capital flows, the EEA loss on forwards and the balancing item, was the enormous sum of £3,676m. This was mainly financed by borrowing on a large scale from the IMF and other overseas monetary authorities.

For the next three years from 1969 to 1971 inclusive the current balance was in surplus and considerable amounts of foreign debt had been repaid. But by early 1972 the current balance was once more in deficit, accompanied by large investment and capital outflows. The deficit in the current balance accelerated during 1973 and for the year as a whole totalled some £842m. However, this was a small deficit in comparison with what was to follow. In 1974 the deficit in the current balance reached £3,650m. By 1975 this had fallen to £1,702m, an improvement on the previous year. Since June 1972 the exchange rate of sterling had been allowed to float. To begin with it appreciated against the US dollar but subsequently declined below the former parity level of $2.40 to the pound. However, the major depreciation in the exchange rate has taken place since the middle of 1974 and early in 1976 it fell well below $1.80 to the pound.

Of the instruments used to try and achieve the various policy objectives the ones of chief interest to this chapter are necessarily the monetary and fiscal. For most of the 1960s and indeed also the early 1970s the authorities would seem to have been sceptical about the effectiveness of traditional monetary and credit policy as exercised through changes in the monetary aggregates or even Bank rate or minimum lending rate as means of or targets to be aimed at in trying to achieve their policy goals. Their attitude would seem to have been vastly influenced by the work of the Radcliffe Committee.[1]

The Committee emphasized the importance of what is described as the 'whole liquidity position' of the system. It appears to have had in mind the borrowing and lending activities of a whole set of financial intermediaries, as well as the provision of trade and other forms of credit, and the apparent ease with which the funds could be conveyed to potential spenders.[2] In so far as monetary aggregates — and in particular the money supply — mattered, they mattered only as part of the overall liquidity picture. The Committee felt that the best way to influence the liquidity picture, apart from dramatic changes in interest rates, which it rejected on the grounds that these might seriously weaken the capital and reserve positions of financial intermediaries, was to strike directly at the major sources of credit supply, which it believed to be bank advances and hire purchase credit. Such measures were indeed the hallmark of official policy for most of the 1960s.[3]

---

1 *Committee on the Working of the Monetary System,* Cmnd. 827, 1959.
2 In an extreme form this suggests that all financial assets and forms of credit are perfect substitutes. On this view control of the money supply becomes relatively unimportant, as indeed does control of *any* particular financial asset or form of credit, except perhaps as a short-run palliative. The Radcliffe Committee would seem at times to have approached this extreme viewpoint.
3 Cf. section II.2 above.

With the introduction of the competition and credit control arrangements the emphasis changed with the quantitative restrictions on advances and hire purchase credit being swept away and more reliance placed on flexible interest rates as a policy target. The monetary aggregates, such as the various money supply aggregates, did not to begin to figure prominently as either targets or indicators of monetary policy, though much greater emphasis has been placed upon them by the authorities in the last couple of years.[1]

For the three years to 1962 inclusive the money supply M_3 (figures for M_1 are not available before 1963) grew at a relatively stable rate of some 2% a year. During 1963 the rate of growth accelerated to over 8% for the year as a whole. The rate of growth, whilst remaining substantially higher than in the early 1960s, declined for the next two years, but for the five years ending in December 1968 the compound rate of growth was some 7% a year, though it was far from being regular on a year to year basis. In 1969 the rate of growth was only about 3%, whereas over the three years to the end of 1971 the average was about 8.5%. For 1971 alone the rate was some 13% and for 1972 and 1973 over 27% in each year. The rate of growth fell substantially in 1974 to around 12.5% and in 1975 fell even further to 7.5%.[2]

From 1963 to 1968 M_1 – the narrower definition of the money supply – grew at a relatively stable rate of about 4% a year. For 1969 the rate fell to zero but for the four years to 1973 the compound rate of growth was almost 10% a year, having been more than 16% in 1971, but only about 5% in 1973, 4% in 1974 and 18% in 1975.[3]

For the monetarist the size and variability of the rate of growth of the money supply – whichever definition is used – during the greater part of the period since the beginning of the 1960s would suggest that it was both inflationary and destabilizing. And many that remain sceptical about monetarism have come to accept that the rapidity of the growth of the money supply in the early 1970s contributed greatly to the pace of inflation in 1974 and 1975 and to the overall state of crisis of the UK economy. The Chancellor of the Exchequer in his April 1976 budget speech has stated that, 'Even before the oil crisis hit us [early in 1974] growth had come to a halt in Britain, our balance of payments deficit by the end of 1973 was already racing up, and inflation, fuelled by a grossly excessive increase in the money supply, was already rising rapidly'.[4] This is in no way to deny the impact on the economy of rising import prices, nor the difficulties that may arise in trying to control the money supply in an open economy, which is subject to large movements of funds in and out of the country.

---

1 There have been at least three official definitions of the money supply, labelled M_1, M_2 and M_3. M_2 is no longer used by the authorities and need not be discussed further. M_1 consists of notes and coins in circulation with the public and UK private sector sterling sight deposits less an allowance for transit items. M_3 comprises notes and coins in circulation with the public together with all deposits, whether denominated in sterling or other currencies, held by UK residents in both the public and private sectors, less a deduction for transit items. See Statistical Appendix Table A5 for figures for M_3.

2 The figures for M_3 are end of the year. This has the effect of inflating them, especially in the last few years, in comparison with say annual averages. Unfortunately, however, annual averages are not available for the early 1960s.

3 The figures for M_1 are annual averages. The figure for 1975 is greatly inflated by changes in the composition of M_1. See *FS*.

4 Parliamentary Debates (Hansard), House of Commons, Official Report, 6 April 1976, col. 239 (parentheses added).

To argue that monetary policy has contributed to inflation may seem strange in the light of the rising trend of interest rates which have been a feature of UK monetary conditions, not just in the last few years but over the whole period under consideration. In the early 1960s the interest rate on 2.5% Consols averaged slightly more than 5.5%, rose to rather more than 6% in the middle 1960s and for the three years 1971 to 1973 inclusive averaged 9.67%, with the average for 1973 being 10.85%, 14.95% in 1974 and 14.66% in 1975. There need not, however, be any inconsistency between an inflationary monetary policy and rising *nominal* interest rates. For if allowance is made for the expected rise in prices the *real* rate of interest may be very low or on occasion even negative. Indeed an inflationary monetary policy may be said to contribute to rising nominal interest rates.

As far as fiscal policy is concerned difficult problems arise in trying to determine whether it is in some sense expansionary, contractionary or neutral. In a growing economy it might be thought useful to describe budgets as being neutral if expenditure and revenue grew in real terms at a stable rate over time, with the rate equal to the potential growth of output. This would imply that the deficit or surplus of each budget would also grow at the same real rate. But this formulation gives rise to problems. It suggests that a surplus or deficit which is growing at more than the potential growth of output is deflationary or expansionary respectively. But it is also important to know the change through time in the rate of change of the surplus or deficit. Thus a reduction in the rate of growth of the surplus or deficit may be described as expansionary or contractionary respectively, relatively to their previous levels, even though the new rates may still be in excess of the potential growth of output; by a similar argument a stable rate of growth of the surplus or deficit may be described as neutral. It would seem to be some such interpretation as the latter which is generally employed by commentators and it is this practice which is broadly followed below.

The foregoing, however, says nothing about how the deficit will be financed or, alternatively, how the surplus will be managed. Yet the effects of, say, a deficit being financed through a net increase in the rate of expansion of the money supply, as opposed to the sale of government debt to the non-bank private sector, will generally be very different. Furthermore, the deficit or suplus on the Consolidated Fund needs to be seen in conjunction with the lending and borrowing activities of the government through the National Loans Fund and the effects that these may have on the economy. Finally, actual Budget deficits or surpluses frequently turn out to be very different to those anticipated, sometimes because of the unforeseen buoyancy of revenue receipts and at other times because of the effects of rising prices on the scale of expenditure. Each of these points — and they are by no means exhaustive — needs to be borne in mind in the following discussion which is only qualitative and far from being comprehensive.

In the early 1960s the Budgets were mildly expansionary, contractionary and more or less neutral respectively.[1] By contrast the 1963 Budget was highly expansionary as it planned for a budget deficit — the first for many years — and a substantial borrowing requirement. By comparison the 1964 Budget was contractionary as it anticipated a small surplus as did the Budget of 1965, whereas the Budget of 1966 planned for a considerably larger surplus than in the previous

---

1   The Budgets referred to are the annual Budgets. However, the authorities have often found it necessary to introduce supplementary budgets.

two years and by intention was thus even more contractionary. The 1967 Budget reversed this trend and to that extent was expansionary. As far as the balance of payments was concerned this would seem to have been a serious misjudgement as the pound had to be devalued in November of that year. The 1968 Budget was contractionary in that it planned for a large surplus and the 1969 Budget for an even larger one. Despite a marked improvement in the balance of payments during 1969, the 1970 Budget was essentially neutral in that it anticipated much the same surplus as for the previous year.

The Budgets between 1970 and 1975 can usefully be looked at as a group. Like its two predecessors the 1971 Budget planned for a substantial surplus, though somewhat less than that of the 1970 Budget, and a *negative* borrowing requirement, thus envisaging a net repayment of debt. During 1971, as for some years previously, the growth of output was sluggish and unemployment began to rise, whilst the balance of payments on current account was strongly in surplus, as it had been for the past two years.

It was against this background that the Budget of 1972 was designed. It was highly expansionary. It planned for a very small surplus and net borrowing of £2,667m – the equivalent of some 17% of the estimated cost of supply services for that year. It was not until 1973 that the economy showed much evidence of a response to this large fiscal stimulus. But during 1972 the overall balance of payments was showing signs of serious weakness. Despite the latter the 1973 Budget carried the expansionary process even further with an anticipated deficit of almost £1,200m, over twice the realized deficit for 1972-3, and net borrowing of some £3,650m.

As has already been seen output grew rapidly during 1973, as did prices, and unemployment fell, whilst the current account deficit on the balance of payments got markedly worse. Inevitably, the 1974 Budget had to try and rectify the position. It planned to turn a provisional deficit for 1973-4 of some £1,700m into a surplus of about £980m and provisional net borrowing of £3,100m into one of around £600m. These were dramatic and large changes in relation to overall budgetary figures, though in the event they were not realized, but taken in conjunction with monetary and other measures probably helped to improve the balance of payments position at the expense of the rate of growth of output and increased unemployment.

The 1975 Budget was prepared against a background of world recession, rapidly rising prices at home with unemployment tending to increase and a massive deficit in the current balance of payments for 1974. The consolidated fund surplus of some £980m expected twelve months earlier had become a deficit of over £3,200m and net borrowing had turned out to be almost £6,000m instead of £3,100m. Despite some increases in taxation the Chancellor planned for a deficit for 1975-6 on the consolidated fund of over £2,700m and net borrowing of some £4,600m. As in the previous year these figures were far from being realized. The 1975-6 deficit on the consolidated fund was actually over £6,600, well over twice what had been planned a year earlier, and net borrowing became £8,750m.

The forecast for 1976-7 is that the consolidated fund deficit will be about £6,700m and net borrowing £10,750m. However, it may be expected that these figures will not be inflated to anything like the extent of the last couple of years since the government has put a strict limit – known as cash limits – on the actual amount of cash that may be spent on a wide range of public services. There is therefore some hope that in the next few years government will bring its expenditure under greater control and reduce the scale of its consolidated fund deficits and net borrowing. These steps should help to reduce the rate of inflation, which is already (Spring 1976) declining, but the price, which is almost certainly a necessary one, may be persistent unemployment and, at least for a time, sluggish economic growth.

Even on the basis of this cursory review of fiscal policy it is hard to resist the impression that it has often been, if not erratic, then certainly far from regular and perhaps at times contributing to the uncertainty facing the economic system. If this is true it supports the views of those who are profoundly sceptical that the authorities or anyone else has at present sufficient knowledge to use fiscal policy for precise short-run economic management. These complex issues are returned to briefly below.

V.2   Policy and the EEC

Whatever may be the judgements about the merits or demerits of past monetary and fiscal policy there is no doubt that as a member of the European Community the UK will be affected by the steps taken to establish economic and monetary union. This has been defined as absolutely fixed exchange rates between members' currencies, free from any exchange rate margins, or alternatively and preferably, a single Community currency; the establishment of a Community system for the central banks, possibly along the lines of the Federal Reserve System of the United States and with analogous powers; the harmonized management of national budgets under a Community decision-making body which would have authority to influence member countries' levels of revenue and expenditure, as well as the methods of financing the deficits and the disposal of surpluses.[1] In general, 'economic and monetary union means that the principal decisions of economic policy will be taken at Community level and therefore that the necessary powers will be transferred from the national plane to the Community plane. These transfers of responsibility and the creation of the corresponding Community institutions represent a process of fundamental political significance which entails the progressive development of political cooperation. The economic and monetary union thus appears as a leaven for the development of political union which in the long run it will be unable to do without'.[2]

These views, though expressed by the Werner Committee some six years ago, would still broadly seem to represent the intentions of the Community. However, a recent report by Mr Leo Tindemans, the Belgian Prime Minister, on European Union shows much greater awareness of the difficulties involved in achieving it. In particular, he feels that a more gradual approach is required, especially towards economic and monetary union where he has suggested a two-tier system, one for the strong members of the Community and one for the weak, namely, the UK, Italy and Ireland. The strong would proceed more or less as outlined in the various stages below, whilst the weak would have more time to catch up with the strong.

---

1 *Report* to the Council and the Commission on the Realization by Stages of Economic and Monetary Union in the Community, Werner Report, Supplement to Bulletin 11-1970 of the European Communities.

2 *Ibid.*, p. 26.

The first stage towards economic and monetary union lasted three years from January 1971 to December 1973. During the first stage the intention was to achieve closer co-ordination of short-term and medium-term economic policies, progress towards tax harmonization, greater freedom of movement of capital, the adoption of measures to alleviate structural and regional problems and a Community approach to international monetary problems. Progress in each of these areas was very limited and in some, like the liberalization of capital movements, non-existent. By and large the member countries were unwilling or reluctant to adopt measures that might, at least initially, affect adversely what they saw as their national interests. But in addition to or in conjunction with this development the Community was greatly disturbed by the upheavals in international monetary arrangements.

The second stage of economic and monetary union commenced on 1 January 1974 and is due to end 30 December 1976, with the third and final stage due to be completed by the end of December 1980. During the second stage it is hoped to establish consultative machinery so that prior discussion can be held before member countries take major decisions about economic and monetary policy. This should include co-ordination of budget policies and possibly the supervision of the size and methods of financing of budget balances. Exchange rates should have fixed but adjustable parities and the maximum permitted spread between currencies should be reduced below the 2.25% which operated amongst some of the members for part of the first stage. The European Monetary Cooperation Fund, established in 1973, should be strengthened by the transfer to it of foreign exchange reserves of the member countries so that it may intervene on the exchange markets and help to develop a Community identity in international monetary matters. These are some of the areas in which the Community hopes to make advances during the second stage towards economic and monetary union, though progress to date has been very slow.[1]

If the goal of economic and monetary union is realized it clearly implies a major shift in economic and political power away from the member states to the Community institutions. This is not necessarily something to be feared provided the Community as a whole ensures that the transfer of economic and political power does not penalize individual countries or regions within them. In particular it requires that the Community should be prepared through its regional, social and other policies to make major transfers of real resources from the richer to the poorer areas as an aid to the development of the latter. That the scale of transfers needed is likely to be massive may be appreciated by the size of the payments that the UK government makes to Northern Ireland, which is part of the economic and monetary union of the UK. For 1974-5 these amounted to some £400m, exclusive of the cost of the army and some payments which do not represent a movement of real resources. These transfers are made to a population of some one and a half million. It is difficult to know what the comparable transfers would amount to on a Community basis, but a factor of forty might not be too far wrong. This would imply funds of the order of £16,000m – some five times the total Community budget for 1975. Unless the members of the Community are prepared to envisage the development of intra-Community transfers of real resources on this kind of scale – or perhaps even larger – than the prospects for either realizing or maintaining economic or monetary union would appear slight.

1   For further information see 'Attainment of the Economic and Monetary Union', *Bulletin of the European Communities,* Supplement 5/73.

V.3   Conclusions

The policy record of the UK for the period since the early 1960s has been extremely disappointing. The simultaneous achievement of the various goals over a sustained period has continuously eluded the authorities. This failure or relative failure raises far reaching questions about the choice of policy goals, the nature and adequacy of the policy instruments at the disposal of the authorities and the limitations on our knowledge of the detailed and interdependent relationships between goals, instruments and targets. Moreover, these questions ultimately go far beyond the realm of the economic. For if a choice has to be made between the different goals in terms of the degree to which they can be achieved then serious political problems may arise. If, for instance, price inflation can only be reduced at the expense of substantial unemployment and sluggish economic growth then the very political institutions of the society may come under strain. However, the last year or so suggests that these strains have been carried more easily than might have been expected.

Furthermore, the discussion in V.1 above suggests that policy errors and misjudgements have contributed significantly to the economic problems of recent years. In particular, both monetary and fiscal policy have from time to time been used in ways which could only be expected to give rise to future economic problems. In the recent past the monetary and budgetary policies of 1972 and 1973 clearly come to mind. Moreover, there seems to be a greater acceptance across a wide range of political opinion that rapid and accelerating inflation imposes serious costs on the community, putting at risk both employment and living standards; and that both monetary and budgetary policy must be managed in ways that contribute to its curtailment. These developments, if they persist, as seems likely, augur well for the recovery of the UK economy over the next several years.

REFERENCES AND FURTHER READING

Bank of England Quarterly Bulletins
Sir Alec Cairncross (ed.), *Britain's Economic Prospects Reconsidered,* Allen and Unwin, 1971.
R. Caves and Associates, *Britain's Economic Prospects,* Brookings Institution and Allen and Unwin, 1968.
D. R. Croome and H. G. Johnson (eds.), *Money in Britain 1959-1969,* Oxford University Press, 1970.
N. J. Gibson, *Financial Intermediaries and Monetary Policy,* Hobart Paper 39 (2nd edition), Institute of Economic Affairs, 1970.
Brian Griffiths, *Competition in Banking,* Hobart Paper 51, Institute of Economic Affairs, 1971.
H. G. Johnson et al., *Readings in British Monetary Economics,* Oxford University Press, 1972.
A. T. Peacock and G. K. Shaw, *The Economic Theory of Fiscal Policy* (2nd edition), Allen and Unwin, 1976.
John Pinder (ed.), *The Economics of Europe: What the Common Market Means for Britain,* Charles Knight, 1971.
A. R. Prest, *Public Finance in Theory and Practice* (5th edition), Weidenfeld and Nicolson, 1975.
Robin Pringle, *Banking in Britain,* Methuen, 1975.
Report of the Committee on the Working of the Monetary System (Radcliffe Committee), Cmnd. 827, HMSO, 1959 Principal Memoranda of Evidence (3 Vols.) and Minutes of Evidence, HMSO, 1960.
Jack Revell, *The British Financial System,* Macmillan, 1973.

3

Foreign trade and the balance of payments

J. S. Metcalfe

I THE UK BALANCE OF PAYMENTS
I.1 Introduction

The importance to the UK of foreign trade, foreign investment and the balance of
international payments will be obvious to anyone who has followed the course of
events since 1960. The growth of the UK economy, the level of employment, and
real wages and the standard of living have been, and will continue to be, greatly
influenced by external economic events. It is the purpose of this chapter to outline
the main features of the external relationships of the UK and to discuss economic
policies adopted to manipulate these external relationships, with the primary focus
of attention being on the years since 1960.[1]

To begin with, it is often said that the UK is a highly 'open' economy, and some
indication of the meaning of this is given in table 3.1. We see that in 1975, exports
of goods and services were 27.8% of GNP and imports of goods and services were
30.6% of GNP, both figures being greater than the corresponding figures for the
mid-1960s and substantially greater than those for 1938.[2] A high degree of
openness implies that the structure of production and employment is greatly
influenced by international specialization. For the UK it also means that about half
our foodstuffs and the bulk of raw materials necessary to maintain inputs for
industry have to be imported. In the sense defined, the UK is a more open economy
than many other industrial nations, e.g. West Germany and France, but less open
than others such as Belgium.

I.2 The Concept of the Balance of Payments

The concept of the balance of payments is central to a study of the external
monetary relationships of a country but, as with many unifying concepts, it is not
free from ambiguities of definition and of interpretation. Such ambiguities stem
from at least two sources, viz., the different uses to which the concept may be put —
either as a tool for economic analysis or as a guide to the need for and effectiveness
of external policy changes — and the different ways in which we may approach the
concept — either as a system of accounts or as a measure of transactions in the
foreign exchange market.

---

1 Earlier editions of this volume contain a discussion of external developments between
  1945 and 1960. See e.g., the 5th edition (1974).
2 In 1938 the export:GNP ratio stood at 14% and the import:GNP ratio at 18.9%.

TABLE 3.1

UK Imports, Exports and National Income (Selected Years)

	1960		1965		1970		1975	
	£m	%	£m	%	£m	%	£m	%
Imports (debits)								
Goods (f.o.b.)	4138	67.0	5071	65.5	7919	65.0	21972	70.3
Services	1416	22.9	1799	23.2	2968	24.4	6403	20.5
Property income net of tax	438	7.1	557	7.2	889	7.3	2071	6.6
Transfers	185	3.0	319	4.1	402	3.3	821	2.6
Total debits	6177	100.0	7746	100.0	12178	100.0	31267	100.0
Exports (credits)								
Goods (f.o.b.)	3737	63.1	4848	62.8	7907	61.2	18772	63.5
Services	1415	23.9	1744	22.6	3368	26.1	7055	23.9
Property income net of tax	671	11.3	992	12.9	1446	11.2	3343	11.3
Transfers	104	1.8	135	1.7	192	1.5	395	1.3
Total credits	5927	100.0	7719	100.0	12913	100.0	29265	100.0
GNP at factor cost (£m)	22875		31672		43809		92840	
Imports of goods & services as % GNP		24.3		21.7		24.8		30.6
Total debits as % GNP		27.0		24.5		27.8		33.7
Exports of goods & services as % GNP		22.5		20.8		25.7		27.8
Total credits as % GNP		25.9		24.4		29.5		31.8

Sources: NIBB, 1975, and *ET,* April 1976.

ᵣ From an accounting viewpoint, we may define the balance of payments as a systematic record, over a given period of time, of all transactions between domestic residents and residents of foreign nations. In this context, residents are defined as those individuals living in the UK for one year or more, together with corporate bodies located in the UK and UK government agencies and military forces located abroad. Ideally, the transactions involved should be recorded at the time of the change of ownership of commodities and assets or at the time specific services are performed. In practice, trade flows are recorded on a shipments basis, at the time when the export documents are lodged with the Customs and Excise, and at the time when imports are cleared through customs. The problem with this method is that the time of shipment need bear no close or stable relationship to the time of payment for the goods concerned and it is this latter which is relevant to the state of the foreign exchange market, although over the year the discrepancies between the two methods are likely to be small. All transactions are recorded as sterling money flows, and when transactions are invoiced in foreign currencies, their values are converted into sterling at the appropriate exchange rate. Because sterling is a 'key' or 'vehicle' currency, and is widely used as an international medium of exchange, it transpires that most of UK exports and roughly half UK imports are invoiced directly in sterling.

Like all systems of income and expenditure accounts, the balance of payments accounts are an ex-post record, constructed on the principle of double entry bookkeeping. Thus each external transaction is effectively entered twice, once to indicate the original transaction, say the import of a given commodity, and again to indicate the manner in which that transaction was financed. The convention is that credit items, which increase net money claims on foreign residents, e.g. exports of goods and services and foreign investment in the UK, are entered with a positive sign, and that debit items, which increase net money liabilities of domestic residents, e.g. imports of goods and services and profits earned by foreign owned firms operating in the UK, are entered with a minus sign. It follows that, in sum, the balance of payments accounts always balance and that the interpretation to be read into the accounts depends on the prior selection of a particular sub-set of transactions. It will be clear, therefore, that there can be no unique picture of a country's external relationships which may be culled from the accounts.

When analysing the balance of payments it can be useful to make a distinction between autonomous external transaction, transactions undertaken for private gain or international political obligation, and accommodating external transaction, transactions undertaken or induced specifically to finance a gap between autonomous credits and autonomous debits. This distinction is by no means watertight, as we shall see subsequently, but it provides a useful starting point when structuring the accounts and when trying to formulate notions of balance of payments equilibrium.

The Structure of the External Accounts of the UK: It is current practice to divide the external accounts of the UK into three sets of items: (i) current account items, (ii) capital account items; and (iii) official financing items. Current account items and all, or part (depending on taste), of capital account items can as a first approximation be treated as if they correspond to autonomous external transactions, while official financing items may be treated as corresponding to accommodating transactions. The structure of the external accounts and figure for 1971-5 are shown in table 3.2.[1] Current account items consist of exports and imports of commodities (visibles) and services (invisibles, e.g. insurance, shipping, tourist and banking transactions), profit and interest payments received from abroad less similar payments made abroad, certain governments transactions, e.g. maintenance of armed forces overseas, and specified transfer payments, e.g. immigrants remittances and foreign aid granted by the UK government. The rationale for collecting these items together is that the majority of them are directly related to flows of national income and expenditure, whether public or private. In particular, visible and invisible trade flows are closely

---

1 For further details the reader may consult the *UK Balance of Payments 1964-1974*, HMSO, 1975. This annual publication is known as the *Pink Book*.

TABLE 3.2

UK Summary Balance of Payments 1971-5 (£m)

		1971	1972	1973	1974	1975
Current Account (credit +/debit −)						
Exports (f.o.b.) (+)		8810	9141	11772	15895	18772
Imports (f.o.b.) (−)		8530	9843	14104	21159	21972
Visible trade balance		+280	−702	−2332	−5264	−3200
Government services and transfers (net)		−527	−564	−798	−880	−997
Other invisibles and transfers (net)		+1305	+1397	+2288	+2494	+2495
Invisible trade balance		+778	+833	+1490	+1614	+1498
Current balance	1	+1058	+131	−842	−3650	−1702
Capital transfers	2	−	−	−59	−75	−
Investment and other capital flows						
Official long-term capital	3	−273	−255	−252	−275	−251
Overseas investment in UK public sector	4	+179	+113	+345	+764	+434
Overseas investment in UK private sector	5	+1052	+752	+1594	+2186	+1428
UK private investment overseas	6	−834	−1409	−1863	−1130	−1937
Overseas currency borrowing (net) by UK banks:						
To Finance UK investment abroad	7	+280	+725	+595	+220	+165
To Finance UK public sector	8	−	−	+827	+594	−19
Other borrowing (net)	9	+201	−254	−63	−519	+67
Exchange reserves in sterling:						
British Government Stocks	10	+55	+65	+74	−124	−15
Banking and money market liabilities	11	+658	+222	+87	+1534	−621
Other external banking and money market liabilities in sterling	12	+709	−91	−7	+148	+550
Import credit	13	+47	+204	+201	+81	+88
Export credit	14	−195	−354	−436	−453	−713
Other short-term flows	15	+15	−430	−195	−229	+414
Total investment and other capital flows	16	+1894	−712	+907	+2797	−410
Balancing item	17	+276	−684	+204	+363	+1020
Total currency flow	18	+3228	−1265	+210	−565	−1092
Allocation of special drawing rights	19	+125	+124	−	−	−
Gold subscription to IMF	20	−	−	−	−	−
Total lines 18-20	21	+3353	−1141	+210	−565	−1092
Official financing						
Net transactions with IMF	22	−554	−415	−	−	−
Net transaction with overseas monetary authorities plus foreign borrowing by H.M. government	23	−1263	+864	−	+644	+423
Drawings on (+)/additions to (−) official reserves	24	−1536	+692	−210	−79	+669
Total official financing	25	−3353	+1141	−210	+565	+1092

Source: BEQB, March 1976.

related to movements in foreign and domestic incomes, the division of these incomes between expenditure and saving, and the division of expenditure between outlays on foreign goods and services and outlays on domestic goods and services.) It should be remembered, however, that trade flows may change not because of changes in incomes, but because of spending out of past savings (dishoarding) or because of the need to build up inventories of means of production, changes in which correspond to variations in holdings of assets. Profit and interest flows are classified in the current account because they correspond directly to international flows of income.

Capital account items can be arranged in several ways. One may distinguish official capital flows (lines 3 and 4) from private capital flows (e.g. lines 5 and 6). Alternatively, one may classify by the maturity date of the assets involved and distinguish long-term capital flows (e.g. lines 3-6 inclusive) from short-term capital flows (e.g. lines 12-15 inclusive). Equally one could, in principle, distinguish capital flows according to the implicit time horizon of the investor undertaking the appropriate decisions. The inevitable limitations of alternative classificatory schemes should not be allowed to hide one basic point, that all capital flows correspond to changes in the stocks of foreign assets and liabilities of the UK, i.e., to changes in the net external wealth of the UK. As such, these capital flows are generated primarily by the relative rates of return on domestic and foreign assets after due allowance is made for the effects of taxation. Flows of direct and portfolio investment in productive capital assets (lines 5 and 6) thus depend on prospective rates of profit in the UK compared to those abroad, and changes in holdings of financial assets depend on relative domestic and foreign interest rate structures. A relative increase in UK profit and interest rates will normally stimulate a larger net capital inflow or a smaller net capital outflow, and vice versa for a relative fall in UK profit and interest rates. One important factor which should not be overlooked here is the influence of anticipated exchange rate changes upon the capital gains and losses accruing to holdings of assets denominated in different currencies. If a sterling depreciation is anticipated, for example, this will provide a powerful incentive for wealth holders to switch any sterling denominated assets they hold into foreign currency denominated assets, in order to avoid any expected capital losses on holdings of sterling assets.[1] The 'capital value' effect is particularly important in creating changes in the flow of short-term capital (lines 7-15 inclusive). It is worth commenting at this stage upon lines 10, 11 and 12 which correspond to changes in sterling balances. Sterling balances arose out of the key currency role of sterling which led to private traders and foreign banks holding working balances in sterling, and which also led governments to hold part of their official exchange reserves in sterling. This latter aspect was, and still is, particularly important for the overseas sterling area countries (OSA) who traditionally maintained their domestic currencies rigidly tied to sterling, maintained the bulk of their foreign exchange reserves in sterling, and pooled any earnings of gold and non-sterling currencies in London in exchange for sterling balances. Furthermore, between 1940 and 1958, OSA countries were linked to the UK through a tightly knit system of exchange controls which discriminated against transactions with non-sterling area (NSA) countries, and especially those in the dollar area. The sterling area was effectively a

---

1 Subject to the possibility that forward exchange cover may have been taken (cf, section III.6 below).

currency union which allowed members to economize on their total holdings of gold and non-sterling currency reserves. One important consequence of this was that the sterling area system created substantial holdings of UK liabilities by foreigners, which have no maturity date and which can be liquidated at a moment's notice, so forming a permanent fund of contingent claims on the UK gold and foreign currency reserves. OSA countries could acquire sterling balances in the following three ways: by having a current account surplus with the UK; as the result of a net inflow of foreign investment from the UK; and from pooling in the UK any gold and foreign currency earned from transactions with NSA countries.[1] At the beginning of the Second World War, the total of sterling balances stood at approximately £500m, by the end of the war they had risen to £3.7 billion, around which figure they fluctuated between 1945 and 1966.[2] In contrast to the stability in the total quantity of sterling balances there were marked changes in the country composition: some countries e.g. India and Pakistan, ran down their wartime accumulation of balances, while other countries, e.g. some Middle East countries, acquired new holdings of sterling balances.[3] The continued existence of the sterling area financial arrangements depended upon two conditions being satisfied. First, the OSA must have a high proportion of their transactions with each other and with the UK. Secondly, there must be a continued confidence in the ability of the UK, in its role of banker to OSA, to match short-term sterling liabilities with an equivalent volume of official reserves or other short term assets. From 1958 onwards neither of these conditions were satisfied. The OSA countries began to transact more intensively with NSA countries and the UK moved into a position of seemingly permanent deficit on her basic balance, so increasing short term liabilities relative to official reserves and other short term assets and creating the conditions for the sterling crises which became frequent in the 1960s.[4] It was not unexpected, therefore, when the sterling area effectively ceased to exist in June 1972.[5]

Recent developments with respect to sterling balances are treated in section III.6 below.

---

1 Ignoring reserve diversification activities, the flow increment of sterling balances is equal to the OSA basic balance surplus with the UK, plus the fraction of their basic balance surplus with NSA countries which is pooled in the UK. The changes in UK official reserves, including any change in official foreign borrowing, less the change in sterling balances (the change in the UK's short-term liquidity position, one might say) is equal to the basic balance of the UK. These relations hold only as an approximation, changes in trade credit, for example, would have to be zero for them to hold exactly. The concept of the basic balance is defined below, section I.3.

2 See Appendix, table A-8 for details of total sterling holdings.

3 Detailed information on this may be found in Susan Strange, *Sterling and British Policy*, Oxford, 1971, Chs. 2 and 3.

4 If official short term and medium term foreign borrowing by the UK government is subtracted from the official exchange reserves, this gives a measure of 'cover' for the sterling liabilities. In 1962 the ratio of 'cover' to total sterling liabilities was 51%. By end 1967, the 'cover' had disappeared entirely, outstanding official borrowing exceed the official reserves by £3.8 billion.

5 Prior to 1972, the OSA consisted of the Commonwealth, except Canada, South Africa, Iceland, Ireland, Kuwait, Jordan and some others. Before June 1972 these countries were known as the scheduled territories, but since June 1972 only Ireland and Gibraltar remain in this category.

We come next to the balancing item (line 17), which is a statistical item to compensate for the total of measurement errors and omissions in the accounts, arising from, for example, the under-recording of exports and the reliance upon survey data for certain items such as foreign investment and tourist expenditures. A positive balancing item can reflect an unrecorded net export, an unrecorded net capital inflow, or some combination of the two. The major source of changes in the balancing item is likely to be unrecorded changes in net trade credit, reflecting discrepancies between the time goods are shipped and the time when the associated payments are made across the exchanges. As can be seen from table 3.2., the balancing item is very volatile and can on occasions be of a magnitude comparable to or greater than the surplus or deficit on current account. The total of investment and other capital flows together with the balancing item is known as the total currency flow (TCF, line 18), which can, in principle, be treated as the net balance of autonomous transactions. Before we come to accommodating transactions, two adjustments to the TCF have to be made, both of which relate to the UK's membership of the IMF. First, we have the allocation of special drawing rights (line 19), which is treated as a credit item since it effectively adds to the official reserves of the UK (line 24). Secondly, we have the gold subscription to the IMF. When the UK subscribes gold to the IMF (one quarter of the UK's quota has to be contributed in gold), the official reserves will fall, and this reduction of assets will be entered in line 24 with a positive sign. The entry in line 20 of the accounts is the requisite double entry to balance the accounts, and can be interpreted as the acquisition of assets in the IMF.[1]

The total of lines 18-20, the adjusted currency flow (line 21), has to be matched by an equal amount of official financing. If, for any year, line 21 has a negative sign, then the authorities must reduce the official external assets or increase the official external liabilities of the UK; they must undertake the reverse operations if line 21 is positive in sign. There are three ways in which the necessary adjustments can be made. First, the UK may draw upon or add to the official gold and currency reserves (line 24). At year-end 1975 the official reserves, including SDR holdings and the reserve position at the IMF, stood at £1.9bn, compared to a post-war peak of £2.5bn at year-end 1971. This represents a very slender reserve base for an economy as open as the UK. At year-end 1975 the reserves would only suffice to finance an amount of imports equal to 7% of the 1975 import bill, compared to a similar figure of 22% at year-end 1963. Not only is the reserve base inadequate, its composition has changed substantially since the mid-1960s. At year-end 1963, 73% of UK reserves consisted of gold and only 6% consisted of holdings of convertible foreign currency; by the end of 1975, the gold proportion had fallen to 16% and the convertible currency proportion had risen to 61%. Unused access to the SDR facility formed 15% of UK reserves at year-end 1975. As a second line of defence, the UK can borrow foreign currencies from the IMF. An amount equal to 25% of the UK's quota may be borrowed automatically, the so-called gold-tranche position which is classed as part of the official reserves.[2] The UK has further access to four credit tranches, each of which

---

1 In January 1976, the requirement that 25% of the quota be contributed in gold was waived. For further discussion of SDR's and the IMF system, see section III.9 below.

2 Automatic borrowing can exceed the gold tranche position to the extent that the total IMF holding of sterling falls below 75% of the UK quota.

corresponds to 25% of quota,[1] but access is dependent upon the UK government adopting economic policies which meet with the approval of the IMF, this being particularly so for drawings beyond the first credit tranche. The maximum amount the UK could borrow at year-end 1975, including the gold tranche position, stood at £1294m. The points to remember about IMF finance are that it is temporary, borrowings have to be repaid within 3-5 years, conditional, and cheap (4%-6%), relative to current commercial rates of interest. Finally, the UK has access to a considerable network of borrowing facilities built up with foreign central banks in the 1960s, primarily as a short-term defence against speculative capital flows. These have proved to be of considerable value to the UK, and have been supplemented since 1973 by direct government borrowing, mostly from the Eurodollar market.

It may already be apparent that the distinction between autonomous and accommodating transactions, upon which this discussion is based, is not entirely satisfactory. For example, by manipulating UK interest rates the government can create an inflow of short-term capital to accommodate a given current account deficit, even though from the point of view of individuals or banks buying and selling the assets the transactions are autonomous. Similarly, autonomous government items such as foreign aid may be deliberately adjusted to accommodate a deficit elsewhere in the accounts. At a more general level, whenever the government adopts policies to change the balance of payments, the effects of these policies will influence the totals of autonomous transactions so that they cease to be independent of the underlying state of the balance of payments. Despite these difficulties the autonomous – accommodating distinction provides a useful starting point for any arrangement of the external accounts.

So far we have examined the external accounts in isolation but they may equally be examined as an integral part of the national income and expenditure accounts, and here two important relationships should be noted. Firstly, the balance of payments deficit (surplus) on current account is identically equal to the excess (shortfall) of domestic expenditure over national income. Secondly, since the difference between national income and domestic expenditure corresponds to the current account deficit or surplus, it also equals the reduction or increase in the net external assets owned by UK residents.[2] It follows that the UK can only add to its external net assets to the extent that it has an equivalent current account surplus. Finally, we should note that, although the accounts separate current account items from capital account items, there are several important links between the two sub-sets of items. We have already pointed out that a non-zero current account results in changes in the net external assets of the UK. As these assets and liabilities have profit and interest flows attached to them, any change in the total of external net assets will lead to changes in the interest, profit and dividend flows which appear in the current account. Furthermore, this also results in equivalent changes in national income and so will affect the current account indirectly through any effects on national expenditure and the demand for imports. Similarly, within the context of a given current account position, capital flows which change the composition of external net assets will change

---

1 See section III.9 below for details of the temporary increase in the size of the credit tranches announced in January 1976.

2 Cf. J. Hicks, *Social Framework,* 1971, Chs. 8 and 21.

the average rate of return on these assets and so react back on the current account. These are perhaps the more important links, but others exist, for example, between trade flows and the balance of export and import credit and between trade and investment flows and changes in total sterling balances. As has often been said, the balance of payments is akin to a seamless web and it can be grossly misleading to treat individual items in isolation from the rest of the accounts.

I.3   Equilibrium and Disequilibrium in the Balance of Payments

It is obviously important, both for purposes of economic policy and historical analysis, to have clear notions of balance of payments equilibrium and disequilibrium. However, the formulation of such notions is not easy. As a first approximation, we could define balance of payments equilibrium as a situation in which, at the existing exchange rate, autonomous credits are equal to autonomous debits and no official financing transactions are required. This definition raises three problems. First, that of the time span over which equilibrium is defined. Clearly, a daily or even monthly span of time would be of little value and it is generally accepted that a sufficient span of years should be allowed so that the effects of cyclical fluctuations in income will have no appreciable net impact on external transactions. Secondly, if the exchange rate is allowed to fluctuate freely to equate the demand with the supply of foreign exchange, then equilibrium is always attained automatically, and any notion of payments disequilibrium becomes redundant. Thirdly, and in contrast, if the exchange rate is managed in some way to make it partially or completely independent of market forces, we must then accept that policies can be adopted to manipulate autonomous transactions in such a way as to make them balance. However, the problem which this raises is that the attainment of external equilibrium, at a given exchange rate, may involve unacceptable levels of employment or inflation, an interest rate structure which is inimical to economic growth objectives and a trade policy inconsistent with international obligations. To take account of these issues we can formulate the following definition of equilibrium. The balance of payments is in equilibrium when, at the existing exchange rate, autonomous credits are equal to autonomous debits over a period of good and bad years, without involving: (i) departures from full employment or price stability; (ii) departures from the desired rate of economic growth; and (iii) adoption of tariffs or subsidies inconsistent with accepted international obligations.

The question now arises of the sets of autonomous transactions to be used in this definition of equilibrium. One possibility is to consider current account transactions alone, but equilibrium would then involve a constant level of net external wealth and there is no particular merit in this, especially for a growing economy. As far as the UK is concerned, two sets of autonomous transactions have been used in discussions of balance of payments performance, the basic balance and the total currency flow.

The basic balance, defined as the sum of the current account and the net flow of long-term capital, attracts attention on several grounds, not least as one indicator of secular trends in external transactions. If the basic balance is in equilibrium, any net outflow (inflow) of long-term capital results in an equivalent increase in the stock of external assets (liabilities) of the UK. Furthermore, all non-zero flows of short-term capital must be matched by equivalent, offsetting changes in official financing.

Thus the basic balance puts below the line all capital flows essentially related to the role of the UK as an international banking and financial centre; capital flows which may be particularly sensitive to accommodating monetary manipulation.

Since 1969, however, the UK authorities have preferred to utilize the TCF as the appropriate indicator of external performance. In contrast to the basic balance, this places all short-term capital flows above the line, so that a zero TCF corresponds to a situation of no change in the total of officially held external net assets. There are several arguments in favour of the switch to the TCF, viz; (i) many short-term capital flows are linked to items in the trade balance, e.g., trade credit, or to the financing of long-term investment, and cannot sensibly be separated from items in the basic balance; (ii) short-term capital flows are inherently volatile, therefore they provide poor accommodation and should not be used for this purpose; and (iii) the TCF avoids the problem of separating the balancing item from the basic balance with the attendant danger of a misleading treatment of any errors and omissions. In the short-term, of course, the TCF is more volatile than the basic balance, but over the longer-run the two measures should coincide, provided that short-term flows net out to zero. A further advantage of the TCF is that it shows the potential increase (decrease) in the UK money supply as a result of a surplus (deficit) in the aggregate of autonomous balance of payments transactions.

The years 1973 and 1974 provide an illuminating example of how the various concepts of equilibrium and disequilibrium can produce markedly different figures. For the two years, the cumulative TCF deficit was £355m, so officially held external net assets must have fallen by this amount. However, the cumulative current account deficit indicates a reduction in the net external wealth of the UK of £4.50 billion, while the cumulative basic balance deficit indicates that short-term net external liabilities must have increased by £3.13bn.

I.4   The Balance of Payments, 1956-75

We shall now use our concepts of equilibrium to assess the balance of payments performance of the UK since 1956. To assist in this, table 3.3 contains average annual figures for selected items in the balance of payments in the periods 1956-60, 1961-64, 1965-67, 1968-71 and 1972-75. The first two sub-periods cover complete short cycles ending in a boom year, while the remaining three are somewhat arbitrary and are separated by the 1967 devaluation and the floating of sterling in June 1972. The averages of course hide substantial annual variations but they will suffice for the present purposes.

In the *Brookings Report,* R. Cooper suggested that the UK balance of payments position, at least up to 1966, could be summarized in terms of four propositions: (i) the UK is normally a net exporter of long-term capital, with a surplus on the current account; (ii) the visible trade balance is normally in deficit, but the invisible balance shows a surplus more than sufficient to offset this; (iii) the role of the UK as banker to the OSA gives volatile short-term capital flows an important position in the balance of payments; and finally, (iv) the trading, investing and international financial activities of the UK are carried out with a very inadequate underpinning of foreign exchange reserves.[1] Of our five periods, that of 1956-60 comes closest to

---

1   R. Caves (ed.), *Britain's Economic Prospects,* Allen and Unwin, 1968, Ch. 3.

TABLE 3.3

Trends in the UK Balance of Payments, Annual Averages for Selected Periods (£m) and Average Growth Rates of Real GDP and World Exports of Manufactures

		1956-60	1961-4	1965-7	1968-71	1972-5
1.	Visible balance	−94	−213	−281	−142	−2874
2.	Government services and transfers (net)	−209	−377	−278	−486	−810
3.	Private invisible (net)	+439	+559	+484	+1124	+2169
4.	Invisible balance (net)	+230	+182	+206	+638	+1359
5.	*Current account balance*	+136	−31	−75	+496	−1515
6.	Balancing item	+91	−13	+49	+129	+226
7.	Balance of long-term capital	−189	−139	−137	−68	+61
8.	Balance of long-term and other capital flows	−130	−181	−498	+337	+611
9.	Basic balance (5 + 7)	−53	−170	−212	+428	−1454
10.	Basic balance plus balancing item (9 + 6)	+38	−183	−163	+557	−1228
11.	*Total currency flow*	+97	−225	−524	+962	−678
12.	Gold subs IMF and SDR's	−18	−	−14	+64	+31
13.	Total lines 11 and 12	+79	−225	−538	+1026	−647
Official financing						
14.	Net transactions with overseas monetary authorities (inc. IMF) and foreign currency borrowing by H.M. government.	−	+143	+420	−628	+379
15.	Transfer $ portfolio to reserves	−	−	+173	−	−
16.	Drawings on (+) or additions to (−) official reserves	−79	+82	−55	−398	+268
17.	Total official financing	−79	+225	+538	−1026	+647
18.	Average annual growth real GDP (1970 prices)	2.36	3.65	2.33	2.27	1.30
19.	Average annual growth world exports of manufactures	8.77	7.95	6.77	10.05	5.57

Sources: UK Balance of Payments 1971 and *ET,* March 1976. World exports from *NIER,* various.

conforming to this view. The net outflow of long-term capital exceeded the current account surplus by an annual average rate of £53m and this was financed by a short-term capital inflow of £59m. After taking account of the balancing item and other factors the UK was able to add to its official reserves at an annual rate of £79m. Certainly the payments position, on either basic balance of TCF definitions, was nearer to a state of equilibrium than in any of the subsequent periods, coinciding as it did with an average unemployment rate of 1.7%.

The next two sub-periods to 1967 show unmistakable signs of a slide into fundamental disequilibrium. The trade balance continued to deteriorate throughout the two periods, despite a sustained growth of world trade, and so did the current account which moved into deficit. A successful attempt by the government to restrict the growth of overseas public expenditure in 1965-7 only prevented the deficit from being worse than it would otherwise have been. To some extent a reduction in the net outflow of long-term capital helped reduce the deficit on the basic balance, but the improvement here was more than offset by massive short-term outflows induced by the sterling crises of 1961, 1964 and each of the three following years. It was, of course, the weakness in the current account and basic balance, and the perpetual fear of a sterling devaluation which was crucial here. An important consequence of this lack of confidence in sterling was the need to incur substantial foreign debts and to liquidate the government's portfolio of dollar securities in order to maintain the parity of sterling.

The inevitable devaluation, which took place in November 1967, was followed by a substantial turn round in the external payments position, although, as we shall see in section III.5, it is not completely clear to what extent this is attributable to the devaluation, or to the acceleration in the growth of world trade, or to measures to restrict demand growth after 1968 (between 1969 and 1971 the average rate of growth of real GDP fell to 1.7%). The visible deficit was almost halved and an increase in the invisible surplus resulted in the current account moving back into surplus. When combined with a halving of the net outflow of long-term capital this created a very strong position in the basic balance, especially when account is taken of the balancing item. Apart from this, confidence in sterling returned after 1968, no doubt helped by the Basle arrangements of that year, and short-term capital flowed back into the UK at an annual average rate of £405m. So strong was the improvement in the payments position, that the UK was able to repay a substantial part of the debts raised in defence of sterling in the previous two periods and, at the same time, add to the official reserves. It cannot be claimed that this period saw a return to equilibrium in the external accounts, simply because of the severe restraint on domestic growth which took place. However, it can at least be argued that the foundations were then laid for a return to equilibrium once the foreign debts had been repaid.

This return to equilibrium has not been achieved, as the figures for 1971-5 indicate. Two features of this period are important. First, the rise in world commodity prices and the depreciation of sterling after June 1972 combined to produce the unprecedented trade deficit of £2.87bn. Fortunately, an improvement in the invisible balance, largely due to additional receipts of foreign profit and interest income, reduced this to a current account deficit of £1.51bn. Secondly, a reversal occurred in the role of the UK as a net exporter of long-term capital with a net capital import of £61m flowing into the UK, largely the outcome of opportunities to exploit North Sea oil resources and substantial foreign currency borrowing by the public sector. The basic balance deficit of £1.2bn (net of the balancing item) was financed in two main ways: (i) a net inflow of short-term capital as oil-producing countries placed part of their surplus resources in the UK; and (ii) resort to substantial foreign borrowing and drawing upon the official reserves. There can be little doubt that this period was one of severe fundamental disequilibrium in the UK balance of payments. The deficits were incurred in a period of deepening recession; from the end of 1973 unemployment rose progressively to reach a rate of 4.8% at the end of 1975, and manufacturing output fell by about 10% over the same period. In addition, gross investment in plant and machinery fell by 12.5% in 1975 and a substantial running-down of manufacturers' stocks took place. Indeed, currently, there seems to be little prospect of substantially reducing unemployment without causing a further deterioration in the external position.[1]

To summarize the experience of the period from 1956 to 1975, the crucial factor appears to be the increasing weakness of the visible trade account which more than offsets the steady improvement in the invisible trade surplus. The consequent deficits in the current account, combined with the propensity to export long-term capital, lead to a steady increase in short-term liabilities (including borrowing from foreign governments) relative to the official reserves. This in turn resulted in a decline in the ability of the UK to maintain its role of banker to the OSA and reduced the willingness of OSA governments to hold sterling as a reserve asset. Clearly trade performance must be improved, or the international financial role of the UK eliminated, if a return to a more stable external position is to be achieved. We should note that, although the short-term external liabilities of the UK exceed short-term external assets, the total of UK external assets still exceeds the total of external liabilities. At year-end 1974, the aggregate net external assets of the UK stood at £1.9bn, compared to figures of £5.9bn at year-end 1973 and £1.4bn at year-end 1962.[2] The UK acts as an international banker, but persistently commits the error of borrowing short and lending long without having an asset structure which prevents crises of confidence.

Before we examine the economic policies adopted to influence the external position of the UK, it will be useful to investigate the possible sources of the underlying weakness in the visible trade balance.

II   FOREIGN TRADE OF THE UK
II.1   Structure and Trends, 1955-75

In this section we shall examine the major structural features and trends in the foreign trade of the UK between 1955 and 1975.[3] In focusing attention upon certain longer term trends, we will find evidence of a marked decline in the international competitive position of UK manufacturing industry; a decline which, it may reasonably be claimed, is the proximate source of the unsatisfactory behaviour of the balance of payments noted in the previous section.

Geographical and Commodity Trade Structure: The traditional picture of UK foreign trade is one in which manufactures are exchanged for imports of foodstuffs

---

1   The Cambridge Economic Policy Group calculate that if 'full employment' had been maintained in 1975, the current account deficit would have reached £6.3bn (*Economic Policy Review*, March 1976, p. 3).

2   See 'An Inventory of UK External Assets and Liabilities: end 1974', *BEQB*, June 1975.

3   Since, over the period, some 65%-70% of total exports and imports reflected commodity transactions, we here concentrate solely on commodity trade. For a treatment of invisible items in the current account see P. Phillips, 'A Forecasting Model for the United Kingdom Invisible Account', *NIER*, No. 69, 1974. Interest, profit and dividend flows are discussed in Section III.7 below. For further details on invisibles, consult the COI pamphlet, *Britain's Invisible Exports*, HMSO, 1970.

and raw materials, with the bulk of the trade being carried out with the Commonwealth and overseas sterling area countries. That this picture is now completely out of date is shown in tables 3.4 to 3.6, which illustrate the radical changes in trading structure which have occurred since 1955. To some small extent these changes reflect the relaxation of wartime import restrictions and the general post-war movement toward free trade that resulted from the several rounds of GATT tariff reductions. But, in general, they are the outcome of more deep-seated changes in competitive forces.

TABLE 3.4

Area Composition of UK Merchandise Trade (Percentages)

	Imports (c.i.f.)				Exports (f.o.b.)			
	1955a	1972a	1972b	1975b	1955a	1972a	1972b	1975b
Western Europe	25.7	43.9	48.1	51.2	28.9	42.9	48.1	49.1
EEC	12.6	24.5	31.6	36.4	15.0	22.9	30.2	32.2
EFTA	11.4	17.5	14.5	12.5	11.6	16.1	13.8	13.1
Other	1.7	2.0	2.1	2.3	2.3	3.8	4.1	3.8
North America	19.5	16.0	16.0	13.3	12.0	16.4	16.4	11.7
USA	10.7	10.6	10.6	9.7	7.1	12.5	12.5	8.9
Sterling Area: Developed[1]	16.6	11.5	7.4	4.9	23.4	12.9	7.9	8.7
Japan	0.6	2.8	2.8	2.8	0.4	1.8	1.8	1.5
Soviet Union + E. Europe	2.7	3.5	3.5	3.1	1.7	2.8	2.8	3.3
Total developed	65.1	77.7	77.8	75.3	66.4	76.8	77.0	74.3
Sterling Area: Developing[2]	22.8	11.8	11.7	9.1	21.6	11.5	11.2	10.1
Latin America	6.1	3.0	3.0	2.6	3.7	3.5	3.5	3.4
Rest of World	6.0	7.5	7.5	13.0	8.3	8.2	8.5	12.2
Total	100.0	100.0	100.0	100.0	100.0	100.0	100.0	100.0

Sources: TI, 16 March 1972 and 22 March 1976; *MDS,* March 1976. Series 'b' differs from series 'a' as follows:
    (i)   Sterling Area: Developed includes Ireland in 'a', but excludes it in 'b'; (ii) EEC 'b' includes Denmark and Ireland; (iii) EFTA 'b' includes Denmark.
Notes: 1 Australia, New Zealand, India and South Africa.
      2 Sterling Area: Developing list from *TI,* 22 March 1973, p. 638.
There are some small discrepancies between the 1975 list of countries and the 1972 list.

The major changes in the geographical composition of UK trade are shown in table 3.4. Several general trends are immediately apparent. In particular, the increase in the proportion of UK trade carried out with the developed nations, (the decline in 1975 is likely to prove a temporary reflection of the increase in world primary commodity prices) and the increase in the proportion of trade carried out with Western Europe. Most striking of all is the increase in the proportion of exports and imports exchanged with EEC countries, a development which has largely been at the expense of trade with the more developed countries of the sterling area. It is worthy of note that trade with EFTA, membership of which has often been presented as an alternative to participation in the EEC, has throughout the period accounted for a smaller proportion of UK trade than has trade with the EEC, even when due allowance is made for changes in the membership of the two organisations. We may also note the increase in the importance of Japan as a trading partner and the decline in the importance of North America as a buyer of UK exports. As far as trade with the developing nations is concerned, the most important feature is the decline in the importance of sterling area countries both as a market for UK exports and as a source of UK imports.

TABLE 3.5

Commodity Structure of UK Imports, Selected Years 1955-75 (Percentages)

SITC Group	Description	1955	1960	1965	1970	1975
0, 1	Food, Beverages, Tobacco	36.2	33.1	29.7	22.7	18.0
3	Fuel	10.4	10.3	10.6	10.5	17.8
2, 4, 5 & 6	Industrial Materials	47.9	44.8	43.1	42.7	34.6
7 & 8	Finished Manufactures	5.2	11.1	15.3	22.9	27.5
9	Unclassified	0.3	0.7	1.2	1.2	2.1
	Total	100.0	100.0	100.0	100.0	100.0

Source: TI, 16 March 1972, p. 437, table 17 and 12 March 1976, p. 755, table 11.
Imports are measured on an overseas trade statistics basis and are valued c.i.f.

The switch toward a greater trade dependence on the industrialized, urbanized, high per-capita income countries of Western Europe, Japan and North America has been matched, not unexpectedly, by significant changes in the commodity structure of UK trade, particularly in respect of imports. The changing structure of UK import trade is shown in table 3.5. Most important here is the increase in the proportion of imports of finished manufactures, the share of which more than quad-rupled between 1955 and 1974, and the decline in the proportion accounted for by foodstuffs, beverages and tobacco. Imports of finished and semi-manufactures now account for some 53% of total UK imports. This same trend has also been experienced by other EEC countries although it remains the case that the UK is more dependent upon imports of non-manufactures than are, for example, France or West Germany.[1] On the export side, table 3.6, changes in structure are less noticeable. While the share of exports of manufactures has increased slightly over the period, this has been matched by a virtually equivalent decline in the importance of semi-manufactures. The only major changes seem to be the rapid decline in the share of textiles and the increase in the share of chemicals in total exports. Looking to the future, the possibility of substantial exports of North Sea

---

1   M. Panic, 'Why the UK's Propensity to Import is High', *LBR,* No. 115, 1975.

TABLE 3.6

Commodity Structure of UK Exports, Selected Years 1955-75 (Percentages)

	1955	1960	1965	1970	1975
Engineering Products[1]	36.5	42.3	43.5	43.5	43.7
Machinery	21.1	24.9	26.5	27.6	29.0
Road Motor Vehicles	8.7	11.1	11.6	10.3	8.7
Other Transport Equipment	5.7	5.0	3.3	3.0	3.4
Scientific Instruments	1.2	1.4	2.1	2.6	2.6
Semi-Manufactures[2]	29.7	27.7	26.8	26.5	20.5
Chemicals	7.8	8.5	9.2	9.7	10.9
Textiles	10.1	6.9	5.8	4.9	3.5
Metals	11.8	12.3	11.8	11.9	6.1
Other Manufactures[3]	12.6	12.0	13.2	14.4	18.4
Non-Manufactures[4]	21.2	18.0	16.4	15.6	17.4
Food, Beverages, Tobacco	6.5	6.0	6.6	6.4	7.2
Basic Materials	5.6	5.1	4.0	3.4	2.8
Fuels	4.6	3.6	2.7	2.6	4.1
Other	4.5	3.3	3.0	3.2	3.3
Total	100.0	100.0	100.0	100.0	100.0

Sources: TI, 16 March 1972, p. 430, table 7, and 12 March 1976, p. 753, table 11. *MDS*, March 1976, table 127.

Notes: 1. Section 7, plus 86.
2. Sections 5, 65 and 67-9.
3. Remainder of section 6 and section 8, less 86.
4. Sections, 0, 1, 2, 3, 4 and 9.

oil over the next five years is likely to raise the share of fuels in total exports and to diminish the share of fuels in total imports.

It will be apparent from this that UK trade is increasingly dominated by an exchange of manufactures for manufactures with the advanced industrialized nations. These structural changes would imply that UK manufacturing industry has experienced and will continue to experience greater foreign competition in home and export markets. They also help to explain the disintegration in the sterling area system which occurred after 1964.

Movements in the Volumes and Prices of Traded Goods: Trends in the volume and value of UK trade are summarized in table 3.7, which represents average annual growth rates of relevant items for four distinct periods, separated by the years of final relaxation of wartime import restrictions, 1960, the devaluation of sterling, 1967, and the floating of sterling, 1972. From 1955 onward we can see a tendency for the volume of imports to grow faster than exports and for imports to increase faster than real GDP. In the case of the unit value indices we have conflicting trends. During the first two periods, export values increased substantially faster than import unit values. However, from 1967, this trend was halted and then sharply reversed. The divergence between the movement of export and import

TABLE 3.7

Annual Rates of Growth of UK Exports and Imports, Selected Periods 1955-75

Average annual rates of increase (%)	1955-60	1960-7	1967-72	1972-4	1974-5
Export volume	2.42	3.24	5.01	6.99	-3.99
Export unit value	2.46	1.60	5.90	15.87	22.00
Export value (f.o.b.)	4.32	4.92	11.17	22.24	18.10
Import volume	4.68	5.10	6.40	8.60	-7.10
Import unit value	0.04	0.87	5.80	29.30	12.70
Import value (c.i.f.)	4.06	5.88	11.18	33.79	3.77
Real GDP (1970 prices)	2.55	3.28	2.22	2.67	-1.61

Sources: Figures for 1955-67 computed from *British Economy Key Statistics,* 1900-1970; post-1967 figures from *NIER* and *ET,* various.

unit values since 1972 is so marked as to require further comment, since it corresponds to an unprecedentedly large deterioration in the terms of trade (ratio of the export unit value index to the import unit value index). Taking 1970 as base, the UK's terms of trade reached a peak of 102.8 in the first six months of 1972 and then fell to a low of 73.1 in the first quarter of 1974, from which level they subsequently experienced a slight improvement. This adverse swing of some 29% is an important factor contributing to the recession, balance of payments difficulties and decline of real incomes recently experienced in the UK. Several conflicting factors were at work to produce the change in the terms of trade. On the side of exports, the rapid increase in UK unit labour costs and prices tended to improve the terms of trade but the favourable effects of domestically generated inflation were more than offset by two factors influencing the sterling price of imports. First, the widespread increases in the prices of foodstuffs and raw materials, of which oil was only one example (and an exceptional one at that, since the oil price increase was largely a reflection of political developments in the Middle East), in response to the world output boom of 1970-73. This raised the index of primary product export prices (in $) from a value of 101.5 at the end of 1971 to a peak of 228.9 at the end of 1974. At the same time, we should not forget that inflationary developments in other industrial countries made a contribution by raising the foreign currency price of manufactures imported into the UK by some 32% between 1970 and 1974. The second major factor was the floating of sterling in June 1972 and its subsequent steady depreciation. Taking these factors together, we can, in a purely arithmetic sense, decompose the movement in the terms of trade between 1970 and 1974 as follows: a 62% rise in export unit values, offset by a 70% average increase in the foreign currency price of the UK imports and a 21% depreciation of sterling against a trade weighted average of other major currencies.[1]

Movements in the volume and unit value indices allow us to gain some impression of the source of changes in the trade balance. Comparing the first and second periods,

1 For details of this 'effective' exchange rate index see 'The Effective Exchange Rate for Sterling', *ET,* June 1974, pp. 29-31.

it is clear that the deterioration in the UK trade balance after 1960 was largely reflected in the decline in the rate of increase of export prices both absolutely and relatively to import prices. Even though the import volume index grew faster in the second period, the gap between it and the growth of the export volume index narrowed. On balance the volume trends were favourable but not sufficiently so to cope with an adverse price movement of the magnitude experienced. In the third period, following devaluation, we can see an improvement in performance with import and export values growing at the same rate. Finally, we see that the deterioration in the trade balance since 1972 is largely the result of the adverse terms of trade movement noted above. Over the whole period we can see a tendency for the rate of growth of export volume to increase almost continuously. Unfortunately, this steady improvement in export performance has not been sufficient to cover the growth in imports, especially in the two periods, 1960-7 and 1972-4, when relative price movements went against the UK. The last column of table 3.7 provides trade volume and value figures for 1974-5 from which, in comparison with the previous years, we should note: (i) the fall in export volume in the face of a widespread world recession; (ii) an even sharper fall in import volume associated with the decline in GDP and the running down of inventories in the UK; and (iii) the continued acceleration in the rate of increase in export prices, a grim reflection of the worsening inflationary situation in the UK.

Changes in export and import volumes are, of course, not independent of changes in export and import prices. Other factors held constant, a deterioration in the terms of trade should tend to accelerate the growth of export volume and retard the growth of import volume, and vice versa for an improvement in the terms of trade. Considerable evidence has now accumulated to the effect that trade volumes and values are sensitive to changes in relative prices, even though prices are not the only factors influencing trade performance.[1] The only difficult point to establish is the speed of response of trade flows to changes in relative prices.[2] In general, one would expect the long-run trade response to exceed the short-run response, because, in the long run, information on price changes is more thoroughly diffused among decision makers, contracts can be renegotiated and new plant can be laid down or written-off as circumstances dictate. In fact, evidence suggests that it can take up to five years for the effects of price changes to be fully reflected in appropriate changes in trade flows.[3] Estimates of trade volume elasticities for the UK suggest a demand elasticity for exports of manufactures of between −1.5 and −3,[4] while a more recent study finds an import volume demand elasticity of −1.6

1 See, e.g., M. C. Deppler, 'Some Evidence of the Effects of Exchange Rate Changes on Trade', *Staff papers IMF*, Vol. 21, 1974, pp. 605-36.

2 H. Junz and R. Rhomberg, 'Price Competitiveness in Export Trade Among Industrial Countries', *AER*, May 1973, pp. 413-18.

3 H. Junz and R. Rhomberg, *op. cit.*

4 H. Junz and R. Rhomberg, 'Prices and Export Performance of Industrial Countries 1953-63', *Staff Papers IMF*, Vol. 7, 1965, pp. 224-71. R. A. Batchelor and C. Bowe, 'Forecasting UK International Trade: a General Equilibrium Approach', *Applied Economics*, Vol. 6, 1974, estimate price elasticities of UK export volume of between −1.13 and −2.80.

for finished manufactures and -1.2 for imports of semi-manufactures.[1] Precise figures such as these must always be treated with caution, because errors in the underlying data and conceptual difficulties in separating price changes from other relevant factors present formidable statistical problems. Furthermore, the estimates are averages computed over long periods and so may yield a completely misleading impression of short-run trade response, especially as they have been computed for a period in which exchange rates and relative prices were more stable than is currently the case. Despite these cautious remarks, one can at least be confident that trade flows are more responsive to price changes than previous pessimistic estimates had suggested.

II.2   The Decline in Competitive Performance

The trend toward an increasing trade deficit in the first half of the 1960s, coming as it did after a relaxation of trade and currency restrictions, has been taken as indicative of a widespread lack of competitive edge in UK industry relative to foreign industry. Further evidence in support of the contention is provided by the continuing decline in the share of the UK in world exports of manufactures,[2] by the rising import propensity in the UK and by, for example, the estimates of Houthakker and Magee, who found, for the period 1951-66, an income elasticity of demand for imports in the UK of 1.66, double the corresponding world income elasticity of demand for UK exports of 0.86. Taken at their face value, which would be misleading, these figures suggest that the UK can only grow at half the world rate if balanced trade is to be maintained.[3]

The statistics of the decline in the UK share in world exports of manufactures are dramatic and show that the share dropped from 20.4% in 1954, to 17.7% in 1959, to 11.9% in 1967 and to 8.8% in 1975. Over the whole post-war period, it seems that an increase in world exports of manufactures of 10% is associated with an increase in UK exports of manufactures of between 5% and 6%.[4]

Of itself, the decline in export share need not give rise to concern, since it may simply reflect a decline in the UK share of world manufacturing production, the natural result, say, of her early industrial start. (In 1899 the UK accounted for 32.5% of world exports of manufactures). However, this is far too complacent a view. Once it is recognized that between 1959 and 1973 the volume of world trade in manufactures grew at the historically unprecedented rates of 7%-10%, and that the UK was alone among the major industrial countries in experiencing a substantial

---

1   A. D. Morgan and A. Martin, 'Tariff Reductions and UK Imports of Manufactures 1955-71', *NIER*, No. 72, 1975. Batchelor and Bowe, *op. cit,* estimate on import elasticity of -0.38 for machinery and -1.08 for other manufactures.

2   'World', in this context, means W. Germany, France, Italy, Netherlands, Belgium-Luxemburg, Canada, Japan, Sweden, Switzerland, USA and UK. In 1974 they accounted for 94% of manufactured exports from all industrial nations. See *TI,* 9 January 1976.

3   H. S. Houthakker and S. P. Magee, 'Income and Price Elasticities in World Trade', *Review of Economics and Statistics,* Vol, 51, 1969, pp. 111-25. This study covered the period 1951-66. For a critique see A. D. Morgan 'Income and Price Elasticities in World Trade: A Comment'. *Manchester School,* Vol. 38, 1970, pp. 303-314.

4   *NIER,* No. 73, 1975, p. 12.

drop in export share, there are grounds for disquiet. Had the UK maintained its 1960 export share, then, in 1967, exports of manufactures would have been 32% higher in value terms than they actually were, and the overall payments position would have been substantially strengthened.

On the import side the evidence for loss of competitive edge is equally disturbing. Even though all the major industrialized nations have experienced a rising import share since 1955, the UK seems to be relatively more import prone than her competitors and to have a relatively high income elasticity of demand for imports.[1]

To explain these developments in any precise sense is not easy; several interrelated factors are involved and the relative weight to be attached to each is difficult to establish and may vary considerably over time. At the most general level, and since it is trade in manufactures which is crucial, there would seem to be three possible sources of a relative decline in industrial efficiency; a relatively slow growth of labour productivity, a relatively low rate of increase in manufacturing output, and an inability to develop, innovate and market new commodities in the face of rapidly changing technical and demand conditions.

It is well documented that, over the period since 1950, the growth of labour productivity in the UK has been inferior to that in the other major industrial nations[2] and that it is this factor, rather than any tendency towards a faster rate of increase of money wages, which is the major reason for the relatively faster increase in UK export prices, at least, that is, until 1967.

Averaged over the period 1959-67, UK dollar export prices rose at an annual average rate of 2%, compared to 1.3% for the other major industrial nations.[3] It follows that the relative price of UK manufactures rose by some 6% over this period and that, assuming an export share elasticity of -2, this could account for 37% of the decline in UK export share between the two dates.[4] The problem with this line of argument is in applying it to developments since 1967. For between then and 1974, UK relative export prices have fallen by 9% and yet the UK export share has continued to decline. Clearly other factors must be at work.

One important factor will be the relative ability to supply exports which, over the long-run, will depend upon the relative growth of manufacturing output in the UK and the other industrial nations. Here again UK performance was disappointing, the percentage increase in UK manufacturing output between 1959 and 1967 being some 45% less than that in the other OECD countries. It is possible that some 25%

---

1 A. D. Morgan, 'Imports of Manufactures into the UK and other Industrial Countries 1955-69', *NIER*, No. 56, 1971 and M. Panic, *op. cit.*, L. F. Campbell-Boross and A. D. Morgan, 'Net Trade: A Note on Measuring Change in the Competitiveness of British Industry in Foreign Trade', *NIER*, No. 68 1974, suggest that since 1963 UK manufacturing industry has never been sufficiently competitive to restore the country's trade situation to the position held in 1963.

2 See, e.g., E. H. Phelps-Brown, 'Labour Policies', in A. Cairncross (ed.), *Britain's Economic Prospects Reconsidered*, Allen and Unwin, 1971.

3 Figures calculated from *NIER* Appendix tables, which also provide a valuable summary of international trends in labour productivity, unit costs and industrial output.

4 An elasticity of -3 would account for 55% of the loss in export share.

of the loss in export share during this period can be attributed to this relatively slow growth of manufacturing output.[1]

Of course, the two explanations of a declining export share are not independent and it is not difficult to weave them together. The below average rate of growth of output can be linked with a below average ratio of investment to output in manufacturing, and hence to a below average increase in output per man. Supply limitations and increasing relative prices each retard the growth of exports and therefore contribute to a below average growth of aggregate effective demand. Profitability is therefore reduced and this, combined with the deflationary effects of policies introduced to correct the associated trade deficit, results in a weakening in the incentive to invest. Hence we come full circle, back to the causes of low growth of output and labour productivity from which we started.

Since 1967 the relatively poor growth performance of the UK has continued to contribute to the decline in export share. Between 1967 and 1972 the percentage increase in UK manufacturing output was 52% less than that of all OECD countries, although between 1972 and 1974 the gap narrowed somewhat to 36%. Against this, however, we must note that since 1967 the UK has exported an increasing share of its total manufacturing output.[2] If this trend continues, it is possible that the UK export share will increase in the future, under the influence of increasing price competitiveness and a narrowing of the gap between UK and other industrial countries' growth rates.

Finally, we must consider the possibility that it is the inability to innovate and market in response to rapidly changing conditions which is the chief source of UK difficulties. The type and quality of manufactures produced, delivery lags and after sales service, and the general quality of marketing effort have each, it is frequently argued, played a significant role in limiting UK trade performance.[3] This is hardly surprising; the shift in the geographic and commodity composition of UK trade noted above is bound to enhance the importance of non-price competitive factors, e.g. advertising and research and development activity, between firms essentially operating under oligopolistic conditions.[4]

Unfortunately, the precise role of these factors has proved impossible, as yet, to determine, although it is interesting to note that similar explanations of poor British competitive performance were employed at the end of the 19th century.[5]

---

1 The remaining 75% must be due, as a matter of arithmetic, to changes in the share of output exported by the UK and her competitors. Since, for the UK, this proportion remained virtually constant, with an average value of 42% over the period, the major loss of share must correspond to her competitors exporting an increasing proportion of their manufacturing output. No doubt the rapid growth of trade between the EEC countries is an important indicator of this.

2 The ratio of UK export volume to manufacturing output (1970 prices) averaged 42% over the period 1959-72, rose to an average of 49% during 1967-72 and reached 58% in 1974.

3 NEDO, *Imported Manufactures,* HMSO, 1965. A. P. Thirlwall, 'The Panacea of the Floating Pound', *NWBR,* August 1974.

4 A survey, carried out by DTI in 1973, found that 44% of UK exports are accounted for by 31 enterprises and 74% by 177 enterprises. Foreign owned companies and subsidiaries accounted for 29% of UK exports. *TI,* 11 April 1975.

5 R. Hoffmann, *Great Britain and the German Trade Rivalry 1975-1914,* Pennsylvania University Press, 1933, pp. 21-80.

Other Factors: While it is the inadequate industrial growth performance which is chiefly responsible for the poor UK trade performance, several additional factors should not be ignored. On the export side, it is possible that an undue concentration on the supply of relatively slow growing markets and on the production of commodities for which world demand was growing relatively slowly could explain the decline in export share. Appealing though this hypothesis is, evidence does not support the view that the structure of UK trade is responsible for poor export performance. A recent NEDO study finds no evidence in support of the view that the UK export structure is biased adversely toward the slower growing commodities in world trade.[1] Furthermore, a study by R. L. Major has shown that only 9% of the total loss in UK manufacturing exports between 1954 and 1966 can be attributed to exporting to relatively slow growing markets.[2]

It may also have been the case that preferential trading arrangements have changed to the disadvantage of UK exporters. Isolated examples of this can be found, for example, in the relaxation by certain Commonwealth countries of import quota restrictions, which led to substantial export gains for Japan and the USA at the expense of UK producers. To set against this, an EFTA study concluded that UK exports in 1965 were 2% higher than they would otherwise have been in the absence of EFTA, although there appeared to be no noticeable effects on UK imports.[3] Of much greater importance has been the formation of the EEC, from which UK exports clearly benefitted, the positive effects of selling to a large and rapidly expanding market more than offsetting the adverse effects of discrimination against the UK.[4]

A factor which may be important in explaining the rising share of imports into the UK is the substantial reduction in tariff and other import restrictions which occurred after 1945. Between 1947 and 1959 the war-time restrictions on imports were virtually eliminated,[5] and from 1955 onwards the UK tariff was progressively reduced in line with agreements concluded through GATT. The UK tariff, introduced in 1932, had developed as a two-part structure with many imports from Commonwealth producers entering the UK duty free, and imports from the rest of the world being subject to duties which, in the case of manufactures, ranged from 10% to 33%.[6] Between 1959 and 1975, the average UK tariff on semi-manufactures fell from 16.2% to 10.5% and that on finished manufactures from 21.4% to 12%. Despite the magnitude of these changes a recent study suggests that their overall

1 M. Panic and A. H. Rajan, *Product Changes in Industrial Countries Trade 1955-68,* NEDO Monograph, No. 2, 1971.

2 R. L. Major, 'Note on Britain's Share in World Trade in Manufactures 1954-66', *NIER,* No. 44, 1968.

3 EFTA Secretariat, *The Effects of EFTA on the Economies of Member States,* Geneva, 1969, p. 162.

4 UK membership of the EEC is treated in section III.8, below.

5 For details see M. F. W. Hemmings, C. M. Miles and G. F. Ray, 'A Statistical Summary of the Extent of Import Control in the UK since the War', *RES,* Vol. 26, 1959, pp. 75-109.

6 In 1957 the average margin of preference on dutiable Commonwealth imports was 9%. See PEP, *Commonwealth Preference in the UK,* 1960. The swing in UK trade toward manufactures and the advanced industrialized nations progressively made this degree of preference less important.

effect has proved to be relatively small, increasing the import values for semi-manufactures by 13% and that for finished manufactures by 9% relative to the values they would otherwise have had in 1971.[1]

Finally, it has been argued that UK trade performance would have been improved if the economy had experienced a more stable pressure of aggregate demand. It is suggested that when aggregate demand presses on the limits of production capacity, the consequent bottlenecks and delivery delays result in a diversion of domestic demand to imports and a diversion of domestic output from exports to the home market, this latter switch being encouraged by an allegedly lower profitability of exports compared to home market sales. This is a complex skein of relationships, difficult to formulate accurately and difficult to judge empirically. It is certainly the case that changes in the rate of growth of manufacturing output tend to be matched by a reduction in the proportion of manufacturing output exported – although 1968 and 1973 provide important exceptions to this rule – and that the share of the UK in world manufacturing exports has declined most rapidly in the years of rapid industrial growth, for example 1964, 1967 and 1973. However, more sophisticated econometric studies have failed to produce very conclusive results and a more definite statement must await further investigation.[2] In support of the hypothesis that exporting is a relatively less profitable activity, there is little conclusive evidence either way. A study by J. D. Gribbin, however, does find that, on average, export profit margins tend to be lower with evidence of a wide dispersion of experience across firms.[3] However, even if this hypothesis should receive more substantial support, it is difficult to know what significance is to be attached to it. For it can be argued that profit margins in home and export markets will be systematically related to the elasticity of demand in these markets and thus, since export markets are more competitive, that the home profit margin will tend to exceed the export profit margin.

1 A. D. Morgan and A. Martin, *op. cit.* It is possible that this study understates the true reduction in protection afforded to UK manufacturing industry because it deals only with nominal tariff rates and not effective tariff rates – the effective rate taking into account the impact of tariff changes on the cost of imported means of production. Recent calculations, for the period 1968-1972, show that while the nominal rate on manufactures fell by 36%, the effective rate fell by 46%. M. Oulton, *Tariffs, Taxes and Trade in the UK: The Effective Protection Approach*, Government Economic Service Occasional Papers, No. 6, 1973, p9.

2 J. Artus, 'The Short Run Effects of Domestic Demand Pressure on British Export Performance', *Staff Papers*, IMF, Vol. 17, 1970, pp. 247-75. R. A. Cooper, K. Hartley and C. A. M. Harvey, *Export Performance and the Pressure of Demand*, Allen and Unwin, 1970, in particular Chs. 4 and 5. The pressure of demand is found to be important in explaining UK import behaviour. See, e.g., R. Marston, 'Income Effects and Delivery Lags in British Import Demand 1955-67', *JIE*, Vol. 1. 1971, pp. 375-99. Imports in the UK are particularly sensitive to fluctuation in stockbuilding activity, see e.g. 'Forecasting Imports: A Re-examination', *NIER*, No. 42, 1967.

3 J. D. Gribbin, *The Profitability of UK Exports*, Government Economic Service Occasional Papers, No. 1., 1971.

III ECONOMIC POLICY AND THE BALANCE OF PAYMENTS
III.1 Introduction

The coverage of this section is limited in two ways. First, pressure of space precludes more than a passing reference to events and policies before 1964. Second, the concept of economic policy is limited to government intervention where the prime concern was to produce alterations in flows immediately affecting the balance of payments. It may be argued that *all* economic policy affects the balance of payments since any non-trivial intervention in the economy is likely to produce at least minor alterations in the balance of forces affecting trade and payments flows. Some policies may well have major implications for trade but, for present purposes, are not regarded as balance of payments policies. Thus, attempts to control inflation or to stimulate efficiency and growth are likely, if successful, to have substantial impacts on trade flows but these problems are discussed elsewhere in this book and, in any case, may be judged desirable for reasons other than those concerned with the balance of payments. Equally, policies which are directed explicitly at trade flows may involve related adjustments in 'domestic' policy, as we shall see in the discussion of devaluation. Manipulation of tariff and other barriers to trade is a legitimate branch of balance of payments policy, but, in practice, government action of this nature is circumscribed by international agreements, and again pressure of space precludes a discussion of what might be done within these constraints. Entry to the EEC is obviously a policy decision of incalculable magnitude affecting all aspects of economic behaviour but this section will confine itself to some balance of payments implications of that decision. The influence of the international monetary system for UK policy is so important that we conclude the section by looking at recent developments in that field.

When interpreting the following discussion it is important to remember that the conduct of balance of payments policy, or for that matter of economic policy in general, is not a matter of 'fine tuning'. In part this reflects the fact that UK balance of payments performance is as much determined by the economic policies adopted in other countries as it is by policies adopted in the UK. On top of this, familiar problems of forecasting the direction and rate of change of economic variables, political and other limitations on the values of policy variables, and conflict between different policy objectives, taken together, mean that practical policy making is more an art than a science.

III.2 The Exchange Market Framework

It is a familiar proposition that modern industrial economies have evolved by means of a progressive division of labour and that one important condition for this is the adoption of a single internal currency, which can act as an intermediary in all economic transactions. The international division of labour has so far, however, proceeded without this advantage. Since nations continue to maintain separate currencies for internal use, it follows that international transactions must proceed with the simultaneous exchange of national currencies, apart, that is, from those transactions conducted in key currencies. This exchange of currencies takes place in the foreign exchange market and it is there that the relative prices of different national currencies, exchange rates, are established.

An important policy issue which faces the government of any country is, therefore, that of the degree of restraint which it wishes to place on the exchange of its own currency with the currencies of other nations. Not only will the chosen restraints limit the type and geographical direction of transaction which domestic residents may make with foreigners, but they will also have an important bearing upon the conduct of policy to achieve internal objectives such as full employment and price stability. Successive UK governments have exercised their options in two ways: by adopting particular forms of exchange rate policy, and by placing restrictions upon the currencies against which sterling may be exchanged for the pursuit of specified transactions, i.e. by exchange control.

Between 1945 and June 1972 the UK operated the foreign exchange market for sterling in accordance with the rules of the par-value system.[1] This required the official adoption of a par, or central, value for the spot market[2] rate for sterling to be expressed in terms of gold or the US dollar of 1944 fineness together with the acceptance of a band of fluctuation of the spot rate around the par value.[3]

Provided the spot rate for sterling, as determined by free market forces, lay within the permitted band, the UK exchange authorities did not need to take any action. Should the exchange rate be under pressure to stray outside this permitted band then the exchange authorities were obliged to intervene in the foreign exchange market, selling foreign exchange from the reserves when sterling was at its lower limit and purchasing foreign exchange to add to the reserves when sterling was at its upper limit. Thus the par value system allowed some degree of variability in the foreign exchange rate but required that the UK keep a buffer stock of foreign exchange reserves, which it could use to keep the exchange rate within the specified bounds.

It must be noted that the par value of a currency is not fixed for all time once a country decides to abide by this system. On the contrary, a country may, when its balance of payments is in 'fundamental disequilibrium' and after consultation with the IMF, change its par value. This UK governments have done twice, devaluing sterling in 1949 and again in 1967. The background to and outcome of the 1967 devaluation are discussed below.

In contrast to what is required in the market for spot exchange, IMF rules place no formal restrictions on the movements of forward exchange rates for a currency. Nor are any necessary. In normal circumstances, the forward exchange rate will stand in a simple relationship[4] to the spot exchange rate, reflecting the role of the

---

1   This is the name given to the exchange rate system adopted by the majority of Western nations after the second world war. The central body of the system is the International Monetary Fund (IMF).

2   A distinction must be made between the spot market and the forward market exchange rates for a currency. The spot exchange rate is the price of foreign currency for immediate delivery, that is, at the time the rate for the transaction is agreed. A forward exchange rate is the price of foreign currency for delivery at a specified date in the future.

3   Until December 1971 the permitted band of fluctuation was 1% either side of par. Under the Smithsonian reforms of that time the band was widened to 2¼% either side of par.

4   This is the interest parity relationship. Given freedom of short-term capital flows, the percentage difference between the spot and forward dollar exchange rates for sterling, say, will tend to equal the difference in short-term interest rates between London and New York.

forward market in providing cover for the exchange risks inherent in spot market transactions.

A major change in UK policy occurred in June 1972, when the par-value system was 'temporarily' abandoned and sterling allowed to take whatever values the balance of demand and supply for foreign exchange might dictate. However, a policy of allowing sterling to float has not meant that the exchange market ceases to be an object of policy concern. The government still has to decide to what extent sterling will float freely, without official constraint, and thus to what extent it is going to manage the exchange rate. Recent UK experience suggests a considerable degree of exchange management to iron out potentially violent fluctuations in the spot rate without, if possible, influencing its longer term trend.

The second aspect of UK exchange policy is that of exchange control. This is a complex issue with a detailed history of evolution, so that space precludes more than the most general remarks.[1] The legal basis of exchange control is contained in the Exchange Control Act of 1947, which assigns to the Treasury the authority to formulate exchange control policy. The day-to-day responsibility for implementing the exchange control provisions is delegated to the Bank of England, while, in turn, the daily volume of foreign currency transactions is handled by authorized exchange dealers, i.e. the commercial banks. The Exchange Equalization Account acts only as a residual purchaser or seller of foreign exchange in order to support a given exchange rate. As far as UK residents are concerned, practice since 1960 has been to allow complete freedom for current transactions[2] but to restrict transactions on capital account in the following manner. Until 1972, capital movements to and from the overseas sterling area were free from restriction but those to and from the non-sterling area were restricted, by not allowing them to pass through the spot exchange market unless official permission was granted. Official attitude toward the exchange control of capital movements has undergone considerable change since 1972, the details of which are discussed below in section III.7.

Exchange control for the UK is greatly complicated by the international reserve and medium of exchange functions of sterling, which result in foreigners holding sterling balances. Since 1958 a distinction has been maintained between two such categories of sterling, external account sterling and resident sterling. External account sterling consists of sterling balances held by non-sterling area residents. This is freely convertible into any currency for current and capital transactions. Resident sterling consists of sterling balances held by residents of the overseas sterling area, who are treated in the same fashion as are UK residents, i.e. full convertibility on current account but restricted convertibility for capital transactions to non-sterling area countries.

From 1958 UK exchange control regulations stayed broadly unchanged. However, with the float of sterling in 1972 several modifications were required, which essentially involved giving the former sterling area countries external account

---

1 A useful historical account of UK exchange control will be found in B. Tew, *International Monetary Co-operation 1945-1970*. Hutchinson, 1971. The interested reader may also consult the IMF *Annual Reports on Exchange Restrictions*.

2 Apart, that is, from certain restrictions on the availability of exchange for foreign travel and for the making of gifts and other transfers to non-sterling area residents.

status. Today the sterling area, for exchange control purposes, consists only of a handful of countries.[1]

III.3   Balance of Payments Policy with Fixed Exchange Rates

In this section we outline the more important aspects of UK balance of payments policy under the par value system. Only occasional reference is made to events prior to 1964 and the discussion focusses upon policies adopted to influence the current account. Balance of payments policy following the floating of the pound in 1972, and policy with respect to the capital account are treated in separate sections.

Implications of the Par Value System: During the period 1945-72 the commitment of successive governments to maintain a par value for sterling had important implications for the way in which the UK economy was linked to other economies and for the appropriate conduct of domestic economic policy. The central point about a regime of fixed exchange rates is that it strengthens the economic linkages between separate national economies, with two important consequences. Firstly, fluctuations in aggregate demand in one country spill over, through changes in trade balances, to influence aggregate demand in that country's trading partners, and secondly, differences in national rates of price inflation have the maximum possible effect upon a country's international competitive strength and its trade performance.

Under any exchange rate regime an increase in incomes in the rest of the world or an increased foreign preference for UK goods will, in the absence of capacity constraints, result in a greater volume and value of UK exports. Under the par value system, however, the increase in exports has two consequences for the UK economy; national income will increase and the balance of trade will improve. Both consequences follow from the theory of the foreign trade multiplier, which in turn is based on the existence of stable import functions relating import expenditures in the UK and foreign countries to the level of each country's national income.[2] The increase in exports will raise UK national income directly through the increased incomes earned in the export trades and indirectly, through the multiplier repercussions which spread to the rest of the UK economy. Thus prosperity or depression in the UK's trading partners will tend to expand or contract national income in the UK. Since approximately 30% of UK output is exported, this is an effect of some potential importance. As far as the balance of payments is concerned, account must also be taken of the effect which additional exports will have in stimulating UK imports. Firstly, one must subtract the proportion of the value of exports which consists of imported means of production and secondly, one must take account of the fact that the export induced increase in UK national income will raise the import bill by an amount which depends on the marginal propensity

---

1   See footnote 5, p. 121.

2   For a detailed discussion of the underlying macro-economic theory consult Kindleberger, *International Economics* (5th edn.), Irwin, Homewood, Illinois, 1973. A proper treatment of the import function for the UK should take into account the differing import content of various categories of national expenditure and in particular, the high import content of stockbuilding.

to import. However, it is a fundamental proposition in foreign trade multiplier analysis that, provided the marginal propensity to save is positive, the total increase in imports will be less than the initial increase in exports so that some improvement to the balance of trade follows. In exactly similar fashion, any increase in UK incomes, which is internally generated, will lead to some increase in foreign incomes and some deterioration in the UK trade balance.[1] The conclusion we are to draw from this is that a system of fixed exchange rates links different national economies together as if they were regions of the same national economy. This linkage, however, is not immutable and it will change in response to divergent trends in national price levels and industrial competitive performance. With a fixed exchange rate, an important determinant of UK trade performances will be the movement in UK export prices relative to foreign export prices. As outlined in section II.2 above, it was the relatively faster rate of increase in UK export prices which was important in explaining both the declining share of the UK in world trade and the rising UK propensity to import[2] in the 1960s.

When account is taken of the UK commitment to maintain the external reserve and trading roles for sterling, adherence to the rules of the par-value system meant that the conduct of macroeconomic policy in the 1960s was primarily governed by the state of the external balance. In turn, the state of the external balance depended on UK economic performance and policy relative to performance and policy in her major trading partners. This interdependence of national economic policies under the par-value system, which accelerated with the return to convertibility and the freeing of trade, must be kept in mind throughout the following discussion. For, as will be obvious, the UK can only improve its trade balance to the extent that other countries are willing to allow their collective trade balance with the UK to deteriorate.

Given the nature of the par-value system, UK governments were left with four broad external policy options, apart from, that is, a change in the sterling parity. Firstly, as a short-term measure, a deficit could be financed by drawing upon the reserves or by foreign borrowing, either in the belief that the deficit was temporary or self-correcting, or as a means of 'holding the fort' while other adjustment policies took effect. Secondly, adjustment policies involving the manipulation of aggregate demand could be employed as an effective short-run method for reducing imports and releasing domestically produced goods for export. Thirdly, longer run measures could be employed to slow down the rate of increase in UK money wages and/or accelerate the growth of UK productivity in order to reduce unit manufacturing costs in the UK relative to those in other nations. Finally, direct controls could be introduced to influence current account transactions. Each of these options was exercised between 1964 and the devaluation of 1967.

Before we turn to a more detailed account of the implications and effects of the

---

1   A full analysis would have to take account of feedback effects on UK exports and national income but this may be ignored in the present context since the qualitative conclusions would remain unchanged. The argument also needs amendment if the full domestic monetary influences of a trade surplus or deficit are allowed to take effect.

2   It is possible to argue that with a fixed exchange rate, the rate of inflation for a country cannot diverge for long from the average inflation rate of her trading partners. As a long-run argument there is undoubtedly some force in the contention, although experience since 1945 would not seem to support the idea of an international convergence of inflation rates.

various policy alternatives, it is worth noting that any fixed exchange rate system implies the existence of an automatic balance of payments adjustment mechanism, at least in principle. At a general level this reflects the fact that a current account deficit for the UK will correspond to an equivalent reduction (increase) in the net external assets (liabilities) of the UK. This reduction in net external wealth will, unless we assume that net wealth has no long-run influence on expenditure decisions, lead to a reduction in national expenditure relative to income and hence to a potential improvement in the balance of payments, a process which will continue until the deficit is eliminated. This is, of course, a process which operates at best in the longest of long runs but it does not seem inappropriate to take account of it when reviewing the balance of payments performance of the UK, say, since 1900. Of greater current interest is a monetary version of this wealth effect mechanism which is essentially a modern variant of the classical gold standard adjustment process. The essential point here is that a payments deficit[1] has to be financed by a liquidation of part of the UK's stock of internationally acceptable liquid assets. To the extent that this involves drawing upon the stock of foreign exchange reserves then, since this reserve stock forms part of the base of the domestic banking system, a contraction in the domestic money supply will normally follow. Effectively the private sector (including the banks) will exchange sterling bank deposits for foreign currency supplied by the Exchange Equalization account. As a result, interest rates can be expected to rise in the UK and domestic currency expenditure to fall, as domestic residents attempt to restore their holdings of money balances to their desired levels. The fall in expenditure relative to national income improves the trade balance and the process continues until the external deficit is eliminated and the reserve loss and monetary contraction halted.

Before applying these monetary principles to the UK several qualifications should be stated. Account must first be taken of the sterling area payments arrangements, and of the role of the UK as banker to the overseas sterling area (OSA) and custodian of OSA exchange reserves. To the extent that UK deficits and surpluses with the OSA are financed by a change in sterling liabilities then no change need occur in UK reserves or in the total of bank deposits with UK banks. Of more importance is the fact that UK reserves may be drawn upon to finance the deficits of sterling balance holders with non-sterling area countries. It is possible for the UK to be in balance, or even overall payments surplus, and yet experience a loss of reserves.[2] The general impact of the sterling area payments sytem is thus to weaken the linkage between changes in the UK reserves and the state of the UK balance of payments.

A second qualification again relates to the relation between UK deficits and reserve losses. Throughout the 1960s, the UK supplemented its gold and foreign currency reserves by substantial borrowing from the IMF and the central banks of Western Europe and North America. In general, such short-term and medium-term foreign borrowing does not of itself prevent a deficit induced contraction in the domestic money supply. Rather it allows the foreign exchange reserves to be

---

1   Meaning, in this context, a deficit on the total currency flow.

2   From 1958 onwards, the visible balances of the UK and OSA with NSA moved increasingly in step, thus aggravating the total of claims on UK reserves and undermining the gains from reserve pooling which accrue to sterling area members. See R. Caves (ed.), *Britain's Economic Prospects*, Allen and Unwin, 1968, pp. 182-4.

maintained intact and so leaves room for the government to break the gold standard rules of the game by actively expanding domestic credit in order to offset the monetary effects of the payments deficit.[1]

The above qualifications are, however, of secondary importance compared to the major policy constraints within which the UK has been placed. The inadequacy of the UK reserves, together with the magnitude and sensitivity of the short-term sterling liabilities, has prevented the UK from enjoying the luxury of a longer-term monetary adjustment to its problems. Any sustained loss of reserves has almost invariably resulted in a flight from sterling and thus to further cumulative reserve losses. Consequently, the UK authorities have had to introduce policies geared to the exigencies of a given short-run situation and to override any longer-run adjustment mechanism, whatever its merits.

Economic Policy and the Current Account: A government has two basic policy options when it wishes to control the current account. It can adopt policies aimed at changing the level of money national expenditure relative to money national income or, alternatively, it can implement policies to change the division of a given volume of expenditure between home goods and foreign goods. It is usual to denote these policies as expenditure changing and expenditure switching.[2] Until 1967, expenditure changing policies formed the predominant method of balance of payments management in the UK. The mechanics of such policies are straightforward. To improve the trade balance a policy of fiscal and monetary contraction is required, to reduce the level, or at least the rate of increase, of domestic money expenditure. The effect will be to reduce expenditure on imports while allowing a greater proportion of domestic output to be exported. The events of 1966 provide a good illustration of this policy, when the package of measures introduced over the year included the following. Commercial banks had limits placed on their total advances, special deposits were called by the Bank of England, Bank Rate was raised by 1% to 7% and hire purchase restrictions were strengthened on two occasions. Similarly, in the 'July measures', indirect taxes were raised by 10% and public authority investment programmes cut by an estimated £152m.[3] In general, such demand management policies have had considerable short-run success in improving the UK current account, but it is important to recognize that this success was bought at a cost. In the short run, output has been sacrificed and additional unemployment generated, while in the long run, the effects have been such as to bring into doubt the rationale of using demand management as the major weapon of payments policy. The point is simply that such policies have a two-fold depressing effect on investment, by raising interest rates and the cost of finance and by reducing the expected profit streams associated with investment. Since it is the

---

1 For details of the relationship between the external deficit, foreign borrowing and the domestic money supply see 'The Domestic Financial Implications of Financing a Balance of Payments Deficit on Current Account', *BEQB*, Vol. 15, March 1975.

2 The distinction refers to the impact effect of the policies only. In particular, expenditure switching policies can only improve the trade balance to the extent that they simultaneously effect a reduction in national expenditure relative to national income.

3 For a detailed account of the effectiveness of fiscal and expenditure changes see M. Artis, 'Fiscal Policy for Stabilization' in W. Beckerman, *The Labour Government's Economic Record 1964-1970*, Duckworth, 1972.

rate of investment which governs, to a considerable degree, the rate of productivity improvement and industrial innovation, it follows that demand management policies may have contributed to the cumulative reduction in the long-run competitive strength of the UK economy. Indeed it is tempting to argue that demand management is, in the long-term, self-defeating as a weapon of balance of payments policy.

This raises a crucial problem of economic management under the par value system, viz, that the objectives of full employment, payments equilibrium and a given rate of economic growth are likely to be mutually incompatible at any arbitrary exchange rate. Certainly at the exchange rate of $2.80 to the £ they were incompatible for the UK in the early and middle 1960s. The general result was that pressure of demand which corresponded to full employment was greater than the pressure of demand needed for the attainment of payments equilibrium.

One way of avoiding this impasse is to introduce expenditure switching policies, to supplement the policies of demand management. To some extent attempts to limit the rate of increase of money wages by an incomes policy fall into the category of expenditure switching policies. If the rate of inflation in the UK is reduced relative to that in other countries then, pro tanto, the UK current balance will improve, as expenditure at home and abroad is switched toward UK goods. It is interesting to note that the various forms of wage restraint introduced over the period 1949-67 each came at a time of balance of payments deficit and were relaxed after the payments situation improved. However, the problem with an incomes policy, as a method of external management, is that it is slow-acting in its effects and thus invariably ruled out by the pressure of short-run events.

Prior to the 1967 devaluation, the only attempt at an expenditure switching policy was the import surcharge introduced in November 1964. The surcharge (tariff) was imposed on imports of most manufactured commodities, amounting to about one-third of the import bill. Initially the rate of duty was set at 15% and was expected to reduce imports by some £200m and to provide the government with £300m of extra revenue in a full year.[1]

The imposition of the surcharge led to a marked display of annoyance by other members of GATT and EFTA, and as a result, the surcharge was reduced to 10% in April 1965 and eliminated completely in November 1966.

Because of the short life of this policy and the announcement effects of its withdrawal, it is more than usually difficult to compute the overall effects. However, it is estimated that the surcharge reduced the 1965 bill (at 1964 prices) by some £130m and the corresponding 1966 import bill by £80m, relative to what it would otherwise have been.[2]

Other, minor acts of policy between 1964 and 1967 were the brief introduction of a scheme of indirect tax rebates on exports and the introduction of SET, with its potentially favourable effect on manufacturing output and exports.

Apart from policies to improve the visible trade balance, the period 1964-70 witnessed a variety of direct measures to improve other items in the current

---

1   Taking the value of imports affected at £1,600m, this implies an import demand elasticity of
    approximately − 0.83. The net effect on the demand for home goods would be deflationary
    to the amount of £100m.

2   Cf. Caves, *op. cit.,* p. 167.

account. In 1966, limits were introduced on the sterling equivalent of the foreign exchange which travellers to the NSA could obtain in a given year. The restrictions, which effectively ended in 1970, are estimated to have improved the current account by some £25m in a full year.[1]

More important quantitatively were the restrictions imposed upon government expenditure overseas. During the period 1958-64 government net current expenditure overseas grew rapidly to reach a deficit of £432m in 1964. Many observers argued that this increase in expenditure was an important 'cause' of UK balance of payments difficulties and implied that these balance of payments difficulties would be greatly reduced if only government overseas expenditure were reduced. The National Plan of 1965 and subsequent policy statements expressed an intention to reverse the growth in expenditure and if possible, to bring about a reduction by 1970. This policy had some success. Current expenditure during the period 1965-9 was held to an annual average of £463m, a marked change in trend. Over the same period, the net outflow on government long-term capital was reduced to an annual average of £61m, compared to £95m over the period 1960-4. In part, this reflected the policy of holding the total level of official foreign aid to an annual average of £211m during the period 1965-72.

While these developments were of importance it is not possible to say that the reductions in net expenditure implied a similar improvement in the current account. Government expenditure and aid is in part 'tied' to the export of UK goods and in addition provides foreigners with extra purchasing power, some of which will have a favourable feedback on UK exports. However, it seems likely that the change of trend did produce some relative improvement in the current account position.

While the government attempted to correct the current account deficit, the slender UK reserve position and the fears of an imminent devaluation, despite repeated official assurances to the contrary, added a further dimension to the UK payments problem. This reflected the need to incur substantial short-term debts in order to support the exchange rate in the face of repeated speculative attacks on sterling. In 1964 and 1966 credits of $3.45bn and $2.6bn were obtained from the Western European Central Banks (through the agency of the Bank for International Settlements) and, again in 1966, the network of inter-central bank swap credits available to the UK was extended from $750m to $1.35bn. The subsequent need to repay drawings on these credits forced the UK to borrow some $1.46bn from the IMF in 1964 and to resort to further borrowing in 1967.

International support for sterling was forthcoming largely because of fears, mainly American, that a sterling devaluation would disrupt the international monetary system and undermine the strength of the dollar as the major reserve currency. From the UK's point of view the borrowing generated a considerable debt burden to add to the other costs of maintaining the sterling parity. Foreign borrowing was merely a costly means of delaying the inevitable decision to correct the past loss in competitive position with a devaluation.

---

1 For some further discussion see A. Peaker, 'Holiday Spending by the British at Home and Abroad', *National Westminster Bank Review,* August 1973.

III.4   The 1967 Devaluation

The previous section has emphasized the importance of expenditure changing
policies in the official attitude toward balance of payments management. However,
1967 saw a change in emphasis with the adoption of an expenditure switching
policy, a change in the sterling par-value, as the primary weapon of external
management. It seems clear, in retrospect, that this marked the beginning of a
period in which flexibility or rather adjustability of exchange rates was received
with more official approval than had hitherto been apparent, not only in the UK
but also in the other major trading nations.

On November 18th the pound sterling was devalued by 14.3% against the
dollar and the defence of the original parity, with its attendant costs of unemployment and international borrowing, was finally abandoned.[1]

During the months leading up to the devaluation, it became obvious that the
stringent demand measures introduced in 1966 were not having the desired
quantitative effect. The current account, after improving through 1966, began to
deteriorate equally rapidly throughout 1967. Unease about the government's
ability to maintain the parity of sterling was exacerbated by a series of unforseeable
events: a dock strike in the UK, the Middle East war and new proposals for the UK
to enter the EEC. These factors, together with increasingly uncompetitive London
interest rates, resulted in an accelerating outflow of short-term capital from April
onwards.

The reserves declined correspondingly, despite drawings on the swap and other
credit facilities provided by overseas central banks. In the months leading up to
devaluation some $1bn was made available in this fashion, adding considerably to
the burden of short-term debt which had already been accumulated. The
deteriorating trade situation and the sustained capital outflow combined to leave
the government no other option. High and rising unemployment levels ruled out
further deflation and fears of foreign retaliation ruled out import restrictions on
the 1964 pattern. Only devaluation remained. In the event, the figure of 14.3% was
decided after discussions with the major industrial countries at the IMF, and was
the maximum the government considered attainable, without risking widespread
retaliation and the withdrawal of sterling support facilities. At the same time, a
total of $2.9bn of foreign exchange was made available for the support of sterling,
of which $1.4bn came from the IMF on condition that the UK adopted additional
demand restraining policies. The package of measures introduced both then and in
1968, together with their rationale, are discussed below.

The Economic Impacts of Devaluation: As with an import surcharge, a devaluation
has its main effects on the balance of trade in goods and services, and operates in
similar fashion, by switching money expenditure from foreign goods to home
goods. Devaluation is, of course, far wider in its effects because it influences *all*
imports and *all* exports of the home country.

A devaluation operates by changing the relative prices of home and foreign

---

1   The 14.3% devaluation of sterling refers to the reduction in the foreign currency price of
    sterling. As a matter of arithmetic the sterling price of foreign currency is raised by 16.7%
    so that this is the increase in the sterling price of UK imports and exports, if their foreign
    currency prices are held constant.

goods, when each are expressed in a common currency. The change in parity allows UK exporters to quote lower foreign currency prices of their products while still receiving the same price in terms of sterling. Conversely, foreign exporters to the UK must raise their sterling prices if they are to maintain the same foreign currency prices for their goods. The net effect is to make UK goods more competitive in both home and foreign markets. It must be noted that the competitive advantage given by a devaluation is of a 'once and for all' kind. To the extent that the loss of UK competitiveness was itself of a 'once for all kind', because of, say, structural change in export markets, then the devaluation can simply restore the status quo ante. But if the loss of competitiveness reflected, say, a tendency for production costs to increase faster in the UK than in other nations, then the devaluation would merely prove a temporary respite. A devaluation is no panacea for a trend of increasing uncompetitiveness and at best will only buy time while more fundamental corrective policies are implemented.

The analysis of devaluation is never straightforward. In the main, this is because the impact of a parity change is not confined to the resource allocation effects of the induced change in the terms of trade. Account must also be taken of the direct effects on money expenditure and the price level and on the total change in the demand for home goods. Analysis of devaluation is at one and the same time a macroeconomic problem and a microeconomic problem. At the microeconomic level the effects of a devaluation follow from the impact upon the relative prices of UK goods and foreign goods. The immediate result of the devaluation will normally be an adverse movement in the terms of trade as sterling import prices are increased while sterling export prices remain constant or at least increase by a smaller proportion than import prices. Corresponding to this movement in the terms of trade there will be an adverse movement in the balance of trade so that the immediate effect of the devaluation is unfavourable. However, to the extent that the devaluation induced change in relative prices leads to an increase in UK export volume and to a decrease in UK import volume, then favourable effects on the trade balance will follow. Whether the trade volume responses are sufficient to outweigh the initial adverse terms of trade effect depends on the values of domestic and foreign demand and supply elasticities for exported and imported commodities.[1] Since, in general, it is to be expected that the potential for trade volume responses will become greater with the passage of time, we have the possibility of a 'J' curve response to devaluation: an initial deterioration in the trade balance is followed by a longer term improvement, provided that the elasticities are of the right order.

This account requires several modifications if it is to be applied to the events of 1967 and after. We must allow first for the possibility that any devaluation advantage may be eliminated as a result of competitive devaluations by the UK's trading partners. Fortunately, in 1967, only eleven countries devalued along with sterling and together they accounted for only 16% of UK trade. Of greater importance is the possibility that firms may offset the effects of the devaluation by changing their pricing policies. UK exporters, for example, may use the devaluation opportunity to increase sterling export prices and take their devaluation benefit in

---

1 In the special case in which there is initial balanced trade and supply elasticities of traded goods are infinite, then the devaluation improves the trade balance provided that the sum of the foreign and domestic elasticities of demand for imported goods exceeds unity. For a more general statement see Kindleberger, *op. cit.,* Ch. 19 and Appendix G.

the form of higher sterling profits on the existing export volume. Similarly, foreign producers may try to maintain their market shares in the UK by reducing their foreign currency supply prices. In a world of imperfect markets and oligopolistic market structures such responses may completely eliminate the resource re-allocating effects of the devaluation but will, nevertheless, improve the current account balance. Following the 1967 devaluation it appears that many firms did respond in the above fashion but that this provided only a partial offset to the terms of trade effects of devaluation.[1]

Account must also be taken of the fact that the post-devaluation increase in import prices will raise costs of production in the UK. Raw materials, fuels and semi-manufactures accounted for 53% of UK imports in 1966, and the 1968 input-output table indicates an average import content for UK manufacturing industry of 21%, with figures as high as 66% for mineral oil refining and 30% for food manufacturing.[2]

It is possible to infer from this that the 1967 devaluation probably increased unit production costs in manufacturing by an average of 3%. Since 84% of UK exports consisted of manufactures this obviously reduced the competitive advantage given by devaluation.

The effects on production costs do not end with the import content linkages. Directly and indirectly, a devaluation will also raise the cost of living, and did so by an estimated 2.9% following the 1967 parity of change. To the extent that this leads to increased pressure for higher money wages, additional increases in domestic production cost may follow to further reduce the competitive advantage yielded by devaluation.[3]

The question of the response of money wages has taken our account toward the macroeconomic impacts of devaluation, which now require further elaboration. We begin by noting that a devaluation will lower the real value of a given volume of money expenditure, simply because it will raise the home currency prices of imports and to a lesser extent the prices of home produced goods. This reduction in the real value of expenditure, combined with the changed relative prices of home goods and imports, will normally result in a reduction in the volume of imports, at least of finished manufactures, and a change in the domestic demand for home goods. At the same time, the reduced foreign currency prices of exports will result in an additional demand for UK goods by foreigners. Now if devaluation improves the trade balance, the important point is that the combined demand for home goods from domestic and foreign residents will be increased. This will introduce two problems as far as the effectiveness of devaluation is concerned. Firstly, to the extent that substantial unemployed resources exist at the time of devaluation,

---

1   For evidence of the response of UK exporters, see P. B. Rosendale, 'The Short-Run Pricing Policies of Some British Engineering Exporters', *NIER*, No. 65, 1973, and the valuable study by D. C. Hague, E. Oakeshott and A. Strain, *Devaluation and Pricing Decisions,* Allen and Unwin, 1974. Professor Cooper has suggested that foreign suppliers cut their prices on average by 4%. See A. K. Cairncross (ed.), *Britain's Economic Prospects Reconsidered,* Allen and Unwin, 1971, p. 181.

2   *E.T.,* January 1971. The 1968 input-output table is based on the results of the 1963 Census on Production.

3   On this wage induced, cost-push effect of devaluation see 'Some Aspects of the Present Inflation', *NIER,* No. 55, 1971.

the increased demand for UK output will have a multiplier effect on domestic incomes and this, via the import function, will raise the volume of imports. This induced income effect will partially offset the favourable relative price effects of the devaluation upon the trade balance. Secondly, the outcome is far worse if the devaluation occurs when the economy is at or near full employment, as the UK appears to have been in November 1967.[1] For then the output of home goods cannot be increased to match the extra demands of home and foreign residents. Unless offsetting action is taken, the net effect must be to create inflationary pressure in the UK, which will only be eliminated when the price of home goods has risen sufficiently to re-establish the pre-devaluation terms of trade.

It is therefore of great importance that a devaluation, when undertaken at or near full employment, should be matched with a package of expenditure reducing policies so that additional output can be exported and resources freed for the production of import substitutes, without creating inflationary excess demand. In part, the needed expenditure reduction can come about directly through the budgetary policies of the government. But restraint also needs to be placed, either through incomes policy or through monetary policy, on attempts to increase money incomes and restore real purchasing power to pre-devaluation levels.

Precisely because of these factors, the 1967 devaluation was accompanied by a deflationary package. This included cuts in planned government expenditure of some £200m per annum, a moderate increase in hire-purchase restrictions, an increase in Bank rate from 6½% to 8% and a ceiling on bank lending; measures which, combined with the devaluation, were considered sufficient to improve the balance of payments by some £500m in a full year.[2]

The Outcome of the 1967 Devaluation: A superficial view of ensuing events would suggest that devaluation was a considerable success. By the end of 1971 the trade balance had improved by £834m compared to the 1967 value, and the current account had similarly improved by some £156m. The current account surplus in 1971 was an unprecedented £1,058m. Unfortunately, any judgement of the devaluation outcome is not as simple as this. The problem is, first, to decide how much of the improvement would have occurred in the absence of devaluation and, once this is settled, how much of the remaining improvement could be attributed to the devaluation and associated measures. Inevitably, the apportioning of effects must be somewhat arbitrary involving, in effect, an exercise in hypothetical history.

In the two years following devaluation the volume of exports responded favourably, to grow at an annual average rate of 11.8%, well above the trend rate of increase of 2.85% for the previous four years. In contrast, the response of import volume was disappointing; total import volume grew in 1968 by 10.5%. This rapid growth of import volume together with the adverse movement of the terms of trade was more than sufficient to offset the favourable export response, and yield an overall trade deficit for 1968 of £667m.

---

1   There is some dispute over the actual degree of demand pressure in November 1967. Although the unemployment rate stood at 2.4% in the last quarter of 1967, and therefore suggested some slack in the economy, there are grounds for believing that the unemployment figures overstated the degree of spare capacity.

2   This was stated in the 'Letter of Intent', sent to the IMF as a necessary prerequisite to obtaining a loan.

The adverse import response created considerable official disquiet about the effectiveness of devaluation, one outcome of which was the import deposit scheme of November 1968. Importers were obliged to deposit 50% of the value of imports with the government, before the goods could be cleared from Customs. The deposits earned no interest, were repayable in full after 180 days and, as with the import surcharge, they only applied to imports of manufacturers. At the then ruling rates of interest, and assuming that all importers had equal access to credit facilities, the scheme was equivalent to an import surcharge (tariff) of 2-2½%. It is doubtful whether this had much effect in reducing imports, especially as the required deposit proportion was reduced to 40% in November 1969 and to 30% in the 1970 budget. The policy was abandoned in December 1970. The main policy response to the continued high import volume took the more traditional form of expenditure reduction. Through 1968, government expenditure was cut, indirect taxes were raised and further restrictions were placed on hire purchase finance and bank lending.[1] The net outcome was to reduce the growth of real consumption expenditure to a mere 0.6% in 1969, compared with the average growth of 2.5% for the previous two years. Not surprisingly, the growth of import volume also fell and, with the sustained growth of exports, the trade balance improved considerably to a 1969 deficit of £157m. It was also in 1968 that the government renewed attempts to establish a statutory prices and incomes policy, in order to maintain the UK devaluation advantage for as long as possible.

Subsequent events suggest that the devaluation advantage had attained a maximum by 1969, for in 1970 and 1971 import and export volume both increased by an average of only 4.6%. By then the full value implications for the trade balance were being realised and substantial surpluses on current account were recorded in 1970 and 1971.

What proportion of the above changes can be attributed to devaluation and what proportion to the other factors which include an increase in world demand for exports of manufacturers of 30% between 1967 and 1969 and the import deposit scheme of November 1968? The most sophisticated attempt so far to unravel the problem has been carried out by the staff of the NIESR whose main conclusions[2] are as follows. By 1970, devaluation had improved the visible trade balance by some £130m and the current balance by some £425m as compared to what would otherwise have occurred. The volume response of trade flows suggest a price elasticity of demand for UK exports of −1.4 and a price elasticity of demand for UK imports of −0.25. Both estimates are lower than was widely thought appropriate at the time of devaluation.[3] In terms of foreign exchange the estimated devaluation improvement in the current account was $1,008m.

Our conclusion is that devaluation worked, but not by as much, nor as quickly, as had been expected. In particular, only when drastic expenditure reducing policies were introduced could the volume of UK imports be cut. It is certain, however, that the government had little option but to devalue in 1967. It is clear too, that, had the old parity been maintained, substantial international borrowing

---

1   Details of the measures and an assessment of post-devaluation strategy may be found in *NIER*, February 1969.
2   See 'The Effects of the Devaluation of 1967 on the Current Balance of Payments', *EJ*, March 1972 (supplement), Vol. 82, pp. 442-64.
3   Cf. A. K. Cairncross (ed), *British Economic Prospects Reconsidered*, p. 90.

would have been required in addition to that already undertaken. No doubt the *quid pro quo* for such credits could have been sustained domestic deflation.

III.5   Balance of Payments Policy with a Floating Exchange Rate

By the end of 1971 it looked as if devaluation might have produced a fundamental transformation in the UK balance of payments situation. Any such optimism, however, was to prove ill-founded. To more careful observers it seemed that the devaluation advantage to UK exports had by then been largely if not completely eroded,[1] and with unemployment at 4% by the end of 1971 and weekly wage rates rising over the year by some 9%, prospects for the balance of payments were not favourable. The expected worsening of the balance of payments appeared at the beginning of 1972, with the visible trade balance moving into substantial deficit. The government was thus faced with the traditional conflict: sacrifice the expansion target for domestic output or sacrifice the exchange rate. In the event, a substantial run on sterling, which developed in June 1972, forced the situation and on June 23 sterling was allowed to float outside the official intervention limits.[2] The float occurred eight weeks after the UK had began to participate in the EEC scheme for limiting currency fluctuations and, no doubt because of this, the float was officially described as 'temporary'. The 'temporary' measure is clearly taking on a more permanent aspect and it is unlikely that sterling will be brought back into the par-value system until the promised reform of the international monetary system takes place.

With sterling only one of many currencies floating against the dollar, there is no simple index of movements in the international value of sterling. Sterling may appreciate in terms of some currencies while, at the same time, it depreciates in terms of others. Current practice is to rely upon the so-called 'effective exchange rate', which is a suitably weighted average of the movements of sterling compared to the currencies of those countries which are most important in UK trade.[3] Until the end of 1972, the effective exchange rate for sterling moved in close step with the sterling/US dollar exchange rate to register a 10% depreciation of sterling relative to Smithsonian parties.[4] Since then the effective exchange rate has continued to depreciate, and by the end of 1975 had fallen by some 30% compared to its end-1971 value. Before we analyze the causes of this sustained depreciation it will prove useful to outline some of the more important economic implications of floating exchange rates.

Floating Rates and Economic Policy: The case for floating exchange rates rests, in large part, upon the alleged simplicity and automaticity of the free market mechanism in re-allocating resources in response to changing circumstances. In a

---

1 *BEQB*, September 1972, p. 306.

2 In the six days prior to the decision to float, the capital outflow reduced the reserves by some £1,000m. *BEQB,* September 1972, p. 325.

3 For details see *ET,* June 1974. Movements in the effective exchange rate appear regularly in *ET* and *BEQB.*

4 So-called Smithsonian parities were established in December 1971. See section III.9 below, for further discussion.

dynamic world in which comparative advantages change rapidly and national
inflation rates differ, changes in exchange rates are necessary if widespread underutilization of productive resources is to be avoided. The advantage of floating rates,
it is argued, is that the necessary changes can occur progressively at a pace dictated
by the costs and profitability of resource allocation, and not, as with the par-value
system, by sudden, discrete jumps dictated by speculative pressure and political
expediency. The resource allocation advantages are only one aspect of the benefits
derivable from the adoption of a floating exchange rate. More important for present
purposes are the implications for the conduct of macroeconomic policy. For it
seems clear that, with a floating exchange rate, the UK could have avoided most of
the policy dilemmas of the period 1960-71 and that the period since 1971 would
have generated impossible policy contradictions had the UK adhered to the par-
value system.

There is, first, the minor point that the government no longer has to decide what
constitutes an equilibrium exchange rate; to a large extent, this will be decided
automatically within the foreign exchange market. One cannot go from this,
however, to suggest that the conduct of domestic economic policy can proceed
independently of developments in the foreign exchange market. The correct
management of domestic demand is just as important with a floating exchange rate
as it is with a fixed exchange rate. Balance of payments problems do not disappear
with the adoption of a floating exchange rate, they are simply manifested in
different forms. Developments that would lead to a loss of reserves with a fixed
exchange rate lead to a depreciation in the foreign exchange value of the currency
if the exchange rate is allowed to float. In the first case, the loss of reserves will
result, unless it is a once and for all loss, in a policy-induced contraction in
domestic income while with a floating rate, the loss in real domestic purchasing
power occurs automatically as import prices rise with the currency depreciation.

The main advantage of a floating rate is that it allows a greater independence of
domestic economic policy making. In particular, full employment objectives may
be more consistently pursued; there being some value of the exchange rate which
will give exactly a zero currency flow at any, non-inflationary, level of employment.
Furthermore, since a floating rate provides the minimum of linkage between the
circular flows of income of different trading nations, it follows that a floating
exchange rate will isolate the level of demand for UK goods from changes in
foreign incomes and preferences for UK goods. An increase in foreign demand
which, under a fixed rate, would generate a multiple expansion in UK incomes,
now generates an appreciation of the sterling rate of exchange such that the final
increase in the value of UK exports is exactly matched by an appreciation-induced
increase in the value of UK imports, i.e., in domestic expenditure on foreign goods.
The total demand for UK goods will remain unchanged.[1] The isolation of domestic
incomes from external changes in demand has, of course, as counterpart the
proposition that the level of domestic income is more sensitive to changes in the
level of *domestic* money expenditure. In this respect, an economy with a floating
exchange rate will behave in the same manner as a closed economy; the effects of
changes in foreign trade upon the circular flow of income are completely negated.

---

1 A more detailed discussion would have to modify this argument in respect of any change in
the aggregate savings ratio which followed the exchange appreciation and any possible
effects on demand of induced changes in international interest rate levels.

The policy consequence of this is that the multiplier repercussions of monetary and fiscal policy will be greater in an economy with a floating exchange rate than in the same economy with a fixed exchange rate.[1] Correspondingly, the cost of mistakes in demand management will be increased with a floating rate and so policy must be conducted with greater attention to underlying economic circumstances.

Other Implications of Floating Rates: The relative merits of fixed and floating exchange rates are matters of considerable controversy among economists. Some of the alleged advantages of flexible exchange rates have already been mentioned. The object of the present section is to deal with two less clearcut aspects of the controversy. In particular, the view that private speculation will convert floating exchange rates into wildly fluctuating rates, and the view that a floating rate increases the uncertainty faced by international traders and investors to the detriment of the international division of labour.

The case for and against floating rates depends essentially on the view taken of the effects of speculators in the operation of free markets. If these markets are to be cleared continuously, without undue fluctuations in the exchange rate, it is essential that speculators take over the role of monetary authorities and operate in a stabilizing manner, selling sterling when the rate is temporarily 'too high' and buying sterling when the rate is temporarily 'too low'. Temporary fluctuations in the exchange rate follow, in part, because daily imbalances in the demand and supply for foreign exchange will result from random and seasonal factors, even if the balance of payments is basically in equilibrium over a longer time span, and because, as mentioned above, short-period trading adjustments to relative price changes are likely to be inelastic. The proponents of floating exchange rates argue that speculative activity will be stabilizing and that speculators will be able to predict the trend value of the exchange rate so as to ensure minimal variations in the actual exchange rate around the trend value. Opponents fear that this will not be the case and the exchange market will be dominated by too much uncertainty for speculators to recognize the appropriate trend. Successive waves of optimism and pessimism will follow the frequent revision of expectations and generate substantial movements in exchange rates, out of all proportion to the volume of trading.

The difficulty with the above arguments is that we have little or no relevant factual evidence to decide either way. However, should private speculation prove to be less stabilizing than is thought desirable, there is no reason why the authorities should not engage in 'official' speculation, if necessary at the expense of private operators. Indeed this is precisely what the authorities do undertake when supporting a par-value against speculative pressure. The implication is, of course, that even with a floating exchange rate the authorities must maintain a stock of exchange reserves. Widespread adoption of exchange management practices would also require the institution of international co-ordination and surveillance of

---

1 Again this is subject to qualifications, depending upon the sensitivity of international capital movements to policy-induced changes in interest rates and the time span considered for analysis. With floating rates a greater degree of interest sensitivity of capital flows enhances the potency of monetary policy and limits the potency of fiscal policy for the management of aggregate demand.

exchange rate practices; this appears neither impossible nor undesirable within the framework of an existing body such as the IMF (see section III.9 below). Finally it must not be overlooked that destabilizing speculation can disrupt any exchange rate framework and clearly did so with the par-value system. One of the major drawbacks of the par-value system was that it gave a one-way option to currency speculators. A currency under pressure would be pushed to one of the official intervention limits. This immediately signalled the possibility of a change in par-value in a direction in which no-one could have any doubt. Naturally, a large and cumulative movement of funds across the exchanges was therefore encouraged. A likely advantage of floating exchange rates is that the problem of a one-way speculative option would be much reduced.

The view taken of the effects of speculation determines the importance of the arguments on uncertainty and the inhibition of trade and investment. Provided that floating rates do not fluctuate wildly there is no reason why the bulk of trade and investment should be seriously affected. After all, exchange risks can always be covered with simultaneous deals in spot and forward markets. For sterling transactions involving the major currencies, the foreign exchange market currently provides active dealings for contracts up to one year in duration. Since some 89% of UK exports are financed on credit terms of less than six months duration,[1] with, no doubt, a similar proportion for imports, there should be no difficulty in traders covering their exchange risks. Longer term trade contracts and international investment projects will face problems, but then in an uncertain world, they always will.[2] In addition, it is argued that, should the forward premium on sterling exceed the appropriate interest differential, the traders will have to face extra costs of finance. There are two counter-arguments to this. First, the difference between forward premia and interest differentials will be smaller, the greater is the response of international capital flows to arbitrage possibilities. Provided that capital controls do not limit such flows, there is no reason to expect the costs of forward cover to be prohibitive. Secondly, suppose it could be demonstrated convincingly that additional exchange rate uncertainty had reduced trade and investment. This could still not constitute an argument against floating rates, until the claimed costs could be shown to be greater than the unemployment and resource mis-allocation costs imposed under the par value system.

Balance of Payments Performance and Policy, 1972-5: Movements in the effective exchange rate and the UK payments performance in this period are the complex outcome of events in the UK and abroad. Consider first the balance of payments record. Although a current account surplus of £131m was achieved in 1972, the

---

1 See the article 'Direct Exporters and the Credit Terms of Exports', *TI*, vol. 7, no. 2, 13 April 1972, pp. 50-2.
2 Since 1960 an increasingly important role in the provision of insurance cover against specified political, commercial and exchange control risks faced by exporters and the banks which extend export credit has been played by the Export Credits Guarantee Department. For details consult D. E. Fair, 'Export Credit Problems', *TBR*, no. 88, 1970; and 'The Finance of Medium and Longterm Shipbuilding Credits', *BEQB*, March 1975. At the time of writing, cover is not provided against risks arising from exchange rate changes. An important innovation was the introduction, in February 1975, of a scheme to cover exporters from domestic inflation in excess of 10% p.a. This applies only to contracts in excess of £2m in value and which take more than two years to complete.

short-term capital outflow of that year, and particularly that in the second quarter, helped to produce a total currency outflow of £1.27bn, of which £692m was financed by drawing on the official foreign exchange reserves. In 1973 a considerable deterioration in the current account position occurred with a deficit of £842m being recorded. Several factors were at work to produce this change, most important of which was the deterioration in the terms of trade. While export volume grew almost twice as fast as import volume during 1973 (8.1% as compared to 4.5%), in spite of the alleged shortage of manufacturing capacity and the existence of supply bottlenecks at the top of the domestic output boom, this favourable development was more than offset by the sharp rise in commodity import prices and by the 7% fall in the effective exchange rate. Even with this worsening of the current account, a sustained net private capital inflow during 1973 meant that the official reserves increased by £210m. Although 1974 began with the miners' strike and the three day week, the most significant event of that year was the quadrupling of the posted price of oil by the OPEC nations, which increased the c.i.f. price of oil to the UK from $3.45 to $8.70 per barrel.[1] The implications of this development were considerable and worldwide, affecting not only individual economies but also the stability of the international monetary system. Some of the wider issues are treated in section III.9 below. As far as the UK is concerned, the effect in 1974 was to increase the oil import bill by £2.68bn more than the average for the previous three years, and to produce the historically unprecedented current account deficit of £3.61bn. Quite remarkably, this was more than covered by foreign currency borrowing, so that the official reserves actually rose by £79m. In 1975, the current account deficit was halved to a value of £1.70bn and this improvement was due essentially to two factors; falling import volume in the face of declining domestic output and real income, and an improvement in the terms of trade of some 9%, the result of declining world commodity prices. So despite the fact that export volume fell by 2.3% during 1975, the overall trade balance improved by some £2bn compared to its 1974 value.

The Oil Price Increase: Since the short-run elasticity of demand for oil imports is unlikely to differ appreciably from zero, the impact effect of the oil price increase is to simultaneously worsen the trade balance and generate deflationary pressure in the UK economy. It is as if the UK government had raised indirect taxes, so cutting the demand for UK output, and had then transferred the tax proceeds to the oil producing nations. In addition, the similar effects on other oil importing economies produced cuts in the demand for UK exports and so provided a further deflationary stimulus; while very little help could be expected in the short-run from the spending of OPEC funds on UK produced goods.

Several options were open to the government to deal with this situation. First it could have attempted to eliminate the current account deficit either by a severe policy induced cut in aggregate demand or by allowing the exchange rate to depreciate, and so improve the non-oil trade balance of the UK at the expense of the other industrialized countries. Neither option has proved to be politically

---

1   The posted price should not be confused with the market price of oil. The posted price is the administrative price from which the OPEC countries assess the royalty payments and tax payments due from the oil extracting companies.

feasible or otherwise desirable, for they would each contribute to a deepening of the general world recession. The only effective policy has proved to be that of substantial foreign borrowing, combined with a neutral stance toward domestic aggregate demand.[1] The net outcome for the UK has therefore been one of rising external indebtedness combined with falling domestic production, as the deflationary effects of the change in the terms of trade worked through to expenditure and demand.

Foreign borrowing has taken place under three separate headings. Prior to 1973, the OPEC oil producers traditionally received about 25% of their oil revenues in sterling and normally deposited this as sterling balances in London. With the increase in oil revenues following the Teheran agreement, the immediate response was to place much of the surplus in London. In 1974 some 37% of surplus oil funds, a total of $21bn, were placed in London. In 1975 the total amount of short-term finance made available in this way declined considerably, in the face of falling surplus oil revenues and an increasing unwillingness to deposit funds in a depreciating currency. In fact, only $4.3bn flowed into the UK, representing 13% of surplus oil funds. The second important source of balance of payments finance has been nationalized industry and local authority borrowing under the Treasury exchange guarantee scheme. Much of this has been in the form of OPEC funds taken out of the Eurodollar market in the form of medium-term (3-7 year) loans. Some $3.4bn was raised in this way in the two years to the end of 1975. Finally, the UK government has itself engaged in substantial borrowing; $2.5bn was raised in the Eurodollar market in January 1974, $1.2bn was borrowed from Iran in January 1975 and, at the end of 1975, $2bn worth of credits were obtained from the IMF – 60% of which represented a drawing from the specially created oil facility. In sterling terms, the public sector borrowed a total of £2bn in 1974 and a further £855m in 1975.

While this policy of foreign borrowing has allowed the UK to accommodate its payments deficit it does imply the need for the rapid emergence of a sustained trade surplus, to meet the burden of debt servicing and amortization payments. Although drawings on the IMF oil facility carry an interest rate of 7.75%, with interest rates of 4-6% on other IMF drawings, the bulk of the foreign borrowing has been raised at higher commercial rates, 10% and upwards. Furthermore, most of the debts incurred by the government, nationalized industries and local authorities are due for repayment within seven years, that is by 1983.[2] A major factor determining the ability of the UK to meet these payments will be the success of the North Sea oil venture which is expected to provide some 10-15% of UK requirements in 1976 and half UK requirements by 1977.[3]

---

1 Although the March 1975 budget was intended to produce substantial cuts in the government borrowing requirement, it can be argued that the net effect on aggregate demand was negligible. See *NIER*, May 1975, p. 11. A more deflationary stance has been adopted in 1976 with further reductions in future public expenditure.

2 The total of outstanding official short and medium-term borrowing from abroad stood at S8.9bn at end 1975, compared to a figure of $2.9bn at end 1973. *BEQB* March 1976, pp. 78-81.

3 The National Institute forecasts that by 1977 domestic oil production will reduce the import bill by £2.3bn or 8% of total imports. Against this must be offset some £350m of profit and dividends remitted to the oil exploring companies. *NIER*, February 1976, pp. 14 and 22.

A further improvement in the UK trade balance can be expected from the rising propensity to import of the OPEC nations, indeed UK exports to the oil producers increased by 64% in 1974 and by 88% in 1975. Of some significance here have been the bilateral trade arrangements negotiated with OPEC states, the latest of which, negotiated with Iran in January 1975, was for UK exports to the value of £500m. Finally, there is the question of the oil price and its future variation. It appears that the OPEC states have agreed to maintain the real price of oil relative to the prices of goods exported by the industrialized nations, and to this effect increased the posted price of oil by a further 10% in 1975. The major question, of course, is whether, in response to falling oil demand and the ambitious development programmes of some OPEC producers, the oil cartel will stay intact, or whether individual producers will be tempted to adopt unilateral price cutting policies to increase their share of the market.

Domestic Inflation and the Exchange Rate: One important implication of the above discussion is that the depreciation of sterling in 1974 and 1975 cannot be put down to the effect of the oil and other commodity price increases. For, to a considerable degree, foreign borrowing has insulated the exchange rate from these price movements, and to the extent that foreign borrowing has exceeded (1974) or fallen short of (1975) the deficit on total currency flow, the authorities appear to have let the official reserves adjust correspondingly.

The chief proximate source of the recent depreciation of sterling must be sought in the excess of the UK's rate of inflation over the rate of inflation in the other industrialized nations. Since the excess is logically equivalent in its effects on the balance of payments to a notional appreciation of sterling, the actual depreciation which follows is the necessary offset to compensate for the excess inflation. In practice this argument requires two qualifications. First, the actual depreciation of sterling over the period since June 1972 has, on average, more than compensated for the excess UK inflation, this being largely due no doubt to changes in capital flows and the volume of imports and exports.[1] Secondly, it is unlikely that the rate of domestic wage increase will be independent of the depreciation of sterling; in fact, there is the danger that depreciation will simply add fuel to an inflationary wage-price spiral. This danger was highlighted by the sharp depreciation of sterling which occurred at the beginning of March 1976[2] – a time of sensitive negotiations on the development of wages policy in the UK and raised serious doubts about the ability of the government to reduce real wages through a sterling depreciation.

In conclusion, it is tempting to argue that the management of the external situation since the end of 1973 has been impressive, even if when measured only by the standards of the early and middle 1960s. However, we should note that the two-fold strategy of foreign borrowing and exchange depreciation in line with excess inflation in the UK is not without severe limitations. We have already suggested that a current account surplus must be attained as a matter of urgency in

---

1 With perfect compensation, the ratio of UK export prices to foreign export prices should stay constant over time. From a value of 106 in the second quarter of 1972, this ratio fell sharply to a low of 91.8 in the fourth quarter of 1973 and then gradually rose to 96.8 by June 1975. See *ET*, March 1976, p. 44.

2 Between the beginning of March and the end of April the depreciation of the effective sterling exchange rate widened from 30% to 37%, compared to 1971 parities.

order to meet the repayment of foreign debts. One immediate way of achieving this would be to reduce the gap between government expenditure and tax receipts but this traditional, deflationary policy would add to the already substantial amount of employment in the UK, and would do nothing to stimulate profitability and the investment which is necessary if the UK is to regain any of the past loss of international competitiveness. Expenditure switching policies would eliminate this employment – balance of payments conflict but may involve the risk of retaliation by other countries and could, in the case of a deliberate devaluation of sterling, seriously reduce the willingness of oil producers to place surplus funds in the UK, and could even result in a widespread liquidation of sterling balances. If this were to happen, the UK would have little option but to suspend convertibility and thus undermine the strategy of foreign borrowing.

In this situation, an alternative policy of general import restriction has much to recommend it.[1] Although import restrictions will not stimulate foreign demand for UK goods they have several advantages; they can be applied selectively to imports of manufactures, so minimizing inflationary pressure on the structure of raw material costs in UK manufacturing industry, they can readily be manipulated to meet changing circumstances and the needs of individual industries, and they do not have the adverse effects on real wages and the price level which are associated with devaluation. In the light of this it is an error of some potential consequence for the UK to have borrowed from the IMF in January 1976 and to have accepted the pre-condition that general import restrictions would not be resorted to. The UK government should make clear in future that the elimination of the UK deficit must impose costs on the rest of the world. If the rest of the world is unwilling to accept these costs, 'it' must be prepared to finance the full-employment UK deficit. If this is not acceptable other countries cannot claim any influence on the methods by which the UK eliminates the external deficit and attempts to return to full employment.

III.6   Short-term Capital Flows and Balance of Payments Policy

Short-term capital movements have traditionally played an important role in the overall UK balance of payments situation. Their importance is the joint result of the UK position as an international financial centre and of the role of sterling as an international reserve asset and medium of exchange. Thus some of the short-term capital flows into and out of the UK reflect changes in the sterling balances which foreign governments and individuals have acquired as matters of commercial and financial convenience. The remainder reflect the role of London as a centre for the Eurodollar and other financial markets, with banks in the UK lending and borrowing extensively in dollars and European currencies.

The significance of short-term capital flows for the conduct of UK policy arises from their magnitude relative to the official reserves and from their volatility. It is convenient to divide the capital flows which influence the UK balance of payments into two broad classes; speculative and non-speculative. The motive behind speculative capital flows is one of making a capital gain from anticipated

---

1 For a detailed comparison of the alternative strategies of devaluation and import restriction see W. Godley *et. al, Economic Policy Review*, University of Cambridge, Department of Applied Economics, 1976, pp. 11-17.

movements in spot exchange rates. If a sterling devaluation is anticipated, holders of sterling assets, to the extent that exchange controls permit, will switch their assets into foreign currency, while importers will accelerate payments to foreigners and exporters will try to delay payments from foreigners. Non-speculative activities, which result in short-term borrowing and lending, are undertaken to avoid exchange risks, in direct contrast to the motives behind speculative activities. The important point about non-speculative flows is that they involve simultaneous transactions in both spot and forward exchange markets. This can be illustrated as follows. Consider an American citizen with dollar funds to invest for three months. He has the choice of investing, say, in New York or in London, by buying a short-term dollar asset in the former or a short-term sterling asset in the latter.

In making his decision the US investor will take into account the different short-term interest rates in London and New York, but relative interest rates are not the only factor to be considered. Any movement of funds across national boundaries must also take into account the possible gain or loss which may result from changes in the exchange rate between the date of purchase of a foreign currency and the future date of sale. If the American investor expects the sterling-dollar exchange rate to have moved in his favour in three months' time, and invests in the UK for this added reason, he will omit to cover his investment in the forward exchange market. He is then acting as a speculator and risks the possibility of a capital loss when he converts back from sterling to dollars, if the *actual* future spot rate differs from the *expected* future spot rate upon which he based his transaction. If he chooses not to speculate he can forego the prospect of an additional gain or loss by simultaneous transactions in the spot and forward markets for sterling. He will purchase spot sterling, in order to acquire the London asset, and simultaneously sell forward the expected sterling proceeds (principal and interest), for delivery in three months' time. In this way the dollar value of his investment is known with certainty at the time of investment. The effect of this operation is to introduce another element into his calculations, the percentage excess of the forward sterling price of dollars over the spot sterling price of dollars. This premium must then be subtracted from the UK interest rate to give an exchange risk free UK interest rate, which he may compare with the interest rate in New York. Then, only if the interest rate advantage possessed by the UK exceeds the forward premium on dollars will it be profitable to invest funds in London.

In sum, short-term capital movements depend on a complex of interactions between national interest rates, spot and forward exchange rates and expectations of future changes in spot rates. Not surprisingly, with expectations such an important factor, short-term capital flows are highly volatile and not necessarily responsive to official attempts at their control.

The importance of short-term capital flows for external and internal policy depends upon the exchange market framework in operation. Under the par-value system the first impact of a short-term capital outflow falls upon the exchange reserves, this being true of both speculative and non-speculative flows. Given the poor reserve/short-term liability situation of the UK, any such loss of reserves, if heavy, almost invariably provoked a change in demand management policy. A 'run on sterling' was normally followed by a policy to contract domestic demand and restore 'confidence'. With a freely floating exchange rate matters are completely different. The impact effect of a change in capital flows falls not upon the reserves but upon the exchange rate. A capital outflow will now work to depreciate sterling and an inflow to appreciate sterling. However, any such change in the exchange rate acts upon the current account in the same way as a policy induced parity change. Hence, a capital outflow has similar effects as a devaluation; encouraging exports, discouraging imports and increasing the rate of circular flow of income. It will be clear that large and sudden capital flows can provide difficult policy problems for fully employed economies operating with floating exchange rates.

An important development since 1958 has been the increasing integration of European and American capital and money markets, and the emergence of London as the focus of Eurodollar activities. This has increased the sensitivity of international capital flows to interest rate differentials and allowed the mobilization of an increased volume of funds for switching between currencies.[1]

This greater degree of financial market interdependence has several implications for the conduct of domestic economic policy. In particular, it reduces the extent to which the UK can manipulate national interest rates to achieve internal objectives. Frequent international discussions on 'interest rate de-escalation' in the middle sixties illustrated the official concern on this matter and, as far as the UK is concerned, the events of July 1973 and after provide a strong case in point. At the beginning of July 1973, minimum lending rate in the UK, the current equivalent of Bank rate, stood at 7½%, a level which was becoming increasingly uncompetitive relative to interest rates in Europe. As a result a capital outflow developed and sterling began to depreciate. In order to halt this slide in the exchange rate domestic interest rates had to be raised. Thus in mid-July minimum lending rate was raised to 11½% and again to 13% in mid-November, when sterling came under pressure. One important domestic repercussion of this was to raise the cost of borrowing to finance capital and other expenditure and, in particular, to precipitate a sharp decline in housebuilding activity.

What can the UK authorities do to influence short-term capital flows? A broad answer would be very little. In the first instance some restraint is provided through exchange control regulations. Residents of the UK and OSA are denied the opportunity to purchase foreign currency except for authorized purposes. In addition, direct limits are placed on the foreign exchange positions which banks and other exchange dealers may undertake.[2] However, this still leaves untouched the activities of non-resident holders of sterling who tend to be the most active in switching funds between currencies.

Two alternatives remain. Manipulation of domestic interest rates is a powerful weapon in current circumstances, given the increasing integration of financial markets. Its use is subject to two limiting provisos: international retaliation and conflict with the level of interest rates needed to attain internal objectives. The remaining policy option is official manipulation of the forward exchange rate, which would allow the authorities to create for the UK a risk-free interest rate advantage on short-term investments, as circumstances dictate. Between 1962 and 1967 the UK achieved some success with this policy, effectively counteracting pressure on the reserves on several occasions. Although such a policy may be run at a modest profit for the UK authorities, technical losses arise if the spot rate is

---

1   Recent estimates put the total amount of privately held international assets available for switching between currencies at some $268 billion, twice OECD member country reserves in 1972. Even allowing for double counting, the magnitude of assets is alarming since they constitute a permanent threat to the stability of any currency.

2   For details see 'Limits on UK bank's foreign exchange positions', *BEQB,* December 1975.

changed while official forward contracts are outstanding. This occurred with the 1967 devaluation, when the sum of £366 million had to be paid out to foreigners who at the time held forward contracts to sell sterling. Since that episode, there has been little indication of official forward activity.

It must be noted that neither interest rate policy nor forward intervention proved of much avail when the par value of sterling came under severe pressure. In these circumstances, policies of this nature merely signal to the foreign exchange market the seriousness with which the authorities view the situation, thus accentuating fears of a parity change and accelerating the capital outflow.

For the conduct of UK economic policy, the behaviour of the sterling balances is of prime importance and will continue to be so as long as the authorities wish to manage the sterling exchange rate. One reason for this is that the UK reserves cannot be treated solely as a buffer stock to finance payments deficits. The reserve function of sterling places the UK in the position of an international banker with the gold and the currency reserves as backing for the short-term external liabilities. As pointed out in section I, the UK's external problems in the 1960s stemmed from a grossly inadequate ratio of reserves to liabilities. The result was a general lack of confidence in the ability of the UK to maintain its banking role, which grew particularly sharp whenever the reserves were used or threatened to be used to fulfil their function of financing a deficit.

Until 1968 the short-term external liability situation of the UK exhibited two important features. First, the overall stability, even in times of sterling crisis, of the sterling balances held as part of the exchange reserves of the OSA countries. Secondly, and, in contrast, the marked volatility of the balances held by NSA governments and residents. It was the latter category which contributed most to the pressure on sterling, particularly after the return to convertibility in December 1958. As it transpired, the more volatile balances diminished in absolute and relative importance in the 60's, forming 42% of total sterling liabilities in 1962 and 32% in 1967. It is possible to argue from this that sterling balances were becoming more stable in total, and thus that the sterling problem was diminishing. Unfortunately, 1968 saw a fundamental change in official OSA attitudes toward their sterling balances.[1] The 1967 devaluation had the side effect of reducing the capital value of OSA reserves in terms of other currencies and gold. As a result, fears of a second devaluation in 1968 led to widespread attempts by OSA countries to liquidate their sterling holdings and diversify their reserves. In the second quarter of 1968 alone, official OSA sterling balances declined by some £230m. For the OSA countries this simply reflected their weakening economic links with the UK. For the UK, however, it represented the demise of a basic ground rule of the sterling payments system, viz, that OSA countries pool their official holdings of gold and foreign currency in London in exchange for sterling balances. Naturally, this development caused much official concern in the UK and inspired negotiations to obtain international support for sterling, the upshot of which were the Basle arrangements of September 1968. Under the Basle arrangements twelve central banks, together with the Bank for International Settlements, extended a credit of $2 billion to the UK, the facility to have a life of ten years. The finance was

---

1   To some extent, reserve diversification had been taking place throughout the 1960s, but mainly via the process of overall growth in OSA official reserves. For a valuable discussion see 'Overseas Sterling Balances 1963-1973', *BEQB,* June 1974.

provided on several conditions, the two most important of which were as follows. First, the credits could only be used to cover the liquidation of private and official balances of the OSA countries and could be activated when the total of such balances fell below an agreed level. Second, to minimize the reserve diversification activities of the OSA countries, each had to negotiate a minimum proportion for the sterling component of its exchange reserves, which varied according to the circumstances of each country. Provided the minimum sterling proportion was at least maintained then, as a quid pro quo, the UK would guarantee the dollar value of that part of each country's official sterling reserves (excluding equity holdings) that exceeded 10% of that country's total reserves. The initial arrangements with OSA countries were for three to five years, all three year agreements being renegotiated in 1971 and extended until 1973. In October 1973 the agreements were extended for six months with, from the UK point of view, an unfavourable change in the dollar rate of exchange at which the balances are guaranteed. The agreements were renegotiated again in March 1974 for the duration of the year, an important change being to guarantee the balances in terms of a basket of currencies and not simply in terms of the dollar, and were finally terminated at the end of 1974.

In effect the Basle arrangements have worked to perpetuate the reserve role of sterling. In every year since 1968 the official sterling balances of the OSA countries have increased, while the proportion of total sterling liabilities used as international reserves has stayed virtually constant, at 59%, over the whole period since 1966.

It is a matter of considerable doubt whether a sterling guarantee was necessary. Holders of sterling fully appreciated the nature of the par-value system, in which a currency could be devalued when in a situation of fundamental disequilibrium. On balance they held sterling because of convenience and because the interest return outweighed any perceived exchange risks. Sterling assets have carried interest yields far superior to those obtainable with alternative reserve media such as gold or even other foreign currencies.[1] The drawings the UK was obliged to make on the Basle facility were repaid at the end of 1969 and the subsequent growth in sterling balances has eliminated any further recourse to this line of credit. But the guarantee left the UK with an uncertain contingent liability, which in the fifteen months to March 1974 cost some £140m in writing up the dollar value of the relevant sterling balances.

Important questions on the future of sterling balances still remain unresolved. The UK has given a commitment to the other EEC members to undertake a reduction in the reserve function of sterling but clearly does not possess the immediate means to achieve this. At the end of 1974, the UK's gold and currency reserves were exactly one third of total official holdings of sterling balances and 94% of other holdings. At a pinch, the resources are only available to terminate the private role of sterling as a trading currency. Paradoxically, in the light of the weakening trade and investment links between the UK and the OSA, total sterling liabilities to OSA governments were 68% greater at end of 1973 compared to their

---

1   The Brookings report points out that over the years 1958-66 UK Treasury bills had an average yield of 4.71%, compared with 3.21% on US Treasury bills and a zero yield on gold. Such rates of return adequately compensate for the effects of a 14% devaluation. See Caves, *op. cit.,* p. 194. The interest cost to the UK of sterling balances increased from £150m in 1963 to some £450m in 1973, under the influence of higher average interest rates and the increase in the total of sterling holdings. See *BEQB, op. cit.,* p. 171.

value in 1968. In 1974 a further annual increase of 27% occurred which reflected the rapid accumulation of sterling balances principally by the oil producing members of the OSA. At the same time the proportion of total reserve sterling holdings held by the oil producers rose from 28% at end 1973 to 69% at end 1975. Effectively, while the oil producers added to their sterling reserves the remainder of the sterling area holders drew upon their sterling balances; in part, no doubt, to finance the increase in their oil import bills. A major issue for the UK remains that of persuading the oil producers to continue to increase their sterling holdings and to prevent any run-down of existing balances, such as happened in the second half of 1975. Whether the promised reform of the international monetary system will contain proposals for the funding of the sterling balances and their replacement by long-term debt of the UK is not clear.[1]

In conclusion it is worth remembering that the management and performance of the UK economy has suffered considerably as a result of the sterling balance problem.[2] Official sensitivity to the country's short-term liquidity position repeatedly forced demand management policy to respond to changes in the reserves rather than to changes in the internal state of the economy. For similar reasons, governments have proved more than willing to incur substantial short-term and medium-term debt to the IMF and central banks, in order to maintain confidence in sterling. Perhaps most damaging, is the argument that perceived 'moral obligations' toward holders of sterling led to a persistent official discounting of devaluation as a policy option. For as we have discussed above, sterling balance holders have been adequately recompensed for any devaluation losses. In sum it appears difficult to avoid a conclusion that maintenance of the international role of sterling has seriously weakened the long-term competitiveness of the UK economy. In this respect adoption of the floating exchange rate in 1972 and a willingness to let the trend in the rate reflect market forces was a welcome development, made even more welcome by the termination at the end of 1974 of the guarantee arrangements on reserve sterling.

III.7   Long-Term Capital Flows and Balance of Payments Policy

In the discussion of balance of payments equilibrium (section I.3), it was shown that a current account imbalance creates a change of equal magnitude in a country's total external net wealth. One important implication of this is that the UK can only add to its net external assets to the extent that it simultaneously has a current account surplus. If the current account should be in balance, a net outflow of long-term investment will not add to the total of UK external assets but rather will change the liquidity structure of these assets. In essence, long-term investments will be made at the expense of a reduction in the reserves, or other offsetting reduction in existing external assets. The purpose of this section is to discuss the balance of payments and other consequences of overseas investment, and to outline the various measures adopted to control overseas investment flows.

---

1   The funding of sterling balances is discussed in B. J. Cohen, 'The Reform of Sterling', *Princeton Essays in International Finance,* No. 77, December 1969.

2   For an account of the internal costs, see S. Strange, *Sterling and British Policy,* Oxford 1971, Chs. 9 & 10.

Any additional flow of overseas investment by the UK will have implications for the current and capital accounts of the UK balance of payments, the mechanism being the linkage between autonomous and induced transactions which was discussed in section III.3 of this chapter. With a fixed exchange rate the impact effect is to reduce foreign exchange reserves, as UK investors acquire the foreign exchange needed for their overseas investment. If we consider direct investment, it is likely that the construction of new capital equipment overseas will involve some increased demand for UK exports of goods and services so that the UK current balance will improve and the charge on the official reserves is reduced accordingly. Should the new flow of foreign investment be associated with a reduction in UK home investment there will be a reduction in the level of economic activity in the UK, and activity will increase abroad if the foreign investment leads to additional investment there. There will then be further repercussions on the UK current balance which stem from the multiplier process at home and abroad and the linkage between changes in activity and imports. In practice, the linkage between the capital account and current account transactions is likely to be such that the current account improves but not by a sufficient amount to finance the capital outflow without loss of reserves.[1] The total increase in net external assets is therefore smaller than the direct investment outflow. If the capital outflow takes the form of portfolio investment, the impact on the current account is likely to be negligible and such investment will be matched by an equivalent reduction in other net overseas assets.

In addition to the linkages between the trade balance and the flow of direct foreign investment, account must also be taken of the return flow of profit and interest income from overseas investment. In the simplest case, in which the overseas assets are acquired without direct resort to foreign borrowing, the return profit inflow will exceed or fall short of the capital outflow according as the rate of return on the foreign investment exceeds or falls short of the percentage rate of growth of the stock of overseas assets. It is not necessarily the case, therefore, that the investment outflow produces a deterioration in the overall balance of payments position, even when we ignore trade linkage effects.[2]

As long as the government aims to maintain a fixed exchange rate, the case for and against control of foreign investment involves a balancing of the short-term gain to the official reserves from limiting the capital outflow, against the cumulative loss through time of the forgone income from the foreign investment. When a floating exchange rate is adopted this particular problem ceases to be relevant. Any

---

1   The theoretical mechanism which underlies this argument is known as the transfer
    mechanism and explanations of it may be found in standard textbooks on international
    economics.
2   For a quantitative investigation of the balance of payments effects of UK direct investment
    overseas, see W. B. Reddaway and Associates, *Effects of UK Direct Investment Overseas:
    Interim Report* (1967) and *Final Report,* (1968) Cambridge University Press. For every
    £100 of foreign assets acquired, it was found that the current account improves by £11
    in the first year (extra exports) and by £4 in every subsequent year (comprising extra
    exports and profit receipts, net of foreign taxation, and interest payments on accommo-
    dating foreign borrowing). These figures suggest that it would take roughly 22 years before
    a steady capital outflow of £100 per annum becomes self financing. With 40% foreign
    borrowing the time period is reduced to 12 years. These figures well illustrate the short/long-
    run dilemma with respect to direct investment, and the desire of the UK authorities to
    encourage the finance of investment by foreign borrowing.

short-term cost to the reserves may be eliminated by an appropriate depreciation of the currency, and this will increase net exports so that the capital outflow may be transferred in real rather than in monetary terms. If full employment is to be maintained by government policy the final increase in net exports will have to be matched by a reduction in domestic investment or consumption. It is then possible to evaluate the costs and benefits of alternative levels of foreign investment by direct comparison of the estimated yields of the foreign investment flows with the forgone yields as resources are moved out of home use so as to accommodate the real transfer. Assuming rational behaviour on the part of investors, it is unlikely that the expected yield (net of risk) on investment abroad will differ substantially from that on the forgone domestic investment. This last argument is subject to the qualification that interest and profits earned overseas generate tax revenues that accrue to overseas governments, whereas home investment generates such revenues for the UK government.[1]

A country may wish to influence the inflow and outflow of long-term capital for a variety of reasons, not least among which relate to the resource allocation effects of foreign investment and the political and economic implications of an increase in the proportion of domestic capital controlled by foreign residents. In the UK the dominant motives for capital controls have been protection of the exchange reserves and improvement of the balance of payments, motives which are approved under the IMF par-value rules. Policy has therefore aimed at encouraging the finance of overseas investment by foreign borrowing and the plough-back of profit earned in existing foreign operations.

Limitations on the outflow of UK capital to the OSA countries may be dealt with quickly. Until 1966 both direct and portfolio investment flows to the OSA were free from exchange restriction. This freedom was a quid pro quo to the OSA for their (unwritten) obligation to pool their foreign exchange reserves in London. In April 1966 a policy of voluntary restraint on UK investment in Australia, New Zealand, South Africa and the Republic of Ireland was introduced. The object of this was to encourage firms to postpone existing investment plans in these more advanced OSA countries, and to encourage discussion of future investment proposals with the Bank of England. This policy was abandoned in March 1972. However, the respite proved to be short lived. The floating of sterling in June 1972 resulted in the majority of OSA countries being assigned external account status, and thereby becoming subject to the same limitations on portfolio and direct investment as the former NSA countries.

As far as portfolio investment in the NSA is concerned, this has been subject to rigorous exchange control since 1945. UK residents are not permitted to buy quoted foreign currency securities with official exchange, nor are they allowed to dispose of the foreign currency proceeds of liquidated direct and portfolio NSA investments at the official exchange rate. Instead, all such transactions must pass through the separate investment currency market, at a price which balances the desire to purchase foreign currency securities with the desire to liquidate existing

---

1 A further qualification is that any depreciation designed to accommodate an additional flow of foreign investment will probably involve the UK in a worsening of its net barter terms of trade which raises the opportunity costs of that investment. Against this, however, must be set any future appreciation of the currency which follows from the return inflow of profits and interest.

holdings of NSA assets. Normally the investment currency rate stands at a premium[1] relative to the spot exchange rate, the magnitude of the premium providing some indication of the degree of restriction on portfolio investment.

Operation of the investment currency system has meant effectively that the UK operates a two-tier foreign exchange market, so that portfolio flows to and from NSA countries are self-balancing and make no claim on the exchange reserves. In April 1965 an important modification was introduced, whereby 25% of the foreign currency proceeds from the sale of NSA securities had to be transferred to the authorities at the official exchange rate. It has been estimated that this 'tax' on the investment currency premium added some $2.25m to the reserves in the period from its inception to March 1974. Since June 1972, the granting of external account status to the OSA countries has meant that portfolio investment in the OSA must pass through the investment currency market. At first, liquidations of OSA securities were not subject to the 25% surrender rule, but this privilege was abolished in the 1974 budget. It is clear that the investment currency system has provided an effective method for isolating the reserves from portfolio investment flows. How long it will remain in force in present circumstances is not clear, although the implicit commitment to participate in the EEC capital market harmonization programme means that it must eventually be terminated. From 1961 onwards, restrictions on direct investment in the NSA took the form of treating proposed investments in terms of three categories. The least restricted category consisted of so-called super-criterion projects, which were expected to bring matching returns to the balance of payments within eighteen months and which could be financed with official foreign exchange up to an effective limit of £50,000. All other projects had to be financed through the investment currency market or by overseas borrowing.[2] These restrictions have been alternatively strengthened and relaxed according to the underlying state of the basic balance. The more important and recent changes occurred in June 1972, when direct investment in the OSA was brought within the same network of limitations, and in the budget of 1974, which resulted in foreign investment in the OSA, NSA and EEC being treated on an equal footing, with official foreign exchange only available for super-criterion projects. It is worth noting that these changes, together with the application of the portfolio surrender rule to OSA securities, mean the end of all elements of discrimination in favour of investment in the OSA and hence the effective termination of the special economic relationship between the UK and OSA countries.

It appears that the restrictions had little impact on the total outflow of direct investment from the UK, nor did the discriminating element in favour of the OSA prevent the swing in the geographical location of direct investment toward the EEC and North America. The most important effect of the restrictions appears to have been in saving foreign exchange. Over the period 1965-71, foreign borrowing financed 56% and internally generated profits financed 47% of all UK private

---

1   The premium is the percentage difference between the investment currency price of sterling and the price of sterling in the spot market.
2   For further details see the C.O.I. pamphlet, *Britain's International Investment Position,* HMSO, 1971.

investment in the NSA, so leaving a small balance to be added to the exchange reserves.[1]

At present, the UK places no legal restrictions upon inward investment, apart from those contained in the 1947 Exchange Control Act which apply to all UK residents. However, inward direct investment is subject to Treasury permission and the criteria upon which permission is granted are aimed at maximizing the contribution which the investment inflow makes to the reserves.[2] The broad details of long-term capital flows into and out of the UK since 1952 are presented in table 3.8.

It can be seen that the UK was a net exporter of long-term capital from 1965 onwards, apart from the period 1968-71. This reversal in the net capital flow was a reflection of a greater inflow of private capital and especially of portfolio and other investment associated with the development of North Sea oil facilities. It can also be seen that the net direct investment outflow expanded continually from 1960 onwards and that there is no obvious support for a view that the UK capital controls have restricted the acquisition of overseas assets by UK firms. During the years 1972-75 the UK returned to being a net exporter of private capital but, in contrast, became a net importer of long-term capital in the aggregate, largely because of substantial borrowing by the UK public sector, a development we referred to in III.5 above. The geographical location of UK foreign investment has changed considerably since 1961. Then, only 24% of the book value of UK overseas direct investments was located in Western Europe and North America but by 1973 this proportion had risen to 46%. In part this reflects a swing toward investment in the EEC which mirrors the changes which have occurred in the pattern of UK trade. The inward flow of investment continues to be dominated by investment from North America and Western Europe which currently account for approximately 95% of the book value of foreign owned direct investments located in the UK.[3] Table 3.8 also contains figures for the flow of profits, dividends and interest into and out of the UK.[4] We can see from these figures that remitted profits earned on the stock of UK direct investments have exceeded the direct investment outflow in each sub-period since 1961, while the direct investment inflow has been almost exactly offset by the overseas remission of profits since 1964. The net contribution of direct investment and associated profit flows is therefore to provide slightly favourable influence on the exchange value of sterling.

Variations in the net profit flow are determined by three factors; changes in the stocks of overseas assets and liabilities under the influence of long-term capital flows, changes in the rate of return on foreign and domestic assets, and changes in the exchange rate. This last factor has been particularly important since 1972, as a sterling depreciation increases the sterling value of UK foreign currency earnings but has no direct effect on the sterling value of foreign currency earnings generated in

---

1   For further discussion see A. K. Cairncross, *'Control of International Long-Term Capital Movements'*, Brookings Institution, 1973, pp. 68-77.

2   M. D. Stenyer, *et. al., 'The Impact of Foreign Direct Investment on the UK'*, HMSO, 1973, Ch. 9. Since 1972, this condition has been waived for EEC companies and investors.

3   For details see *TI*, 25 October 1975 and 15 March 1975.

4   The category 'other', includes interest payments and receipts on short-term liabilities and assets.

Foreign trade and the balance of payments

TABLE 3.8

UK Long-Term Capital Flows and Related Flows of Profits, Interest and Dividends. Annual Averages for Selected Periods (£m), 1956-75

	1956-60	1961-4	1965-7	1968-71	1972-5
(a) Long-term Capital Account[1]					
Government outflow[2]	−56	−93	−74	−140	−258
Overseas investment in UK					
public sector[3]	n.a.	+33	+26	+46	+414
Private investment in UK	+165	+240	+287	+782	+1490
Direct	n.a.	+172	+187	+348	+594
Portfolio	n.a.	+3	−39	+110	+138
Other[4]	n.a.	+65	+139	+324	+758
UK investment abroad	−298	−319	−376	−757	−1585
Direct	n.a.	−234	−288	−545	−1283
Portfolio	n.a.	+15	+39	−96	+123
Other[4]	n.a.	−100	−127	−116	−425
Direct private investment (net)	n.a.	−62	−101	−197	−689
Total private investment (net)	−133	−79	−89	+25	−95
Balance of long-term capital	−189	−139	−137	−69	+61

(b)   Current Account − interest, profit and dividend flows

	1956-60	1961-4	1965-7	1968-71	1972-5
Credits	633	790	982	1343	2794
Direct	n.a.	306	422	661	1390
Portfolio	n.a.	135	153	166	202
Other[5]	n.a.	349	407	516	1202
Debits	380	445	577	868	1652
Direct	n.a.	158	218	347	602
Portfolio	n.a.	59	82	111	219
Other[5]	n.a.	228	277	410	831
Total net flow	+253	+345	+405	+475	+1142
Net flow as % GDP	1.24	1.31	1.22	1.12	1.80

Sources: UK Balance of Payments, 1971 and ET, March 1976.

Notes: 1. Assets, increase − /decrease +. Liabilities, increase+/decrease −
2. Figures are net prior to 1961.
3. Prior to 1961, included in private investment in UK.
4. Oil and miscellaneous.
5. Including oil.
n.a. Not available.

the UK.[1] It is interesting to note that the net foreign income of the UK is now barely 2% of GDP. Finally it is to be expected that the profit outflow from the UK will increase substantially in the next few years, in response to the successful development of North Sea oil facilities.[2]

III.8   The UK and the EEC

The subject of UK membership of the EEC has always been controversial and the controversy has shown little tendency to abate since the UK became a full member in January 1973. On gaining office the Labour government of 1974 declared its firm intention to renegotiate the original terms of entry,[3] completed the renegotiations in March 1975[4] and then settled the question in favour of membership with a referendum in June 1975. In this section we shall only comment upon the balance of payments implications of membership – other implications are treated in Chapters 2 and 4 of this volume.

It was apparent at the time of the pre-entry negotiations that the full effect of entry into the EEC would imply a deterioration in the current account and possibly a deterioration in the long-term capital account of the balance of payments. To offset this, the UK would have to depreciate the exchange rate or employ direct policies of expenditure reduction in order to achieve the cut in real income and expenditure necessary to eliminate the adverse balance of payments effects of entry. Against this 'real resource cost' could be set the dynamic benefit of selling in a greatly enlarged market: a benefit which, it was argued, would result from greater economies of scale in production and which would be manifested in an increase in the UK growth rate.[5] Improved growth performance, it was thought, would possibly yield some offsetting dynamic gains to the basic balance. Unfortunately, while it proved possible to provide plausible estimates of the balance of payments cost, measurement of the potential dynamic gains has so far eluded any precise assessment. At the time of writing, belief in the benefits of entry remains an act of faith.

The effects on the UK current account can be discussed under three headings: changes in the pattern of trade in manufactures, adoption of the common agricultural policy, and contributions to the Community budget.

The main implications for trade in manufactures follow from the customs union aspects of the Community; all tariffs on trade between the UK and the other members have to be reduced to zero by 1977 and the UK has to adopt the common

---

1   A further factor which should be noted is that of changes in the international taxation arrangements which the UK concludes with other nations. It should also be noted that unremitted profits are entered twice in the balance of payments statistics, as an item in the current account and then as a fully offsetting item in the long-term capital account.

2   Cf. *NIER*, no. 75, 1976, p. 22.

3   *Renegotiation of the Terms of Entry into the European Economic Community*, Cmnd. 5593, April 1974.

4   *Membership of the European Community: Report on Renegotiation*, Cmnd. 6003, March, 1975.

5   *Britain and the European Communities: An Economic Assessment*, Cmnd. 4289, February 1970.

external tariff (CET) on trade with non-Community countries by the same date.[1]
It is impossible as yet to say what the final effects on the UK's pattern of trade will
be. Not only are we still in the transitional phase of tariff alterations, we must also
take into account the discrimination which is now imposed against former
Commonwealth countries (excluding signatories of the Lomé convention) and the
associated loss of UK export preferences in the same countries. We have already
shown, in section II.1, that the direction of UK trade in the 1950s and 1960s swung
progressively toward Western Europe and away from the traditional markets in
North America and the OSA. It seems clear that entry into the EEC has accelerated
the process. Over the years 1969 and 1972 UK exports to the EEC increased at an
average annual rate of 12.5%, while imports from the EEC increased by 17.7%.
However, between 1973 and 1974 these growth rates increased dramatically with
exports to the EEC increasing by 36% and imports from the EEC increasing by 48%.
The period 1974-5 provides much lower growth rates for UK trade with the EEC
(in part the result of the general world recession): imports increased by 14% and
exports by 16%, but the interesting point is that total UK imports only increased
by 4% over the period while total UK exports increased by 20%. It will be interesting
to see whether this will become a more permanent feature of the UK trade pattern,
the UK becoming more import-dependent on the EEC but, at the same time, less
export-dependent. Such a trend, it will be noted, would be consistent with the
hypothesis that UK industry is becoming increasingly uncompetitive relative to
industry in the rest of the EEC and that it is therefore forced to find markets
outside the EEC.

Assessments of the balance of payments cost of entry for the UK have tended to
concentrate upon the effects of adopting the CAP system of agricultural support in
place of the deficiency payments method formerly used by the UK. Under the
deficiency payments method the UK imported foodstuffs at world prices, free of
any import duty. Under the CAP the UK is obliged to import all foodstuffs at the
common EEC prices and to impose import levies on imports from non-EEC sources,
to bring their prices up to EEC levels. At the time of negotiation for entry it was
estimated that EEC prices were between 18-26% higher than world market prices
and that, given an inelastic demand for imports of foodstuffs, the UK import bill
would be increased accordingly.

Finally, the UK is obliged to contribute to the budget of the Community and
this involves a transfer of funds across the foreign exchanges, the gross contribution
of the UK being assessed with reference to the share of the UK in the total GNP
the Community. The net contribution will be smaller than the gross contribution to
the extent that the UK receives reverse transfers from the EEC, for example, in the
form of regional aid and industrial development aid.[2]

Estimates of the static balance of payment cost of entry produced widely

---

1 The necessary tariff changes are to be achieved in stages, for details see '*The United
   Kingdom and the European Communities,* Cmnd. 4715, July 1971, paras. 79-80. The
   average final level of CET on UK imports of manufactures will be 8½%.

2 Cf. Cmnd. 4715 paras. 91-96 and Annex A.

varying results, although most suggest a substantial balance of payments burden[1] and thus an implied real resource cost of UK entry to be imposed by a devaluation or other means. It was in the light of the assumed advance balance of payments implications that the UK government renegotiated the original terms of entry. The most concrete results of the renegotiation were the creation of a mechanism for reducing the gross budgetary contribution of the UK in line with the UK's share in the total GNP of the Community, and the guarantee of continued access to the Community for Commonwealth sugar and dairy products from New Zealand.[2]

It is remarkable how inaccurate the initial estimates of the balance of payments cost have proved to be. Three factors are relevant here. First, and most important, the rise in world commodity prices between 1971 and 1975 brought world food prices up to the level of EEC prices and so eliminated any potential cost of CAP on the UK's import bill for foodstuffs. Second, the attempt to offset the effect of the depreciation of sterling on CAP prices has led to a substantial net transfer of funds from the EEC budget to the UK. The reason for this is as follows. EEC food prices are set in terms of units of account and are then translated into national currencies at representative exchange rates, determined by administrative decision. Since June 1972, the depreciation of sterling relative to the dollar has not been matched by an equivalent depreciation of the representative exchange rate for sterling, the so-called green pound, the percentage gap between the two rates reaching as much as 20% in July 1975.[3] The effect of such a sterling depreciation is to raise the sterling price of food imports into the UK above CAP levels and to create the possibility of profitable arbitrage between commodities, sterling and other EEC currencies. To prevent these disruptions to CAP, subsidies are paid to the UK to keep down the sterling price of imported foodstuffs to the level dictated by the representative exchange rate, while, at the same time, the UK is obliged to tax any agricultural exports in order to maintain their representative prices in terms of other EEC currencies. Since the UK is a large net importer of foodstuffs it has received more in the form of import subsidies than it has had to levy in export taxes and subsequently transfer to the community budget.[4] Third, and finally, the UK has begun to benefit in the form of payments from the regional fund, receiving a total of £35.8m of regional aid in the first year of its operation.

The net effect of these reverse transfers has been to substantially reduce the net budgetary cost of entry below the amounts estimated in 1971. In 1974, for

1 The 1970 White Paper, Cmnd. 4289, suggests a balance of payments cost ranging between £100m to £1.1bn per annum. For a comparison with other, less extreme estimates see J. Pinder (ed), *The Economics of Europe*, Charles Knight, 1971, Ch., 6 by M. Miller. For a more optimistic assessment see R. L. Major and S. Hays, 'Another Look at the Common Market', *NIER*, no. 54, November 1970.

2 Cmnd. 6003. For additional details of the Lomé convention which grants tariff preferences on exports to the EEC of industrial products, and some agricultural products from signatory developing countries, see P. Coffey, 'The Lomé Agreement and the EEC: Implications and Problems', *TBR*, No. 108, December 1975.

3 For a time series of the percentage premium of the green pound over the official sterling exchange rate, see R. W. Irving and H. A. Fearn, *Green Money and the Common Agricultural Policy*, Wye College, Occasional Paper No. 2, 1975.

4 It has been estimated that the UK received £190m in 1975 in the form of net agricultural subsidies, known officially as monetary compensation amounts (*Financial Times*, 24 March 1976).

example, the actual net contribution was £31m, compared to a 1971 estimate of £165m, while the estimated net contribution for 1976 has been put as low as £25m.[1] Over the three years to end 1975, the net balance of payments charge in the form of service and transfer payments from the UK to the EEC averaged £35m, less than 5% of the average net outflow on government account. In addition, one must take account of borrowing by UK bodies from EEC institutions, e.g., the sum of approximately £300m borrowed by the UK steel and coal industries from the European Coal and Steel Community and the European Commission.

It is entirely another question whether the UK will be so fortunate in future years. It does not seem possible that world food prices can be maintained at EEC levels, nor is it likely that the system of monetary compensation will continue unchanged. In the light of this it would appear to be in the UK's interest to press for a more flexible approach to CAP and to try and force EEC food prices to fall in line with productivity gains in the most advanced farming units. Failure on these fronts will simply raise again the potentially formidable cost of UK membership.

Although the CAP and budgetary contribution questions have tended to dominate practical discussion on EEC membership, it is important to recognize that the issue of monetary unification is potentially of greater significance to the UK. In 1971, the European Commission, following guidelines laid down in the Werner Report of 1970, adopted the goal of full monetary union to be achieved by 1980. In its fullest form this would involve the irrevocable fixing of the parities of EEC countries one to another, full currency convertibility for current and capital account transactions and the creation of a Community central bank with full powers to determine monetary policy in each region of the EEC. In many respects the case for monetary union is an integral part of the case for a common market in commodities. Creation of a single currency (de facto by fixing exchange rates, or by the adoption of a new currency unit) reduces transactions costs and promotes exchange and the division of labour which, it could be argued, is necessary if the dynamic gains from membership are to be maximized.

Furthermore, it can be argued that once the members of the EEC develop intensive trade and investment links with one another then adoption of a fixed pattern of exchange rates is the only foreign exchange market policy consistent with price stability. Stable EEC parities are, of course, a very necessary part of the operation of CAP and other Community-wide policies. Whatever the merits of these arguments it should be realized that the costs of monetary unification are considerable.[2] As part of a monetary union the UK would abandon the right to change its parity unilaterally against other currencies, having already surrendered the ability to impose import restrictions and export subsidies for balance of payments purposes by adopting the CET. Expenditure switching instruments are therefore eliminated from the armory of feasible economic policies. Adjustment to payments deficits must then be by domestic deflation and the creation of unemployment, with the harmful and ultimately self-defeating implications noted in section III.3 above. At best, a high degree

1 Cmnd. 6004, para. 43. For the 1976 estimate see *Public Expenditure to 1980,* Cmnd. 6393, 1975.

2 The interested reader may consult, Y. Ishiyama, 'The Theory of Optimum Currency Areas: A Survey', *IMF Staff Papers,* Vol. 22, 1975, pp. 344-83. For a discussion of the monetary union between the UK and Eire see O. Whitaker, 'Monetary Integration: Reflections on Irish Experience', *Moorgate and Wall St.,* Autumn 1973.

of labour mobility to the other EEC countries may mitigate the effects on unemployment, while it is possible that sustained financial support from other Community members may ease, but not eliminate, the burden of adjustment. Equally, the commitment to capital market integration would rule out restrictions on capital transactions in order to improve the basic balance.

Progress to date has been non-existent and, one could say, illustrates the folly of the whole conception. The most concrete move, taken in March 1972, was to limit the margin of fluctuation between the strongest and weakest of the EEC currencies to a maximum of 2.25%.[1] The scheme has proved to be ill-fated. Sterling defected in June 1972, after only eight weeks of membership, the lira is floating independently and the French franc has been forced out of the snake twice, the most recent occasion being in March 1976. The lesson from this is that it is pointless to fix exchange parities between countries with divergent rates of inflation, and that uniformity of inflation rates will not come about without the prior emergence of national rates of wage increase which exactly offset national differences in productivity growth. To some extent the adoption of a common central bank and co-ordinated fiscal policies may assist in this regard but such developments are likely to fall foul of the fundamental issue of national sovereignty in the formulation and implementation of economic policy.

III.9   The Reform of the International Monetary System

The quarter century from 1945 witnessed the recreation of an integrated world economy to replace the system shattered by the collapse of the gold exchange standard and the world depression in the late 1920s and early 1930s. An important role in the process of international reconstruction was played by the system of international financial rules known as the Bretton Woods system, the supervisory institution of which is the International Monetary Fund (IMF). Under the aegis of this body the wartime restrictions on trade and capital flows were dismantled and, following the general return to currency convertibility in 1960, world production expanded over the next decade at an average annual rate of 5%, while the volume of world trade increased at the historically unprecedented annual rate of 8½%. At the same time, the flow of international investment increased substantially and international capital markets became more integrated.[2]

Two main features characterized the Bretton Woods system. Firstly, each country was required to adopt a par-value for its currency, defined in terms of gold, and the authorities in each country were responsible for maintaining the spot market value of their currency within 1% of the par-value. The par-value was not meant to be immutable but could only be changed in the face of a 'fundamental' balance of payments disequilibrium, a concept nowhere adequately defined in the IMF Articles

---

1   This scheme was known as the 'snake in the tunnel', the 'snake' representing the closely linked EEC currencies which, under the pressure of market forces, is free to move up and down relative to the dollar in the 'tunnel' defined by the Smithsonian exchange rate limits. (See section III.9) The 'tunnel' disappeared in March 1973 when the EEC currencies engaged in a joint float against the dollar.

2   For a clear statement of the increasing interdependence of the world economy during this period consult R. N. Cooper, *The Economics of Interdependence*, McGraw-Hill, 1968.

of Agreement, and only then after consultation with the IMF. Secondly, the IMF would provide finance for temporary payments imbalances up to defined maxima, provided that the country requesting finance was prepared to accept IMF surveillance of its economic policies. In general, therefore, the contribution of IMF finance was temporary and conditional.

Throughout the 1960s it became clear that the IMF system suffered from potentially lethal inconsistencies and that, in particular, it placed the United States in an economic position which the European industrial nations became increasingly unable to accept. The first weakness was the general unwillingness of the main industrial countries to adjust par-values in the face of obvious fundamental disequilibria until the force of events, aided by currency speculation, forced governments into belated action. The case of sterling in the mid-1960s and of Germany and Japan in the late 1960s are obvious example of this failure to use the par-value adjustment mechanism in the way originally intended by the architects of Bretton Woods. Not unrelated to this was the asymmetry between deficit and surplus countries, in that the pressure of reserve losses bore far more heavily on the deficit countries than did the converse phenomena of reserve gains in the surplus countries. In practice the 'scarce currency' provisions of Article 7 of the IMF Agreement, which were meant to act as a sanction against persistent surplus countries, were never invoked.

The second weakness involved the supply of global reserve media, which under the IMF system consisted mainly of gold and foreign exchange holdings, and in particular, of course, of US dollars. The problem was that the supply of monetary gold depended on the vagaries of mining and speculative activity, and the supply of foreign exchange depended upon the balance of payments deficits of the US, which could prove to be temporary and, more important, unrelated to global reserve needs. In the light of this there was considerable discussion in the 1960s of the alleged inadequacy of world reserves, which took as its basis the observed decline in the ratio of world reserves to world imports, from a value of 68% in 1951 to one of 24% in 1974; the latter being less than the equivalent ratio for the depressed years of the 1930s. The problem with this type of discussion was that it failed to make clear that the demand for foreign exchange reserves is a demand to finance balance of payments *disequilibria,* not a demand to finance the volume of trade. It failed, therefore, to recognize that the demand for reserve media will be smaller the more frequently exchange rates are adjusted in line with economic pressure, the more co-ordinated are national policies of demand management, and the greater the willingness of national governments to engage in mutual international borrowing and lending to finance payments imbalances. In the limit, for example, with a perfectly freely floating system of exchange rates the demand for official reserves would be zero.

Finally, there was the so-called 'confidence' problem, which followed from the increasing degree of dependence of world reserve growth on foreign exchange in the form of the dollar and to a lesser extent sterling. The problem was simply that by 1964 the total of outstanding dollar liabilities exceeded the gold reserves of the United States and from then on this disparity between dollar liabilities and gold 'cover' increased. By December 1971 the US gold stock amounted to only 16% of the total of US short-term dollar liabilities held by overseas monetary authorities. *De facto* this meant that the dollar was no longer convertible into primary reserve assets and so the willingness to hold dollars in official reserves decreased and the danger of a dollar crisis increased. As R. Triffin pointed out in 1958, the gold-exchange standard contained an automatic self-destruct mechanism,[1] with the potential risk of a severe liquidity crisis in which dollar and sterling reserves were liquidated and destroyed, while a given total of gold reserves was redistributed between countries.

It is important, when trying to understand recent events and proposals for reform, to realize that the Bretton Woods system had the effect of placing the United States and the dollar in a unique position in the international monetary system. Opponents of the United States have argued that the reserve currency status of the dollar enables the United States to conduct internal policies independently of its balance of payments position and to finance an outflow of direct overseas investment on advantageous terms. In contrast, it has been argued that the USA has no choice but to adopt a passive balance of payments policy and run a payments deficit of sufficient magnitude to satisfy the global demand for dollars as an international reserve asset. Whatever the merits of these viewpoints two aspects of the situation are clear. Firstly, because the dollar was extensively used as the intervention currency for stabilizing exchange rates, the USA had no need to concern itself with supporting the external value of the dollar. Secondly, the one option open to the USA to cure its deficit, namely a devaluation of the dollar relative to gold and therefore relative to other currencies, was steadfastly ruled out on political grounds, until, that is, the events of December 1971.

Throughout the 1960s the strains inherent in the system manifested themselves in a variety of ways. Most significant, perhaps, were the ad hoc measures taken by the industrial countries to supplement the existing sources of balance of payments finance. At one level were the General Arrangements to Borrow, organized in October 1962, in which the Group of Ten countries (UK, France, Germany, Britain, Netherlands, Italy, US, Canada, Sweden and Japan) agreed to lend their currencies to the IMF should the latter run short of one of their respective currencies. These arrangements have been renegotiated on several occasions, most recently in October 1975 with the amount of support involved totalling SDR 5.5bn. In addition to this have been the currency swap arrangements between the US and the central banks of other countries, whereby each agrees to lend or acquire currency balances for an agreed time period. In June 1975 several such arrangements existed between the US and other countries and totalled $20bn. The UK has benefited considerably from the availability of this short-term financial aid, the UK-US swap facility being increased to $3bn in March 1974. The UK has also been able to draw upon credits provided by European central banks from 1961 onwards.

A second manifestation of strain related to the official price of gold and the possibility that it could be raised should there be a widespread attempt to liquidate dollar exchange reserves. In 1961 a gold pool was formed in which the major central banks stood ready to intervene in the private gold market in order to maintain the market price at the official level of $35 per oz. Speculative pressure following the 1967 devaluation of sterling, and the loss of some $3bn of monetary gold stocks, sold in an attempt to stabilize the private market between November 1967 and March 1968, led to the collapse of this arrangement. Replacing it was the Washington gold agreement of March 1968 which created a two-tier market for gold. The central banks agreed to transact between themselves at $35 per oz and to refrain from transactions with the private market whenever the price in that market stood

---

1   R. Triffin, *Gold and the Dollar Crisis,* Yale, 1958.

above $35 per oz. The free market price was left to be determined by the balancing
of supply, and speculative and industrial demand. Apart from a brief respite in
1969, speculative pressure, reinforced no doubt by the dollar devaluations of 1971
and 1973, and the example of increasing world commodity prices, pushed the free
market price progressively upwards to a peak of $195.5 per oz in December 1974,
compared with an official price of $42.22 per oz. The discrepancy between the
official and free market prices put considerable strain on the willingness of some
central banks to abide by the Washington agreement, which effectively prevented
the use of monetary gold for the finance of payments imbalances, and in November
1973 it was abandoned. The question of the demonetization of gold is treated
further below.

The final, and some would say most significant, manifestation of strain was the
increasing volume of speculative capital flows which from 1967 onwards repeatedly
disrupted the working of foreign exchange markets and threatened the parities of
the deutschmark, the yen and the dollar. It became increasingly clear that the
par-value system could not survive unless more effective methods for adjusting
exchange rates in line with changing economic circumstances could be devised and
unless some means could be found for absorbing an increasing volume of short-
term capital flows.

Proposals for Reform: Plans for reform produced in the 1960s centred upon two
issues, the adjustment of exchange rates and the creation of alternative reserve
assets to supplement or replace gold and foreign exchange. Proposals for improving
the adjustment mechanism ranged from abandoning par-values completely and
resorting to freely floating exchange rates, to more practicable alternatives of
widening the margins of fluctuation around par-values and creating a mechanism for
the automatic adjustment of par-values. This latter approach to greater exchange
rate flexibility has become known as the sliding parity proposals of which there
are several variants.[1] The main feature of this device is the achievement of exchange
rate adjustments not by discrete jumps, which provide a profitable one-way option
for speculation, but by small annual amounts of the order of, say, 2%: 'small' in
this context meaning that the magnitude of the change in exchange rates can be
compensated by feasible interest rate differentials so that the incentive to short-
term capital flows is eliminated. Attractive though these proposals are they are not
without drawbacks. In particular, there is no guarantee that the path of exchange
rate adjustment which eliminates incentives to speculation is the same as the path
of adjustment which is optimal from the point of view of the internal economic
situation of a country. The crawling peg may adjust too slowly and in addition
require a substantial backing of international reserves to support it.

Discussions at the level of the IMF provided a lukewarm response to the proposals
just discussed, and little progress was made on the adjustment problem. A study by
the executive directors of the IMF concluded by reaffirming faith in the viability
of the par-value system, with the only concessions to flexibility being the suggestion
of wider margins of fluctuation around par-values and the temporary abrogation of
par-value obligations.[1]

---

1 *The Role of Exchange Rates in the Adjustment of International Payment: A Report by the
Executive Directors*, IMF, 1970.

By far the most important development of the 1960s was international agreement on the creation of a new reserve asset, the Special Drawing Right. The outcome of several years of discussion, this scheme came into operation in 1970.

Special Drawing Rights: SDRs are book entries in the Special Drawing Account of the IMF by means of which countries can give and receive credit on a multilateral basis to finance balance of payments deficits. At the moment SDRs are held only by those national monetary authorities which participate in the IMF arrangements and which agree to accept the provisions of the SDR scheme. The total of SDRs is agreed collectively by the members of the IMF, so that the supply of this new reserve asset is agreed by international decision; the basis for their creation being the provision of an adequate, but not inflationary, long-term rate of growth of world reserves. SDRs are thus superior to gold and foreign exchange in that their supply is not arbitrary but the outcome of rational discussion. The total of SDRs is revised on a five-year basis with the first allocation of $9.3bn being made in three stages between 1970 and 1972.[1] Each country is assigned a net cumulative allocation of SDRs, in proportion to its quota in the general account of the IMF, and can treat this allocation as 'owned reserves' to finance payments imbalances. A country in deficit, for example, may use its SDR quota to purchase needed foreign exchange from other countries. One of the most ingenious features of the scheme is that utilization of a country's SDR quota is subject to the supervision of the IMF, the object being to ensure a balanced and widespread activation of the SDR facility. Use of SDRs is thus subject to three provisions: (i) they must be used for legitimate balance of payments purposes and not, for example, to diversify exchange reserve portfolios; (ii) a country need not accept SDRs in excess of twice its net cumulative allocation; and (iii) a country's average holding over a period of five years must not fall below 30% of its net cumulative allocation — essentially to prevent the persistent, as distinct from temporary, financing of a deficit with SDRs. To give effect to these provision two types of transactions in SDRs are allowed, designated transactions and non-designated transactions. With designated transactions, the IMF decides the countries that will add to their SDR holdings and so provide the currencies required by the country running down its SDR holdings, the choice of countries for designation being decided on the basis of their balance of payments strength and the adequacy of their reserve holdings. In contrast, non-designated transactions involve the transfer of SDRs between countries without recourse to the IMF where the objective is to redeem the currency liabilities of the transferor.

It is perhaps too early to say whether the scheme is successful but initial indications are promising. At the end of the first five year reconstitution period, no participant had violated the 30% minimum average holding rule and a balanced utilization of SDRs had been achieved. As one would have expected, the industrial countries, with the exception of the UK and USA, had been net recipients of SDRs and the less developed countries had been heavy net users of their SDR allocation.[2] More interesting questions relate to the future status of SDRs relative to gold and foreign currencies, especially the dollar. At end 1974, SDRs provided 5% of total

---

1 The revised Articles of Agreement to incorporate SDRs may be found in the IMF *Annual Report* for 1968, or in the book by F. Machlup listed at the end of this chapter.

2 For details consult IMF, *Annual Report 1975*, Washington, tables 1-3 and 1-6.

world reserves compared to gold which accounted for 20% and the dollar which accounted for 35%. The question is, are SDRs simply to co-exist with other reserve assets or are they to be developed as a replacement for either or indeed both?

In the initial arrangements SDRs were effectively a gold substitute, they had a gold guarantee and carried a low rate of interest on net holdings of 1½%. On the understanding that the dollar is not devalued relative to gold then SDRs are inferior to the dollar as a reserve asset because of their lower interest yield and lesser convenience of usage. However, the dollar devaluations of 1971 and 1973 upset this situation, as did the resort to a general floating of the important currencies relative to gold. In response to these changed circumstances the IMF announced, on 1st July 1974, that the value of the SDR would be computed as a weighted average of sixteen currencies, that the link with gold would be terminated, and that the interest rate on net holdings of SDRs would be increased to 5%.[1] These changes provided scope both for the elimination of gold as a reserve asset and for the replacement of the dollar and other reserve currencies by SDRs. As and when SDRs come to be held by private traders and banks, it would then be quite sensible for the major countries to use SDRs as an intervention currency to stabilize their exchange rates, a development which would essentially involve the stabilization of the effective exchange rate of a currency.[2]

The 1971 Crisis and A Forum for Reform: Any illusions that the creation of the SDR scheme had inaugurated a new period of stability for the par-value system were quickly shattered. Following a period of considerable uncertainty in foreign exchange markets and massive short-term capital outflows from the US, the US government announced in August 1971 that the dollar was no longer convertible into gold and that to eliminate the disequilibria in the international economic system other countries must revalue their currencies relative to gold. To add pressure toward this end a 10% surcharge was imposed on US imports of manufactures and the US proclaimed its intention to obtain trade concessions from Japan and the EEC. Detailed and intensive official decisions culminated in a meeting of the finance ministers of the Group of Ten countries at the Smithsonian Institute in Washington in December 1971. The main points agreed were: (i) a new set of values of exchange rates which involved a revaluation of the deutschmark and the Japanese yen; (ii) that 'pending agreement on longer-term monetary reforms' the permitted IMF margins of fluctuations around par values would be increased to ± 2.25%; (iii) that the US would devalue the dollar in terms of gold by 7.89% so creating a new official price for gold of $38 per oz and that this would form the new par value of the dollar; (iv) that the 10% import surcharge would be abolished; and (v) that new discussions should be undertaken, under the auspices of the IMF, to consider the long-term reform of the international monetary system in all its major aspects.

The forum for discussion of international reform was set up in June 1972 and became known as the Committee of Twenty, holding meetings between September

---

1 For details of the composition of the currency basket and of the formula for changing the interest rate on SDRs in line with commercial rates in international money market see 'The New Method of Valueing Special Drawing Rights', *BEQB*, September 1974.

2 Cf. J. H. Williamson, 'The Future Exchange Rate Regime', *Banco Nationale del Lavoro Review*, June 1975. For further treatment of the future role of SDRs consult F. Hirsch, 'An SDR Standard: Impetus, Elements, and Impediments', *Essays in International Finance No. 99*, Princeton, 1973.

1972 and June 1974 when the final report was presented. Three items dominated the deliberations of the C-20. Firstly, methods of absorbing and re-cycling short-term capital flows. Secondly the creation of an exchange rate system with stable but adjustable par values and with recognized and widely acceptable criteria for instigating changes in par-values. Thirdly, the future reserve base of the international monetary system and in particular the role of the SDR in any reformed system. The deliberations of the C-20 could hardly be described as successful, the final report made clear that substantial differences of view existed on fundamental issues.[1] The most concrete outcome of the C-20 activities has been its perpetuation in the form of an Interim Committee which continues to discuss proposals for reform. However, it would have indeed proved remarkable had any concrete reform proposals emerged, for the reform discussions were overtaken by two important events; the adoption of generalized floating by the major industrial countries in March 1973 and the massive increase in the price of oil in December 1973.

Managed Floating and the Oil Price Issue: Confidence in the Smithsonian exchange parities proved to be short-lived and in the period to March 1973 frequent speculative crises disturbed the international monetary system. The only effective counter to the disturbances proved to be the widespread adoption of floating exchange rates. Apart from the floating of sterling in June 1972, the major changes occurred as a result of the speculative crisis of February and March 1973. By the end of March, the Italian lira and Japanese yen were floating independently, the EEC countries (less UK and Italy) had undertaken a joint float against the dollar and the dollar had been devalued for the second time in two years, to a value of $42.22 dollars per ounce of gold. Thus by April 1973 the par-value system had been abandoned by the major trading nations, perhaps a predictable outcome of the 1971 events which effectively placed the world on a dollar standard.

The experiences of 1972 and 1973 have underlined a major problem faced by any exchange rate system in current circumstances, viz, coping with the massive volume of short-term funds which can be switched very rapidly between financial centres. Short-term capital flows forced the abandonment of Smithsonian parities and have played an important part in the fluctuations experienced by floating rates. Various attempts have been adopted to limit such flows, for example, a two-tier foreign exchange market by Italy, direct controls on overseas borrowing by Germany and an extension of inter-central bank currency swap arrangements, but these are of a somewhat *ad hoc* and inadequate nature.

The inception of a period of managed floating raises several difficulties for the international monetary system, in particular those of mutually inconsistent exchange rate stabilization policies, the possibility of competitive, beggar my neighbour, exchange rate management and the problem of exchange instability in the face of speculative pressure. To help avoid these problems the IMF issued guidelines for exchange rate management in June 1974.[2] The guidelines emphasized the point

---

1 The final report of the C-20, 'Outline of Reform', was published in IMF *Survey*, June 1974. See also, *International Monetary Reform, Documents of the Committee of Twenty*, IMF, 1974.

2 Cf. IMF, *Survey*, 17 June 1974, pp. 181-3.

that exchange rate policy is a matter for international consultation and surveillance by the IMF and that intervention practices should be based on three principles: (i) exchange authorities should prevent sudden and disproportionate short-term movements in exchange rates and ensure an orderly adjustment of exchange rates to longer-term pressures; (ii) in consultation with the IMF, countries should establish a target zone for the medium-term values of their exchange rates and keep the actual rate within that target zone; (iii) countries should recognize that exchange rate management involves joint responsibilities. The experiences of the period of managed intervention have been mixed. On the one hand, short-term movements in exchange rates have been more volatile than advocates of flexible rates would perhaps condone while, on the other hand, exchange rates have been managed without any overt clashes of national interest and have changed to compensate substantial national differences in inflation rates.[1]

More damaging to the reform movement is the increase in the price of oil which created an unprecedented imbalance in the international economic system, in the form of a massive payments surplus for the oil producers and a corresponding deficit for the oil importing countries. The problem is simply that the ability of the oil producers to spend their oil revenues on imports of goods and services has not so far matched the increase in revenues. Thus the oil producers enjoyed aggregate payments surpluses of $56.5bn in 1974 and $31.5bn in 1975, and it is estimated that by 1980 their cumulative payments surpluses could total as much as $300bn, expressed in terms of 1974 dollars.[2] Too much weight should not be placed on such estimates but it is salutary to note that the figure of $300 billion is almost twice the total of world reserves at the end of 1975. Since, as is generally agreed, the OPEC countries have no serious alternative but to invest their surplus revenues in the advanced industrialized nations, so returning on capital account the purchasing power extracted from the current accounts of the oil important nations, the oil problem raises three serious issues for the stability of the international monetary system. First, there is the potential havoc which would be brought to foreign exchange markets if surplus oil funds are invested in liquid assets and switched between currencies in search of interest return and the expected capital gain from exchange rate alterations. Clearly some means must be found of placing the funds in less liquid investments and/or creating sufficient central bank co-operation to undertake large scale re-cycling operations. Secondly, and more important, is the fact that the attractiveness of different oil importing nations as havens for OPEC investment need bear no relation to the way in which their respective current account balances have been affected by oil price increase. The possibility is therefore reinforced that individual countries will try to eliminate their deficits by deflation or currency depreciation, the only outcome of which would be a worsening of the world recession. Finally, there are the problems faced by the developing nations

---

1   IMF, *Annual Report,* 1975, pp. 23-33. On the volatility of exchange rates see F. Hirsch and D. Higham, 'Floating Rates – Expectations and Experience', *TBR*, June 1974.
2   A compendium of widely differing estimates of OPEC financial accumulation by 1980 is in T. D. Willet, 'The Oil-Transfer Problem and International Economic Stability', *Essays in International Finance,* No. 113, Princeton 1975.

which have seen the real values of aid inflows virtually eliminated by the increase in oil prices.[1]

In March 1974, the IMF put forward proposals to borrow, from the oil export-ing countries and those industrialized countries in a relatively strong payments position, on a medium-term basis, and for making the proceeds available to the countries most severely affected by the oil price increase. The first oil facility, which expired in December 1975, raised $2.8 billion and was drawn upon by forty countries. In April 1975, the IMF undertook to arrange a second oil facility, for the period to April 1976, of the order SDR £5.6 billion. Borrowings from this second oil facility have to be repaid within three to seven years and carry interest charges on a scale increasing from $7\frac{5}{8}$ to $7\frac{7}{8}$ %. A country can borrow up to a maximum of 125% of its IMF quota or 85% of the calculated increase in oil import costs — whichever is the smaller — and all borrowings are conditioned upon IMF approval of the medium-term balance of payments policies adopted by the borrowing country. The countries financing the oil facility are paid interest at $7\frac{1}{4}$ % per annum. The second oil facility promised to be used heavily and, by the end of January 1976, some SDR 3.3 billion had already been taken from the facility, including the sum of SDR 1 bn borrowed by the UK. In addition to arrangements conducted though the IMF, the OECD countries arranged in March 1975 a SDR 20 billion 'safety net' fund to finance their respective oil deficits. Although the industrial countries have managed to arrange balance of payments finance without too much difficulty, major problems still face the less developed countries despite a rising total of OPEC disbursements to the third world.

Recent Developments: The final report of the C-20 advocated an evolutionary approach to the problems of world monetary reform and, despite the problems noted in the previous section, substantial progress, it seems, is now being made. During 1975 the Interim Committee held several meetings and agreement on four important issues was reached in January 1976. It was first agreed to increase the global quotas in the general account to SDR 39 billion, an increase of 32.5%, and within this total to double the quotas of the oil producing nations. Furthermore as a temporary measure, until the increase in quotas is ratified, the size of each credit tranche at the IMF is to be increased from 25% to 36.25% of quota, so raising the size of each country's borrowing facility from 100% to 145% of its quota. This will provide some $1.5 billion to $2 billion extra conditional finance to cover payments deficits.

Also agreed at the 1976 meeting were some longer-term measures of considerable consequence which relate to the role of gold and the permissible types of future exchange rate regime. On gold it has been agreed that countries need no longer supply 25% of their quotas in gold, nor are they obliged to use gold in other transactions they may undertake with the IMF. The IMF is also to sell one sixth of its gold stock on the free market over the next four years and use the proceeds to establish a Trust Fund, the object of which will be to provide balance of payments

---

1 For discussion of the adverse effects on developing countries and possible means of easing their problems consult C. Michalopoulos, 'Financing Needs of Developing Countries: Proposals for International Action', *Essays in International Finance*, No. 110, Princeton 1975.

assistance on concessionary terms to the poorer countries, i.e. those with per-capita income not greater than SDR 300 in 1973.

A further one-sixth of the IMF gold stock is also to be transferred to IMF members at the official price. The way has thus been paved to eliminate gold from the international monetary system and to establish the SDR as the principle reserve asset.[1] Of considerable long-term significance is the proposal to amend Article 4 of the IMF agreement. The main points involved are as follows:[2] (i) a general return to stable but adjustable par-value can take place with the support of an 85% majority in the IMF; (ii) par-values may not be expressed in terms of gold or other currencies but can be expressed in terms of SDRs, the margins of fluctuation around par-values remain at ± 2.25%; (iii) with the concurrence of the IMF, any country may abandon its par-value and adopt a floating exchange rate; (iv) the exchange rate management of a floating currency must be subject to IMF surveillance and must not be conducted so as to disadvantage other countries; and (v) the agreed practices with respect to floating rates will operate until such time as a general return to par-values is attained. In effect floating exchange rates have been legalized within the framework of the IMF system and without any diminution of the powers of the IMF.

These represent important developments and reflect well on the ability of nations to co-operate in their long-term interests, despite the disruptive short-term pressures they face. It would be foolhardy, however, to conclude that little remains to be achieved. Progress must still be made on the control of capital movements, particularly with the prospect of a mixed par-value floating exchange rate system, on criteria for changing par-values and on the future role of SDRs and the elimination of the foreign exchange component of current world reserves. Without these additional measures there can be little prospect of re-creating a stable international monetary system.

1　The Group of Ten has also agreed that there will be no action to peg the price of gold and that the stock of monetary gold in their reserves will not be increased. IMF *Survey*, 19 January 1976, p. 19.

2　The text of the proposed new Article 4 is contained in IMF *Survey*, 19 January 1976, pp. 20-21.

REFERENCES AND FURTHER READING

S. Brittan, *Steering the Economy,* Pelican, 1971.
Sir Alec Cairncross (ed.) *Britain's Economic Prospects Reconsidered,* George Allen
   and Unwin, 1971.
Sir Alec Cairncross, *Control of Long-Term Capital Movements,* Brookings Institution,
   1973.
R. E. Caves and Associates, *Britain's Economic Prospects,* Brookings Institution and
   George Allen and Unwin, 1968.
H. G. Johnson and J. E. Nash, *UK and Floating Exchanges,* Hobart Paper, 46,
   Institute of Economic Affairs, 1969.
C. P. Kindleberger, *International Economics,* Irwin, 1973.
F. Machlup, *Remaking the International Monetary System,* Committee for
   Economic Development and Johns Hopkins, 1968.
C. McMahon, *Sterling in the Sixties,* Oxford University Press, 1964.
J. E. Meade, *UK, Commonwealth and Common Market: A Reappraisal,* Hobart
   Paper 17, Institute of Economic Affairs, 1970.
W. B. Reddaway, *Effects of UK Direct Investment Overseas: An Interim Report,*
   Cambridge University Press, 1967; *Final Report,* Cambridge University Press,
   1968.
B. Tew, *International Monetary Cooperation 1945-70,* Hutchinson, 1970.
S. J. Wells, *British Export Performance,* Cambridge University Press, 1964.

OFFICIAL PUBLICATIONS

Bank of England Quarterly Bulletin.
Economic Trends (regular analyses of balance of payments in March, June,
   September and December issues).
IMF, Annual Report
NEDC reports, especially *Export Trends* (1963) and *Imported Manufactures* (1965).
Report of Committee on the Working of the Monetary System, Radcliffe Report,
   Cmnd. 827, 1959.
Trade and Industry (weekly) (previously *Board of Trade Journal*).
UK Balance of Payments Pink Book (CSO annually).

4

Industry and commerce

J. R. Cable (assisted by M. Waterson)

I   INTRODUCTION: SOME THEORETICAL BACKGROUND

Whenever we attempt to analyze the behaviour of firms and industries we have, at some stage, to rely on theoretical models. Orthodox theory has it that firms behave as if their objective was to maximize profit. The theory offers us many insights and can lead to important policy implications for the government and others. But there are alternative models which will be drawn upon in this chapter for additional insights.

One strand of recent theoretical development has resulted in a group of 'managerial' models. These recognize that in modern, large firms there has been a divorce of ownership (by shareholders) from control (by salaried executives).[1] In this situation profit remains important to policy makers within the firm both for survival and also because it may be directly linked to executive salaries through incentives such as stock-option schemes and bonuses linked to profits. But it is argued that where top management exercises the degree of control over policy that it appears to do in practice, firms are most likely to behave as if maximizing the value of variables yielding utility to managers, subject to some profit or other financial constraint. The variables in question vary from model to model. In Baumol's model the firm is assumed to maximize sales revenue, subject to a profit constraint.[2] Marris has developed an alternative, growth maximizing model, with a security (stock market valuation) constraint.[3] Williamson put forward a more general model of managerial utility, in which the objective function incorporates salary, the number and quality of subordinates, control over discretionary investment and expenditure on managerial perquisites.[4]

Firms pursuing such objectives would usually arrive at equilibrium outcomes which differ from those of a profit-maximizer, e.g. in terms of price and output levels. In some cases they would also adjust decision variables in the opposite direction to a profit maximizer, in response to changes in the business environment, e.g. changes in tax rates. Hence in analyzing firms' behaviour and in assessing the effects of government policy we may reach different conclusions depending on which theoretical model of behaviour we apply. Unfortunately there is at the

---

1   See A. A. Berle & G. C. Means, *The Modern Corporation and Private Property,* revised edition, Harcourt, Brace and World, N.Y. 1968; and P. Sargent Florence, *Ownership Control and Success of Large Companies,* Sweet and Maxwell, 1961.

2   W. J. Baumol, 'On the Theory of Oligopoly', *Economica,* Vol. XXV, No. 99, August 1958, pp. 187-98, and *Business Behaviour Value and Growth,* Macmillan, 1959.

3   R. Marris, 'A Model of the Managerial Enterprise', *Quarterly Journal of Economics,* May 1963, and *The Economic Theory of Managerial Capitalism,* Macmillan, 1964.

4   O. E. Williamson, 'Managerial Discretion and Business Behaviour', *American Economic Review,* December 1963, and *The Economics of Discretionary Behaviour: Business Objectives in the Theory of the Firm,* Prentice-Hall, 1964.

moment no clear way of telling which model should be adopted. Empirical testing of the hypotheses so far has produced some evidence in support of each, but none of the theories – including profit maximization – has yet been accepted as demonstrably superior. In this situation perhaps the most we can do when looking at the behaviour of firms and industries is to be very clear on the theoretical assumptions we make and, especially when appraising public policy issues, consider the various responses which might be expected under different theoretical assumptions.

Alongside the managerial theories is another, somewhat more radical, new theoretical departure. The 'behavioural' theory emphasizes the organizational aspects of firms and the limited amount of knowledge available in decision-making.[1] In the behavioural theory the firm is seen to pursue a number of goals in the form of independent, aspiration-level constraints, e.g. a particular sum of profits, or level of sales, or a target rate of return on capital, which firms attempt to 'satisfice'. Goals are imperfectly rationalized, may conflict, and receive sequential rather than simultaneous attention. Over time, aspiration levels for a particular goal will change according to past achievements in relation to past aspirations. The firm is seen as an adaptive organism, solving pressing problems rather than attempting to apply plans leading to optimal equilibrium values or growth paths of decision variables, as in more conventional approaches. In a situation of imperfect knowledge, search (the acquisition of information) is neither continuous nor determined optimally as an investment decision. Rather, search is 'problemistic', requiring to be motivated e.g. by adverse feedback on goal fulfilment or by some external event or evidence of failure. Search is 'limited' or 'narrow'; solutions are sought at first in the neighbourhood of problem symptoms and current alternatives and search widens only as satisfactory solutions fail to be found. In choosing among alternative strategies 'satisficing' procedures are adopted, the first acceptable strategy being selected. The firm's behaviour is constrained by standard procedural rules governing search, choice, etc. and these are abandoned only under duress. However, in the long term organizational learning occurs, and search and choice rules are adapted in the light of experience. Typically, firms exhibit organizational slack in the form of excess resources within the organization.

In order to derive quantitative predictions of firms' behaviour from the behavioural model it is necessary to develop specific computer simulation models. However, the theory does permit of some qualitative analysis without this. Like the managerial theories, the behavioural theory is important because it may lead us to conclusions about firms' behaviour which are different from those of other models. However, one distinguishing feature of the behavioural model is that it specifically sets out to embody the decision process. Thus, unlike all the other models so far mentioned, the behavioural model *does* attempt to tell us how various outcomes are arrived at as well as what the outcomes will be.

The theoretical approaches to firms' behaviour so far discussed have generally been conceived with the private sector of the economy in mind, and especially 'secondary' manufacturing industry rather than the 'primary' sector (agriculture and extractive industries) and the 'tertiary' sector (transport, distributive trades,

1 H. A. Simon, 'A Behavioural Model of Rational Choice', *Quarterly Journal of Economics,* February 1955; R. M. Cyert and J. G. March, *A Behavioural Theory of the Firm,* Prentice-Hall, 1963, and H. A. Simon, 'Theories of Decision Making in Economics and Behavioural Science', *American Economic Review,* June 1959.

professional and other services, government administration, etc.). Nevertheless there
are some insights which they can give in all areas of industry and commerce,
whether public or private, and the scope of this chapter is not limited to the private
manufacturing sector. Some of the issues we shall consider do mainly concern the
private sector (e.g. the question of monopoly control). But in another section we
also consider the public sector issue of pricing and investment criteria for
nationalized industries. And a number of the issues considered are common to both
the public and private sectors and all industry and commerce, e.g. the whole
question of efficiency, productivity and technical progress.

II   THE SIZE STRUCTURE OF INDUSTRIES AND TRADES

An idea of the size structure of UK industrial groupings is given in the first column
of table 4.1. Size is measured in terms of output. Alternative measures would be

TABLE 4.1

Size Structure and Growth of UK Industries, 1957-75.

	Annual Rate of growth 1957-75 (%)	*GDP by industrial origin, 1974 (£m)*[3]
Agriculture, forestry and fishing	2.76[1]	2,116
Mining, quarrying	−2.41	1,021
Manufacturing:		
Food, drink, tobacco	2.44	2,410
Chemical and oil products	5.33	2,012
Metal manufacturing	−0.45	1,271
Engineering and allied industries	2.35	8,981
Shipbuilding and marine engineering	−0.83[1]	466
Vehicles and aircraft	1.23	1,883
Textiles	1.38[1]	1,119
Clothing	1.30[1]	639
Other manufacturing	3.56[1]	4,213
Total manufacturing	2.41	20,645
Construction	2.09[1]	5,645
Gas, electricity, water	4.69	2,255
Transport and communication	3.09[1]	6,648
Distributive trades	2.69[1]	7,003
Insurance, banking, finance	5.32[1] ⎞	6,750
Professional and business services	3.23[1] ⎠	
Miscellaneous services	2.03[1]	8,735
GDP[2]	2.70	72,625

Sources: NIBB and *NIER.*

Notes: 1   1957-74 only.

2   Includes public services and administration, defence, ownership of dwellings,
adjustment for financial services and residual error.

3   Contribution of each industry to GDP before providing for depreciation but
after providing for stock appreciation. Figures for individual manufacturing
industries are estimates.

employment and capital stock. In some cases these would produce a rather different picture, because of inter-industry differences in capital/labour ratios. For instance, in 1972 the UK coal, petroleum and chemical industries together accounted for 21.4% of total capital employed in manufacturing but only 5.7% of manpower and 11.4% of output. Evidently there is need for some care in choosing the most appropriate size measure for any particular given purpose.

Industry boundaries are based on the Standard Industrial Classification for the UK. The SIC groups the UK economy into Orders, which are subdivided into Minimum List Headings. The latter are generally the nearest one can get in official statistics to what we would normally mean by an 'industry', although even these subdivisions are too broad in some cases. The industry groups in the table are mostly Orders, or even groups of Orders, and it must be remembered that they may be composed of a very large number of sub-trades, often quite disparate. Although there may be quite strong technological links among the industries concerned, it is by no means certain that their various products necessarily have high cross-elasticities of demand. In general official industrial classifications tend to be production-oriented.

In comparison with other major European countries the UK has a relatively small agricultural sector, reflecting a greater reliance on food imports in the past (see below, p. 194), but some larger tertiary industries, notably finance, insurance, etc. The manufacturing sector as a whole is not large in relation to GDP by international standards, and certainly accounts for a much smaller share of all economic activity than in West Germany.

TABLE 4.2

Relative Importance of Manufacturing Industries, UK and Selected European Countries, 1970[1]

| | *Percentage of manufacturing output* | | | |
	UK	France	W. Germany	Italy
Food drink and tobacco	11.24	–	10.37	11.80
Chemicals	8.72	28.04	18.12	13.45
Basic Metals	7.68	15.16	8.08	7.06
Iron and steel	5.73	12.17	6.77	5.84
Non-ferrous metals	1.95	2.98	1.31	1.21
Metal Products	42.78	23.51	41.38	31.53
Non-electrical machinery	13.42	–	11.46	11.58
Transport equipment	11.81	9.43	8.52	7.94
Textiles, clothing, leather	10.21	12.17	7.86	16.98
Other manufacturing	19.38	21.12	14.19	19.18
All manufacturing	100.00	100.00	100.00	100.00
Manufacturing Output in thousand millions of I.U.A.[2]	34.3	49.9	79.2	23.9

Sources: *Industrial Production: Quarterly Supplement to Main Economic Indicators of 4th Quarter, 1975,* OECD, and *General Statistics 1975,* Statistics Office of the European Commission.

Notes: 1 The figures have been extracted from tables containing weights for mining, electricity and gas, as well as manufacturing.

2 International Units of Account are an EEC monetary unit based on the gold content of the US dollar prior to its devaluation in December 1971.

Table 4.2 enables more detailed comparisons to be made among the major West
European countries for the manufacturing sector. The outstanding features of this
table are the comparatively small UK chemicals sector, and the comparatively
large metal products group, which includes the engineering and allied industries.

Changes in the size distribution will obviously occur when industries grow at
different rates. As the next section will show there have been considerable differences in growth experience among individual UK industries since the early 1950s.
These have produced some changes in the proportion of GDP originating in broad
sectors of the economy. The share of manufacturing fell from 36.7% in 1955 to
33.7% in 1974, and that of other industrial production (agriculture, mining and
construction) also declined, from 14.1% of GDP to 13.0%. Public utilities and
commerce (distribution, transport, insurance, etc.) increased their share of GDP
from 26.6% up to 28.2% and the share of miscellaneous services, public administration and defence also rose.[1]

III   INDUSTRIAL OUTPUT GROWTH 1957-74
III.1   General Output Trends

The growth of UK industrial output over the past two decades, at a rate of
approximately 2.8% per annum, has been extremely modest by international
standards. Table 4.3 compares the annual growth rates for total industrial production (manufacturing, mining, electricity and gas) between the UK and the six
original EEC members. Most of the other countries grew at around twice the UK
rate or more, except for Belgium and Luxembourg, and of these two the Belgian
rate was also well above the UK's. If differences in growth rates such as these
persisted for only short periods there would be little change in relative output

TABLE 4.3

Output Growth and GDP per head in the UK and EEC

Country	Annual growth of industrial production[1] 1957-74 (%)	Total growth of industrial production, 1957-74 (%)	GDP per head (in IUA) 1960	1974
UK	2.80	60	1374	2700
France	5.54	150	1337	4056
Germany	5.38	144	1298	4915
Italy	7.00	216	696	2163
Belgium	4.39	108	1253	4307
Netherlands	6.68	200	979	4094
Luxembourg	2.96	64	1568	4761
EEC (the Six)	5.64	154	1110	3806
EEC (the Nine)	–	–	1168	3561

Sources: *Industrial Production,* OECD; *National Accounts of OECD Countries,* OECD; and
          General Statistics 1975-12, Statistics Office of The European Community.

Note: 1   Includes manufacturing, mining, electricity and gas.

1 For a stimulating and controversial discussion of Britain's alleged structural malaise, with
   too few resources committed to marketed goods, see R. Bacon and W. Eltis, *Britain's
   Economic Problem: Too Few Producers,* London, Macmillan, 1976.

levels and, ultimately, living standards among the various countries. When they persist for a time period as long as that covered in table 4.3 the differential impact is large. Whereas UK industrial production grew by about 60%, that for the EEC as a whole rose to two and a half times the original level while the Italian and Dutch production more than trebled. At the beginning of the period (and indeed up to 1967) national income per head was higher in the UK than in the EEC as a whole, although the French and German GDP per head had exceeded the UK's since 1961. By 1972 the UK had become one of the poorer European nations.

Table 4.1 shows a fair measure of diversity among the growth rates for various industry sectors in the UK over the same period, with the chemical industry and the public utilities expanding at around twice the average rate, and with three industries actually declining. Yet even the faster growing sectors have scarcely matched the average performances in the EEC countries previously discussed. As one would expect, examples of more impressive expansion do emerge upon further disaggregation, e.g. plastics, electronics and man-made fibres. The physical quantity of synthetic resin production increased more than eight-fold between 1950 and 1974, and total production of man-made fibres has more than trebled since 1958.

What will be the eventual effects of EEC membership on individual UK industries is hard to say. Various forecasts were made at the time of UK entry. One of the most comprehensive has produced a ranking of some 230 manufactured products in order of those most likely to benefit from entry.[1] The products belong to nine industrial sectors: chemicals; manufactures of leather, wood, rubber, paper, etc; textiles and clothing; iron and steel; non-ferrous metals and metal manufactures; mechanical engineering; electrical engineering; transport equipment; and a miscellaneous category. The broad conclusion is that none of these industrial sectors is likely to fare much better or worse than any other across the board. Rather, each sector has its more promising and more vulnerable parts. This result accords well with previous findings that the creation of the EEC influenced the economies of the original partners mainly by a redistribution of resources within rather than between industries.[2] However, the findings for individual products do not in all cases agree with an official list of products thought likely to benefit from entry.[3] This included footwear, machine tools and food-processing equipment, all of which figure among those expected to do least well of all among the 230 products in the first study.

III.2   Agricultural Development and Policy

As in almost all other developed countries, UK agricultural production has been maintained and developed since the war at a higher level than would otherwise be the case, given the costs of domestic production and world price levels for agricultural products. The method by which support was given prior to the entry of the

---

1   S. S. Han and H. H. Liesner, *Britain and the Common Market* University of Cambridge, Department of Applied Economics, Occasional Paper No. 27, 1971.

2   B. Balassa, 'Tariff Reductions and Trade in Manufactures among the Industrial Countries,' *AER,* June 1966, pp. 466-73, and I. Walter, *The European Common Market: Growth and Patterns of Trade and Production,* New York, 1967.

3   *BTJ,* 8 July 1970, pp. 41-3.

UK into the EEC differed in some respects from the Common Agricultural Policy (CAP) operated by the EEC.

Under the UK scheme up to 1973, farmers received assistance in two main ways, through deficiency payments and through direct grants for capital investment and farm improvement schemes. The deficiency payments scheme operated as follows. Agricultural products sold in the UK at world price levels, with more or less free access to the UK market for foreign producers, and some preferential treatment for Commonwealth producers. Where these prices were below the level of a guaranteed price, set by the government to encourage a certain level of home production taking production costs and farm incomes into account, farmers received from the government a deficiency payment equal to the difference. Thus the UK maintained open markets to foreign producers and consumers enjoyed the relatively low world food price levels, but home production was encouraged and farm incomes were stabilized and controlled. The cost fell on the Exchequer and varied inversely with the level of world prices. Early experience of the mounting cost of an open-ended support scheme, with no upper limit on quantities produced at home and hence on the liability of the Exchequer, led to a modification in the early 1960s. Around 1963 'standard quantities' were introduced for most products, and the guaranteed price fell as these were exceeded.

The farm capital grants scheme provided assistance for investment in farm buildings, fixed machinery, land drainage, hill-land improvements and remodelling works for farm amalgamations, etc. The rates of grant-aid tended to differ among projects, although steps were taken in 1970 towards a comprehensive scheme with a basic rate of 30%. In addition to capital grants, subsidies were offered for certain current expenditures, for example those associated with the use of fertilizers and lime. The guaranteed prices, grants and subsidies were reviewed annually and published in the *Annual Review and Determination of Guarantees.*

One overall result of the old UK policy was certainly to make domestic production higher than it would have been without official support (and assuming other countries continued to support their own farmers). The policy also affected the composition of agricultural output and the efficiency of the industry. In the later years of the policy especially, guaranteed prices were manipulated to produce selective expansion. Similarly, selective use was made of grants and subsidies to bring about desired changes in the structure of the industry, and to mechanize and modernize it. The fact that between 1955 and 1972 output grew by 2.7% per annum and capital by 3.0% while employment fell by roughly 3.1% is some indication of the extent to which this happened.

The EEC arrangements for agricultural support under the CAP have objectives which are very similar to those of the previous UK policy. Article 39 of the Treaty of Rome mentions securing increases in agricultural efficiency, stabilizing agricultural markets, guaranteeing regular supplies, and ensuring reasonable prices to consumers and fair living standards for the agricultural population. The two policies are also similar in that support to farmers comes partly in the form of price guarantees and partly in capital and current grants or subsidies. However, the methods of operation are different, especially on the price-support side.

The CAP was designed to bring about free intra-Community trade in agricultural products, with uniform prices among the members and a common external tariff. Since the early 1960s 'target' prices have been negotiated for many products which, like the UK guaranteed prices, make domestic production profitable. However, under the EEC arrangements consumers pay the full target price, or a price close to it. To ensure that this is so, there is a system of variable levies on imports from the outside world, broadly designed to equalize the supply price of foreign produce (including transport costs) and the target price. In addition, there is provision for support-buying of unsold produce when prices fall below an intervention-price level. In some cases the intervention price is set close to the target price. For instance, the intervention price for grain is within 5–7% of the target price. For some products, however, such as fruit and vegetables, prices can fall significantly before support buying occurs. The central authority responsible for the policy is the European Agricultural Guidance and Guarantee Fund. Price-support is managed by the Guarantee wing of this authority. The fund receives its income from the Exchequers of member nations, contributions being determined partly by negotiation and partly in proportion to the size of the import levies arising from each nation's external trade in agricultural products.

Grant aid to farmers comes under the Guidance wing of the EAGGF but grants are actually made by each national government. Up to 1971 the assistance schemes of each country had not been harmonized, but over the 1960s an increasing proportion of the relevant expenditure was reimbursed by the Fund. The rate of grant aid for approved schemes varied up to a maximum of 25%, and as in the UK some grant aid was available for current expenditures (i.e. towards the cost of non-capital inputs).

The relative merits of the two systems are worth underlining. From a world standpoint many observers have commented unfavourably on the protectionist attitude of the CAP towards non-community produce, in contrast to the 'open-door' aspect of the earlier UK policy. Secondly, the high domestic price characteristic of the CAP has been adversely compared with the former UK 'cheap food' policy, especially as food expenditure accounts for a higher proportion of total expenditure among poorer families. (In fairness, however, it should be added that the main precondition for cheap food in the UK in the past was the low levels of world food prices which prevailed then, but which in most cases no longer prevail today). Thirdly, many observers would say that compared with the UK system the CAP is an inefficient scheme in a number of technical respects.

Thus one problem is that of surpluses of major products. The CAP's high prices and support-buying arrangements stimulate production and remove the normal market sanction on oversupply (i.e. downward price adjustment) while simultaneously discouraging demand. In the absence of other non-market controls on supply, such as the 'standard quantities' under the old UK system, this produces a chronic tendency towards the appearance of surpluses. At one time or another there have in fact been surpluses of butter (purchased to sustain a high target price for milk), grains, sugar, beef, fruit and wine. A second technical deficiency, which also arises from the open-ended nature of the support system, is that there is in principle no upper limit to the cost of support. Thirdly, the CAP as at present operated places much less emphasis on raising farm efficiency than did the old UK system. Despite the *Mansholt Plan* of 1968, which was designed to shift the emphasis of CAP away from price support towards structural reform, price support retains the major share of expenditure. Thus the guidance wing of the policy accounts for only around a third of the total cost, compared with the 60% or so going on grants and subsidies under the old UK system.

The CAP has always been a source of problems among the member countries, with their differing domestic agricultural situations and interests. Setting suitable common target prices against a background of widely differing productivity levels from country to country has been a major and recurring problem. Lengthy and often heated negotiations also occur over the size of the Farm Fund, and of individual member contributions to it, in a situation where West Germany in particular, and also Britain and Italy, are net losers in terms of budgetary contributions and receipts, and the remaining countries either benefit or receive roughly what they give. In the 1970s currency problems have also loomed large: since agricultural prices are fixed in IUA, changes in official parities within the community create a need for adjustments to maintain agricultural price uniformity in real terms. In the case of Britain, the 'green pound' – the exchange rate between sterling and IUA for agricultural purposes, which does not float – was devalued by a total of 15% in 1974 and 1975 alone.[1]

TABLE 4.4

Degree of Self-Sufficiency in Agricultural Products in the UK and EEC (Value of domestic consumption as % of domestic production)

| | 1973/74 (%) | | |
	UK	EUR-6	EUR-9
Wheat	62	114	103
Rye	38	95	94
Barley	93	110	103
Oats	99	95	95
Potatoes	98	101	100
Sugar	35	111	91
Whole Milk	100	100	100
Cheese	66	106	107
Butter	11	116	93
Eggs	97	100	100
Meat	73	96	98

Source: *Yearbook of Agricultural Statistics, 1975,* Statistics Office of the European Community.

As well as sharing in the general problems of the CAP Britain is also still undergoing problems of adjustment from the old to the new systems. Two main aspects of this problem are the phased adjustment to higher domestic prices and an endeavour to raise the UK's degree of self-sufficiency towards the EEC level (see table 4.4). For instance, the 1976 *Annual Price Review* involved an estimated 2% increase in the average family food bill, the majority of which was attributable to the phased adjustment to CAP price levels rather than to changes in those price levels themselves. And expansion of agriculture to save imports – with emphasis on milk, beef, sugar beet, cereals and sheep meat – was the major theme of a government *White Paper*[2] which envisaged a reduction in food imports of £530 million (13%) or more by 1980.

III.3   Energy

The growth of total energy consumption, at a fraction over 1% p.a. over the past fifteen years (table 4.5), has clearly been much less than the expansion of GDP over

1   See also T. Josling and S. Harris, 'Europe's Green Money', *TBR*, March 1976.
2   *Food From Our Own Resources,* Cmnd. 6020, April 1975.

the same period. The introduction of technical economies in fuel use, and relatively slow growth in some fuel-intensive industries such as iron and steel and rail, are among the factors which explain this differential growth.

The discovery of natural gas and then oil in the North Sea, together with the quadrupling of world petroleum prices by OPEC countries in 1973-4, have produced dramatic changes in UK energy procurement. Gas was the first industry to be affected, moving from stagnation to resurgence in the mid-1960s as cheap, imported gas became available to replace town gas. Growth then accelerated under the impact of even cheaper and growing North Sea supplies in the 1970s. From 1969 to 1974 sales rose at some 21% p.a. and by the latter date nearly 85% of gas used was natural. First signs of a check in this growth were seen in 1975, mainly attributable

TABLE 4.5

Total UK Inland Energy Consumption, 1960-74: Heat Supplied Basis (million therms)

Type of fuel	1960	(%)	1965	(%)	1970	(%)	1974	(%)	% change 1960-74
Coal (direct use)	23,433	(46.4)	17,409	(32.4)	11,839	(20.4)	7,519	(12.9)	−67.9%
Gas	3,187	(6.3)	3,868	(7.2)	6,182	(10.7)	12,123	(20.7)	+280.4%
Electricity	3,372	(6.7)	5,022	(9.4)	6,567	(11.3)	7,282	(12.5)	+116.0%
Petroleum (direct)	12,385	(24.5)	19,820	(36.9)	27,198	(46.9)	27,193	(46.5)	+119.6%
Other fuels[1]	8,154	(16.1)	7,568	(14.1)	6,167	(10.6)	4,371	(7.5)	−46.4%
Total	50,531	(100.0)	53,687	(100.0)	57,953	(100.0)	58,488	(100.0)	+15.7% (= 1.05 p.a.)

Source: AAS

Note: Includes coke, breeze, solid smokeless fuel and liquid fuels derived from coal.

to reduced demand by industry. On present indications a further significant increase in the share of gas in total energy use seems unlikely.

Direct use of coal was in very sharp decline over the whole period 1960-74. (The reduction in coal output was much less rapid however (cf. tables 4.5 and 4.1) because coal has been retained, by a deliberate act of government policy, as a primary energy source in electricity generation. Up to the mid 1970s there was rapid growth of electricity demand, and the electricity industry's share in total coal sales rose from 21.8% in 1957 to 56.9% in 1974.) The reason for coal's decline over the period was primarily that after 1956 petroleum had become relatively much cheaper. The 1973-4 oil price rises, however, restored coal's price competitiveness, and the industry's prospects have also been improved by the discovery of large reserves at Selby, and by technical developments in mining technology. Current plans are for re-expansion of coal production to provide an extra 42 million tons p.a. by 1980 (a 38% increase on the 1975 production level) of which 10 million tons is expected from a new pit at Selby. However, by early 1976 much of coal's price advantage over oil had been lost, and the *actual* development of coal up to 1980 will depend very much on trends in UK inflation rates, mining productivity and the level of world oil prices.

The availability of North Sea oil should not be expected to lead to any dramatic change in the future pattern of fuel use. This is because the oil, though of high quality, is expensive and in the narrow sense of the word economically viable only if world price levels are high. (Production costs of North Sea oil are approximately ten times those of the most accessible Middle East sources). In fact oil consumption in 1980 is expected to be not much different from the 1974 level. The main benefits to the UK of North Sea oil lie in other directions, particularly the balance of payments and government revenue.[1] At the time of writing new discoveries continue to raise the estimated size of the reserves and there is much talk of Britain being 'self-sufficient' in oil (best interpreted as meaning no longer a net importer of oil, since certain essential types of crude are not found in the North Sea) by 1980. However, the claims and arguments must be treated with caution. Because North Sea oil is expensive, the amount that is worth extracting — i.e. the usable reserves — is likely to remain much less than the amount it would be technically feasible to produce. Hence estimates of *usable* reserves and of the socially desirable extraction rate can vary widely according to different projections of extraction costs, the price of imported oil, and of world political developments which affect the strategic value of a secure, domestic source of supply.

Energy consumption per head in the UK is higher than in Europe, over 9% higher in total than in the nine EEC member countries, and 10% higher in the household consumption sector.[2] However, UK dependence on imported fuel is much less, 49% as against 63%. This is the result of an even more rapid rundown of coal production and switch to petroleum on the continent than in the UK. In 1950 coal supplied nearly 75% of energy needs in the Six, and petroleum only 10%. In 1971 the proportions of coal and oil among the different primary fuels in gross inland consumption in the UK and in the Nine were:

	UK	EEC-9
Hard Coal	32.6%	20.9%
Crude Petroleum	48.6%	59.4%

Comparatively speaking, therefore, the 1973 oil crisis was less serious for the UK than for the European countries.

Like agriculture, energy is the subject of a common policy in the EEC. However, the energy policy is rudimentary compared with the elaborate CAP. It is also very different in that the Community opted for a cheap energy policy during the 1960s based on imported crude oil, with some subsidies to internal coal producers. These characteristics typify the UK agricultural support system rather than CAP. One reason for the rather limited agreement over energy policy which has been achieved is that before 1967 responsibility for the various fuel industries was divided. Coal was the responsibility of the European Coal and Steel Community (ECSC); oil, natural gas and electricity were covered by the EEC; and nuclear power was the province of the European Atomic Energy Community (Euratom). After the merger of the three communities in 1967 the full extension of the Treaty of Rome to the energy sector was agreed; i.e. a common market in energy was created. Since then the European Commission has undertaken short- and medium-term forecasts of energy demand and supply, analyzed the problems likely to occur up to 1985, and identified various policy options. A number of directives, orders, regulations and decisions have also been made. Through these, members have agreed to maintain certain levels of oil stocks (ninety days by 1 January 1975) and to

---

1 For an excellent summary of the economics of North Sea Oil, see *MBR*, May 1975, pp. 11-19.
2 The gap is closing however: comparable figures for 1971 are 15.6% and 19.7% respectively.

supply regular information on oil and natural gas imports and on certain investments in oil refineries, oil and gas transport and storage facilities, and in electricity
production. Support of coal production by member governments has been
authorized, e.g. by financing stocks, and a subsidy introduced for EEC production
of coking coal and coke. Other proposals not yet adopted at the time of writing
include harmonization of fuel taxes (at a proposed level lower than the present UK
fuel-oil tax) and a detailed package containing forty-six measures, proposed in
1972, covering such things as environmental protection, developing relations between
petroleum exporting and importing countries, and defining medium-term guidelines
for the coal industry.

In the nuclear energy sector Euratom was set up to promote and co-ordinate
research, help disseminate technical information, facilitate capital investment,
establish a common market in specialized material and equipment, free movement
of capital and manpower in the nuclear field, and maintain links with other
countries and international organizations. Some progress has been made in each
of these areas, but generally less than was envisaged originally. In particular
Euratom has not been successful in co-ordinating the national nuclear R and D
programmes of members.

III.4   Transport

Provision of transport services has actually grown much faster than the output
series for the transport and communications sector suggests, at least on the
passenger side (cf. tables 4.6, 4.7, and 4.1). This is mainly because the output
series takes no account of private motoring, which is where the main increase in
passenger mileage has occurred, until checked in 1974 by the very sharp increase
in fuel costs. The impact of rising incomes on car ownership has been a major
factor. (The number of private cars currently licensed rose from 4.2m in 1957 to
13.6m in 1974). Before 1974 relative price movements would have also been a
reinforcing factor; both rail and bus fares rose very much faster over the period
than did private motoring costs. In the inland freight sector the two growth rates

TABLE 4.6

UK Inland Passenger Mileage, 1957-74[1] ('000m passenger - miles)

| Year | Air | Rail | Road | | Total |
			Public service vehicles	Private transport	
1957	0.3 (0.2%)	25.9 (19.7%)	45.5 (34.6%)	59.9 (45.5%)	131.6 (100.0%)
1965	1.0 (0.5%)	21.8 (10.6%)	39.2 (19.0%)	144.7 (70.0%)	206.7 (100.0%)
1974	1.5 (0.5%)	22.4 (8.1%)	34.2 (12.4%)	217.5 (78.9%)	275.6 (100.0%)
% Change 1957-74	400%	−13.5%	−24.9%	263.1%	109.4% = 4.4% per annum

Source: AAS

Note: 1   % figures in brackets show respective contributions to the total in any one year.

TABLE 4.7

UK Inland Freight Transport, 1957-74[1] ('000m ton—miles)

Year	Road	Rail	Coastal shipping	Inland waterways	Pipelines[2]	Total
1957	22.9 (42.5%)	20.9 (38.8%)	9.8 (18.2%)	0.2 (0.4%)	0.1 (0.2%)	53.9 (100%)
1965	42.1 (57.1%)	15.4 (20.9%)	15.3 (20.8%)	0.1 (0.1%)	0.8 (1.1%)	73.7 (100%)
1974	53.0 (65.1%)	14.3 (17.6%)	11.9 (14.6%)	0.1 (0.1%)	2.1 (2.6%)	81.4 (100%)
%Change 1957-74	131.4%	−31.6%	21.4%	−50.0%	2,000%	51.0% = 2.5% per annum

Source: AAS

Notes: 1 % figures in brackets show respective contributions to the total in any one year.
         2 Excludes the movement of gases by pipeline, and pipelines less than 10 miles long (prior to 1965).

are much more nearly in line, but there too there has been a major re-allocation of traffic towards road services (table 4.7).

Because so much of public transport is nationalized, developments in the transport sector are more than usually subject to government policy.[1] The current official thinking on transport policy was set out in a long consultative document published in April 1976.[2] This highlighted a number of problems. One was the lack of a proper framework for the co-ordination of transport policy, at both the national and local levels. A second were the problems facing certain vulnerable groups, in particular the 50% of households without a car, whose mobility has been reduced as the growth of private motoring adversely affected the revenue base of public transport and the level of services provided. This problem is especially severe in rural areas (where the proportion of households without cars is 30%). Thirdly, environmental problems were listed as requiring a greater degree of priority in the future. Finally, the document stressed the problem of transport subsidies, which rose from £300m in 1968 to £630m in 1975. The bulk of this money has gone to the railways; despite subsidies and the writing off of more than £3,000m debt over twenty years, the rail subsidy had risen to over £400m in 1975. The document stressed that these subsidies, especially to rail users, do not necessarily represent transfers to the poorer sections of the community; thus the richest 20% of households account for 50% of rail travel, whereas the poorest 40% are responsible for only 15%.

The document did not detail specific proposals, although some suggestions and probable directions of future policy were intimated. The idea of switching freight from road to rail was rejected, mainly on the ground that the impact would be slight. Thus, even if all journeys over a hundred miles were transferred to rail, only a 2—4% reduction in road traffic would result. Also, the document did not suggest

1 See also section IV.
2 'Consultative Document on Transport Policy', Department of the Environment, 13 April 1976.

that any drastic measures to curtail private motoring were being contemplated. Continued subsidies to rail transport were described as unjustifiable, and further rail fare increases are clearly to be expected, especially as the document claimed that 1975 experience showed that demand for rail services is price inelastic.[1] On the other hand, subsidies for bus operations may increase, these being more likely to find their way to poorer people and those without cars. Other forms of encouragement for buses and local transport are also envisaged, perhaps including some relaxation of the licensing system. Heavier taxes on lorries were mooted, especially heavy lorries with few axles for which current tax levels do not cover resource costs, let alone environmental costs. In road building environmental considerations may lead to more investment in by-passes around sensitive and congested areas. Finally, the document proposed that a National Transport Council be set up as a forum for policy formulation. A further paper, presumably with more definite policy proposals, was to follow after consultations with interested parties.

EEC transport policy originates from a European Commission memorandum of 1961 (the Schaus Memorandum) and an Action Programme of the following year. One of the general aims was to prevent transport from blocking the development of an effective common market for other goods and services. Transport is an important element in the cost of many commodities. If, for instance, transport undertakings in one country gave preferential treatment to certain industries or firms, this would frustrate attempts to secure competition among member states on equal terms. A second general aim was the more positive one of fostering transport developments which would stimulate trade and the opening up of markets, e.g. in the development of transport networks. Thirdly, the Community was to endeavour to create in the transport sector (as elsewhere) 'healthy competition of the widest scope'.

Subsequent detailed agreements have gone only part of the way towards achieving these objectives. Prohibitions have been introduced on discrimination in the transport sector on grounds of nationality, and on tariffs designed to give the kind of preferential treatment outlined above. An inquiry was held into the way costs of infrastructural investments were met in the member countries, in the first instance to see whether the costs fell broadly on those to whom the benefits accrued, or whether, on the other hand, infra-structural developments tended to result in tariff structures not truly reflecting the costs of providing the relevant services. There has also been harmonization of the regulations governing lorry-drivers' ages, qualifications, hours, rest periods etc. Some agreement has been reached whereby bilateral arrangements between members for quotas for public service licenses would be replaced by Community-wide agreements. Some uniformity in tariffs has also been agreed, e.g. in the form of maximum and minimum road haulage rates, between which any rate negotiated between contractor and customer should settle. It has been established that the EEC rules of competition apply to the transport sector. Finally, agreement has been reached on the 'normalization' of railway accounts to take account of any social burdens placed on the systems, with common rules for granting subsidies in such cases and a common definition of obligations that could be imposed in return for such subsidies.

---

1   Prices rose by 50% and traffic fell by 5%, implying a price-elasticity of demand of 0.1.

IV   POLICY TOWARDS THE NATIONALIZED INDUSTRIES
IV.1   Their Size and Importance

The proportion of UK economic activity which is under state control is now very large. Public enterprise, or state ownership and control, may be defined as where there is an undertaking which is publicly owned and directed by a branch of the government or a body especially set up for the purpose by the government. This definition would clearly include public administration (all central and local government activities) and defence and the public health and education services. It would also include a number of government agencies such as the British Tourist Authority, the Forestry Commission, the Herring Industry Board etc.[1] Our concern is with the nationalized industries proper, whose activities are run along commercial lines, in some sense of the word. Thus we are dealing with the Post Office, the coal, gas and electricity industries, British Airways and the British Airports Authority, the railways and other nationalized sections of transport (the Passenger Transport Authorities, the Docks Board, British Waterways, the National Freight Corporation and the National Bus Holding Company) shipbuilding and aerospace and the major part of the steel industry. Together, value-added in these industries accounts for some 10.7% of GDP. Annual gross fixed capital formation by the nationalized industries is nearly £2.7 billion per annum, compared with £3.3 billion invested by all manufacturing industries.

The extent of the public sector is, of course, a sensitive political issue, and tends to vary at the margin according to the preferences of the government of the day. Steel and freight transport have both moved in and out of public ownership. The 1970-4 Conservative Government for a while espoused a policy of 'hiving off' or selling to private concerns parts of nationalized industries which could reasonably (or profitably) be run by private enterprise. For example the coal industry was divested of some of its ancillary activities and Thomas Cook, the travel concern, was sold to a consortium of firms in May 1972. In contrast, the post 1974 Labour Government nationalized the shipbuilding and aerospace industries, formed the British National Oil Corporation and also created the National Enterprise Board, with powers to take state holdings in private companies and take over responsibility for companies such as British Leyland, Rolls Royce and others, in which the government had acquired an interest prior to the NEB's establishment.[2]

In EEC countries it is fairly general for there to be state control of electricity, gas and water, postal services, railways and parts at least of broadcasting and the national airlines. Steel, however, is generally in private hands. The French have a particularly large public sector and own among other things the Renault car manufacturers; the Italians have two giant state companies, IRI — a wide-ranging holding company — and ENI, an oil and chemicals firm. There is also the uniquely continental phenomenon of a state monopoly in certain goods for taxation purposes; that is, the state retains a monopoly profit as part of its fiscal revenue. The match industry (in France, West Germany and Italy) and the tobacco industry (in France and Italy) are examples.[3]

---

1   See R. Maurice (ed.), *National Income Statistics: Sources and Methods,* Central Statistical
    Office, HMSO, 1968.
2   See below, p. 233.
3   See D. Swann, *The Common Market* (2nd ed.), Penguin Books, 1972.

IV.2   Price and Investment Policy: Theory

The well-known economists' prescription for nationalized industry pricing is that prices should be set equal to marginal cost.[1] A simple rationale can be given for such a policy. On the one hand the demand curve for a nationalized industry's product tells us how much consumers will pay per unit for different quantities supplied, and so we interpret the demand curve as consumers' evaluation of the good or service as output is varied. On the other hand the marginal cost curve tells us the incremental cost of producing each unit, and if we can equate the money costs actually incurred by the undertaking with the true opportunity cost of diverting extra resources from alternative uses to the undertaking in question, we can construe the marginal cost curve as recording consumers' evaluation of the forgone alternative product. If consumers value the public enterprise's good more than the alternative (demand price exceeds marginal cost) then consumers' welfare can be increased by diverting more resources to the public enterprise, so increasing output, and vice versa. Hence, for an optimum level of output, price should equal marginal cost.

Unfortunately, this apparently straightforward principle is also well-known for the difficulties it raises. Firstly, an optimum is reached only if a large number of other conditions are met, including the equality of all other prices with marginal cost. Otherwise the 'second best' solution will very likely require a price not equal to marginal cost.[2] A modification of the marginal cost pricing rule which takes some of this into account is to set price equi-proportional to marginal cost. Thus if price is on average, say, 10% above marginal cost in the economy, this same margin should be included in public enterprise prices. So long as we are concerned only with the relative output levels in commodity markets this has some merit. But it will not produce an overall optimum, since income/leisure preferences will be affected and the supply of labour (and hence also total output) will be less than is consistent with an ideal; that is, optimum conditions will be fulfilled in commodity markets but not in factor markets.

Secondly, even if all necessary conditions are met, the ensuing resource allocation is optimal only within the existing distribution of income among consumers. If this distribution is not accepted as being ideal, it would be perfectly justifiable for the government to modify some or all nationalized industry prices in the name of social justice. It could be argued that this is precisely what the government does in not charging or making only token charges for some public sector goods and services, e.g. health and education.

Thirdly, price must be set equal to marginal social cost, rather than marginal private cost. Where, for instance, increased output in one industry confers external benefits by reducing production costs in other industries, marginal private costs in that industry will exceed marginal social costs, and vice versa for an industry imposing net external costs. Therefore, even if all other necessary conditions for a welfare maximum were met, a nationalized industry equating price with marginal private cost would be producing too much, from the community standpoint, if it gave rise to net external costs and too little if it conferred net external economies.

---

1   For a fuller discussion, see Ralph Turvey, *Economic Analysis and Public Enterprise,* Allen and Unwin, 1971 and *Public Enterprise,* Penguin Books, 1968.
2   See R. G. Lipsey and K. Lancaster, 'On the General Theory of Second Best', *RES,* Vol. XXIV, 1956-7, pp. 11-32.

Hence, for maximum welfare, external effects of this sort must be taken into account in both the nationalized sector and elsewhere.

Fourthly, economists are themselves divided as to whether price should be equated with short-run marginal cost (the rate of change of total costs in the short run, i.e. when some factor or factors are fixed) or with long-run marginal cost (the rate of change of total costs in the long run, when there are no fixed factors). Finally, except where there are constant returns to scale, neither short-run nor long-run marginal cost pricing will automatically ensure that total costs will be recovered from revenue. Marginal and average costs are equal only at that output at which average costs are at a minimum. Hence marginal cost pricing will exactly equate total costs and revenues only if, by chance, the output level which results happens to be this one. Otherwise, either a deficit (marginal cost is less than average cost) or a surplus (marginal cost exceeds average cost) will result. In practice, most of the nationalized industries are thought to be ones where average costs decline continuously over the relevant range of outputs, so that marginal cost is less than average cost and a deficit is likely to result. Since there is no agreed method of financing deficits (or distributing surpluses) in a way which will not affect resource allocation, there is a basic conflict between financial rectitude and pricing policies designed to optimize resource allocation.

For optimal investment by public enterprises, the two main requirements are that the costs and benefits of any project over its life are correctly evaluated, and that estimates of future costs and benefits are correctly related to the present decision-making period.[1] In evaluating costs and benefits, due account must be taken of external effects on other producers and consumers. Moreover, since market-determined prices in a 'second best' world will not necessarily reflect the true worth of inputs and outputs to the community, it will usually be necessary to attempt the difficult task of adjusting these on a socially desired basis.[2] The method of relating together costs and benefits in different periods that is generally thought best is to express the returns to an investment project in terms of net discounted present value.[3] Generally speaking, the rate of time discount used in evaluating public sector projects should be the same as is used elsewhere (and any allowance made for uncertainty should also be the same). Otherwise the relative merits of private and public sector projects will be distorted.[4]

Even if public sector projects were treated scrupulously in the desired manner outlined, the maximum benefit would not be derived from the total of funds

---

1   For a description of the methods used to evaluate investment in nationalized industries see R. Pryke, *Public Enterprises in Practice*, MacGibbon and Kee, 1971, ch. 15.

2   For an extended discussion of cost-benefit analysis see A. R. Prest and R. Turvey, 'Cost Benefit Analysis: A Survey', *EJ*, December 1965.

3   Net discounted present value (R) for any project with a life of n years is given by

$$R = \sum_{t=1}^{n} \frac{B_t - C_t}{(1+r)^t} - I$$

where B_t, C_t are benefits and costs respectively in year t, r is the rate discount and I is the initial cost. The main merits of this method over its chief rival (internal rate of return or marginal efficiency of capital) are that it always gives a unique solution and always ranks projects correctl

4   A discussion of the implications of using different rates of time discount appears in R. Pryke, *op. cit.*, ch. 16.

available for investment in the economy unless private projects were treated in
exactly the same way. In practice, private sector investments will almost invariably
be evaluated with no regard for external effects; various ways of treating uncertainty
are likely to be used; and a substantial amount of decision-making will be undertaken by rule-of-thumb methods.[1] In so far as the government is unable to regulate
all private sector investment appraisal appropriately, the best that can be hoped for
is a form of sub-optimization, the correct principles being applied in the public
sector only.

IV.3   Price and Investment Policy: Practice

A White Paper published in 1967 sets out the basis for current policy.[2] For the
first time explicit price and investment rules were laid down. On pricing, the
marginal cost principle was in fact adopted, though in addition accounting costs
were to be covered by revenue. Two- or multi-part tariffs or unit prices proportional
to marginal cost were recommended for the apportionment of fixed costs among
consumers where this is necessary to cover total costs. Social cost-benefit analysis
was proposed for investment appraisal, and it was stated that the returns on investment projects should be expressed in terms of net present value. A test discount rate
of 8% was laid down for project appraisal and later raised to 10%. The rate chosen
was expressly intended to match the return looked for by private industry on
marginal, low-risk investment. Because of differences in financing methods and tax
liability the equivalent private sector rate will be higher than any given nationalized
industry rate; the original 8% was held to be the equivalent of 15-16% in the private
sector.

The White Paper explicitly recognized that most nationalized industries undertake a mixture of commercial operations and social responsibilities. For instance
the electricity industry has had a statutory duty to extend supplies to more remote
areas, regardless of whether it is really economic to do so. The point here is not
that such activities are necessarily wrong, but that when they are undertaken both
the decision and the related costs should rest with the community at large, and
not interfere with decisions and charges relating to commercial operations. The
White Paper was very clear on this point; it stressed the need to distinguish the
two sorts of activities and provided for the government to take financial responsibility for non-commercial operations, e.g. by specific subsidies where current
costs were involved.

An existing system of financial targets for the industries was retained in the
White Paper, which since 1961 had been specified as rates of return on assets
employed. However, it was recognized that if appropriate price and investment
procedures are applied there should be little need for further safeguard to the
financial outturn, expressed as a rate of return. The main reason why financial
targets were retained appears to have been for them to act as a measure of expected
performance for comparison with actual achievement. Finally, the White Paper
specifically retained for the government the right to bring national economic
considerations to bear on the nationalized industries, e.g. by rephasing investment.

1 See NEDO, *Investment Appraisal*, HMSO, 1967.
2 *Nationalized Industries: A Review of Economic and Financial Objectives*, Cmnd. 3437,
   HMSO, November 1967.

In view of the theoretical difficulties and disputes, it would be impossible to produce a practical policy which would receive universal endorsement by economists. The White Paper could certainly be described as fairly remarkable for its attention to the kind of things thought to be important by economists; it could also be said to ride roughshod over many of the difficulties, without offering appropriate solutions.

In the first year or two after the publication of the White Paper there seems to have been some progress towards revising pricing methods, especially by British Rail and the Post Office;[1] towards eliminating cross-subsidization; and towards distinguishing commercial from other activities. By the early and mid 1970s, however, macroeconomic and financial considerations had become of overriding importance once more, as they had tended to be before 1967. Thus under the 1970-4 Conservative government nationalized industry prices were subjected to more stringent price restraint than in the private sector. This must have curtailed the freedom of the nationalized industries to adjust their price structures on marginal cost principles. It also left them in a parlous financial state. Also, the nationalized industries' investment plans were among the victims of the emergency budget of December 1973, which cut £264m from the 1974 investment programme.

This 'interference' with the nationalized industries' price and investment policies did not contravene the 1967 White Paper's recommendations, in that these explicitly reserved the right of the government to intervene on national economic grounds. Under the post 1974 Labour government the primary focus has continued to be on financial considerations. Beginning from the 1974 Budget, the attempt has been mainly to hold and then eliminate Exchequer support to the industries via price increases and economy measures. The price increases in virtually all the industries have been large, including an 87% increase in British Rail's overall charges in the two years to April 1976, and a rise in letter postal rates from 3½p to 8½p in a period of less than eighteen months. In most cases there was a significant improvement in the financial performance of the industries, one exception however being British Rail, which continued to operate at a large loss of around £500m in the year 1975-6.

Given the large size of the nationalized industries it is easy to see how governments are tempted to use them directly to help manage the economy. It is also easy to see how this can distort competition between the industries and their private sector rivals, and undermine efforts to pursue economically sound pricing and investment policies.

IV.4   Organization, Control and Productive Efficiency in the Nationalized Industries

The performance of the nationalized industries receives a great deal of attention and comment. The high degree of interest shown can no doubt be attributed to the political sensitivity of the public ownership issue, and to the fact that more information is published about the nationalized industries than about private industry. A high level of interest and concern is undoubtedly justified. Because of the extremely large scale of the operations under one administrative control, there are

---

1 The *Annual Reports* of the various industries give some idea of this progress. See also the 1968 *Transport Act*.

immense organizational problems in the nationalized industries, exceeding those of all but a few, giant, private firms. Moreover, because of the amount of real resources controlled by any one nationalized industry, the social consequences of a wrong decision or any shortfall of efficiency are more severe than those arising from similar shortcomings in most individual firms in the private sector. However, many of the problems involved in securing efficiency in the nationalized industries, whether of a technical or organizational nature, resemble those met in private enterprise undertakings. The whole question of productive efficiency is discussed in general terms in section VII below. Here we look at some particular problems which arise for nationalized industries.

It is sometimes suggested that the nationalized industries will tend to be inefficient because of their monopoly positions. But while there is often no direct competition with other 'firms' making the same product, the nationalized industries (with the possible exception of the Post Office) do face competition from close substitute products, e.g. in the energy market. Evidence that the nationalized industries are inefficient, for whatever cause, is sometimes found in the fact that at least some of them incur regular deficits. However, this is not necessarily conclusive evidence of inefficiency. It is clear from the discussion of the previous sections that a nationalized industry might be perfectly efficient and yet incur a deficit, this deficit being the inevitable outcome of the policy imposed upon the industry, and the activities required to be undertaken. In any case, surpluses of nationalized industries are not exactly comparable with profits in the private sector. Since interest, depreciation, redemption of capital and provision of reserves are chargeable against revenue, some items are excluded which would be met from private sector profits.

However, there undoubtedly are certain special difficulties associated with publicly owned industries, and these may have given rise to some losses in efficiency. The need to reconcile operating efficiency with public accountability is one problem. The one arguably requires maximum autonomy, delegation and decentralization in nationalized industries; the other inhibits this. In 1968 the Select Committee on the Nationalized Industries concluded that in the past ministers have tended to do the opposite of what Parliament originally intended.[1] Whereas they were supposed to lay down policies, but not intervene in management, they have in practice given very little policy guidance but been closely involved with many aspects of management. At the time of writing there are still widespread complaints about the nature and degree of government intervention, and this factor seems to have been an important contributory cause of the creation in early 1976 of a 'Nationalized Industries Chairman's Group', popularly referred to as a state bosses' 'union'.

Secondly, weakness in government policy — the lack of clear financial objectives, especially before 1961, and the confusion and intermingling of commercially viable and other activities, etc. — may well have reduced managerial efficiency and general morale and productivity. Thirdly, an inadequate salary structure for top and middle management may have reduced the nationalized industries' ability to recruit, retain and suitably motivate high-calibre management. In 1969 a report of the NBPI found that top salaries and retirement pensions were substantially lower in nationalized industries than in private industry, and that the difference was not due to differences

---

1 *Ministerial Control of the Nationalized Industries*, H. of C. 371-I, II and III, 1968.

in responsibilities.[1] Large increases for chairmen of the main undertakings were recommended and implemented from £11,000 or £12,500 to £17,000 or £20,000 respectively. Later on, however, the government did not adopt the recommendations for increases of a further, independent study published at the end of 1974,[2] and the relatively low salaries offered have been advanced by many observers as a major cause of recent difficulties in finding candidates to take over the running of, for instance, the Post Office, BSC, British Leyland and the NEB.

The 1967 White Paper discussed in the preceding section made some explicit references to general efficiency. Some specific items were mentioned, including the efficient use of qualified and skilled manpower; and the need for labour saving, flexibility on both sides of the industries towards manning practices and the abandonment of restrictive practices, etc. In addition, the heavy emphasis on correct methods of investment appraisal may be regarded as specific guidance on an important aspect of efficiency. A sanction on the efficiency of the industries under the 1964-70 Labour Government was the involvement of the NBPI, charged with both a general task of carrying out efficiency audits, and a specific duty of examining the underlying justification for price increases, their timing, and the extent to which costs could be reduced by increased efficiency. These tasks have to some extent now been transferred to the Monopolies Commission and the Price Commission.

On the organizational side there have been a number of important developments over recent years. Several were embodied in the 1968 Transport Act which, inter alia, eliminated the regional divisions of British Rail; set up a National Freight Corporation and Freight Integration Council; created Passenger Transport Authorities for four major conurbations (now increased to five) and transferred the London Transport Board to the GLC making, effectively, a sixth, and established a National Bus Company for England and Wales, and a Scottish Transport Group. Then from October 1969 the Post Office, previously a government department, became a public corporation, to be run on more commercial lines. The British Steel Corporation was reorganized into a system based on product divisions[3] (four steel-making, one for constructional engineering, and one for chemical activities). Formerly there were four large groups, under which system most products fell within more than one group. Finally, there has been a major reorganization of the gas industry. The Gas Council and the area boards have been replaced by a single authority, the British Gas Corporation. A recurring theme in these organizational changes was clearly to provide for better coordination and planning throughout the whole of the particular industries concerned.

IV.5   EEC Provisions

The EEC members have not so far devised a common policy on the control and financing of public enterprise. On the other hand the publicly-owned industries and firms are, of course, affected by Community policies towards industry, such

---

1 NBPI Report No. 107, *Top Salaries in the Private Sector and Nationalized Industries,* Cmnd. 3970, March 1969.
2 *Report on Top Salaries,* Cmnd. 5846 Dec. 1974. This would have given the chairmen of BSC and The Post Office £40,000 per annum.
3 See British Steel Corporation, *Third Report on Organization,* H. of C. 60, 1969-70.

as the competition and regional policies, and the common policies towards energy and transport. All of these are discussed elsewhere in this chapter. Two other issues are of relevance for the UK in this context.

The first concerns the use of subsidies by member governments. As we have seen these are an important feature of the UK policy, but they are contrary to the spirit and rules of the Community. This is because if one particular member government subsidizes a loss-making industry of its own the free play of competition within the Community-wide industry would be inhibited. However, in practice it can be hard for the Community to apply meaningful sanctions on such behaviour. Moreover, it could be that UK subsidies for the strictly non-commercial activities taken by the nationalized industries would be sanctioned, e.g. under the 'harmonization of accounts' procedure agreed for railways.[1] On the other hand some limitations could be set on the precise nature of the social obligations placed upon the industries. More difficulty is likely to arise over any remaining annual revenue supports to cover operating deficits after allowance for social obligations is made, and cases where, from time to time, the accumulated deficits of UK industries like coal and rail in particular are written off, or interest payments suspended.

Secondly, two of the UK nationalized industries come within the sphere of influence of the ECSC, the history and role of which is some importance.[2] The ECSC is the oldest of the three communities (ECSC, EEC and Euratom) and was the first step towards European integration, i.e. the first common market. Among other things, the 1951 Treaty of Paris abolished duties and quotas on trade in coal and steel among member states; discrimination in prices, delivery terms and transport rates; and restrictive practices leading to collusive sharing or exploitation of markets. Up to 1967 the ECSC had separate institutions but the relevant bodies are now those of the three merged communities, the European Commission and Parliament, the Council of Ministers and the European Court of Justice. One additional body which survived from the earlier period was a high level consultative committee, composed of producers, consumers, workers and dealers.

The ECSC maintains a policy of free trade in coal and basic iron and steel products. Producers are required to publish all prices at selected basing points, and transport charges also have to be published or notified. Levies are made upon coal and steel producers, currently equivalent to around 0.2% of production value but with some variation according to product. Various kinds of central benefits are paid out, in the form of assistance to redundant or transferred coal and steel workers (provided this is at least matched by the member government); contributions to technical research projects; and loans at attractive rates for investment projects capable of employing redundant ECSC workers in the declining coal and steel areas, housing for ECSC workers and investment projects to facilitate the capital investment programmes of the coal and steel industries. At the time of writing redundancy assistance has been agreed for UK steel workers and is under negotiation for coal workers. Also, contributions have been received for steel industry research undertaken in 1973, and other discussions are in progress. As in most EEC affairs, it seems that much depends on the process of negotiations, in this case between the European Commission and the UK government.

The ECSC regulations obviously provide an additional set of considerations for

---

1 See above, section III.4
2 See P. M. Topley, 'The E.C.S.C.: the oldest of the Communities', *TI*, 17 January 1974.

the industries, affecting pricing in particular. In steel and to some extent coal and transport modifications of existing practices have been required. In principle, however, there is no reason why the ECSC requirements should clash with the basic marginal-cost pricing rules and investment procedures which are now recommended practice in the UK nationalized industries.

V   COMPETITION POLICY AND CONSUMER PROTECTION[1]
V.1   Introduction

A recent wide-ranging piece of legislation has brought together and extended policy measures in two main areas that were previously separate: control of anti-competitive market structures and practices, and other consumer protection. The 1973 Fair Trading Act is now the basis of the law dealing with dominant-firm monopoly, merger and restrictive trade practices. It also codifies and extends previous legislation offering a variety of safeguards to consumers. The following discussion begins by examining the need for such legislation, in the light of the theories outlined in section I. Some background information on the degree of competitiveness in UK markets is then presented, before the UK legislation is described and its past achievements assessed. The discussion concludes with an outline of EEC policy measures in this area.

V.2   The Need for Policy Measures

Whichever theory of the firm we take, monopolistic market structures and practices can be shown to raise questions of public policy. The precise criticisms, however, vary somewhat according to our choice of theoretical model.

Under profit maximizing assumptions there are four main criticisms of monopoly. First, price exceeds marginal cost, with consequential resource misallocation and reduced consumers' welfare. Secondly, supernormal profits may be earned (if price also exceeds average cost), so that income is redistributed in favour of producers. Thirdly, possession of market power permits firms to undertake practices such as price discrimination among consumers and cross-subsidization among activities. These can also reduce welfare and, furthermore, can be used to protect a monopoly position. A fourth argument is that monopolists will tend to be inefficient, costs being higher than they need be because the presence of excess profits blunts the desire to seek out and apply cost-minimizing techniques. However, this argument is not strictly consistent with profit maximization, since it implies pursuit of some other objectives, e.g. leisure, at some point.

The main significance of monopoly under the managerial theories is that the existence of market power is likely to increase the tendency for firms to pursue managerial objectives other than profit. The criticisms of monopoly derived from the profit maximizing model may not apply, but managerial behaviour need not lead to genuine cost-minimization (e.g. in Williamson's model organizational slack is

---

1   See also J. D. Gribbin, 'Recent Anti-Trust Developments in the U.K', *Anti-Trust Bulletin* Vol. XX, No. 2, Summer 1975; Alex Hunter, *Competition and the Law,* Allen & Unwin, 1966, and *Monopoly and Competition,* Penguin, 1969.

typically present)[1] and, in general, a part of the stream of resources being generated by the firm is diverted for the satisfaction of managerial aims (sales, growth, discretionary investment, staff, slack, etc.) and away from consumers' welfare. The behavioural principle of 'satisficing' behaviour suggests that although monopoly potential may exist it will not necessarily be exploited. Whether the type of market structure will affect efficiency under the behavioural theory would depend on the effect on search and decision procedures, and little is known about this at present. In general, if the behavioural theory is adopted, the whole basis for discussing monopoly in terms of resource allocation and supernormal profits is lost.

Exactly why firms merge has never been explained satisfactorily in the theoretical models. But clearly one effect may be to create monopoly situations (though this need not be the sole objective), with consequences as outlined above under the different theories. Official thinking on mergers[2] emphasizes the potentially anti-competitive effects of both horizontal and vertical mergers, but recognizes that there may be substantial efficiency gains from scale economies, rationalization of production, etc.[3] Conglomerate mergers are seen as a special category. Both the anti-competitive effects and the potential for increased efficiency are considered likely to be smaller than for horizontal and vertical mergers, but there is concern that many may take place for purely financial reasons, and yield very little benefit in terms of increased efficiency, but at some anti-competitive risk. Moreover, it is argued that conglomerate mergers could lead to substantial losses in operating efficiency.[4]

Under profit maximization the argument against restrictive trade practices is, broadly, that by concerted action a group of firms may achieve the same result as a single firm monopolist. Thus the formal model explaining joint profit maximization by two or more firms turns out to be identical with the one explaining multi-plant monopolist behaviour.[5] Moving away from the formal model, it is also argued that if prices are set at a level which allows the least efficient to survive many firms will earn abnormal profits without difficulty, the inefficient will not be eliminated, and the general competitive spur to efficiency will be lost; and that restrictive

---

1 See above, p. 186.
2 See *Annex* to Monopolies Commission, *The Rank Organisation Limited and De la Rue Company Limited,* 298, H. of C. 1968/9, and Board of Trade, *Mergers: A Guide to Board of Trade Practice,* HMSO, 1969.
3 Horizontal mergers are between competitors in the same market, vertical mergers are between customer and supplier. The first will, other things being equal, increase market concentration (the share of supply in the hands of a few large suppliers). Vertical mergers threaten competition where, for instance, a manufacturer takes over the firm supplying raw material both to himself and to his competitors, and would be able to charge disadvantageous prices to them, or where a manufacturer secures control over the sales outlets for both his own and his competitors' products.
4 Conglomerate mergers are those where there has previously been neither vertical nor horizontal links between the parties. Efficiency gains would probably be mainly financial and managerial; efficiency losses might arise because of the complexity of operations under one control. Competition might be harmed if the conglomerate firm, by virtue of its size, became accepted as a price leader in a particular market, or fought its way to a monopoly position in that market via a price war, accepting temporary losses in that market, compensated for by profits earned elsewhere. See also J. D. Gribbin, 'The Conglomerate Merger', *Applied Economics,* 1976, 8, 19-35.
5 See, e.g. K. J. Cohen and R. M. Cyert, *Theory of the Firm,* Prentice-Hall, 1956, p. 235. In practice the degree of coordination of activities required is greater than would normally occur under a restrictive agreement between firms.

agreements may also provide a base for collusive action to forestall the entry of new competition, suppress new techniques and developments, etc. How the managerial theories might qualify these arguments has yet to be shown. In a behavioural analysis we should probably be much less suspicious of the motives underlying restrictive practices than if we assume profit maximization. Assuming profit maximization, restrictive practices would not exist unless profits were thereby raised; under behavioural analysis this need not be so. Moreover, restrictive practices fit fairly easily into the behavioural concept of the 'negotiated environment', the implication being that they are primarily uncertainty-reducing phenomena, perhaps with advantages in facilitating forward planning, etc.

Clearly the criticisms of monopoly and monopolistic practices do vary somewhat according to our choice of theoretical model. Moreover, one of the problems confronting policy-makers is that whichever model we take, monopoly or monopolistic practices may confer advantages as well as disadvantages. For instance, against adverse effects of monopoly on resource allocation and income distribution under the profit maximization hypothesis is the fact that, if scale economies are to be exploited, there may be room for only one firm of minimum optimal scale in some markets. Moreover, it has been vigorously argued (though not universally agreed) that the security and profitability of monopoly is an important enabling condition for technical progress.[1] It has also been pointed out[2] that an active merger market may make firms more efficient than they would otherwise be, for the companies most likely to be taken over are those which are operating at a high level of slack, have a correspondingly low level of profit, and so are poorly rated on the stock market. A 'take-over raider' who hopes to make the firm more efficient will thereby make a capital gain. However, such a threat, presumably accompanied by threatened displacement of management, may well serve to keep the present management 'on its toes'.

A further problem confronting policy makers, though one arising only if profit maximizing assumptions are retained, concerns the 'second-best'. Where competition does not prevail in every other market, removal of an individual monopoly or monopolistic practice cannot be relied upon to increase welfare (as a result of the ensuing change in resource allocation), and may indeed reduce it.[3]

The control of anti-competitive market structures and practices is itself a form of consumer protection, since the exercise of market power is typically at the expense of the consumers' interests. This aspect apart, economic theory does not place much emphasis on the need for consumer protection. In the theory consumers are assumed to have a complete ordering of their preferences for different goods and services based on full information about the characteristics of the commodities and the utility to be gained from consuming them. Consumers then attempt to maximize their utility, faced with their income and market-determined prices. Provided these prices (including the price of labour and hence income) are competitively determined, the theory implies that all is well with the consumer. In

---

1 See Section VII below and J. Schumpeter, *Capitalism, Socialism and Democracy,* Allen and Unwin, 1943; J. K. Galbraith, *American Capitalism,* Hamish Hamilton, 1956 (revised edition), Ch. 7; J. Jewkes, D. Sawers and R. Stillerman, *The Sources of Invention,* Macmillan, 1969; and C. F. Carter and B. R. Williams, *Industry and Technical Progress,* Oxford, 1957, Ch. 11.

2 See B. Hindley, 'Capitalism and Corporation', *Economica,* November 1969.

3 See above, p. 201 and R. G. Lipsey and K. Lancaster, *op. cit.*

practice the consumer is not fully and costlessly informed, and may not be able to judge the utility he will derive from a certain good. He may not, for example, realize that a drug may be unsafe under certain conditions, or that food may be too old for use and he may be faced by confusing packaging or subjected to misleading claims by advertisers or retailers. Lastly, he may not be able to choose how much or how little service he obtains with a good.

There is nothing to guarantee that it is in the manufacturers' best interests for consumers to exercise a totally free and informed choice. It is this potential divergence of interests which creates the need for policy measures.

V.3   Structural Conditions in UK Markets

According to orthodox micro-theory the main structural characteristics of markets which determine market conduct and performance are the degree of actual competition, measured by seller concentration; the degree of potential competition, reflected in the height of barriers to the entry of new competition; the extent of product differentiation in the market; and the rate of growth or decline of demand.[1] All of these have a bearing on the degree of market power enjoyed by firms in a market, and it is control over the exercise of such power that competition policy attempts. Unfortunately, systematic information on structural conditions in the UK is limited to the first characteristic only, seller concentration.

TABLE 4.8

Seller Concentration in Selected UK Markets, 1968[1]

Concentration class[2] (range of five-firm concentration ratio, %)	Number of product groups in class	%
0 – 9	0	0.0
10 – 19	8	2.4
20 – 29	20	5.9
30 – 39	28	8.2
40 – 49	34	10.0
50 – 59	47	13.8
60 – 69	36	10.6 ·
70 – 79	38	11.2
80 – 89	46	13.5
90 – 100	83	24.4
TOTAL	340	100.0

Source: Census of Production, 1968.

Notes: 1 The markets included are sub-Minimum List Heading product groups in mining and quarrying and manufacturing, for which five-firm concentration ratios are available.

2 The meaning of this column is that there are no product groups in which the largest five firms account for less than 10% of total sales, eight in which they account for 10–19%, and so on.

---

1 See J. S. Bain, *Industrial Organization,* 2nd edition, Wiley, 1968, and R. Caves, *American Industry: Structure, Conduct and Performance,* 2nd edition, Prentice-Hall, 1967.

The most comprehensive source of concentration data is the Census of Production. The 1968 Census gave five or seven firm concentration ratios (combined market shares of the largest five or seven sellers) for 340 markets, or product groups. Table 4.8 summarizes the information given, showing the numbers of markets within specified concentration ranges and the proportion of the total in each class. The striking feature of table 4.8 is that in almost one-quarter of the 340 markets five firms held 90% or more of total sales, while in only 16.5% of markets was the top five firms' share under 40%.

From an analytical viewpoint the main question is how far the UK markets fall into the 'atomistic', oligopolistic or monopolized categories, for which theoretical models exist. Since concentration ratios tell us nothing about the size distribution among the largest firms, Census data can tell us only about the division between atomistic and non-atomistic markets, the latter including both oligopoly and monopoly. Without supplementary information even this division is not easily made. The first two concentration classes are almost certainly atomistic, but when the five firm ratios exceed 30% the possibility of some recognized interdependence among the market leaders, or of one firm among the five exerting some form of leadership, must be recognized. When the ratio exceeds 50%, the probability of this must be reckoned very high. Thus, on the basis of the markets included in table 4.8 no more than 8.3% of the three hundred and forty markets can safely be assumed non-atomistic. An alternative approach is to base the division on previous empirical results relating seller concentration in different markets to their performance and especially to differences in profit rates, which we should expect from neoclassical theory to be higher in non-atomistic markets. One pioneering study for the US found systematic differences according to whether or not the seven firm concentration ratio exceed 70%.[1] Making a notional adjustment for the fact that table 4.8 has five firm ratios, we might guess that at least 40–45% of the three hundred and forty markets came above the critical line in 1968.

One snippet of information on the incidence of single, dominant firms was contained in a Parliamentary answer in 1970. This suggested that in 1965 there were one hundred and fifty-six product areas where one firm had 50% or more of the market.[2]

Concentration data prior to 1963 generally related to MLH categories of the SIC, i.e. broad industry groupings rather than markets. And before 1958 official concentration statistics were published in the form of three-firm ratios based on employment shares, rather than shares of sales. All of this makes it difficult to monitor changes in seller concentration accurately. However, the general conclusion of various published studies is that concentration has been increasing over time, and at a much faster rate since the late 1950s than previously. Thus, one early study found that in forty-one out of two hundred industries for which accurate comparisons were possible concentration increased in twenty-seven trades over the period 1935-51 and fell in only fourteen.[3] Between 1951 and 1958 there was apparently a somewhat similar tendency, concentration increasing in thirty-six of sixty-three industries and falling in sixteen, with two showing no change and nine

1 J. S. Bain, *op. cit.*
2 *Hansard*, April 1970. Reprinted as Appendix A in G. Walshe, *Recent Trends in Monopoly in Great Britain*, C.U.P., 1974.
3 R. Evely and I. M. D. Little, *Concentration in British Industry*, C.U.P., 1960.

undetermined.[1] A recently published analysis of the period 1958-63 reveals that the unweighted average concentration ratio for two hundred and fourteen market or product areas rose from 55.7% to 58.6% (in terms of the average weighted by total sales in each market, the rise was from 65.8% to 69.0%).[2] Analysis of a sample of thirty markets out of the two hundred and fourteen suggested that merger activity had been responsible for around one third of the net change in concentration overall and one half of the total change in those cases where concentration had increased. Between 1963 and 1968 there was a further and more rapid increase in concentration levels, especially pronounced where concentration levels were already high, and giving rise to the situation described in table 4.8.

Alongside this trend towards a higher degree of seller concentration in individual markets there has been a similar, accelerating increase in overall concentration, as measured by the share in net output of the hundred largest firms in the economy. Before the first world war this was less than 20%, and rose by some five percentage points every ten years up to around 1958, when the figure was 33%. Over the next twelve years the rate of increase roughly trebled, so that in 1970 the hundred largest firms accounted for no less than 50% of net output. The precise connection between overall concentration and seller concentration in individual markets is not well documented. But a recent source indicates that of the hundred largest manufacturing companies between 1968 and 1974 approximately half were known to have two or more 'monopolies' (25% shares in particular markets) and of these twenty companies had five or more monopolies.[3]

TABLE 4.9

Seller Concentration in Selected Markets, UK and some EEC Countries, 1963[1]

Concentration class (range of four-firm concentration ratio, %)	UK No.	%	France No.	%	Italy No.	%	Netherlands No.	%	Belgium No.	%
0 – 9	7	5.98	42	43.30	36	36.73	13	13.40	13	13.83
10 – 29	47	40.17	43	44.33	43	43.88	44	45.36	34	36.17
30 – 59	43	36.75	11	11.34	18	18.36	23	23.71	32	34.04
60 – 100	20	17.08	1	1.03	1	1.02	17	17.52	15	15.96
Total number of industries	117	(100.0)	97	(100.0)	98	(100.0)	97	(100.0)	94	(100.0)

Sources: M. C. Sawyer, 'Concentration in British Manufacturing Industry', *OEP,* November 1971 pp. 352-78 for the UK figures and Louis Phlips, *Effects of Industrial Concentration, A Cross Section Analysis for the Common Market,* North Holland, 1971.

Notes: 1 The markets are roughly equivalent to Minimum List Heading level for the UK and the other countries. The figures are derived in very similar ways.

1 See W. G. Shepherd, 'Changes in British Industrial Concentration 1951-58', *OEP,* 1966, and K. D. George, 'Changes in British Industrial Concentration 1957-58', *JIE,* July 1967.
2 P. E. Hart, M. A. Utton and G. Walshe, *Mergers and Concentration in British Industry,* C.U.P. for the *NIESR,* 1973.
3 J. D. Gribbin, 'The Conglomerate Merger', *Applied Economics,* 1976, 8, pp. 19-35.

The inescapable conclusion is that UK economic activity is relatively highly concentrated in the hands of a fairly small number of firms, and that this concentration is increasing. Less up to date data suggest the level of market concentration is much higher than in at least two of Britain's major European partners, France and Italy (table 4.9). Concentration in Belgium and the Netherlands is much the same as in the UK, but high concentration in these countries is to be expected in view of the much smaller total markets; if firm size is governed at all closely by minimum efficient scale of production, which varies little from country to country, seller concentration is bound to be higher where total market size is less. No comparable data is available for West Germany.

V.4   Policy Measures

The Fair Trading Act of 1973[1] provided for the appointment of a Director General of Fair Trading, to centralize the application of competition and consumer protection policies. Previously this responsibility had been rather widely shared.

The 1973 Act repealed the earlier Monopolies Acts of 1948 and 1965, which had created powers of control over dominant firm monopolies. However, the 1973 Act contained provisions similar to but more wide-ranging than those enacted in the earlier legislation. Monopolies in the UK are not presumed illegal per se, as they are in the United States, but there is provision for review of monopoly situations by the Monopolies Commission (MC), which is an independent administrative tribunal, supported by a research staff. Monopoly references may be made either by ministers or the director general (subject to veto). The latter is expected to provide a broader-based view of the state of competition in the economy, to which end he has a responsibility to collect data on market structure and the behaviour of firms, on which the MC may draw. Merger references, on the other hand, are the sole prerogative of the secretary of state.

Dominant-firm situations may be referred if the firm holds at least one quarter of total sales in the relevant market. (Prior to 1973 the figure was one third). The market share rule also applies to reference of proposed merger cases, which may alternatively be referred if the gross assets are £5m or more. One new feature introduced by the 1973 Act is that the market share test may be applied to sales in a particular local area, rather than at the national level only. Responsibility for acting upon the recommendations of MC reports rests with the appropriate minister whose task it is to make the necessary statutory orders. In practice the Director General of Fair Trading has been asked by the secretary of state to discuss the recommendations with the firms concerned, and when appropriate secure undertakings to implement them.

Anti-competitive practices of firms are now subject to constraints imposed under the 1973 Fair Trading Act, the 1956 and 1968 Restrictive Trade Practices Acts and the 1964 Resale Practices Act. Under the legislation, uncompetitive practices adopted by firms in their capacity as employers, uncompetitive practices adopted by nationalized industries and restrictive labour practices are liable to investigation by the MC. In the latter case, however, the intention is to stimulate informed discussion only, and there is no power to make orders based on the MC's conclusions.

---

1   A useful summary of the Act appears in *TI,* 9 August 1973, pp. 301-5.

Other types of anti-competitive practice are dealt with by the Restrictive Practices Court, originally set up under the 1956 Act. At that stage the scope of the legislation was limited to the supply of goods: specifically it embraced agreements under which two or more persons accept restrictions relating to the price of goods, conditions of supply, quantities or descriptions, processes, or areas and persons supplied. In 1968 'information agreements' were also included, that is agreements under which no restrictions are accepted, but information concerning prices, conditions etc., is exchanged. The 1973 Act permitted the extension of the legislation to cover the supply of services, and action implementing this provision was taken in early 1976.

The general procedure with restrictive agreements is that they must be registered, and it is the director general's responsibility (formerly that of the Registrar of Restrictive Practices) to bring them before the court. This has the status of a high court, and consists of five judges and ten other members appointed for their knowledge and experience of industry, commerce or public affairs. Agreements are presumed contrary to the public interest, and the onus is on the parties to prove the reverse by seeking exemption under one or more of eight escape clauses or 'gateways'. Valid grounds for exemption may be found if it can be shown that the restriction gives protection from injury to the public; benefits consumers; is necessary to counteract measures taken by others to prevent competition, or to counterbalance a monopoly or monopsony; avoids local unemployment; promotes exports; is required to maintain some other restriction which the court finds to be not contrary to the public interest; or does not directly or indirectly restrict or discourage competition to any material degree. If a case is made out on one or other of these grounds, the court has to be further satisfied that, on balance, benefits to the public outweigh detriments. Otherwise the agreement is declared void, and continuation would be in contempt of court.

There is a time limit for the registration of agreements,[1] and penalties for non-registration, and interim orders may be made on registered agreements, while a final decision on them is being made. The relevant minister may exempt certain agreements which he deems to be in the national interest or intended to hold down prices.

One particular restrictive practice is the subject of its own act. This is 'resale price maintenance' dealt with by the Resale Prices Act 1964. Prior to 1964 it was the manufacturers' general practice to specify actual (as opposed to maximum) prices at which their product should be retailed, with sanctions for non-compliance. The act itself was very similar in form to the law on restrictive practices in general including a general prohibition and 'escape clauses'. Although resale price maintenance remains in a few trades, for instance in the supply of books, it has in many cases been superseded by the device of 'recommended' retail prices, which are in effect maximum prices. This device has been investigated by the MC which concluded that it operated with different effects in different industries, not always contrary to the public interest.

Monopoly and restrictive practice legislation is now both comprehensive and detailed, after a quarter of a century of modifications to remedy shortcomings and fill in perceived gaps in the earlier acts. By contrast, the concept of overall

---

1 The 'call up' for registration of agreements relating to commercial services specified a three month period from 22 March to 21 June 1976.

government responsibility for consumer protection (as opposed to piecemeal responsibility) is quite new. The 1973 Act is accordingly much more general in this area. The Director General of Fair Trading is again assigned a key position.

He has a duty to collect and assess information about commercial activities, in order to seek out trading practices which may affect consumers' economic interests. If he finds areas in which there is cause for concern, he then has two options. The director general may either make recommendations to the relevant minister as to action which might be useful in altering the malpractice, whether it concerns consumers' economic interest or their health, safety and so on. Or, presumably where more severe action is demanded, he may set in motion a procedure which could lead to the banning of a particular trade practice. To do this he makes a 'reference' along with proposals for action, which goes to a new foundation of the Act, the Consumer Protection Advisory Committee, which considers whether his proposals are justified, given that the practice is covered by the legislation. This body, after taking evidence from interested parties, reports to the relevant minister, who then makes an order, when appropriate, with the agreement of Parliament.

Another of the director general's main functions in the area of consumer protection is to make sure that those who are persistently careless of their existing legal obligations to consumers mend their ways, either by his seeking written assurance or, failing this, in the courts. Lastly, the director general has obligations to pursue an informal dialogue with industry; to publish information and advice for consumers; and to encourage trade associations to use voluntary codes of practice to protect consumers.

Finally, the Fair Trading Act contains a section outlawing those schemes whereby salesmen gain commission mainly by recruiting subordinates, known as 'pyramid selling'. The director general is not involved, and this section of the act is rather outside the scope of our discussion.

V.5   Policy Impact

A total of nearly fifty monopoly situations had been investigated by the Monopolies Commission by the end of 1975. In addition, several hundred merger cases had been screened since 1965. However, only a small proportion were actually referred to the Commission; for instance, between November 1973 (when the Fair Trading Act came into force) and the end of 1975 over three hundred merger cases were screened, of which only eleven were referred. The total number of restrictive practices registered by the end of 1975 was 3,103, of which 2,788 had been abandoned. Of course, not all these cases were heard by the court. Many were terminated voluntarily after the results of key cases became known, and others were simply left to expire.

On the consumer protection side, three references to the CPAC were made between 1973 and the end of 1975, concerning the purported exclusion of inalienable consumer rights; pre-payment for goods; and the sale of goods without revealing that the sale was in the course of a business. Voluntary codes of practice were introduced in a number of trades, including the servicing of electrical appliances, package holidays and the sale of new and used cars. Over the same period, the Office of Fair Trading investigated various other practices (e.g. bargain offer claims, party-plan and door-to-door selling, and one-day sales) and reviewed the conduct of seventy-eight individual companies, of which nineteen subsequently gave assurances about their future business practices. In addition, the working of the

1968 Trades Descriptions Act was reviewed, and the Office of Fair Trading issued nine consultative documents concerning the implementation of the 1974 Consumer Credit Act.

In very bare outline, these are the results of competition policy as developed in the UK over nearly thirty years. Bearing in mind the comparatively small number of single-firm monopoly cases investigated, reservations about the quality of the analysis in some cases,[1] and an unaggressive approach in applying remedial measures, it seems unlikely that this particular strand of the policy has had a marked general effect on seller concentration levels or on the behaviour of dominant firms. In the merger field, a small number of proposals has been stopped, or allowed to proceed only after certain assurances had been given. Again, in purely numerical terms the impact of policy can hardly be said to have been widespread. If the official assessments of the public interest and the likely consequences can be relied upon, one could argue that it is only in a very small minority of cases that mergers have undesirable effects. However, it can be said that the merger area is one in which there is a strong need for more research into causes and effects. Until this is forthcoming, the success or otherwise of merger policy is hard to judge.

The control of restrictive practices has undoubtedly done away with a great mass of overt price-fixing that had existed before 1956. But this is not necessarily conclusive evidence of success. Firstly, both the escape clauses in the 1956 Act and the quality of the court's reasoning and decisions have been adversely criticized.[2] Indeed, doubts have been expressed over the suitability of judicial practices for resolving complex economic issues. Secondly, it is questionable how far the abandonment of restrictive practices has actually affected behaviour in the markets concerned. Especially where the practices abandoned are in fairly concentrated, oligopolistic markets, they may merely formalize the mutually accommodating behaviour which would in any case occur. Removal of an agreement in these circumstances would not touch the underlying, structural cause of this behaviour.[3]

The variety and detail of the consumer protection activities undertaken since 1973 is in some ways impressive. As expected, the overwhelming emphasis has been on voluntary solutions: negotiated codes, assurances and the like. The advantages of this approach, its flexibility, cost-effectiveness and constructiveness, are heavily stressed by the Director General of Fair Trading in his first two annual reports.[4] Its main drawback is perhaps that voluntary cooperation is most likely to be forthcoming and effective where it is least needed.

V.6   EEC Provisions[5]

Articles 85 and 86 of the Treaty of Rome set out EEC regulations dealing with

---

1 See C. K. Rowley, *The British Monopolies Commission,* Allen and Unwin, 1966 and A. Sutherland, *The Monopolies Commission in Action,* C.U.P., 1970.
2 See, e.g. R. B. Stevens and B. S. Yamey, *The Restrictive Practices Court,* Weidenfeld and Nicolson, 1965, and D. Swann *et al, Restrictive Practice Legislation in Theory and Practice,* Allen & Unwin, 1974.
3 See J. B. Heath, 'Restrictive Practices and After', *M.S.,* May 1961.
4 H. of C., 370, 21 May 1975 and H. of C., 288, 7 April 1976.
5 For a useful summary of the Community's competition policy see D. W. McKenzie, 'Fair Competition in the EEC', *TI,* 13 December 1973. See also D. Swann, *op. cit.,* pp. 55-68 and 159-75.

monopolies, mergers and restrictive practices. The European Commission is the body responsible for applying the policies and investigating breaches in them.

The most fully developed parts of the regulations are those relating to restrictive practices. These prohibit all agreements, such as price fixing and market sharing, which prevent, restrict or distort competition in the EEC and extend over more than one member country. As in the UK however, exemption may be gained via a 'gateway' if the agreement improves production or distribution or promotes progress. There is also provision for block exemptions. At present these apply in two narrowly-defined cases — one deals with certain types of exclusive dealing agreement between a supplier and a distributor, and the other with certain arrangements for specialization of production. Finally, the Commission has indicated that certain general areas of agreement are not caught by the regulations, mainly because of their limited impact on inter-member trade, or because they deal with rather peripheral or partial co-operation between firms. Firms wishing to test whether their agreements conflict with the legislation are invited to apply for 'negative clearance' while their cases are being investigated.

EEC monopoly regulations are less clear-cut since, although any abuse of a dominant position within the EEC is prohibited if it affects trade between member countries, it is not clear as yet what sort of market share criterion constitutes dominance, or what abuses will be covered by the regulations. Even less clear up to 1971 was the position of mergers. Until the case of Continental Can (an American firm) in that year it was unsettled whether Articles 85 and 86 could be applied to merger cases. Although this particular merger was allowed on appeal to the European Court of Justice, the implicit extension of the legislation to mergers was accepted. Since then a proposed regulation concerning mergers has been approved by the European Parliament.[1] This empowers The European Commission to prohibit mergers involving combined assets of 200 million I.U.A. or 25% of a national market where the merger in question creates or strengthens a position of the parties 'to hinder effective competition in the common market or in a substantial part thereof', and to exempt such anti-competitive mergers in particular cases where this is 'indispensable to the attainment of an objective which is given priority treatment in the common interest of the Community'. It further provides for a compulsory system of advance clarification in cases of large mergers involving combined assets of 1 billion I.U.A. unless the acquired firm has assets of less than 30 million I.U.A.

It is perhaps appropriate that EEC competition policy should focus rather more on restrictive practices than monopolies, given the lower seller concentration levels in at least some EEC countries, and given the long history of cartelization in countries such as Germany. Besides, economic integration of the member countries obviously involves breaking down many such restrictive agreements. Even in the area of restrictive practices however, it is only comparatively recently that the Commission has been shown to have any teeth in dealing with severely anti-competitive cartel practices, by imposing fines on such groups as the 'Aniline Trust' who negotiated more-or-less simultaneous price increases in the Market, and on a group of firms fixing prices and market shares in the market for quinine. Some agreements between UK firms may well fall foul of the EEC regulations. For

---

1 For a discussion of the regulation, which is under consideration by a special working party of experts from member states, see Kurt Market, 'EEC Competition Policy in Relation to Mergers', *Antitrust Bulletin,* Vol. XX No. 1, spring 1975.

example, the agreement by which Imperial Tobacco and British American Tobacco shared common brand names, but only sold cigarettes in certain specified agreed markets, has undergone extensive modification.

EEC case-law on monopoly is virtually non-existent as yet. This is partly due to the concern in the community that EEC industry should be competitive in world markets with US industries, and the arguments that this needs large firms, in order to obtain full economies of scale. It could be argued, however, that some of these scale economies, such as economies of scale in Research and Development, might better be achieved by means of common research work, since this particular kind of restrictive agreement is not proscribed in the treaty.

VI   REGIONAL POLICY AND THE LOCATION OF INDUSTRY
VI.1   The Regional Problem and the Rationale for Government Action

According to one writer a regional problem might be said to exist when there is somewhere a sense of regional grievance.[1] This could arise over regional discrepancies in unemployment and activity rates, average income per head, output growth, net emigration and so on. Statistical information on some of these disparities will be found in chapter 5, section I.3. A major influence on the character of the UK regional problem since the mid-1950s has been the decline of certain staple industries, especially coal, cotton textiles and shipbuilding, and falling agricultural employment. However, the UK regions are nearly all mixed urban-rural areas with a fair spread of activities and by international standards the imbalance between them is fairly slight.[2] For instance there is nothing to compare with the 'southern problem' in Italy, where income per head was estimated to be only half the national average in the mid-1960s and only one seventh of that in the richest part of the EEC in the late 1950s. Other main aspects of the EEC regional problem are some low-income agricultural areas in France and the Irish Republic, and certain older industrial areas developed around iron ore and coal – the Ruhr, Saar and Lorraine.[3] The industrial centres of the EEC outside the UK lie mainly along the Rhine-Rhône valleys, from the Netherlands to Northern Italy. These are estimated to have accounted for some 60% of the Gross Product of the EEC before its enlargement in 1973.

The original objective of UK regional policy was to reduce the very high unemployment rates in the regions in the 1930s. Although there are now other policy considerations, such as securing economic growth, the efficient utilization of national resources and demand management, concern over regional unemployment is still very much to the fore. Persistent regional unemployment indicates a continuing labour market disequilibrium, with excess supply of labour at the ruling wage levels. One justification for government intervention is that such disequilibria

---

1   A. J. Brown, 'Surveys in Applied Economics: Regional Economics, with Special Reference to the United Kingdom', *EJ*, Vol. LXXXIX, No. 316, December 1969. See also the same author's *The Framework of Regional Economics in the UK,* C.U.P. 1972; G. McCrone, *Regional Policy in Britain,* Allen & Unwin, 1969; H. Richardson, *Elements of Regional Economics,* Penguin, 1969 and *MBR,* November 1975, pp. 11-19.

2   The standard regions of the UK are: Northern, Yorkshire and Humberside, E. Midlands, E. Anglia, S. East, S. West, Wales, W. Midlands, N. West, Scotland and N. Ireland.

3   D. Swann, *op. cit.*

have proved themselves non-self-curing through normal market mechanisms. Presumably this has been due to the immobility of capital and, especially, of labour for various reasons, including social ties, imperfect knowledge of job opportunities elsewhere and, perhaps, downward rigidities in wage rates.

A second justification for government regional policy is the likely divergence of social and private costs and benefits in firms' location decisions. Thus, left to their own devices firms might choose locations which permitted minimum cost production (or at least a satisfactorily low level of costs) when the costs actually entering their accounts are the only ones considered. But when the social costs are taken into account (e.g. arising from increased congestion and differential effects on unemployment as between high and low employment areas) we might find that the most desirable location was a quite different one.

VI.2   Regional Policy Measures

These have been implemented by the Special Areas Act 1934, the Distribution of Industry Acts since 1945, the local Employment Acts since 1960 and various Finance Acts. Current policy is laid down by the 1972 Finance Act and also the 1972 Industry Act, which gave effect to the White Paper *Industrial and Regional Development* (Cmnd. 4942) published in that year. The history of regional policy since 1945 is one of repeated experiment. The following description looks first at the types of area designated to receive assistance, and then at the forms this assistance has taken.

Up to 1966 the criterion used for designating areas for assistance was simply the level of unemployment. Since then the criterion has been widened to 'all circumstances, expected and actual', which allows population migration, for example, to be taken account of as well. The first areas to be selected were the pre-war 'special areas' (South Wales, North-East England, West Cumberland, and the Clydeside-North Lanarkshire area). In 1945 these were extended to produce fairly large 'development areas'. These were replaced in 1960 by some one hundred and sixty-five smaller development districts, based on local employment exchange areas, the idea being to channel assistance to the most severely affected centres of unemployment. But this change in the policy gave rise to considerable uncertainty about the continuing status of individual districts, and in 1966 there was a reversion to the policy of specifying broad development areas. This remains the basis of current policy, although two other types of areas have been designated, in addition to the development areas. These are the 'special development areas' and the 'intermediate areas'. Special development areas, lying within the development areas, were first created after 1967 in areas affected by colliery closures because of the imminence there of high and persistent unemployment, but were later extended to other areas. Intermediate areas were designated after the Report of the Hunt Committee in 1969,[1] being areas outside development areas suffering problems similar in kind if not in acuteness, and likely to decline relative to areas which either had natural advantages or were already receiving assistance.[2]

---

1 *Report on the Committee on Intermediate Areas,* Cmnd 3998, HMSO, 1969.
2 A fourth type of area, the North Midlands 'Derelict Land Clearance Area', received certain subsidies to encourage the modernization and construction of industrial buildings from 1972 to 1974.

The geographical extent of the assisted areas at the time of writing is as follows: development areas cover all of Scotland and the Northern Region of England; Wales (except for its eastern fringes, both north and south); the northern part of Yorkshire and Humberside; and North Devon and Cornwall. Special development areas exist in West Central Scotland (centred on Glasgow); the Tyneside-Wearside area and West Cumberland in the north of England; Merseyside; part of North Wales including Anglesey and a large area of South Wales around Cardiff. Intermediate areas cover those parts of the North West, Yorkshire and Humberside and Wales not already mentioned, as well as the Chesterfield area and part of Devon. Altogether, the assisted areas account for 43% of total employment in Great Britain. Northern Ireland is treated as an additional, special case.

In looking at the assistance measures which have been adopted at one time or another it is convenient to distinguish between measures designed to prevent expansion in areas considered to be sufficiently developed, and financial assistance designed to encourage expansion in the regions. The principal member of the first group is the Industrial Development Certificate (IDC), required for factory building or extension. Up to 1972 they were required in all areas for projects above a certain minimum size, and after 1966 their issue was strictly controlled in the Midlands and South East. From 1972 IDC's have not been required in development areas, and since 1974 a three-tier system has applied to the rest of the country, the maximum size-limit for exemption being 15,000 square feet in the intermediate areas, 5,000 in the South-East planning region and 10,000 elsewhere. The 1974 change represented a tightening of the system in the non-assisted areas, although in the recession situation which followed IDC control has apparently not been applied strictly.

In some ways similar to IDC's are the permits required for office development. This control began in London in 1964, and was later extended to certain other areas, although it subsequently lapsed in some. In February 1969 the exemption limit in outer London was raised from 3,000 to 10,000 square feet. This form of control was retained in 1972 in view of the planning pressures in the South-East. However, control of office development has never been regarded as a major policy instrument for dispersing jobs to the regions, and has tended to operate more with regard to intra-regional considerations.

Up to 1963 the financial inducements offered to firms moving to or located in the assisted areas were mainly in the form of discretionary grants and loans which were conditional upon the creation of sufficient employment (at a capital cost not exceeding certain limits, albeit flexible ones). In addition, there was government provision of 'advance factory units' for sale or lease to firms at attractive rates. From 1963-6 these measures were supplemented by a system of tax allowances favouring firms in development areas. In January 1966 the tax allowances were replaced by a system of cash grants on plant and machinery, combined with initial allowances[1] on industrial buildings. From September 1967 manufacturers in development areas have also received a regional employment premium (REP) the value of which was doubled in 1974. For a time they also benefitted relatively to firms elsewhere under Selective Employment Tax. In October 1970 cash grants gave way once more to differential tax allowances in the regions, but in 1972 these

---

1 An initial allowance is an additional proportion of the cost of an asset which may be written off for tax purposes in the year in which the capital expenditure takes place. See chapter 2, section IV.6.

latter benefits were made nation-wide. Extra assistance for the regions was then added in the form of grants. In 1973 a special scheme was introduced to assist removals to the assisted areas by firms in service industries, offering fixed grants per employee transferred and rent free periods in the new premises.

The full list of the incentives offered is now a formidable one.[1] It includes regional development grants for buildings, new plant and machinery; selective assistance loans or interest relief grants; removal grants; advance factories; tax allowances on machinery and industrial buildings; finance from European Community funds (e.g. from the European Investment Bank or the European Coal and Steel Community); REP; manpower training assistance; help for transferred workers; the contract preference scheme relating to contracts placed by government departments and nationalized industries. Obviously not all of these will apply in every case. Some are conditional on the amount of employment created and the rates of benefit vary among the different types of area, Northern Ireland generally offering the highest rates.

In terms of both the size of the areas covered and the variety and scope of the assistance measures, regional policy could hardly be more comprehensive. However, the regional measures described so far have existed alongside another, to some extent competitive, policy. Under the New Towns Act 1946 and Town Development Act 1952, some twenty new towns have been established and rather more enlarged. The principal objective here has been to relieve congestion and assist urban renewal in large conurbations. But this policy impinges on regional policy since the new and enlarged towns have by no means all been in development areas, and their creation may have been a counter-attraction to firms which might have moved to development areas.

VI.3   Some Issues in Regional Policy

One criticism that has been made of government intervention in the location of industry is that it will give rise to an efficiency loss in the form of higher real costs of production.[2] This real cost must be set against the social benefits of regional policy, and might overwhelm them. The argument makes two assumptions. The first is that firms will locate at cost-minimizing sites if left alone, and the second is that location significantly affects costs.

There is some evidence, on the first of these, that firms do not approach location as a cost-minimizing exercise, but, in practice, more as is predicted by the behavioural theory of the firm.[3] Thus, apparently, firms do not seek an optimum location but rather an adequate site which satisfies certain minimum requirements. Choice is usually from among a very limited number of alternatives, perhaps no more than two or three. The decision to move is usually stimulated by some problem such as expiry of a lease or a cramped, physically constrained site, rather

---

1 For full details see Department of Industry: *Incentives for Industry in the Areas for Expansion*, HMSO, March 1975, and *Regional Development Incentives*, HMSO, Cmnd. 6058, May 1975.

2 See, e.g., A. C. Hobson, 'The Great Industrial Belt', *EJ*, September 1951.

3 See B. J. Loasby, 'Making Location Policy Work', *LBR*, January 1967; W. F. Luttrell, *Factory Location and Industrial Movement*, NIESR, London, 1952; and R. M. Cyert and J. G. March, *op. cit.*, pp. 54-60.

than by the attractions of alternative locations alone. Search for a new site is 'narrow' in the literal sense of not spreading far from existing operations. By itself this evidence does not enable us to dismiss the argument that interference necessarily results in an efficiency loss. For the sites selected might be lower cost locations than ones to which government policy directs firms, although not optimal ones. On the other hand, they might be higher cost locations. Thus, once cost-minimizing assumptions are abandoned, it becomes impossible to predict whether intervention will on balance lead to an efficiency gain or loss, assuming that location significantly affects cost.

On this second question there is some evidence to suggest that location may not significantly affect costs, at least for the majority of manufacturing. One study estimated that some 70% of manufacturing is 'footloose', i.e. not critically affected by costs at different locations.[1] Another writer suggests that some two-thirds of manufacturing is probably footloose with respect to transport costs, which are obviously an important consideration in this context and have always received much attention in location theory.[2] A third, very comprehensive study found little evidence of continuing excess costs on plants which had moved in relation to the levels in parent or original plants, although it could take five years for initial excess costs to disappear.[3] Thus it appears that a serious efficiency loss would not be inevitable if at least a good deal of manufacturing industry were relocated though there could obviously be specific exceptions.

A second criticism of UK regional policy has been over its capital bias. Prior to 1967 the various grants, loans and tax allowances offered as financial incentives related exclusively to capital expenditures. As a result the policy was especially attractive to firms with capital-intensive operations, and this was clearly not helpful to the policy objective of creating new employment. Moreover by lowering the relative price of capital inputs, the policy would tend to increase capital/labour ratios of firms receiving the assistance, perhaps causing this ratio to depart from what it should be for efficient utilization of resources. However, REP (and, for a short time, SET subventions) would have worked in the opposite direction.

A number of other issues have arisen concerning the nature of the policy instruments used at various times.[4] Firstly, the widening of financial incentives after 1963 to include tax allowances or cash grants for investment and the REP etc. has been criticized on the ground that a larger and larger proportion of the aid given has become unconnected with the creation of new jobs; it is available to firms already in development areas as well as to those moving in. As this has happened, it is argued, the cost-effectiveness of the policy in creating new jobs must have fallen. However a profit maximizing firm, with reasonably full information and already situated in a development area, would presumably now find it profitable to expand output and employment and seek to do so, and even satisficing firms with only limited perception would tend to do so in so far as aspiration levels adjust to what is attainable and if there is sufficient publicity surrounding the new measures. Secondly, it has been argued that where tax allowances give way to cash grants assistance is paid to the inefficient as well as the

---

1 R. J. Nicholson, 'The Regional Location of Industry', *EJ*, 1956. But see A. J. Brown, *op. cit.*, on the reliability of this result.

2 L. Needleman, 'What are We to do About the Regional Problem?', *LBR*, January 1965.

3 W. F. Luttrell, *op. cit.*

4 See also T. Wilson, 'Finance for Regional Industrial Development', *TBR*, September 1967.

efficient, since their receipt does not depend on profits being earned, as do the benefits through tax allowances. Thus a policy including grants may result in propping up ailing firms. On the other hand, the arguments in favour of grants carry some force. Broadly, these are that grants are more likely to be taken into account in decision making, since there is evidence that returns on investment are often calculated pre-tax;[1] that grants are more conspicuous and the benefits offered easier to calculate; and that the longish time-lag in the 'payment' of tax allowances can be avoided, as can the uncertainty of benefits under the allowance system, since these depend on future, unknown, profitability. Especially if firms' location policy is on behavioural lines, it could well be that a system of grants is necessary for incentives to be effective, even if on other grounds tax allowances might be preferable. Thirdly, it could be argued that the use of a negative prohibition like the IDCs as a policy instrument may be less acceptable than positive financial incentives. For, if rigidly applied, IDCs could do harm by choking off investment and expansion altogether in some cases (e.g. in non-footloose trades). Financial incentives on their own would not entail this risk, and, moreover, footloose industries would presumably select themselves, thus automatically minimizing the real costs of, e.g., achieving a given reduction in regional unemployment. This argument is quite strong so long as profit maximization is assumed. On a behavioural analysis, however, the IDC comes off rather better in some respects. If firms 'satisfice' financial incentives on their own are unlikely to succeed, or will work only sluggishly. For although higher profits are made attainable in development areas, the response (especially from existing firms) may well be slight if adequate profits can still be earned elsewhere. On the other hand, failure to secure an IDC, like expiry of a lease, is exactly the kind of problem to which firms are stimulated to respond in the behavioural theory, and the obvious response is to move. Two pieces of empirical evidence may be cited in this context: the conclusion that the stimulus to move comes from the 'exporting' area not the 'importing' area[2] and the belief among the administrators of the policy that at least up to the mid-1960s it was the IDC rather than the financial incentives which had most effect. Thus, like cash grants, the IDC's may be necessary for an effective policy, even if there could be other drawbacks. Moreover, on a behavioural analysis the IDC or similar controls may have other merits. Thus, we no longer assume cost-minimizing location decisions and, by promoting wider search than would otherwise occur, the IDC could increase the chances of lower cost locations being found. Indeed, it could even be that the IDC is a necessary adjunct to financial incentives because it plays an attention-focusing role in bringing their existence to the notice of firms.

Finally, let us look at two rather contentious issues in regional policy. One is that offering incentives to individual firms is not an effective way of inducing them to move to areas which are otherwise unattractive to them. More effective would be to create positive, real attractions like new towns or other 'growth points', and by the government undertaking more infra-structural investment in roads, docks and other items of social capital stock.[3] Resolution of this argument requires a good deal more knowledge than we have at present about firms' motivation.

---

1 See NEDC, *Investment Appraisal*, HMSO, 1965.
2 B. J. Loasby, *op. cit.*
3 See, e.g., *Report on the Scottish Economy, 1960-61* (The Toothill Report), Edinburgh, 1962.

Secondly, there has been some dispute over the respective merits of the present 'work to the workers' policy and of the alternative solution of encouraging migration ('workers to the work'). The alternative policies may be thought of as eliminating unemployment (excess supply of labour) by shifting the demand curve to the right (work to the workers) and shifting the supply curve to the left (workers to the work). The migration solution, even if successful in eliminating regional unemployment, would not necessarily remove all inter-regional differences. In particular it would increase net emigration from some areas. Arguments against the migration solution would be that the most mobile workers are probably also the fittest and most skilled, so that the areas they leave become even less attractive to firms; that social overhead capital might be wasted; that congestion in receiving areas would intensify; that the community life and culture in the emptying regions would deteriorate, and so on. However, some limited sorts of migration might avoid these effects (e.g. marginal population movements from large, old, industrial centres to expanding towns outside major conurbations in the prosperous regions). It is very unlikely that a thorough comparison of the costs and benefits of migration and of existing policy would indicate that present policy should be scrapped. But it may be that the two policies are not mutually exclusive and, especially in view of the very small scale of assistance towards migration at present,[1] it could be that some readjustment of the relative weight given to the two policies is desirable. The 1972 policy changes did include more financial help for workers moving house in search of work, but did not go very far in this direction.

VI.4   The Effectiveness of Regional Policy

The statistical evidence shows that, despite the existence of regional policy, the regional problem is still with us. There has been no long term trend for regional disparities in unemployment to disappear. None of the depressed regions acquired rates of output-growth significantly faster than the UK average, though regional policy has undoubtedly helped Scotland to equal, and occasionally overtake, the overall rate in the 1960s, after a period of very slow relative growth in the late 1950s. Except for Northern Ireland and the South-West, the 'problem' regions all had higher personal incomes in relation to the UK average in 1954-5 than in the subsequent ten years. Finally, although the drift to the South-East was checked in the later 1960s, net emigration from Scotland, the worst affected region in this respect, increased markedly in the 1960s.

Yet studies do suggest regional policy has had some impact. Two studies of investment grants in the period 1966-68 concluded that planning regions showing predominantly 'development area' status enjoyed a greater level of investment in plant and machinery per employee than the other planning regions,[2] with the marked exception of the South-East in the case of one study. A third study analysed patterns of relocation of manufacturing over the period.[3] From 1945-51

---

1 See chapter 5, section I.3.
2 See A. Beacham and T. W. Buck, 'Regional Investment in Manufacturing Industries', *Yorkshire Bulletin of Economic and Social Research,* May 1970; and C. Blake, 'The Effectiveness of Investment Grants as a Regional Subsidy', *Scottish Journal of Political Economy,* February 1972. The former relates to 1966, and the latter to the 1967-8 period.
3 R. S. Howard, 'The Movement of Manufacturing Industry in the UK 1945-65', *Board of Trade,* 1968.

about two-thirds of all moves in manufacturing were to development areas. But this was largely because in this period of post-war reconstruction the chief factor stimulating moves was the availability of factory space, which was under government control and mainly in development areas. Between 1952-9 this control had disappeared, the shortage eased, financial inducements under regional policy were not yet strong and IDCs were not too difficult to get outside development areas. As a result the proportion of moves to development areas fell below 25%. But stricter control over IDCs and larger financial incentives subsequently raised this figure to 50% by the mid 1960s. More recently published studies tend to confirm that regional policy has had a significant effect, suggesting that the strengthening of the policy in the 1960s may have increased the number of moves to development areas by 70-80 per annum (in relation to a maximum of around 160 per annum) with a total employment effect of about 220,000 jobs by 1970. Apparently all three major policy instruments — IDCs, financial incentives and REP — exerted a separate, significant influence.[1]

If the regional problem remains, but regional policy has had some mitigating effects, there is only one conclusion. But for the existence of the policy, the regional problem would now be worse than it is.

VI.5   EEC Provisions

Subsidies given to assist the development of backward regions are explicitly permitted by the Treaty of Rome. In the early development of the EEC and up to 1969 the member governments gave a variety of regional aids with very little supervision or guidance from the central EEC institutions. As a result there was very little harmonization of attitudes towards regional problems and of types and rates of assistance. There is even some evidence of competition among member governments to attract foreign investment to their own problem regions. However there was some activity at community level. The European Investment Bank, provided for in the Rome Treaty, financed projects in less developed regions and made loans to firms for rationalization required because of the creation of the Common Market; these loans were at commercial rates of interest and intended to top-up funds raised from other sources to the required level. Also, some of the activities of the ECSC and Agricultural Guidance and Guarantee Fund contributed to the community regional policy effort, especially as the EEC regional problems have much to do with agriculture and the coal and steel industries. Finally, the Social Fund financed training schemes for unemployed workers, though mainly on an industry-by-industry rather than regional basis.

In 1969 a memorandum from the European Commission expressed the need for a more cohesive policy and made certain proposals. These included annual examination of each nation's regional problems; the establishment of a standing committee to review aid schemes; and a Regional Development Rebate Fund to give financial aid to member governments from community sources (in the form of abatements of interest) for approved aid schemes.

Lengthy and inconclusive negotiations over EEC regional policy measures took

1   B. Moore and J. Rhodes, 'Evaluating the Effects of British Regional Policy', *EJ*, Vol. 83, 1973, pp. 87-110 and 'Regional Economic Policy and the Movement of Manufacturing Firms to Development Areas', *EC*, 43, pp. 17-31, February 1976.

place in late 1973 and early 1974, ultimately being suspended because of elections in Britain and France. The size of the Regional Fund was a major source of disagreement, the UK originally proposing a large sum of £1,500m over three years compared with the £250m proposed by West Germany when negotiations broke down. Agreement was finally reached at a meeting of heads of government in December 1974. The Fund was established from 1 January 1975 at a level of £540m for the three years 1975-7. The UK share was set at 28%, the second largest after Italy (40%), and the net gain to the UK will be about £60m after deducting our contribution through the EEC budget. This figure compares with a total of around £500m spent on regional aid within the UK in 1975. Moreover, receipts from the Fund go to the government rather than to the promoters of individual projects, and so form part of the UK total spending rather than an addition to it.

At one time there were some doubts about the compatibility of UK regional measures with overall EEC policy, but this issue has now been resolved. In general the EEC philosophy appears to favour selective rather than automatic aids, and aids directed towards investment rather than operating costs. Thus automatic aids like the UK Regional Development Grants do not find favour, while the REP, which is both automatic and related to operating costs, is positively disliked. Nevertheless, the existing UK measures have been accepted in the EEC, albeit after a certain amount of rewording of the community's principles during the renegotiation of the UK's terms of entry.[1] EEC policy distinguishes between 'central' and 'peripheral' areas, with 20% and 30% ceilings on the level of assistance respectively. In the UK non-assisted and intermediate areas have been classified as central, and development and special development areas as peripheral, with Northern Ireland being treated as a special case.

VII INDUSTRIAL EFFICIENCY
VII.1 Introduction

In earlier sections of this chapter we have seen that industrial growth in the UK has proceeded at a very modest rate by international standards, to the point that in terms of GDP per head Britain has now to be regarded as one of the poorer countries in Western Europe. In the search for explanations various questions have been asked. Has Britain fallen behind because of a lack of technical progressiveness and R and D spending? Are UK firms too small to compete with those of other countries in world markets? Does UK management and workforce exhibit inefficiency to an unusually large degree? There are no complete answers to these questions, but in the following pages we shall consider some of the evidence relevant to them and especially the role of the government.

In the following sections five aspects of the problem and their accompanying strands of policy are isolated and discussed. These are R and D performance; industrial structure (in particular the size distribution of plants and firms): problems of financing investment; the role of planning and of information exchange; and the micro-level significance of price control.

When considering these matters we should, of course, bear in mind the view that industrial growth may not be unambiguously beneficial. For many people it is an

---

1 See *Membership of the European Community: Report on Re-negotiations,* Cmnd. 6003, March 1975, pp. 9-10 and 20-21.

open question how long the richer industrialized countries can continue to grow
with little regard for the position of developing nations in the third world.
Moreover, some would argue that the current pursuit of industrial expansion will
lead to its own downfall, and to the breakdown of society, by irreversibly
disrupting the life systems on the planet.[1]

VII.2   R and D and Technical Progressiveness

By international standards the UK has a good performance in terms of R and D
effort: among advanced capitalist countries Britain and America research the most.
Comparison of the two countries reveals some interesting similarities.[2] In 1969-70
some 2.7% of GDP was spent on R and D in the UK, a total of £1,082m. In the US
the figure for 1966 was around 3% of GDP. In both countries private industry
carried out most of the R and D work — 59% in the UK, 70% in the US — but the
majority of the finance came from government funds — 52% in the UK, 53% in the
US. (A major factor underlying these statistics is government purchases of R and D
on defence and, in the US, space projects). The breakdown of R and D expenditures
by industry in the two countries is also similar. The league table in the UK was
headed by electrical engineering (26.6%, with electronics and telecommunications
alone contributing 17.4%), followed by aerospace (24.7%), chemicals and allied
industries (15.2%), mechanical engineering (8.8%), and motor vehicles (7.1%).
Other industries had less than 4%. Finally, R and D activity is very much the
preserve of large firms in both the UK and US. For the UK a survey in 1959 of
nearly 5,000 firms showed that three hundred and fifty large firms (employing
over 2,000 workers) accounted for about 85% of the total R and D expenditure,
with medium firms contributing only a minor share, and small firms virtually
nothing.

However, a high level of R and D effort does not necessarily go hand in hand
with rapid growth of GNP. Thus America and Britain, which research most, have
grown less rapidly in recent years than has Europe, which invests less in R and D.
It is not clear to what extent this simply reflects the fact that technical progress is
not contained by national boundaries, but it would be true to say that Britain and
especially America are creditor countries in R and D, while Europe is in deficit.[3]

Nevertheless, encouragement of research activity is a longstanding element in
government policy. The large share of R and D which is government-financed has
already been mentioned. The benefit to private industry from this work would not
be as great as if, for instance, grants of equivalent value were made for firms' own
projects. Nevertheless, a substantial overspill of new developments into the firms'
other operations does occur, especially in such fields as aircraft, electronics,
metallurgy, engines and machine tools. In some cases, notably computing, aircraft
and machine tools, the government has provided funds for the development of

---

1 'A Blueprint for Survival', *The Ecologist*, Vol. 2, No. 1, January 1972, and E. Goldsmith
   (ed.), *Can Britain Survive?*, Sphere Books, 1972. For a criticism of this standpoint see
   'The Case Against Hysteria', *Nature*, Vol. 235, No. 5333, 14 January 1972.
2 Sources for these comparisons are: A.A.S.; F. M. Scherer, *Industrial Market Structure and
   Economic Performance*, Rand McNally, 1970, and C. Freeman, 'R and D: A Comparison
   between British and American Industry', *NIER*, May 1962.
3 See C. Kennedy and A. P. Thirlwall, 'Technical Progress: A Survey', *EJ*, March 1972.

firms' own projects. Additionally, the government sponsors work on behalf of industry in its own research establishments; funds research through various Research Councils; gives grants to cooperative research associations in various industries; and via the National Research and Development Council (NRDC) finances development of inventions made in government laboratories and by private individuals, where this is in the public interest.

All of the measures impinge directly on R and D activity. Two other strands of government policy may have had an indirect bearing; policies to encourage larger firm size and competition policy. These policies are discussed elsewhere.[1] Here we consider only the reasons for their connection with R and D.

As we have seen R and D activity is heavily concentrated in large firms in Britain and America, and one school of thought is that large firm size is a necessary condition for technical progressiveness, primarily because of the large financial requirements.[2] However, not all stages of the innovation process are expensive. Invention itself can still involve only negligible expenditure. It is the subsequent stage of development up to the point of commercial application, and the actual introduction of the new product or process which are typically expensive. In the past many important inventions have been the work of individuals or small firms. This sort of evidence puts the contributions of large firms, as measured by R and D inputs, into a different perspective. There is some evidence that in Britain and elsewhere large firms are a comparatively minor source of fundamental break-throughs,[3] and that the R and D resources they commit are devoted mainly to relatively minor product improvement and modification.

The question of large absolute size and technical progressiveness intertwines with the argument that market power (large size relative to market supply) is an important facilitating condition.[4] Empirical tests of this hypothesis and its rival — that competition is conducive to technical progress — have so far proved very inconclusive.[5] It is difficult to say why this is so. It might be because of practical difficulties in measuring technical progressiveness, of which there is no direct measure. Alternatively, the explanation could be that both competition and market power carry with them both advantages and disadvantages from the point of view of securing technical advances, and the balance between them is either roughly equal or varies from case to case. Thirdly, it may be that there are other important factors at work. Some case-study evidence certainly would suggest that there are, the quality of management being an important one.[6]

---

1 See sections VII.3 and 5.
2 See J. K. Galbraith, *American Capitalism,* Hamish Hamilton, 1956; and Lord Blackett's evidence to the Select Committee on Science & Technology, Minutes of Evidence, 14 March 1968, *Defence Research,* HCP 139-V, 1967/8.
3 See, e.g., J. Jewkes, D. Sawers and R. Stillerman, *op. cit.,* and F. M. Scherer, *op. cit.*
4 See also section V above.
5 The evidence is mainly for the US. Scherer, *op. cit.,* after providing an excellent summary, notes 'that market concentration has a favourable impact on technological innovation in certain situations. How much concentration is advantageous remains to be determined. Obviously there is no general answer . . .' (p. 376).
6 See C. F. Carter and B. R. Williams, *Industry and Technical Progress,* O.U.P., 1957; also *Investment and Innovation,* O.U.P., 1958; and *Science in Industry,* O.U.P., 1959.

VII.3   Scale, Unit Cost and Structural Reorganization

The ideas that there are widespread and large economies of scale in production, and
that they fairly frequently fail to be exploited, are recurring themes in discussions
of UK industrial growth. The extent of potential scale economies can be gauged
either by observing the physical relationship between inputs and output in
production (i.e. by estimating production functions) or by direct observation of
long-run average costs as scale is varied. To assess how fully such scale economies as
exist are exploited we would need to relate additional information on the actual
size distribution of plants and firms to these estimates of potential scale economies.
There is a fair amount of information on the first of these questions. The second
has received very little attention in the literature, but certain limited conclusions
can be drawn from Census of Production data.

In general, empirically estimated production functions in both the UK and most
other countries have revealed remarkably few results that are inconsistent with a
constant returns hypothesis.[1] By contrast, empirical cost functions have suggested
that average costs decline rapidly at first as scale increases, but that the rate of
decline lessens as scale is increased further, the cost curve tending to flatten out
until it is virtually horizontal. Thus an 'L' shaped long-run average cost curve is
observed, indicating substantial economies to increases in scale over smaller size
ranges; further, but less substantial, economies at higher size levels; but with no
evidence of eventual diseconomies of scale.[2] According to the evidence there is
much inter-industry variation in the magnitude of scale economies. One study
shows the percentage increase in total cost per unit faced by plants producing at
only 50% of estimated minimum efficient scale (m.e.s.) for various industries;[3]
in brick production, for instance, costs would be some 25% above the level of m.e.s.
whereas for a sulphuric acid plant the increase would be only 1%. In view of this

TABLE 4.10

Size Distribution of Manufacturing Units[1] by Employment Size, UK 1972

Size category	No. of units	%	No. employed	%
11 – 19	17,155	28.7	246,722	3.3
20 – 24	8,150	13.6	179,045	2.4
25 – 99	20,637	34.5	1,049,668	14.2
100 – 199	6,246	10.4	867,511	11.7
200 – 499	4,894	8.2	1,509,389	20.4
500 – 999	1,589	2.7	1,101,187	14.9
1,000 – and over	1,121	1.9	2,433,682	32.9
TOTAL	59,792	100.0	7,387,204	100.0

Note: 1   A manufacturing (local) unit is 'any factory or plant at a single site or address'.

1   See A. A. Walters, 'Production and Cost Functions: An Econometric Survey', *Econometrica*, 1963.

2   *Ibid;* see also J. Johnston, *Statistical Cost Analysis*, McGraw-Hill, 1960; C. F. Pratten, *Economies of Scale in Manufacturing Industry*, Cambridge University Press, 1971; and Z. A. Silberston, *EJ*, March 1972.

3   C. F. Pratten, *op. cit.*, M.e.s. is the point on the L-shaped long-run average cost curve at which average costs cease to fall.

inter-industry variation, only very rough generalizations can be made. But from the available evidence it seems that scale economies in most trades are likely to have been secured by plants five times as big as the smallest, and even where economies continue to be enjoyed at larger size levels, they will almost certainly have been exhausted by plants ten times the size of the smallest.

This tentative conclusion enables us to draw from Census data some equally tentative inferences about the degree of exploitation of scale economies. Table 4.10 details the size distribution of plants in 1972. It shows that small plants are numerically predominant. This can mean one of several things. Either these plants are all in industries, or subsections of industries, where there are few, if any, economies of scale; or the larger plants are run inefficiently, so that there is room for small efficient plants which nevertheless fail to exploit scale economies fully; or the owners of these small plants are content to accept a very low rate of return on their investment; or, finally, scale economies are of very little importance, so that the size distribution is the outcome of purely random effects.[1] Attempting to allow for the first suggestion, we might say that the smallest plants which generally exist in an industry employ one hundred workers. Then, if we take plants employing more than five hundred workers and apply the conclusion of the previous paragraph, we find from table 4.10 that nearly 48% of total employment is in plants in which the bulk of scale economies can fairly safely be assumed to have been exploited. On the same basis, approximately 33% of total employment is in fact accounted for by plants at least ten times the size of the smallest. The same general picture emerges for manufacturing enterprises (groups of establishments under common ownership). Without close study at the individual industry level, firm conclusions should not be drawn. But it could be that the efficiency loss believed to arise from the existence of sub-optimal scale may have been exaggerated.

However, over time, there has been a fairly marked trend towards larger plants and firms. Plants with over 1,500 workers accounted for 15.2% of total employment in private sector manufacturing industry in 1935, and for nearly 30% in 1968; those with under a hundred employees accounted for 25.6% in 1936 and for 18.4% in 1968. Perhaps, therefore, the importance of plant scale economies is increasing, but if so the evidence indicates it is being taken up to some extent. Also, it is interesting to observe that the number of establishments (plants) per enterprise is quite small, 1.33 in 1968,[2] so that if firms *are* efficient then economies of multi-plant operation must be very limited in most industries.

As a means of securing greater efficiency and growth, structural reorganization has tended to receive emphasis under Labour governments, particularly from 1964-70. Thus an Industrial Reorganization Corporation (IRC) was set up, which initiated and aided a number of mergers including some spectacular ones such as Leyland-BMC and GEC-AEI-English Electric. The 1968 Industrial Expansion Act was also designed to provide government support for schemes which would improve

---

1 It has been pointed out that the configurations we observe are similar to those one might expect if firms, initially of equal size, were subjected over a longish period to a succession of pieces of good or bad luck, each having a proportionate effect on firm size. For a discussion of this idea see: H. A. Simon and C. P. Bonini, 'The Size Distribution of Business Firms', *AER*, September 1958; P. E. Hart, 'The Size and Growth of Firms', *EC*, February, 1962, and F. M. Scherer, *op. cit.*, on Gibrat's law.

2 *Census of Production*, 1968.

economic efficiency, expand productive capacity and promote technical improvements, and a specific programme of grant-aided help was provided to reorganize the shipbuilding industry under a 1967 Act.

Under the 1970-4 Conservative Government emphasis tended to swing away from 'structural' solutions to industrial problems in favour of a greater reliance on the pressure of competition, and the IRC was dissolved in May 1971. The main emphasis of current government policy is described in section VII.5.

VII.4   Finance for Investment

Orthodox economics suggests two possible reasons for government intervention in private sector capital formation. One would be that, for some reason, the social returns on investment projects undertaken by firms are greater than the private returns. If so it is legitimate to reduce the cost of capital services to the firm in order to raise the level of investment in capital goods from the privately-optimal to the socially-optimal level. The divergence between social and private benefits might arise from the impact of investment on unemployment, or on the balance of payments or even on national prestige. Secondly, intervention would be justified if there was evidence of 'market failure' in the supply of funds for investment: that is, if shortcomings in the organization of financial institutions, or in the information flows on which they base their decisions, left firms unable to borrow at 'appropriate' interest rates given the profitability and degree of risk of their investment plans.

Alternative explanations, implicitly drawing on rather different theoretical models of the firm, might be that firms facing an uncertain future simply tend to under-estimate the private returns to investment, or that investment policies resulting from the gradual adjustment of firms' aspirations to their past achievements would result in growth rates that were unacceptably low to the government.

The current official view, shared by many other observers, is that the rate of investment in UK manufacturing has been too low. Also, new investment has tended to result in relatively poor returns, and the capital markets are believed to be subject to imperfections, mainly affecting the supply of medium- and longer-term funds. Measures to improve investment performance are now embedded in a broader government industrial strategy, outlined in a White Paper published in November 1975.[1] The investment measures themselves stem from the Industry Acts of 1972 and 1975. The 1972 Act affirmed the (Conservative) government's determination to provide a substantial and lasting impetus to profitable industrial expansion, modernization and a higher growth-rate by increasing the government's incentives to investment in all regions of the UK. The main investment incentive was the allowance of free depreciation (whereby firms set capital expenditure against tax at whatever rate suits them best)[2] on new plant and machinery and an initial tax allowance of 40% (later raised to 50%) on industrial buildings and structures throughout the UK, measures which had previously applied only to the assisted areas.[3] Further, there was a system of grants to industry for capital

---

1 *An Approach to Industrial Strategy,* HMSO, Cmnd. 6315, November 1975.

2 In most cases free depreciation amounts to a 100% initial allowance.

3 See also section VI and chapter 2, section IV.6.

expenditure in the assisted areas and in some cases elsewhere. A special provision of the act was a system of short-term, tapering grants to ship-builders until a longer-term solution for this industry had been worked out.

One other provision of the 1972 Act was that grants might be given only in exchange for state shareholdings in the companies concerned. This provision was not used by the Conservative Government, but has been used subsequently by the Labour Government, most noticeably in its rescue of British Leyland in 1975.

The 1975 act greatly increased the emphasis on extending state ownership in the provision of assistance to industry. Part I of the act set up the National Enterprise Board,[1] with initial finance of up to £1,000m to assist firms, or the reorganization of industries, exercising the powers of selective financial assistance under the 1972 Act. A controversial feature of the NEB is that it is empowered to extend public ownership not only to companies asking for help (as Upper Clyde Shipbuilders, Rolls-Royce and British Leyland had earlier done) but also into profitable companies. The NEB is required to promote industrial democracy in the undertakings controlled by it, and to hold and manage securities and other property in public ownership which is transferred to it (including Rolls-Royce, Alfred Herbert, Ferranti, and BL). The act required the NEB to earn an 'adequate' return on its capital, and made acquisitions exceeding £10m in a company or 30% of a company's shares subject to the consent of the secretary of state.

At one time there was optimism in the left-wing circles and apprehension elsewhere that the NEB would lead to a major extension of public ownership, to include at first one hundred and then twenty-five of the biggest UK companies. It is now clear that the NEB as presently organized and financed cannot and is not intended to attempt such a task. At present it has only around £225m per annum at its disposal up to 1980, after allowing for commitments to the companies transferred to it. Moreover guidelines for its operations published in early 1976 restricted its freedom of action without reference to the Secretary of State for Industry to £0.5m in cases of share purchases contested by shareholders. As and when fixed investment in manufacturing recovers from the recession levels of the mid 1970s it seems likely that the generous tax incentives under the 1972 Act will provide more of a stimulus than will the NEB.

So far only government activity to improve investment performance has been mentioned. In late 1975 there was a City initiative to help the flow of funds to industry: the proposed 'Equity Bank' (although the funds would be administered through the government body Finance for Industry). Precise details of its operation are unclear at the time of writing. The idea is essentially to improve the flow of funds from institutional investors to companies wishing to raise new equity finance. The indications are that it would operate on a fairly small scale at least initially.

VII.5 Information Exchange and Planning

In most textbook descriptions resource allocation takes place in market economies without the need for economic agents to meet, exchange information and co-ordinate their behaviour in any direct way. Planning is effected via the price mechanism. In the UK, especially under Labour governments, steps have been

---

1 Other parts of the act dealt with planning agreements and information disclosure, which are discussed in section VII. 5.

taken to supplement the impersonal price signals in the market with other types of information, and to create a measure of non-market planning in the resource allocation process.

The first major effort in this direction was the National Plan of 1965. As a planning exercise this was short-lived. However some of the institutional structure associated with the plan survived, in particular the Economic Development Committees for different industries. Twenty-one EDCs were set up, under the *aegis* of the central National Economic Development Council, and they undertook a wide range of activities. These have included regular demand and supply forecasts and publication of information on export performance, sales opportunities in particular markets, and import trends. Other topics which have been covered include manpower problems; standardization; stockholding procedures; factors affecting investment; R and D; and the effect of decimalization, taxation and devaluation. The information has been disseminated within industries via newsletters and reports, and there has also been some exchange of information between industries.

A more recently introduced policy instrument is the Planning Agreement, first mooted in a White Paper on *The Regeneration of British Industry*.[1] Planning Agreements are intended as a means of exchanging information between the government and individual companies on long-term objectives and medium-term expectations and plans.[2] Agreements would be concluded annually, though subject to revisions, and they would also be voluntary. However, companies may find themselves under considerable pressure to volunteer, in order to secure maximum benefits from government assistance measures. Thus, for instance, the 1975 Industry Act provided safeguards to firms with Planning Agreements over the rate of grant and qualifying conditions for regional development grants and selective financial assistance. Moreover part IV of the same act provided a procedure – albeit a cumbersome and lengthy one – whereby companies may be compelled to disclose information of a planning nature. (In return it obliged the government to publish 'in due course' a model of the economy so that the public can make forecasts using their own assumption about GDP, unemployment, the balance of payments, retail prices, average earnings and other matters. Access to the model will not be restricted to companies with Planning Agreements.)

More generally, government philosophy on planning was described in a 1975 White Paper *An Approach to Industrial Strategy*.[3] As the White Paper stresses this is not a strategy but a programme for developing a strategy. It proposes as a first step the provision of a systematic statistical and analytical framework, embracing the past performance of thirty or so individual sectors of manufacturing, and the implications for each of alternative medium-term growth assumptions. Choice of the sectors will be a matter of 'picking winners' – industries 'intrinsically likely to be successful', or with the potential of being so (together with industries 'whose performance (as in the case of component suppliers) is most important to the rest of the industry'). The White Paper then envisages government-industry consultations at three levels: national, industry, and company. Frequent references are made to

1 Cmnd. 5710, 1974.
2 For a description of the possible contents of such agreements, see *TI*, 8 August 1975, pp. 338-42.
3 Cmnd. 6315.

the role of the EDC's, the NEB and Planning Agreements. The whole exercise is intended as an annual 'rolling-plan' procedure.

It is hard to say what will come of all this. Amongst non-involved observers (including economists) there is often marked disagreement about the relative merits of market solutions versus planning, and there is a dearth of objective theoretical knowledge and empirical evidence to help resolve the issues. Moreover, it is particularly hard to evaluate mixtures of planning and the market mechanism such as present policy in the UK implies, as distinct from 'ideal' stereotypes.

On the one hand, it is possible that the government, if it succeeds in discovering more about the micro-implications of its macro policies, could avoid some of the past errors which the White Paper lists: unduly sharp and frequent changes of economic regulators; pre-emption of resources for the public sector and personal consumption; and intervention in the nationalized industries. It is possible also that companies, if better informed about government intentions and less prone to suffer from the errors listed above, could improve their own planning and resource utilization. On the other hand, the White Paper makes little effort to conceal that the government is only feeling its way towards a planning system, and the eager cooperation of companies is unlikely to be forthcoming. The process of finding the policy is thus bound to be a slow one, and perhaps prone to interruption should a change of government occur.

VII.6 Some Microeconomic Implications of Price Controls

Statutory price controls were first introduced by the Labour Government in 1966, after a period of voluntary control. Applications for increases were reviewed by the now disbanded National Board for Prices and Incomes (NBPI). Subsequently, statutory controls gave way to voluntary arrangements until November 1972 when the Conservative Government reintroduced a statutory policy. In the first stage there was a virtual standstill on most prices other than food for five months. Manufacturing prices were allowed to rise only to meet increases in import costs. Stage II of Conservative policy saw the creation of a Price Commission (PC). Firms with sales of over £50m a year (or in service industries, over £20m a year) were to give prior notification of proposed price increases to this body. These price rises were accepted only on the basis of 'allowable' cost increases, that is a rise in the price of materials, fuel, rents, transport etc. and a proportion of labour costs, and as long as profit margins did not exceed a 'reference level' — the average level in the best two of the previous five years. Smaller firms had to report prices intermittently, and the smallest to keep records for inspection. As with the Labour policy, there was also a control on dividends and there were certain exceptions to the codes outlined above where, for example, firms were making losses.

Stage III of the price code was still in force at the time of writing (though due to expire, unless renewed, in mid-1976), and introduced few changes in the previous position. Under Stage III more firms have to report to the PC any intended price rises. However, the code was made slightly easier in two directions in the hope of encouraging investment: reductions in profit margins were limited to 10%, and depreciation costs could be taken into account when the PC made its decision. As well as continuing with the statutory scheme which it inherited, the post-1974 Labour Government took two additional steps. For a time the prices of certain foods, including bread, were pegged, with subsidies for the relevant manufacturers.

Later, in February 1976, a 'selective price restraint' scheme was introduced, the prices of certain well-publicized items (accounting for a claimed 15-20% of consumer expenditure) being guaranteed not to rise more than 5% over six months.

The primary objectives of price control policies are, of course, macroeconomic ones. From time to time claims are made that the PC has rejected or modified price increases worth £x millions to the consumer. These claims should not be taken at face value, however, for they appear to be based on an extreme assumption of perfectly inelastic demand. At the same time, it would be unreasonable to suggest that the policy has had no effect. Its maximum impact was most likely to have been in the last peak of economic activity in 1973-4. In the recession situation of the 1975-6, on the other hand, the binding constraint on price levels was almost certainly depressed trading conditions rather than price controls. Thus, in the third quarter of 1975 company profit margins were below 50% of their reference levels.

However, our present interest is less in the macroeconomic significance of price controls than on their incidental microeconomic effects, especially their impact on industrial efficiency. If orthodox theoretical arguments are employed, we should expect these to be small or non-existent. If firms are already maximizing profits and pursuing cost-minimizing policies, the extra sanction of price controls is superfluous, from the point of view of securing industrial efficiency. The main effects of price control will be on output and employment levels and on investment. Thus, if costs increase but prices do not adjust to the same extent, the profit maximizing output and employment levels will generally fall. And if current and expected future profit levels fall, the incentive to invest is weakened, while at the same time the surplus available for re-investment is less.

Other models lead to somewhat different conclusions. As was noted earlier, in section I, the managerial and behavioural theories suggest that there is generally some discretionary expenditure and/or slack in the firm's operations. In the behavioural theory in particular, firms do not generally operate at or close to maximum efficiency, in the sense of choosing cost-minimizing factor ratios and obtaining the maximum output it is possible to get from any given bundle or resources. One set of empirical estimates of the degree of technical inefficiency — or X-inefficiency in the writer's own terms — suggests that it may amount to 25% of output in many cases and up to 80% in some.[1] If these estimates are anywhere near the truth, the scope for raising efficiency is clearly considerable, and the sanction of price controls is one possible way of achieving it. Thus, in the Williamson model, the introduction of price controls could result in a more adverse business environment, causing discretionary expenditures to contract. In behavioural terms, price control could be exactly the kind of 'problem' to which firms will respond by cutting slack and widening search for new and better production methods. However, the gains will not always be unambiguous ones. For instance, where firms are forced to abandon managerial objectives there will be some loss of managerial utility to offset the social gain arising from cost savings, and organizational slack may serve a useful social function to some extent as a form of contingency reserve. Moreover, cutting slack will tend to have employment implications, with the attendant social costs, especially at times when unemployment is already high.

---

1 H. Leibenstein, 'Allocative Efficiency vs. X-Efficiency', *AER,* 1966.

What the actual effects of price control have been is hard to assess. Certainly the NBPI found itself with a good deal to say in its reports by way of specific recommendations for improved efficiency and long-term productivity benefits. This is much less true of the PC which, however, has less scope for independent initiative than had the NBPI, because the controls and exemptions which it operates are set out in far more detail.

REFERENCES AND FURTHER READING

F. M. Scherer, *Industrial Market Structure and Economic Performance,* Rand McNally, 1970.

R. Turvey, *Economic Analysis and Public Enterprise,* Allen and Unwin, 1971; and *Public Enterprise,* Penguin, 1968.

R. Pryke, *Public Enterprise in Practice,* MacGibbon and Kee, 1971.

Nationalized Industries: A Review of Economic and Financial Objectives, Cmnd. 3437, HMSO, 1967.

A. Hunter, *Monopoly and Competition,* Penguin, 1969.

D. Swann *et al, Competition in British Industry,* Allen and Unwin, 1974.

A. Sutherland, *The Monopolies Commission in Action,* C.U.P., 1970.

A. J. Brown, *The Framework of Regional Economics in The UK,* C.U.P., 1972.

H. W. Richardson, *Elements of Regional Economics,* Penguin, 1969.

C. F. Pratten, *Economies of Scale in Manufacturing Industry,* C.U.P., 1971.

C. Kennedy and A. P. Thirlwall, 'Technical Progress: A Survey', *EJ,* March 1972.

D. Swann, *The Common Market* (2nd edition), Penguin, 1972.

And for information on current developments in industry and commerce:

Trade and Industry

National Institute Economic Review (especially the annual survey, February issue in each year).

Midland Bank Review, notes on 'Government and Business'.

5

Labour

David Metcalf and Ray Richardson

I   THE LABOUR FORCE
I.1   Total Employment

In September 1975 the working population in Great Britain was estimated to be 25,581,000[1]. This aggregate was composed of employees in employment (22,131,000), employers and self-employed (1,916,000), HM Forces (340,000) and the registered unemployed (1,194,000). Since 1971, when a new method of estimating the number of employees in employment was introduced, there has been a definite tendency for the estimated working population to rise. On the face of it this implies a re-establishment of the post-war experience that lasted until 1966 and a break with the sustained fall in working population that is estimated for the period 1966-71.

To some extent these changes in trend may reflect measurement and estimation mistakes. For example, it is difficult to estimate accurately the number of self-employed workers and it has been suggested that certain tax and national insurance changes have given substantial incentives for people to switch into self-employed status. If this has happened it is quite possible that the estimated changes in working population are misleading because they would capture the fall in employees but not the rise in the self-employed. It is, however, appropriate here to assume that the estimates are broadly correct and to discuss what determines the size of and changes in the labour force.

One influence is the size and demographic composition of the population. For example younger males and older males are less likely to be in the labour force than are males aged between 25 and 55. In order to abstract from demographic changes, it is convenient to discuss these issues in terms of activity rates (sometimes called labour force participation rates). These express, for any age and sex group, the proportion of working to total population. There are two influences on male activity rates to consider here, the trend in economic growth and fluctuations around the trend.

Economic growth tends to reduce male activity rates. In particular, younger males stay in the educational system longer and older males retire earlier, especially when growth is accompanied by improved retirement pensions. These changes predominantly reflect the fruits of economic growth.

Superimposed on this inverse relation between growth and male activity rates is a complex reaction to fluctuations in growth. Over the last ten to fifteen years there has, if anything, been a positive relation between growth and activity rates. Thus, growth fell in the second half of the 1960s and tended to rise in the early 1970s; more recently it has begun to fall again. A slightly different picture over time is produced if one considers real take-home pay rather than GNP growth but

---

1 *DEG*, February 1976, p. 186.

it is still the case that the male labour force tends to contract in recession and expand (or contract less rapidly) in prosperous times.

These two relations between growth and activity rates, the inverse and the positive, are not contradictory, as they might seem at first sight. The first concerns people's responses to a permanent increase in wealth levels; the second concerns people's responses to what is presumed to be a temporary fall in employment prospects. This is an application of the fundamental notions in economics of income and substitution effects. If a worker is not planning to supply the maximum amount of labour at all times, he can choose the most advantageous periods when the supply is to be offered. On many calculations the most advantageous periods occur when wages are high and jobs are easy to find, that is, in expansionary conditions. Consequently, a recession is a period during which there is less point in offering one's services. This view therefore predicts that over the business cycle the size of the labour force will be positively related to the state of the economy. It is usually termed the 'discouraged worker effect', meaning that as the economy turns down, the number of people in employment falls by more than the increase in the number counted as unemployed.

There is an alternative and opposite view to the one just described, labelled the 'added worker effect'. It suggests that as 'primary' (i.e. permanent) members of the labour force are made unemployed in recessions, 'secondary' (i.e. temporary) workers are drawn into the work force so as to provide a source of income for the family; the result is that the number of *un*employed rises more than the number *dis*employed. This view obviously has some validity but it is basically a qualification to the 'discouraged worker' hypothesis. It stresses that many households plan imprecisely, that unpredicted events are important and force changes even in carefully laid plans, and that savings, credit and social welfare payments may be inadequate to maintain family living standards for more than a relatively short period. These and other factors are all of obvious practical importance, but they should not be taken to imply that the 'discouraged worker' hypothesis, with its emphasis on rational calculation, is thereby unrealistic and likely to be misleading. In fact, when careful statistical analysis is carried out, the evidence strongly suggests that it is the 'discouraged worker' effect which dominates the 'added worker' effect.[1]

I.2   Female Employment

For many years now there have been substantial differences between male and female employment changes. Concentrating on the estimates of employees in employment it can be seen that the number of male workers in Great Britain rose fairly consistently from 13,447,000 in June 1950 to 14,704,000 in June 1966;[1] by June 1975 the figure had fallen, again fairly consistently, to 13,182,000.[2] The net result over the twenty-five years was a fall in the number of male employees in employment. Female employees, on the other hand, have not had prolonged periods of decline and have risen in number from 6,871,000 in June 1950 to 8,935,000 in June 1975, a rise of 30%. Around that long-run trend there have

---

1   B. Corry and J. Roberts. 'Activity Rates and Unemployment: the experience of the UK 1951-66', *Applied Economics*, vol. 2, no. 3, 1970.

2   *DEG*, February 1976, p. 186.

been years of increases and occasional falls but over the period as a whole the percentage of the working population that is female has risen from 32 to 38.

It should be noted that by far the most dramatic rise in participation has come from married females; since 1931 activity rates of married women in each of the important age groups have increased by at least 300%.[1] This was not solely a wartime phenomenon, as the increase continued strongly after 1951. For example between 1961 and 1971 the proportion of middle-aged married females in the labour force rose from 35% to 55%.[2] Unmarried women (i.e. single, widowed and divorced) have had a more mixed experience, with the younger groups having a falling activity rate since 1951 and the older groups a rising rate.

Of course, in absolute terms activity rates for unmarried women are still much higher than those for married women. Given that the experience of the two groups, married and unmarried, has been different it seems likely that the major explanation of the increase in the number of working wives is not something that affects women generally, such as a decline in anti-female discrimination. Whether or not such discrimination, usefully defined, is extensive, there have been no conclusive studies showing changes in its extent.

Concentrating, therefore, on influences primarily affecting married women, we can point first to the fact that the average number of children per family has fallen over time. Whether this is a cause or effect of higher participation is not known. What is known, for America, is that activity rates have also risen for married women with young children. This suggests that declining family size is, at best, only a partial explanation of rising activity rates.

A second possibility is that, due to the introduction of new products, there has been a rise in the productivity of the housewife, effectively allowing her to produce the same amount of housewifely services as before but in less time. By itself this improved productivity does not necessarily make for greater participation by the wife in the labour force because, at the same time, everyone's income has risen. With the rise in income one might expect both the family's demand for housewifely services and the housewife's demand for personal leisure to increase, thereby decreasing the incentive to join the labour market. Only if the domestic productivity effect is strong will the net effect be to release housewives for market work. With this possibility there is again the question of whether the product improvements were cause or effect. That is, did they appear autonomously or were they induced and hurried along by the independent effect or a rise in working wives caused by some other factor? To our knowledge, no study has given a satisfactory answer to this question.

A third possible explanation of the rise in activity rates for married women is that social attitudes have become increasingly tolerant of wives, even mothers, working. This explanation is probably the most popular of all of the explanations and there is certainly no doubt that attitudes have indeed changed. Again, however, there is the difficulty of deciding the extent to which changes in attitudes were an independent cause or were themselves a response to changes in practice. It does seem plausible that the two world wars were very influential in this matter. They were, as far as the labour market was concerned, exogenous events inducing many women to join the market for the first time. This process surely changed social

---

1 *BLS*, pp. 206-7.
2 *DEG*, January 1974, pp. 8-18.

attitudes, encouraging working wives. It is also notable that over the last twenty years the largest increases in activity rates for married women are associated with older women, who experienced to the full the turmoil of wartime. However, one note of caution is worth sounding as to the impact of wartime exigencies. The available data are very sketchy, but they suggest that the increase in the proportion of wives who work in the market is very much an international phenomenon, extending even to countries for whom the impact of the wars was quite modest.

The above explanations all run in terms of supply influences, implying that progressively more married women are willing to work in the market. Demand influences may also have been important. One possibility is that the attempts by successive governments to induce greater regional evenness of employment have been successful in bringing some work to women who previously had virtually no job opportunities at all. Related aspects of this view are discussed in section I.7 below, but here are two qualifications to be noted. First, if this argument has much weight one would expect that, region by region, more or less equal increases in activity rates for married and unmarried women would have occurred. It is not clear that this has happened. Second, if the point were merely that there has been a geographical redistribution of jobs one would expect a decline in female activity rates in the prosperous, job-losing regions. This has certainly not happened in absolute terms, but it is true that over the period 1954-64 female activity rates rose most rapidly in areas where they had initially been low.[1] In fact there has not been merely a redistribution of jobs. Since the end of the 1930s, the UK economy has been run at unprecedented and persistent tightness. It seems most plausible to us, in the absence of hard statistical confirmation, that it is this influence rather than deliberate geographical dispersion that explains a major part of the rise of women in the labour force.

A second, structural argument relating to demand influences could be made. It might be suggested that female activity rates have risen because expansion has been particularly marked in industries employing a high proportion of female to male workers. It is shown below, in section I.4, that these female-intensive industries have indeed enjoyed a relative expansion, certainly since the second world war. However, most of these sectors are not inherently female-intensive and we should again put principal stress on the general expansion of the economy when considering demand influences which account for the rise of female participation in the labour market. Essentially what has been happening here has been the tapping of a labour reserve.

Recently there has been some interesting research in this area, specifically in explaining the variation in married females' activity rates across one hundred and six towns and cities in Great Britain.[2] It was shown that wives' activity rates were greater, the higher were female wage rates and the lower were male wage rates; wives' activity rates were also higher for the foreign born, for those with little wealth, for those who lived in the larger cities and for those who lived in towns with low male unemployment rates. In general where labour markets are tight, as judged by unemployment or wages, married women are more likely to be in the labour force.

---

1 J. Bowers, *The Anatomy of Regional Activity Rates, Regional Paper 1, NIESR,* 1970, ch. 3.
2 C. Greenhalgh, 'Labour Supply Functions for Married Women in G.B.' *EC.* (forthcoming, 1977).

I.3   Spatial Employment Patterns

The national pattern of jobs and workers in Great Britain is changing rapidly both within regions and across regions. For example, between 1964 and 1974 the number of employees in employment in the manufacturing sector in Greater London fell by more than 425,000, or more than a quarter. Many of these losses for London were gains for the rest of the South East region. Similar developments have taken place in many of the large British cities, sometimes in response to natural market forces and sometimes as a result of deliberate planning policy. Thus in the period since the second world war there has been a great planned expansion of new towns that ring many of our major cities. Often firms have wished to expand their operations around their existing inner city sites but have been denied planning permission and have therefore been obliged to move either to a nearby new town or to a more distant depressed region. Of course, many firms have moved for reasons other than planning difficulties, for example because suitable nearby land was not physically available, or because labour was increasingly scarce locally or because local transportation facilities were deteriorating.

The loss of workplaces in many of the major cities may or may not imply higher urban unemployment. For example, in London there has been no obvious change in unemployment, relative to other areas, during the period of major job loss. This implies either that the population is leaving London at the same rate as jobs or that commuting patterns are changing. Clearly some cities are suffering from the loss of jobs, (Glasgow is often said to be in this category) while others benefit from the reduction of congestion that decline implies. Overall, what is happening is that within most regions jobs and population are being more evenly spread and less heavily concentrated in particular areas.

Until recently, when specific urban problems became more acutely perceived, the most noticed national aspect of employment was the inter-regional one. In the latter context the pattern of unemployment across regions was of most concern but attention was also paid to variations in activity rates by region.

In considering the activity rates of different regions a certain degree of care must be taken. The calculation of activity rates for adult, male employees by region produces a significant variation, from a high of 81% in the Midlands to a low of 67% in Northern Ireland. However, with the inclusion of the self-employed, family workers and the armed forces, the variation is much reduced, from a high of 89% for the Midlands to a low of 83% for the South West. Refining the computations further to take account of students and the aged, the regional variation virtually disappears, to give the familiar result that nearly all prime males are economically active. Nevertheless, it is not without significance for the efficient allocation of resources that as many as 16.4% of male workers in Northern Ireland were estimated to be self-employed. The greater importance of agriculture in that region is unlikely to account fully for such a high figure, and the suspicion exists that so much self-employment represents considerable under-employment of labour resources.

For females the picture is more complicated. First, the variation in activity rates across regions is much more pronounced. In 1961 rates for married female employees varied from 34% in the north-west to only 17% in Wales.[1] An adjustment for the self-employed, the aged and the students does not, as with all female groups, appreciably affect the picture. For unmarried females the rates are much higher and

---

1   Bowers, *op. cit.,* p. 22.

have a smaller regional variation; nevertheless in 1961 they varied from 54% in both the Midlands and Scotland to 41% in Wales. A second feature of the pattern of regional employment for females is that the rise in activity rates has been particularly pronounced in those regions with very low rates initially. Consequently, regional variation is being progressively reduced.

I.4   Employment by Industry and Occupation

In September 1975 the manufacturing sector of the British economy employed only 33% of all employees at work.[1] Adding the number of employees in agriculture, mining, construction and gas, electricity and water we still get only 44.5% of all employees, implying that the service sector now accounts for well over half of the employment in the country. The tendency for the service sector labour force to grow relative to the whole labour force began in the mid-1950s at which time the manufacturing and service sectors each employed about 42.5% of the total number of employees.

Within the service sector the main growth areas have been professional and scientific services, particularly in education and medicine. Between June 1971 and September 1975 the numbers employed in education and medicine rose by nearly 550,000, almost the amount by which employment in manufacturing fell. Between 1959 and 1975 more than 1.4 million workers joined the education and medical sectors.[2] Some service sectors have become smaller over this period, for example, transport and communication (due mainly to the rapid decline in railway employment) but the general tendency is for growth. In contrast, virtually all the main manufacturing sectors have declined.

Another way of examining the composition of the labour force is to examine the breakdown between the private and the public sectors. For the UK working population there was an increase in the proportion of public sector workers from 25% in 1959 to 27.2% in 1974. Within that aggregate figure there has been a substantial increase in local authority workers (from 7.5% of the employed labour force in 1959 to 11.3% in 1974), a small decline in the number of workers in the public corporations (i.e. roughly, the nationalized industries) and no net change in the proportion of central government civilian employees.[3]

These structural changes are reflected in the relative growth of female employment, referred to above, because much of the service sector has made intensive use of female labour. Thus, approximately 70% of the employees in professional and scientific services are female, as against 20% in agriculture and only 5% in mining and shipbuilding. It is true that the textile and clothing industries are also female-intensive, but their decline has not been so great in contrast to service expansion. It is also worth emphasizing that a significant amount of female employment, particularly in the rapidly expanding service sectors, is part-time employment. Thus, in September 1975 more than half of the 1.2m females working in education and 45% of the nearly 1m in medicine were part-time workers. This is more than double the proportion of part-time females in manufacturing and

---

1   *DEG*, January 1976, pp. 20-3.
2   *DEG*, February 1976, pp. 188-9 and *DEG*, March 1975, pp. 196-202.
3   *ET*, February 1976, pp. 119-127.

it may suggest that the sectoral shifts that have occurred are not so much an active move away from manufacturing as an entirely appropriate tapping of a previously unused labour reserve that would not be available for full-time work or perhaps even for part-time work in other sectors.

I.5   Hours Worked

To clarify discussions of hours of work one should distinguish between normal basic hours, normal hours and actual hours of work. The first term relates to the number of hours a man is expected to work at basic rates of pay; the second includes any guaranteed overtime paid at premium rates; the third, and for most purposes much the most interesting notion, includes all overtime, guaranteed or not. Actual hours are typically in excess of normal hours, but by including absenteeism and sick days in the picture the situation may be reversed.

As with activity rates, two lines of enquiry can be distinguished for hours worked by the labour force as a whole. First, one wants to explain the trend; second, one wants to explain temporary variations around it. Further, it is revealing to examine the structure of hours worked, e.g. by occupation or wage level.

Over a long period average actual hours of work have fallen, from around sixty hours per week in the early part of the century to approximately forty-one hours by 1975. Initially, the fall was in hours per day; subsequent reductions have been first in days worked per week and second in weeks per year. There is therefore a clear tendency for extra leisure to be bunched, there being 'economies of scale' in leisure activities.

Normal hours have fallen much more rapidly than actual hours, implying an increase in the number of hours labelled 'overtime'. For example, between 1938 and 1966 actual hours fell from forty-eight to forty-six hours per week while normal hours fell from forty-seven to forty hours.[1] That such a change is to be deplored is highly debatable. The rise in overtime would seem to reflect two forces. First, with increasing National Insurance contributions, redundancy payments provisions, training costs and other fixed employment costs it is sensible for the employer to spread the higher fixed costs of hiring labour over more hours per man. Second, individual circumstances of both employers and workers vary a great deal; overtime arrangements permit greater flexibility and allow these circumstances fuller expression. A different view suggests that much overtime comes from a desire to waste time at work in order to obtain a living wage. The idea here is that some work at overtime rates is necessary for a 'living wage' to be secured. Seeing that on this view neither employer nor worker gains from such an arrangement, as compared to less work with constant earnings, it is surprising that it continues.

There is some tendency, conclusively documented for the US and also discernible in the UK, for the decline in the actual work week to be slowing up over time. This development probably reflects two forces. First, the greater enjoyment that many derive from work as the structure and skill levels of the labour force change; second, a possible slowing down of the relative fall in the price of recreational goods and services, which are complements to leisure. It is also true that measurement problems might obscure the true fall in work time. For example sick days and absenteeism

---

1   E. Whybrew, *Overtime Working in Britain, Research Paper Number 9* to the *Royal Commission on Trade Unions and Employers' Associations* (The Donovan Report), HMSO, 1968.

both show a tendency to increase over time,[1] and they are not easily caught within official hours of work data.

Hours of work fluctuate a good deal from year to year. The changing tempo of the economy is the principal explanation of these variations, with work weeks falling in recessions and rising in expansions. In addition there have recently been changes in government taxation policies, such as higher National Insurance contributions, which tend to raise average hours.

There are wide variations across industries in actual hours worked. In 1973 the average *annual* hours worked per employee in Great Britain was 2,289 in construction as against 1,432 in mining.[2] It is also clear that operatives work more hours than white collar workers and males more than females.

Some of the variation observed in such a cross-section is caused by the different experience of different industries in the business cycle. Additionally, some industries have relatively old labour forces whose work weeks are naturally shorter. Nevertheless, there are persistent real variations across industries and occupations in hours worked and these certainly affect the attractiveness of the different jobs. Some research work is beginning to explain such variations. In a recent study[3] it was shown for a sample of ninety-six industries in Britain that the number of hours offered by the average manual male worker was positively affected by the hourly wage rate and low skill levels and negatively affected by the number of fellow workers employed in the factory, residence in the South East and Midlands and residence in conurbations. Further, the number of work hours demanded from the male worker was greater when the worker was more skilled, aged between twenty-five and fifty-four and working in industries that were fast growing or highly concentrated; fewer hours were demanded from young males and from those who tended to work alongside females.

I.6 The Quality of the Labour Force

As time goes on the average skill level of members of the labour force rises. This is one component of the increased quality of the working population, implying that from a given number of workers and a given quantity of supporting factors of production potential output grows over time. Other important sources of higher quality are better health levels, an improved spatial distribution of employment and, up to a point, shorter working weeks. In quantitative terms the increases in skill levels has had much the largest impact on productivity of any of these sources.

There is no precise, independent measure of the increase in average skill level in the UK over any period and no comprehensive indication of the allocative efficiency of labour between various skill levels. In recent years, however, a number of studies have been made, mainly of the educational system. The formal education sector is not the only source of skill augmentation but the model testing its efficiency has general applicability. The problem at issue may be described as follows. If the sector is organized efficiently the net social value of the marginal pound's expendi-

---

1 For an interesting discussion of absenteeism see R. Jones, *Absenteeism*, Department of Employment, Manpower Papers No. 4, 1971.

2 *DEG*, September 1975, p. 882.

3 D. Metcalf, S. Nickell and R. Richardson, 'The Structure of Hours and Earnings in British Manufacturing Industry', *OEP*, July 1976.

ture will be the same for all types and levels of education. What we must do, therefore, is to equalize the social profit rate on all educational activities.

The terminology employed here may be disagreeable to some people. However, as long as account is taken of all sources of cost and benefit, whether they be material or psychic, no real objection is involved. It is true that some sources may not be measurable in practice and that others may be measured only imperfectly. These defects do not suggest that no measurement should take place, merely that decisions and judgements should not be based solely on what is measurable.

In fact the measurement of the profitability of education and training programmes is decidedly imperfect. The usual measure of benefits is some estimate of the expected increase in monetary earnings enjoyed by the trainee, i.e. his expected full earnings minus the earnings he would otherwise expect were he not to undertake the training under consideration. To take a concrete example, in estimating the profitability of a university degree a comparison is made between the observed earnings of people already graduated and those of people who stopped just short of going to university. This provides an earnings differential for each age group which stands for the earnings increase expected by the current trainee at each stage of his working life.

This estimate is extremely crude and a number of adjustments can be made to improve upon it. For example, not all of the crude differential can be attributed to education because ability and motivation levels differ between the two groups from which the data are drawn. Consequently, an effort should be made to estimate the independent effect of ability differences.

Once the estimate of benefits has been obtained it is necessary to estimate the costs of the training. The principal cost is the output that could have been produced by the trainee had he been in full-time work. Its value is usually measured by the monetary earnings he foregoes while being trained or educated. Added to the foregone earnings are the direct costs of instruction, represented by salaries of teachers, cost of buildings etc.

The two most substantial research efforts for the UK are by Blaug[1] and Morris and Ziderman[2] and both contain a clear account of the procedures and difficulties involved. The latter was more comprehensive and among its conclusions were (1) that postgraduate qualifications were not very profitable for society and (2) that higher national certificates were very profitable indeed. If these calculations are correct they imply that society would be better off if there were more resources involved in HNC work and less in postgraduate work. At present, these calculations suggest, the UK educational system in inefficiently structured and is turning out the wrong mix of graduates.

The importance of adequate supplies of skilled labour has been increasingly recognized in public discussion in the last ten to fifteen years. In 1964 the Industrial Training Act was passed in an attempt to increase the quantity of skilled manpower and improve the quality of training. Under the Act, Industrial Training Boards were set up for a number of industries. The Boards impose a levy on the firms in the industry and with the proceeds approved training schemes are financed. More recently the government has set up the Training Services Agency with substantial

---

1   M. Blaug, 'The Rate of Return on Investment in Education in Great Britain', *MS*, September 1965.
2   V. Morris and A. Ziderman, 'The Economic Return on Investment in Higher Education in England and Wales, *ET*, no. 211, May 1971.

funds to provide a wide range of training programmes. None of these attempts to improve the skill structure has yet been evaluated very thoroughly.

I.7 Unemployment

Unemployment is conventionally divided into three types: frictional, structural and deficient demand.

Frictional or search unemployment may be defined as that unemployment which exists when workers have to spend relatively small amounts of time and money searching for a job and do not expect to take a wage cut in their new job. It is short-duration unemployment, and some amount is necessary to ensure the efficient functioning of the labour market. A worker may quit his job voluntarily to search for improved conditions; he may have insufficient experience to get a permanent job immediately after leaving school; he may be laid off temporarily either because of a strike in another section of his plant or in a supplying firm, or because of timing factors — as with dockers, when ships are not constantly in harbour, or because of seasonal factors — as with holiday and construction workers in winter; he may be fired because the employer is dissatisfied with his performance.

Frictional unemployment will exist at 'full employment'; indeed, its extent probably increases when the economy expands because workers then quit their jobs in the confident expectation of better job opportunities elsewhere.

Structural unemployment occurs because of shifts in the relative supply of, and demand for, labour in particular regions and industries. A substantial increase in the minimum wage set by a Wages Council[1] may result in structural unemployment because the value of a worker's services is less than the wage the firm must pay him.

The demand for labour in any activity may shift because of technological advance (automation); for example as diesel engines replace steam engines the fireman becomes redundant. Also, the depletion of natural resources and the rise in foreign competition can lead to structural problems; thus the uneven incidence in unemployment by region is partly attributable to the decline of the coal, textile and shipbuilding industries.[2] Such unemployment will be particularly severe if those who become unemployed are relatively old, and will therefore tend to be less mobile and less likely to invest in retraining. As one might expect, the average age of the work force tends to be higher in declining than in expanding industries.

Supply shifts in the labour market also change the amount of structural unemployment. For example, the substantial increase in the birth rate in the immediate postwar years resulted in a large increase in the flow of degree holders in the late 1960s and early 1970s, thereby contributing to graduate unemployment in nearly all fields.

Deficient demand unemployment is a very familiar notion, but even though most commentators have an idea as to what constitutes adequate aggregate demand in the economy, the concept is slippery. For some time the orthodox Keynesian view has been that total employment can virtually always be augmented, and hence

---

1 These institutions exist in many industries with low levels of unionization. They provide collective bargaining for workers in these industries. See also section II.9.

2 The uneven increases in unemployment by region are analyzed by J. Bowers *et. al.*, 'The Change in the Relation Between Unemployment and Earnings Increases: A Review of Some Possible Explanations', *NIER*, No. 54, November 1970.

unemployment reduced, given an injection of purchasing power by the government into the economy. However, beyond a certain level of employment and output further expansion is thought to imply unacceptable, but not accelerating, rates of inflation. A different view, most prominently associated with Professor Milton Friedman, is that increases in employment beyond a certain level are not sustainable without continually accelerating inflation. As a separate point, Friedman suggests that the employment level in question is lower than that which most governments have become accustomed to think acceptable. This is not universally accepted among economists, but certainly most observers are less sanguine than they used to be as to the extent to which unemployment can be reduced permanently by expansionary policies.

Although the types of unemployment so far discussed are illuminating for some purposes it is not easy to discover how many workers, and what sorts of workers, are suffering any one type at a particular time. A different approach to understanding the incidence of unemployment would be to drop the above categories and proceed in the following way.

The unemployment rate in any area, or at any time, is the product of (1) the probability of workers becoming unemployed and (2) the average duration of unemployment. Clearly (1) and (2) are each effected by both demand and supply influences. More fully, the unemployment rate is the result of four separate possibilities: (a) the probability of being laid off or fired (i.e. involuntary separations); (b) the probability of quitting (voluntary separations); (c) the probability of being offered a new job; (d) the probability of accepting an offer.

A large number of forces affect these four probabilities, including various personal characteristics of individual workers (e.g. age, skill, sex and race characteristics) and various market demand characteristics (e.g. product, demand, rates of technical change and merger activity). In a recent study of unemployment rate differences across seventy-eight English towns,[1] it was found that unemployment rates were higher in those towns with relatively many unskilled workers and older workers and lower where there were relatively larger numbers of married workers and immigrants.

One important feature of unemployment has recently become much better understood. In any period, for example in any single month, the *net* change in unemployment is dwarfed by the number becoming unemployed and the number leaving the unemployed register. Thus, between March and April 1974 net registered unemployment rose by 55,000 but more than 350,000 came onto the register and nearly 300,000 left it. These so called 'flow' statistics emphasize the enormous turnover in the stock of unemployed that takes place at all times.

Recently, there has been increased attention paid to the problems involved in producing accurate measures of the amount of unemployment prevailing at any time.[2] One difficulty is that unemployment is both an economic and a social problem, so that a single measure may not give an adequate account of the two problems simultaneously. Thus, a large number of men each unemployed for a short period could give rise to the same unemployment rate as a small number of men each unemployed for a long period. However, the social and economic

---

1   D. Metcalf, 'Urban Unemployment in England', *EJ*, September 1975.

2   *Unemployment Statistics*, Report of an Inter-Departmental Working Party, November 1972, Cmnd. 5157.

implications would be different, both between the two cases and for either one taken separately.

Another measurement problem is to define unambiguously what one would like to measure, whether it be for social or economic purposes. One definition would be those without a job who would like one at prevailing wages; another definition would be those without a job who are looking for one; yet another definition would include in the unemployed total those in work who were not currently being fully used, either because they were not working as many hours as they would like or because they were not using to the full their productive potential.

The usual measure of unemployment used in Britain is the monthly total of those who register as unemployed. In March 1976 there were 1,300,000 workers on the register of unemployed. The main motives for registering are to qualify for unemployment benefit or other social security payments and to get access to the government's job placement services. It follows that those who are ineligible for benefit or do not want help locating a job tend not to register, even though they may in every sense be unemployed. This applies particularly to married women and young persons in the labour market for the first time. On the other hand some of those registered may not be interested in work; in this category are some of those under sixty-five years of age in receipt of an occupational pension who want their national insurance contributions paid for them so that they will be entitled to a full state retirement pension at age sixty-five.

In the monthly figures, therefore, there are elements of both under- and over-representation of those not in work but seeking it. Unfortunately, it is likely that the extent of the under- and over-representation varies over time so that even changes in the number of registered unemployed have to be interpreted with caution. For example, it is thought that the introduction of earnings related unemployment benefit may have changed the incentive to register so that a larger fraction of any true amount of unemployment is now registered. Also it is possible that registering habits differ across the country so that the reported pattern of unemployment rates by region overstates the true pattern of waste or hardship.

For these and other reasons there has been some pressure for governments to supplement the usual figures by taking monthly or quarterly surveys of the whole population, essentially to get at the unregistered unemployed. The nearest we have to this at the moment is the annual General Household Survey (the 1973 version of which was published in early 1976) This indicated for 1973 that those who declared themselves to be unemployed but not registered, accounted for 20% of male unemployment and 62% of female unemployment.[1]

II   WEALTH, INCOME AND PAY

The distribution of wealth, income and earnings are topics which excite great controversy. In this section we describe the (unequal) distributions of wealth, income and pay and discuss some of the theories advanced to account for these distributions. Our analysis of labour earnings looks at the pay structure by industry, occupation and sex, wages in local labour markets and poverty and low pay.

---

1   O.P.C.S., *The General Household Survey*, 1973, p. 70.

II.1   Distribution of Wealth[1]

The measurement of personal wealth, and its distribution, is notoriously difficult. There are three main methods by which the distribution of personal wealth can be estimated. First, a sample survey could be undertaken of individuals' assets and liabilities to determine net wealth (sometimes referred to as net worth). Such a survey is desirable in principle but would be difficult to execute because of such problems as a low response rate and the composition and valuation of items to be included in wealth. Second, the investment income method works backwards from statistics on investment income to determine the distribution of capital from which this investment income is derived. Third, under the present British tax system the only time an individual's wealth becomes known is at death when a return is filed for capital transfer tax. These estate returns to the Inland Revenue form the basis of most of our knowledge on the distribution of wealth. The calculations assume that the wealth of the individuals who die comprises a sample of the assets of the living. Some problems with this approach will be elaborated below.

The Inland Revenue wealth data based on estate returns demonstrates the inequality in the distribution of wealth. In 1974 this conventional measure showed that the richest 1% of the adult (aged eighteen and over) population owned 24% of the personal wealth and the richest 10% owned 65% of the wealth. In absolute terms the Inland Revenue estimated personal wealth in 1973 to be £164 billion, which implies an average holding of about £4,000 per head of the adult population (see table 5.1). There were 31,000 individuals with assets worth £200,000 or more and on average these people possessed wealth valued at £600,000 — some one hundred and fifty times the overall average. These figures refer to *individual* wealth. Clearly, if wealthy men marry wealthy women the distribution of wealth among families is likely to be yet more concentrated.

The main items comprising the 1973 figure of personal wealth (£164 billion) are dwellings (32.2%), securities and shares (18.2%) and life assurance policies (14.3%). The relative importance of each item varies according to the range of net wealth. For example, National Savings and household goods account for relatively high proportion of the wealth of the poorest groups while shares and land are more important for richer people.

One graphic method describing the extent of some wealth holdings is to compare such holdings with lifetime earnings. This comparison below ignores taxes and inflation: it merely brings out some rough orders of magnitude. In 1973 adult male manual earnings were approximately £2,000 p.a. If an individual entered the labour force in 1973, worked for fifty years and received £2,000 per year plus real growth in earnings of 2% per year his (undiscounted) earnings after a lifetime of work would total slightly less than £200,000. In contrast we see (table 5.1) that in 1973 31,000 individuals had personal wealth of at least £200,000. These individuals comprise the richest 0.1% in Britain. If their wealth brought no annual return these people could nevertheless sustain a consumption level equivalent to that of the typical manual worker even if they opted for a life of leisure. In fact, most

---

1   The two main sources for the discussion contained in this section are A. B. Atkinson, *The Economics of Inequality*, Oxford University Press, 1975, and Royal Commission on the Distribution of Income and Wealth (Chairman Lord Diamond), *Initial Report on the Distribution of Income and Wealth*, Cmnd. 6171, HMSO, 1975. These are referred to as Atkinson and Royal Commission.

TABLE 5.1

Inland Revenue Estimates of Personal Wealth GB, 1973

Numbers of wealth holders and amounts of net wealth, by range of net wealth; 1973

Range of net wealth (lower limit) £	Total		Males		Females	
	Number (000)	Amount (£000m)	Number (000)	Amount (£000m)	Number (000)	Amount (£000m)
Nil	3,599	1.6	1,774	0.7	1,825	1.0
1,000	4,804	8.5	2,542	4.5	2,262	4.0
3,000	2,279	9.0	1,350	5.3	929	3.7
5,000	4,082	29.8	2,584	19.1	1,498	10.7
10,000	2,229	27.7	1,496	18.4	743	9.3
15,000	782	13.9	465	8.5	317	5.3
20,000	415	9.8	241	5.9	174	3.9
25,000	629	20.9	381	12.7	248	8.2
50,000	211	13.1	125	7.7	86	5.4
100,000	79	10.0	43	5.6	36	4.5
200,000	31	19.4	18	10.9	13	8.5
Under 10,000	14,764	49.0	8,250	29.6	6,514	19.4
10,000 and over	4,375	114.8	2,759	69.7	1,617	45.2
Total	19,140	163.9	11,009	99.3	8,131	64.6

Source: Royal Commission, p. 472.

forms of wealth do bring an annual return and there are around 100,000 people who could sustain such a consumption level without ever working by virtue of the return on their holdings and the gradual erosion of their wealth over their lifetime.

These data also show a trend towards greater equality in the distribution of wealth at particular points in time. The share of the richest 1% (10%) has declined from 69% (92%) in 1911-13 to 24% (65%) in 1974:

	Share of personal wealth owned by		
	Top 0.1%	Top 1%	Top 10% of adult population
1911–13	–	69	92
1924–30	–	62	91
1936–38	27	56	88
1954	16	43	79
1960	15	38	77
1966	12	32	72
1972	–	30	72
1974	–	24	65

Source: Royal Commission.

There are a number of reasons why the degree of inequality in the distribution of wealth measured at particular intervals has lessened over this century. First, the rates of estate duty have risen steeply: Atkinson states that in 1911 an estate of

£1 million paid duty of 14% while in the early 1970s the rate was 75%; it seems
likely that such an increase in tax liability has sharpened the incentive to avoid
the duty by distributing the estate among heirs prior to death. Second, the
proportion of owner-occupied dwellings has risen from around 10% in 1900 to over
50% in the 1970s and this, coupled with the rise in house prices, has caused a sharp
narrowing in the distribution of (net) wealth. Third, it is likely that some of the
reduction in top wealth holdings between 1972 and 1974 is attributable to the
decline in share prices in 1973-4. It cannot be assumed that the trend towards a
more equal distribution of wealth will automatically persist in the future: if the
rate of increase in the proportion of householders who are owner-occupiers
declines, or if house prices fall significantly, or if share prices rise dramatically
(as they did in 1975) people will have to look at alternative measures, such as the
proposed wealth tax or capital transfer tax, to ensure that the trend towards a
more equal distribution of wealth is sustained.

The Royal Commission argued that the Inland Revenue figures tend to overstate
the true concentration of current wealth and they made a number of corrections to
the data. The results of these corrections are summarized in table 5.2.

TABLE 5.2

Royal Commission Modifications to Inland Revenue Wealth Data, 1972

	GB	
	% Share of personal wealth owned by:	
Modification	*Top 1%*	*Top 10%*
Inland Revenue data	30	72
Correction for bias in Inland Revenue estate multiplier method (e.g. property may be undervalued)	28	67
Impute wealth (an average of £700 per person) to those whom Inland Revenue assume to have zero wealth		
Allow for wealth in form of Occupational Pensions	26	64
Allow for wealth held in form of State Pensions	17	46

Source: Calculated from Royal Commission.

It will be seen that imputing some wealth to those assumed by the Inland Revenue
to have none and correcting the estate multiplier method only has a modest impact
on the concentration of wealth. When allowance is made for the imputed value of
the future stream of benefits locked away in occupational and state pension schemes
the share of personal wealth accounted for by the richest 1% (10%) declines from
28% (67%) to 17% (46%) while the share of the bottom 80% rises from 18% on
the Inland Revenue basis to 41%. This is because the inclusion of state pension
rights adds £154 billion (1972 figures) to the stock of wealth and this particular
wealth is more evenly distributed than the other forms of wealth.

It is an open question whether wealth in the form of future pension rights should
be included in these calculations and, if they should be included, the method by
which they should be calculated. Unlike wealth held as stock, land, houses, etc.,
this (anticipated future) wealth is not marketable (if it were marketable, ownership

of one individual by another would be implied). Further, if we are prepared to impute a value to the stream of future pension benefits why not also impute the (non-saleable) wealth associated with being a member of a powerful craft union or which occurs because of individual investment in education or health?

The attempts to explain the current (cross section or snapshot) distribution of wealth have concentrated mainly on the pattern of wealth accumulation over the life cycle and on inheritance.[1] Polanyi and Wood emphasize the role of the life cycle pattern of savings and asset accumulation. Even if income and inheritance were equal, some inequality in wealth would occur because older people would have saved absolutely larger amounts than younger people. This factor is important (on reasonable assumptions it can generate a situation where 10% of the population in this egalitarian society hold 30% of the wealth) but it is far from the whole story. In particular, the distribution of wealth *within* age groups is itself concentrated and similar to the overall wealth distribution, yet if the life cycle explanation is correct we should find higher wealth holdings occurring disproportionately in the older age groups.

It is possible, conceptually, that the distribution of wealth within age groups is accounted for by the dispersion of earnings and unequal savings patterns. However, this hypothesis must be rejected on the basis of the age distribution of the very rich: of those with wealth in excess of £125,000 in 1968 (the top 1% of wealth holders) one third were aged under 45. It is extremely unlikely that such wealth could have been accumulated by savings out of higher earnings. It is clear, therefore, that inheritance plays a large part in explaining the share of the very rich in the current distribution of wealth: evidence suggests that one third of the top wealth holders in Britain (top 0.1%) are self made while two thirds owe their position to inheritance.

II.2   Income Distribution

The distribution of total income from all sources (i.e. from employment, pensions, dividends etc.) is less concentrated than the distribution of wealth. This is because earnings from employment are the main source of total personal income and these earnings are more equally distributed than the investment income provided by personal wealth.

The composition of total personal income in the UK may be seen from the following figures:

Source of income	Percentage distribution		
	1951	*1971*	*1974*
Employment	71.4	70.1	69.4
Self employment	12.1	9.2	10.3
Rent, dividends, interest etc.	10.5	10.7	9.6
National insurance benefits etc.	6.0	10.0	10.7
Total personal income	100.0	100.0	100.0

Source: Social Trends, No. 6, 1975, table 5.2.

1   For a discussion of life cycle accumulation see G. Polanyi and J. Wood, *How much Inequality?*, Institute of Economic Affairs, London, 1974 and J. S. Flemming and I. M. D. Little, *Why we need a Wealth Tax,* Methuen, London, 1974. For an analysis of the role of inheritance see C. D. Harbury and P. C. McMahon, 'Inheritance and the distribution of personal wealth in Britain', *EJ,* vol. 83, 1973.

The main change which has occurred in the postwar period is the increased importance of national insurance and other state benefits in total personal income. This mainly reflects the higher unemployment levels prevailing in the 1970s and the larger number of pensioners and higher pensions.

The distribution of personal incomes is shown in table 5.3. The data are derived from Inland Revenue data supplemented by information on incomes which are not taxable (for example unemployment benefits) or are below the tax threshold. The data refer to tax units, i.e. generally consider a married couple as one unit. It will be seen that in 1972-3 the majority (59%) of pre-tax incomes were between £1,000 and £4,000 and only 3.2% of the 28m tax units had incomes over £4,000. The fact that there are relatively few people with high incomes makes the redistribution of income, and greater provision of desirable health and education services, very

TABLE 5.3

Distribution of Personal Incomes Before and After Tax, UK, 1972-3

	Pre-tax income by pre-tax range		Post-tax income by post-tax range	
	Numbers (000 tax-units)	Amounts (£m)	Numbers (000 tax-units)	Amounts (£m)
Income ranges				
Lower limit of range (£)				
Under 595	4,868	2,104	4,871	2,105
595	2,265	1,573	2,594	1,797
750	3,409	3,020	4,164	3,688
1,000	2,648	2,981	3,227	3,647
1,250	2,491	3,423	2,945	4,057
1,500	2,406	3,903	2,686	4,366
1,750	2,238	4,179	2,280	4,264
2,000	3,500	7,803	3,154	7,018
2,500	2,133	5,812	1,273	3,466
3,000	1,472	5,009	769	2,611
4,000	455	2,022	183	813
5,000	157	860	95	517
6,000	146	999	81	553
8,000	68	605	20	178
10,000	39	426	5	53
12,000	26	345	3	36
15,000	17	289	0.5	8
20,000 and over	13	411	0.5	15
All ranges	28,351	45,764	28,351	39,192

Decile shares	Pre-tax	Post-tax
Top 10%	26.9	23.6
11-20%	15.8	15.8
21-30%	13.1	13.2
31-40%	11.0	11.2
41-50%	9.2	9.5
51-60%	7.5	8.0
61-70%	5.9	6.5
71-80%	4.8	5.5
81-90%	3.1	3.6
91-100%	2.8	3.3

Source: Social Trends, No. 6, 1975; table 5.7.

difficult. While it may be possible to squeeze many thousands of pounds out of a rich individual there are so few of them that the total revenue raised by squeezing them harder is small.

The bottom part of table 5.3 provides information enabling us to compare the distributions of incomes and wealth. The top 10% (1%) of individual wealth holders accounted for 72% (30%) of conventionally defined wealth in 1972 (section II.1). In contrast the top 10% (1%) of the income distribution by tax units accounts for only 26.9% (6.4%) of total income before tax and 23.6% (4.4%) after tax. Thus income distribution is much less concentrated than the distribution of wealth. Nevertheless, the share of the top 20% of the income distribution, with 42.7% of income, is seven times the share of the bottom 20% who account for only 5.9% of the total. Likewise, the top half of the income distribution has three times the share of the bottom half. It should be borne in mind that these figures refer to the current distribution: many of those in the bottom half of the distribution in 1972-3 (e.g. some pensioners and students) will be in the top half at other points in their life. The inequality in lifetime incomes is less than the inequality of the income distribution observed at any particular point in time.

The government attempts to redress some of the inequality in income via taxes on income and expenditure and benefits in cash and in the form of services such as education and health. The relationship between taxes paid and income and benefits received and income is given in table 5.4. All taxes combined are only slightly progressive. (With a progressive tax system the ratio of tax paid to income received rises as income rises. The reverse is true for a regressive system). This is because although income tax is progressive, national insurance contributions by employees and indirect taxes are regressive.

Social service benefits as a whole are very progressive. The benefits include here: family allowances; national insurance benefits (pension, sickness, unemployment,

TABLE 5.4

Taxes and Benefits as a Proportion of Original Income, UK, 1973

	All households in sample	
Range of original income (£)	Total taxes as % of original income plus cash benefits	Total benefits as % of original income plus cash benefits
Under 381	21	126
381-556	24	84
557-815	25	66
816-1,193	30	48
1,194-1,748	32	32
1,749-2,560	33	22
2,561-3,749	33	15
3,750 +	33	9
Averages over all income ranges	32	23

Source: ET, no. 254, December 1974, tables D and E.

Note: The figures are not actually total taxes and total benefits. Some taxes such as company taxes and death duties are excluded. Similarly some benefits, particularly those that cannot be easily assigned to specific individuals, e.g. defence, are excluded.

industrial injury, maternity benefits, etc. death grants); non-contributory old age pensions; supplementary pensions and allowances; war pensions, service grants and allowances; national health services; state education; housing subsidies. The progressiveness of these benefits is primarily because flat-rate benefits are a larger proportion of low than of high incomes. Note, however, that the higher income group receive similar absolute benefits to lower income groups. The expansion of state education at higher levels which is mainly used by the middle and upper income groups is an important reason for this.

Atkinson and the Royal Commission provide evidence on trends through time in the distribution of income. The biggest change in recent years occurred between 1938 and 1949 when the pre-tax share of the top 1% fell by one third and the share of the top 10% fell from 40.5% to 32.1%. Subsequently the share of the top 10% has continued to fall but at a very modest and decelerating pace.

TABLE 5.5

Distribution of Income, Before and After Tax, UK, 1949, 1967, 1972-3

| | *Percentage share of total income (by tax unit)* | | | | | |
| | *Before tax* | | | *After tax* | | |
	Top 10%	*Next 60%*	*Bottom 30%*	*Top 10%*	*Next 60%*	*Bottom 30%*
1949	33.2	54.1	12.7	27.1	58.3	14.6
1967	28.0	61.6	10.4	24.3	63.7	12.0
1972-73	26.9	62.4	10.7	23.6	64.0	12.4

Source: Atkinson, table 4.1 and *Social Trends,* No. 6, 1975, table 5.7.

It is interesting to note (table 5.5) that the decreased share of the rich has not resulted in an equivalent gain for the poor; rather it is the middle income groups which have increased their share in total income. There has been surprisingly little discussion about the trends in income distribution detailed in table 5.5. The increased income share of the middle 60% is probably due to two important postwar features of the labour market. First, the full employment policy has (until 1975-6) ensured that there are not a large number of workers forced into the lower tail of the distribution by prolonged unemployment. Second, the increased labour force participation rates of (especially married) women have boosted the family incomes of those of labour force age.

The income figures presented and discussed in this section should be treated cautiously for the following reasons: (i) the data ignore income in the form of imputed rent from owner-occupied houses, fringe benefits, home production and capital gains; (ii) the data are uncorrected for tax evasion and misreporting; (iii) the data refer to money but not real incomes. This is important because inflation affects people differently according to the basket of goods they consume. For example over the last twenty years the price of housing, food and fuel have risen faster than the overall index of retail prices. As pensioners and low income families spend relatively large amounts of money on these items the changes in the distribution of real incomes will be different from those in the distribution of money incomes; (iv) income alone does not capture other aspects of welfare such as leisure, security and job satisfaction; (v) family composition has changed over time such that there are now more old and young people living alone; this will tend to increase the dispersion in income observed over time; (vi) the data refer to current and not lifetime income distributions.

II.3 Distribution of Earnings

The distribution of earnings, like the distribution of income, is positively skewed (median earnings are less than mean earnings). However, the earnings distribution is more equal than the distribution of income because the latter includes a return on wealth which, as we have seen, (section II.1) is very concentrated.

The dispersion of earnings in April 1975 (full time workers, men aged 21 and over, women aged 18 and over, whose pay for the survey week was not affected by absence) was as follows:[1]

| | Median earnings per week (£s) | As a % of median | | | | |
		Lowest decile	Lower quartile	Upper quartile	Highest decile	Mean
Men	55.9	67.0	81.0	125.3	157.6	108.6
Women	34.1	67.4	81.5	125.2	164.5	109.6

Both men and women towards the bottom of the distribution (specifically those at the lowest 10% point) earned two thirds of median pay while the best paid 10% earned at least half (men) or two thirds (women) more than the corresponding median.

There are two particularly important and interesting facts concerning the distribution of gross weekly earnings of male manual workers. First, the dispersion of the distribution has been remarkably stable for almost a century:[2]

| | Distribution of weekly earnings, manual men (% of median) | | | |
	1886	1938	1965	1974
Lowest decile	68.6	67.7	69.7	68.6
Lower quartile	82.8	82.1	82.9	82.2
Median	100.0	100.0	100.0	100.0
Upper quartile	121.7	118.5	121.4	121.0
Highest decile	143.1	139.9	143.9	144.1

1 *DE, New Earnings Survey 1975*, Part A, Table 15. The data discussed in this section refer to individuals, not families or Inland Revenue income units. Many people only work part time or only work part of the year and therefore the distribution of annual earnings of those who worked at any time during the year is different from the distribution above because the annual earnings distribution has a concentration of people in the lower tail.

2 *Social Trends*, No. 6, 1975, table 5.15. 1974 data refer to GB, other years refer to UK. A very full discussion of the evidence on the distribution of earnings and evaluation of theories seeking to explain this distribution is contained in A. R. Thatcher, 'The New Earnings Survey and the Distribution of Earnings', paper presented to Royal Economic Society Conference on Income Distribution, Lancaster, July 1974. We draw freely on this paper in the text.

This stability suggests that we might seek to explain the distribution of earnings by factors such as differences in ability, motivation and luck, which might be expected to remain fairly stable from one generation to the next, rather than by appeal to institutional factors such as the growth of unionism, or social forces such as the extension of public intervention, which have changed dramatically in the last century.

Second, the position an individual occupies in the distribution changes from year to year. Evidence on the gross weekly earnings of all full time adults who were in the New Earnings Surveys in 1970, 1971 and 1972 indicates that the lowest paid workers received the largest percentage increases in earnings between one survey and the next, while the higher paid workers tended to experience a decline in earnings. Such movements are known as 'regression towards the mean'. Of those manual men who were in the lowest tenth in 1970 less than half were also in the lowest tenth in both 1971 and 1972. These movements refer to weekly earnings of full time workers and therefore reflect the variable nature of many components of manual workers' earnings (e.g. overtime, short-time, bonuses, piecework), the effects of job changes and the incidence of wage settlements. Movements in individuals' hourly earnings, which may more nearly reflect skill and motivation, or in annual earnings, which may reflect the incidence of unemployment, could be more or less dramatic than the fluctuations in weekly earnings.

One important explanation of the skewed distribution of earnings relates to the coupling of natural ability and training. In a smoothly functioning, competitive labour market earnings will reflect productivity at the margin. Among all the determinants of marginal productivity we may concentrate here on a worker's 'natural ability' and training. If, for a given level of formal training, a man comes to the labour market with relatively great motivation, ability and drive he will tend to earn more than the average worker. Further, it is established that on average the more naturally gifted man tends to undertake more than average amounts of training. An unskewed distribution of ability combined with a skewed distribution of training produces a skewed distribution of productivity. The last, in an approximately competitive market, produces a skewed earnings distribution.

This simple picture is only a partial explanation of the actual earnings distribution. First, not everyone has equal access to the educational and training sectors, even where natural ability is the same for all. One implication is that relatively bright working-class children have difficulty in getting sufficient secondary and advanced education. This means that ability is not properly harnessed with education, thereby reducing the degree of earnings inequality.

Second, in some activities, including many of the professions, free entry of labour is restricted and earnings are pushed above the competitive level. This will raise inequality, at least as measured by comparing the bottom 20% of wage-earners with the top 20%, because the low paid can only rarely restrict entry.

Third, luck plays a significant part in determining earnings, particularly in any one year. The last qualification is important because a more valid measure of material well-being than current earnings is the discounted sum of lifetime earnings. If a man is lucky one year but unlucky the next we should derive a misleading view of his well-being by looking at either year in isolation. Similarly, if a man is receiving low wages currently because he is training, but expects to do well when he is trained, it would be mistaken to view him as a poverty case. The same may apply to people approaching retirement. When measured by lifetime earnings the distribution of material rewards is substantially more equal than when measured in cross-section by current earnings.

There has recently become available in Britain a rich new data source, the General Household Survey, which provides each year information on individual earnings and related individual characteristics such as age, schooling, work experience, race and family background. Some preliminary research has been undertaken analyzing this data.[1] Approximately one third of the variation in the annual earnings of the 7,000 or so male employees in the survey is explained by years of schooling (for which the individual receives a compensating wage differential to make up for his foregone earnings while undertaking extra schooling) and work experience; these two variables measure the human capital embodied in the individual. A further third of the variance in earnings is explained by differences in the number of weeks worked in a year by each individual (which may itself be explained by human capital factors: for example skilled workers experience less unemployment than unskilled workers).

One particularly important finding concerns the influence of colour and country of birth on pay. Other things equal (i.e. holding constant age, experience, weeks worked, years of schooling, marital status etc.) nonwhites receive annual earnings 9.3% lower than whites and people born outside Britain receive 5.1% less than the British born. The composite differential for nonwhites born outside Britain is 13.9%. These differentials occur because black and brown workers tend (like women) to be crowded into low paying occupations and industries. This in turn discourages them from undertaking extra schooling or training because the payoff to such investment is lower than it is for whites. Further their occupational status may lead potential employers to conclude that nonwhites are feckless when in fact their higher average turnover rate or higher average absenteeism rate are characteristics of their occupations and industries and not inherent racial characteristics. For example a study of labour turnover at London Transport[2] showed that, other things being equal, blacks had a longer duration of employment than whites. It seems clear that the occupational composition of black and brown workers, as compared to white workers, will shortly (quite rightly) become a pressing policy issue. The problem is in many ways analogous to that facing women (see section II.6).

A nice contrast to the inferior economic status of nonwhite workers in Britain occurs if we examine the pay of the chief executives (i.e. highest paid director) in UK companies. The highest paid director in every industrial order (in 1971) was paid over £32,000 and the top man in the Green Shield Trading Stamp Company received £282,035. This executive pay information is quite new and has recently been analyzed to determine the extent to which economic forces are important in explaining the pay structure of these top earners.[3] The main influence on pay is company size (measured by assets or sales) which alone explains half of the variance in chief executive salaries. The relationship between profitability and pay, while positive, is much weaker. Further, *ceteris paribus,* executives in monopolistic or

---

1 Mark Stewart, 'Determinants of Earnings in Britain', WP/88, June 1975, mimeo, and G. Psacharopoulos and R. Layard, 'Human Capital and Earnings: British Evidence and a Critique', January 1976, mimeo. The research is being undertaken at the Centre for the Economics of Education, London School of Economics.
2 J. Smith, *Labour Supply and Employment Duration in London Transport,* Greater London Paper No. 15, 1976.
3 A. Cosh, 'The remuneration of chief executives in the UK', *EJ,* vol. 85, No. 337, March 1975.

oligopolistic industries (as measured by industrial concentration) do not receive higher rewards than those in other industries. The Confederation of British Industry and other employers' groups continually bemoan the low level of profitability of British industry. It would appear that some part of the remedy for this low profitability lies in their own hands: why not reward chief executives more on the basis of their company's profits and less on the basis of their size?

The Royal Commission on the Distribution of Income and Wealth has investigated the pay of those earning over £10,000 a year.[1] In 1974-5 there were 65,000 individuals who earned £10,000 or above. They comprised 0.3% of the labour force and accounted for 2.1% of the total employment income received by all persons. Only one in fifty of these high earners were women. These people were disproportionately represented in London and the South East and tended to work in managerial occupations. The evidence shows that the inequality in the distribution of earnings has declined modestly since 1959. For example the pay of the highest millile (i.e. top 0.1%; implying in turn that the pay of 99.9% of males fell below the following figures) rose from £5,854, or ten times median earnings, in 1959-60 to £12,590, or eight times the median, in 1972-3. Further, the real disposable earnings (i.e. after allowing for income tax and the increase in the retail price index) of those in the top 0.1% of the distribution actually fell a little in the decade prior to 1973-4 while median earnings rose some 18%. This was one reason why industrialists and other pundits expressed concern that the 1975-6 pay policy, which permitted no pay rises for those earning over £8,500 per year, would seriously erode the incentive to extra effort and responsibility among our top managers. Nevertheless, despite this trend towards greater equality in the distribution of earnings it should be remembered that, post tax, the earnings of the top 1.0% of males in 1973-4 were over three times median earnings while those in the top 0.1% earned over seven times the median.

We now turn to examine some more narrowly defined aspects of the distribution of earnings. The next four sections analyze the pay structure by occupation, industry, sex, and in local labour markets. The lower tail of the income distribution is studied in the final sections on poverty and low pay.

II.4   Wage Structure by Occupation

The foundations of wage theory are contained in two famous principles. First, Adam Smith's principle of *net advantage* states that when competition exists in the labour market the 'whole of the advantages and disadvantages' of different occupations will continually tend towards equality. Note that this principle does not imply that wages will tend towards equality, but that (suitably discounted) lifetime returns to one occupation will tend to equal those in another occupation. The returns that make an occupation attractive or unattractive are both pecuniary and non-pecuniary. Second, we have the principle of *non-competing groups,* which evolved from the work of John Stuart Mill and Cairnes; this states (broadly) that certain non-competitive factors may inhibit the tendency towards equality in net advantages.

Linked to these two principles are two sets of reasons for the existence of

---

1 Royal Commission on the Distribution of Income and Wealth (Diamond Commission) 3rd Report, Cmnd. 6383 HMSO, January 1976.

occupational wage differentials: compensatory wage differentials and non-compensatory wage differentials.

Compensatory wage differentials are those differentials which are consistent with competition in the labour market.[1] If individuals were not compensated for the factors listed below (in the form of higher wages when at work) then the supply of labour to those occupations would tend to be deficient. All other things being equal, individuals will tend for example to be compensated in the form of higher wages for entering occupations that (1) require long periods of education and/or training, (2) are dangerous or dirty, (3) are subject to lay offs or have a relatively short working life. (4) Also if they are risk averters, they will desire to be compensated in terms of the mean earnings of the occupation if the dispersion of the earnings around the mean is very large. (5) Differentials will also accrue to wholly exceptional workers, such as professional sportsmen and entertainers', this being an example of economic rent applied to the labour market.

Non-compensatory occupational wage differentials are different. They occur for institutional or economic reasons inconsistent with perfect competition. For example, *ceteris paribus:* (1) legislation which raises the school leaving age will tend to raise the wages of teenagers relative to non-teenagers; it reduces the supply of teenagers below what it would otherwise have been. (2) Minimum wage legislation will tend, at least in the short run, to raise the pay of (employed) unskilled workers relative to skilled workers. (3) Equal Pay for Women legislation will tend to raise the pay of (employed) women relative to men. (4) If a union is able to exercise strict control over the supply of entrants to an occupation the earnings of those in that occupation will be higher than they would otherwise have been.

Earnings by broad occupational group are presented in Table 5.6. It will be seen that the earnings of the non-manual occupations are greater than those of manual workers. This reflects in some large part the relative education/training intensities of the two groups. There is also evidence of other compensating differentials. Within group 12, furnacemen earn 136.0p per hour while plumbers earn 126.1p per hour. The furnacemen are being compensated for the unpleasant conditions in which they work. Bricklayers (group 14) earn 127.6p per hour, while general labourers (group 16) earn 101.4p: the bricklayers are being compensated for their relatively low earnings while apprenticed. Within group 7, firemen earn 124.7p per hour while security guards earn 107.7p. The firemen are being compensated because their job is dangerous.

There is also evidence of individuals being compensated for being more able, or having more alternative job opportunities or undertaking a more skilled task, even though the length of education and training is similar to that of their less skilled colleagues. In group 2, for example, teachers in further education earn 300p per hour which is 33p more than secondary school teachers earn. Within group 15, the earnings of a lorry driver are positively related to the size of vehicle: drivers of heavy goods vehicles (over 3 tons) earn 10p per hour more than other goods drivers.

Trade unions are able to influence the occupational earnings structure if the demand for labour is inelastic and/or if they can control the labour supply. For

---

1   The extent to which the occupational pay structure is the outcome of competitive forces or of custom excites considerable controversy. Two good articles on the controversy are M. Fisher, 'The Human Capital Approach to Occupational Wage Differentials', *International Journal of Social Economics,* vol. 1, no. 1, 1974 and G. Routh, 'Interpretations of Pay Structure', *International Journal of Social Economics,* vol. 1, no. 1, 1974.

TABLE 5.6

Earnings by Occupation: Full Time Adult Men, April 1975

Occupation		Average gross weekly earnings (£)	Average gross hourly earnings (p)
Non Manual			
1	Professional and related management and administration	79.6	211.5
2	Professional and related in education, welfare and health	74.3	222.0
3	Professional and related in science, engineering and technology	72.4	183.6
4	Managerial	67.7	170.7
5	Clerical and related	52.1	126.4
6	Selling	54.2	132.0
7	Security and protective service	62.2	138.3
Manual			
8	Catering, cleaning, hairdressing	46.9	99.2
9	Farming, fishing and related	42.2	89.7
10	Materials processing (excluding metals)	53.9	118.0
11	Making and repairing (excluding metal and electrical)	55.2	123.3
12	Processing, making, repairing (metal and electrical)	59.7	129.0
13	Painting, repetitive assembling, product inspection	53.9	120.5
14	Construction, mining	59.1	126.2
15	Transport operating	55.4	112.2
16	Miscellaneous	51.8	110.2
	Total: Manual	55.7	119.2
	Total: Non-Manual	68.4	174.6
	Total: All occupations	60.8	139.3

Source: DE, *New Earnings Survey 1975,* Part A, table 8.

Note: Both sets of figures exclude those whose pay was affected by absence. The gross hourly earnings figure excludes the effect of overtime.

example, the hourly earnings of occupational groups 5 and 14 are identical but miners (group 14) earn 180.8p, which is 62.6% more than postmen (group 5) earn. This reflects, in part, the strength of the National Union of Miners, conferred by the inelastic demand for domestic coal which results from the currently used methods of electricity generation, together with limitations on imports. In contrast the lengthy postmen's strike of 1972 certainly did not bring the country to a halt, partly because telephonists and other postal workers continued working and tolerable substitutes were therefore available for the postal workers' services.

II.5   Wage Structure by Industry

There are a number of reasons for studying the industrial wage structure. First, it is important to know whether labour can be allocated among industries independently of wages or whether expanding (contracting) industries must pay higher (lower) wages to get the labour they require. Such information is useful in designing a pay policy. Second, how are the gains in labour productivity distributed? They can go to labour in the form of higher wages or firms in the form of higher profits or consumers in the form of lower prices. Analysis of the industrial wage structure provides evidence on the topic. Third, it is important to know whether, independent of the characteristics of the individuals working in the industry, highly concentrated industries or industries with large plants pay higher wages; such data would be useful in, for example, designing our monopoly legislation.

Wage Changes and Employment Changes:[1] Price theory implies that in the long run, given competitive conditions, each industry will, *ceteris paribus,* pay for a given grade of labour a wage identical to that paid by other industries. The *ceteris paribus* assumption implies that there are no differences in the non-pecuniary attractions of different industries or locations or in the cost of living by location. In the long run therefore the growth in industry wage levels should not be correlated with the growth in the amount of labour employed. In the short run an industry which expands its demands for labour will tend to have to raise the wages it pays because of short-run inelasticities in labour supply. Therefore the theory predicts a positive association in the short run between changes in employment by industry and changes in wages by industry.

The OECD found that in all cases but one the short run (i.e. one year) associations between changes in earnings and changes in employment were positive in the UK in the 1950s. Reddaway examined the employment changes and earnings changes in 111 minimum list heading industries between 1951 and 1955 and found a positive association (r = + 0.43). Finally Phelps Brown and Browne made a similar calculation for 132 industries over 1948 to 1958 and found a tendency for the relative earnings of expanding industries to rise and contracting industries to fall (r = + 0.24). These studies suggest therefore that the market labour supply curve does slope upwards in the short run but that in the long run an industry can get all the labour it requires at the going wage rate. Thus a pay policy which hoped to avoid labour shortages developing might need to permit labour shortage sectors to pay above the norm.

Wage Changes and Productivity Changes: An industry may react to an increase in physical productivity by lowering its relative product price or raising the relative wages it pays. If wage changes among industries are significantly (positively) related to movements in value productivity (i.e. variations in physical productivity and product prices taken together) this implies that non-competitive forces, such as ability to pay, determine the wage structure. In contrast, if the differential wage changes are unrelated to change in value productivity by industry this implies that

---

1   OECD, *Wages and Labour Mobility,* 1965, pp. 85-118; W. B. Reddaway, 'Wage Flexibility and the Distribution of Labour', *LBR,* October 1959; E. H. Phelps Brown and M. Browne, 'Earnings in Industries of the UK 1948-1959', *EJ,* vol. 72, September 1962. These references also contain information on earnings and productivity cited below.

competitive forces dominate in the explanation of wages. We anticipate such forces will be important because there is no reason, on equity or efficiency grounds, to expect that sectors with high labour productivity or growth in labour productivity will, *ceteris paribus*, pay high wages: working with bigger machines, if the intensity of work is unchanged, is no reason for higher pay (see also section III.2).

Neither Phelps Brown and Browne (using observations from one hundred and thirteen industries) nor OECD (using observations from eighty-six industries) found any relationship between changes in male average hourly earnings and changes in the gross value of output per worker over the period 1948-54. The correlation coefficient (r) in the OECD study was .05. This is clear evidence in favour of the competitive hypothesis: differential inter-industry wage changes appear unrelated to differential productivity changes. A more recent study[1] also found no association between industrial capital: labour ratios and earnings. Individuals who work with a lot of capital do not receive higher pay, *ceteris paribus*, than individuals working with little capital. These findings are reassuring. They suggest that workers who cannot increase their productivity easily (such as musicians or nurses) do not find their relative position in the pay structure worsening persistently. Further, they also indicate that, after allowing for general inflation, the gains from increased labour productivity flow mainly to consumers.

Industry Characteristics and Wage Levels: There has been considerable interest recently in the idea that the labour market is segmented into two (or more) sectors, one of which is high paying, with well developed internal labour markets allowing for promotion within the firm, employing high quality labour with low quit propensities and the other with opposite characteristics. Some recent studies on the structure of earnings in British manufacturing industry throw some light on this idea.[2]

Differences among industries in the demographic composition of their work-forces are partly responsible for inter-industry wage differentials. Industries which employ skilled prime age workers pay, on average, higher wages than other industries. What is more interesting is that even after allowing for the influence of personal characteristics, industries with large plants or which are highly concentrated tend to pay higher wages than industries with small plants or which are atomistic.

Highly concentrated industries might pay higher wages, *ceteris paribus*, for two reasons (though both appear *a priori* unlikely to us). First, if the high concentration reflects monopoly power and supernormal profits are earned by concentrated industries, the managers of those industries might attempt to purchase good industrial relations by sharing those profits with their employees. Second, the high wages paid in concentrated industries might be an attempt by the existing firms to forestall entry by new firms. Industries with large plants have a high proportion of shift work and workers on payments-by-results schemes which both boost average

---

1   W. Hood and R. D. Rees, 'Inter Industry Wage Levels in the UK Manufacturing Industry', *Manchester School*, 1974.

2   D. Metcalf, S. Nickell and R. Richardson, 'The Structure of Hours and Earnings in British Manufacturing Industry', *Oxford Economic Papers*, July 1976; M. Sawyer, 'The Earnings of Manual Workers: A Cross Section Analysis', *Scottish Journal of Political Economy*, vol. XX, No. 2, June 1973; J. Shorey, 'Wage Differentials by Plant Size', mimeo, Cardiff University 1975; A. Tylecote, 'Determinants of Changes in the Wage Hierarchy in UK Manufacturing Industry: 1954-70', *British Journal of Industrial Relations*, vol. XIII, No. 1, March 1975.

pay but even after allowing for these institutional arrangements large plant industries still have relatively high pay.

This evidence provides modest support for the notion of a segmented labour market. Big firms in monopolistic industries (the so-called primary sector) pay high wages relative to small firms in unconcentrated industries (the secondary sector). This wage differential is attributable, apparently, to higher labour quality, the disutility of working in large plants, the higher profits of concentrated industries and the higher density of union membership in the primary sector. However, the policy implications of such findings are far from clear. Should we, for example, encourage unionization in the secondary sector or discourage it in the primary sector? Should we encourage small plants to merge? Further to the extent that labour quality is important the evidence does not tell us which firms will choose a low wage, low labour quality, low productivity strategy as against a high wage, high quality, high productivity strategy. Clearly, there is a lot more work to be done before we can fully understand the factors underlying the structure of earnings across industries.

II.6   Wage Structure by Sex[1]

Evidence: Females account for 40% of employees in employment in Britain, yet less than 2% of those earning over £10,000 per year in 1974-5 were females. Females earn less than males in each broad occupational and industrial group: the data in table 5.7 show that the hourly earnings of full time female adult workers were, on average, 70.6% of male hourly earnings and that the percentage differential between male and female pay is higher for non-manual workers than for manual workers.

There are two broad reasons why average male pay exceeds average female pay. First, and more important, women are crowded into the low paying occupations and industries. Second, within occupational groups women tend to be paid less than men. In education, for example, women are disproportionately represented in the relatively low paying primary segment and within primary school teaching women earn 213p. per hour, which is 53p. (24.8%) less than men in primary teaching. It must be noted, however, that even within primary teaching the main reason for the differential is not that women are paid less than men for doing the same job but rather than women are underrepresented in the higher paying headship and deputy headship jobs. This example could be repeated for other occupations and industries.

Reasons women earn less than men: The main reason women earn less than men is that their attachment to the labour force is weaker than that of men. This relatively weak attachment is in large part because it is widely believed that it is the role of women rather than men to drop out of the labour force to care for young children: the lower lifetime commitment of women to the labour force is a response to centuries of social conditioning rather than an inherent trait. Attitudes on the roles

---

1 In view of the importance of this issue there has been surprisingly little research on it in Britain. A useful summary of the existing literature is B. Chiplin and B. Sloan, 'Equal Pay in Britain', in B. Pettman, *Equal Pay for Women: Progress and Problems in Seven Countries,* MCB Books, Bradford, 1975. This volume discusses the labour market status of females in Britain, US, Germany, Canada, Australia, New Zealand and Japan.

TABLE 5.7

Male — Female Hourly Earnings, Full Time Workers, April 1975

	Female (p)	Male (p)	Female/Male (%)
Total manual	81.1	119.2	68.0
Total non-manual	105.9	174.6	60.7
Total	98.3	139.3	70.6
All Wage Boards and Wage Councils			
Manual	70.3	97.9	71.8
Non-manual	73.1	125.3	58.3
Occupations: non-manual			
Professional: management	154.7	211.5	73.1
Professional: health, education, welfare	151.5	222.0	68.2
Professional: science, engineering, technology	123.9	183.6	67.5
Managerial	99.7	170.7	58.4
Clerical	94.5	126.4	74.8
Selling	68.9	132.0	52.2
Occupations: manual			
Catering, cleaning, hairdressing	80.5	99.2	81.1
Materials processing (excluding metals)	78.5	118.0	66.5
Making and repairing (excluding metal and electrical)	79.1	123.3	64.2
Processing, making, repairing (metal and electrical)	86.5	129.0	67.1
Repetitive assembling etc.	81.9	120.5	68.0
Transport etc.	85.0	112.2	75.8

Source: DE, *New Earnings Survey, 1975,* Part A, tables 8 and 9.

Note: Data refers to adult workers whose pay in the survey week was not affected by absence and excludes the effect of overtime.

of the two sexes can certainly be influenced by economic factors; for example the two world wars, which caused the demand for female labour to rise substantially, were particularly important in raising the labour force status of women. This suggests that the respective roles of men and women are thus amenable to change via economic and other influences. The observed weaker labour force attachment causes females to be crowded into the lower paying segments of the labour force and, in some cases, to be paid less than men in a given task. Some manifestations of the relative labour force attachments of men and women, which partially determine their occupational composition, include the following.

Labour turnover is higher for women than for men. Such turnover imposes costs on the employer; at a minimum these costs will be the hiring costs incurred when replacing employees. The *New Earnings Survey* shows that in April 1974 the number of female employees who had been with their employer under twelve months was 28.5% while the corresponding male figure was 18.6%.[1] It is often

1 *DEG,* January 1975, p. 25-26.

argued that these figures reflect a composition effect, i.e. that females are disproportionately represented in industries and occupations which themselves have high turnover. This appears not to be true: in every industry and every occupation except one female turnover is greater than male turnover. An alternative possibility, however, concerns the age composition of the labour force. Young workers have dramatically higher turnover rates than prime-age and older workers. Therefore some of the observed higher female labour turnover may occur because younger workers account for a higher fraction of the female labour force than the male labour force.

Females are also more prone to absenteeism. In April 1970, for example, 23.8% of full-time adult women were paid for less than their normal working hours because they were absent from work owing to sickness (certified or uncertified), late arrival or early finish, holidays or other approved absence, or unspecified reasons. The corresponding figure for men was only 15.9%. Absenteeism also causes costs to employers, for example, by disrupting production schedules.

Because women have higher turnover rates than men, employers have less incentive to pay for female training. A profit-maximizing employer will be willing to pay for his employees' training if he can get a return on his investment by paying the trainee less than the value of his services when the training is completed. Given that women are more likely to quit or to be absent from a firm than men employers will prefer to train men. This is compounded by hours legislation prohibiting women from working over a certain number of hours per week or at certain times.

Similarly, girls have less incentive to finance their own education and training. Staying on at school or university or taking a computer programming course entails costs, for example tuition costs or foregone earnings (i.e. earnings that could have been received if working). If a woman has children this will involve a period out of the labour force; further, women retire at a younger age than men. Thus the time over which she will receive benefits (in the form of higher earnings) from the training is less than for a man. Thus, of those young persons entering employment in 1974, 44.3% of the boys entered apprenticeships to skilled occupations or employment leading to recognized professional qualifications, while only 8.3% of girls followed this route. In contrast 40.0% of the girls are immediately segmented into clerical employment. The contrast is even clearer if we consider highly qualified people (i.e. those holding an academic or professional qualification of degree standard). The DE estimates[1] that in 1971 the stock of such highly qualified males was 1,060,000, compared with 352,000 females.

If females go out of the labour force for a period in their twenties or thirties they will accumulate less experience and seniority (on the job training, learning by doing) than males. On all these grounds, females will tend to be less productive than males. They will therefore earn less within a given occupation and will be less likely to progress up the occupational hierarchy.

Females will also tend to be paid less than men if the firm draws them from a limited geographical area: they will incur lower transport costs on average than will men. Also, women may tend to work in more pleasant conditions.

The structure of the industries in which females work is a further element in the explanation of the sex differential. Females are disproportionately represented in small plants and atomistic industries, which tend to pay less and offer poorer career

---

1 DE, *Employment Prospects for the Highly Qualified,* Manpower Paper No. 8, HMSO, 1974.

prospects than larger plants and concentrated industries; also a relatively low proportion of the female labour force is unionized, which reflects in part the higher costs of organizing in industries consisting of small plants.

Discrimination: It is frequently alleged that the main cause of the pay differentials is that discrimination exists against women. However, it seems unlikely that discrimination *in the labour market* is an important cause of their low pay and lack of promotion. Employer discrimination means that if the net value of the woman's service is identical to that of the man the latter receives a higher wage. The only way that the woman can offset the employer's discrimination is to accept a lower wage. If *all other things are equal* yet firms pay, because of discrimination against women, higher wages to men than to women, then higher profits will accrue to the firm that replaces men with women. Male sales assistants are paid 105p per hour whilst females are paid 65p per hour. It is unlikely that if both males and females were equally productive, firms would not substitute female labour for male labour.

It should be noted that none of the above discussion implies that women are not discriminated against in society at large — they obviously are. The crucial question is how that discrimination can be ended, and the problem here concerns the causal relationship. We believe that if females could be given greater incentives than they have at present to remain in the labour force, accumulate experience, undertake training, travel longer distances etc., then this will cause the distinction between the traditional roles of men and women to be eroded fairly speedily.

The equal pay and equal opportunity legislation which effectively came fully into force in 1976 should provide some incentive to stronger female labour force attachment. However, should this legislation prove too frail other policies exist to improve the lot of women in the labour market and these will be considered below.

The purpose of the Equal Pay Act is to eliminate discrimination against women in connection with wages and fringe benefits. A woman is to receive equal treatment when she is employed (a) on work of the same or broadly similar nature to that of men; (b) in a job which, though different from those of men, has been given an equal value to men's jobs under a job evaluation exercise. Thus the act is designed to ensure that if the net value of a woman's services is identical to that of a man both will receive identical wages and conditions. While this act may be of some use in eliminating any blatant wage discrimination against women it is unlikely to have far-reaching effects.

If discrimination does exist it is based on hostility to women employees or lack of information (e.g. employers think that women will be more likely to be absent or to quit and therefore pay them less than men or refuse to promote them). The Equal Pay Act by itself is likely to lead to a reduction in information about the relative performance of men and women both because of segregation and because female unemployment may rise because of the higher costs of employing women.

On two grounds, at least, the act may result in reduced employment of women, especially where men and women are doing the same job. First, if employers do discriminate against women then the legislation will protect men's jobs by reducing the possibilities of women replacing men by accepting lower pay. Second, female employment may fall if the cause of the pay differentials is not discrimination but lower female productivity or the higher costs of employing females. If this is the case then female labour costs per unit of output might rise and women be replaced by machines or men.

Further, the intentions of the act can be overcome in a number of ways. Men and women can be segregated by job: this is clearly happening already. The standard occupational classification lists over two hundred occupations but the 1975 New Earnings Survey reports only thirteen occupations with sufficient men and women to provide comparisons of their earnings. It seems possible that this act will therefore compound rather than reduce occupational segregation. If women believe that they are nevertheless doing work of equal value the jobs can be subjected to a job evaluation scheme. But the employer can give a relatively high weight in such a scheme to attributes such as physical strength where men have a relative advantage, and a low weight to manual dexterity where women have the advantage (although there is a right of appeal on the 'fairness' of the job evaluation scheme). Legislation precludes women from night work and limits the number of overtime hours women may work; an employer may therefore pay large shift work or overtime supplements. It is likely therefore that the Equal Pay Act will only have a modest impact.

The Sex Discrimination Act will probably be more important in overcoming the current underrepresentation of women in high paying sectors. It covers education and the supply of goods and services as well as employment. The act says that women must be given equal treatment in the arrangements for selecting a candidate for a job, in the terms on which a job is offered, on access to promotion, transfer and training or any other aspects of the job and on dismissal. The act establishes the Equal Opportunities Commission with fairly wide powers: it can help individuals to bring cases if it considers them of wider interest; it can conduct formal investigations compelling people to give evidence; it can serve non-discrimination notices and seek injunctions against persistent discriminators.[1]

The Employment Protection Act (1976) should also favourably influence women's labour force commitment. It provides for six weeks' paid maternity leave and twenty-nine weeks unpaid leave with no loss of seniority or status. This legislation is of particular significance for women in highly skilled sectors.

If the legislation proves inadequate the government could consider a number of alternative strategies to improve the labour force status of women. First, it might encourage them to join unions. It has recently been shown that the male-female wage differential is, *ceteris paribus*, much smaller in those industries which are highly unionized.[2] Second, more girls could be encouraged to take apprenticeship or college training by providing them with differentially large training grants. Third, female quotas, especially in the higher occupational grades, could be enforced. Finally, women's pay could be forced up relative to men's pay by subsidizing women's employment.

II.7 Local Labour Markets

A local labour market may be defined as 'the geographic area containing those actual or potential members of the labour force that a firm might induce to enter its employ under certain conditions, and other employers with which the firm is in

---

1 For more details on equal pay and equal opportunity legislation see DE, *A Guide to the Equal Pay Act 1970*, HMSO, 1975; Home Office, *A Guide to the Sex Discrimination Act 1975*, HMSO, 1975; *The Economist*, 27 January 1975.

2 S. Nickell, 'An Analysis of the Industrial Wage Structure for both Men and Women', *BJIR*, March 1977.

competition for labour'.[1] Evidence suggests that, for a given occupation, substantial dispersion of earnings exists within the local labour market. For example Robinson, examining earnings in ten occupations in engineering plants within an (unspecified) local labour market, finds that the range in pay between the highest and lowest paying plants is never less than 55% and is over 100% on two occasions.

Mackay,[2] examining engineering plants in Birmingham and Glasgow, confirms that such dispersion in earnings is normal. These authors also find (1) the rankings of plants by wage levels is stable through time; (2) high wage plants with respect to one occupation tend to be high paying with respect to other occupations; (3) wage dispersion is as high in Glasgow, where unemployment is relatively high, as in Birmingham where it is relatively low.

What are we to make of these findings? In particular, do the findings help us to accept or reject the hypothesis that earnings are determined by competitive forces in the labour market? If the observed earnings differentials reflect inter-plant differences in labour quality, or in non-monetary advantages or in monetary fringe benefits (e.g. pensions), or in short-run shifts in labour demand, we may accept the competitive hypothesis. If, on the other hand, they are related merely to plant size or ability to pay, we must reject the competitive hypothesis. It is quite possible that the observed wage dispersion indicates the existence of healthy competition in the labour market, in contrast to an institutional domination of wage determination which would establish a common rate across all plants. It may also reflect the fact that information about wages and conditions in other plants is costly to obtain, thus allowing inter-plant wage differentials to persist for a long time.

Evidence from another source shows that earnings in local labour markets in engineering are positively related to plant size.[3] The rank correlation coefficients found between earnings and plant size by industry were:

Electrical machinery	+0.85	Radio and telecommunications	0.00
Motor vehicles	+0.78	Mechanical engineering	+0.19
Insulated wires	+0.65	Metal working	+0.37
Scientific instruments	+0.73		
Miscellaneous electrical	+0.73		

The rank correlation coefficients for the industries on the left-hand side are statistically significant. Before such evidence is used to refute the hypothesis that wages are determined by competitive factors it is necessary to show that the quality of labour is the same in all plants: it could be that the large plants pay high wages to get superior quality labour. Indeed in their conclusions the authors stress the importance of competitive conditions in determining engineering wages: 'There was recurring evidence in all the studies of the need for earnings to conform in some degree to prevailing local levels. In engineering it was found that if the average

1   D. Robinson, 'External and Internal Labour Markets', in D. Robinson (ed.), *Local Labour Markets and Wage Structures*, Gower Press, 1970, ch. 2. This book contains a wealth of evidence on earnings within local labour markets and within individual plants.

2   D. Mackay, 'Wages and Labour Turnover', in *ibid.*, ch. 3. Mackay's findings are reported more fully in D. Mackay, D. Boddy, J. Brack, J. Diack and N. Jones, *Labour Markets under Different Employment Conditions*, Allen and Unwin, 1971. This excellent book contains precise summaries of previous literature on local and internal labour markets and an elegant synthesis of theory and facts. It also contains a full discussion of factory (i.e. intra-plant) wage structures and labour turnover which pressure on space forces us to omit here.

3   S. Lerner, J. Cable and S. Gupta, *Workshop Wage Determination*, Pergamon, 1969, p. 32.

earnings in a works were below the modal level for a district, this was usually sufficient grounds for securing a wage increase from the local employers' association'.[1] Thus firms which paid less than the going rate in an area tended to find that they experienced problems recruiting and retaining adequately qualified labour.

Clearly therefore competitive forces do exert an influence on earnings differentials among plants in a local labour market. However, the strength and extent of noncompetitive forces remain an open question. Do they dominate competition or are they of trivial importance? Mackay believes that one important set of factors in pay determination inconsistent with competition is 'the circumstances of the individual plant', particularly its profit levels or whether 'higher wages can be passed on through higher prices due to favourable product market conditions'. However, 'imperfect knowledge, inertia on the part of employees, collusion between employers through anti-pirating agreements, discrimination in favour of employees against non-employees' are certainly not important causes of plant wage differentials in those local labour markets in the midlands and in Scotland studied by Mackay. It will be a long time before we have sufficient evidence to reach firm general conclusions on this interesting and important question.

II.8   Poverty[2]

One aspect of income distribution which causes widespread concern is the problem of poverty. Low earnings from work are only one part of the poverty problem, which also encompasses hardship faced by, for example, old people, sick or disabled people, families with large numbers of children, fatherless families, and the unemployed.

The Current Position: Currently poor or disadvantaged people are aided by the state in five ways. (i) National Insurance benefits, mainly retirement pensions, unemployment and sickness pay; these benefits are paid as a right to those satisfying the statutory conditions. Payments vary according to marital status and number of children. (ii) Supplementary benefits to persons over sixteen who involuntarily fall below a prescribed 'tolerable' level of income laid down by Parliament below which it is felt to be wrong that any family's income should be allowed to fall. These benefits are paid only after investigation of the individual's family circumstances. (iii) Family allowances are paid for all dependent children other than the first, up to a maximum age of nineteen. Under the 'clawback' scheme these benefits are taxed specially and therefore are of greater net absolute money value to poor than to rich people. (iv) An array of benefits in kind exists in housing (e.g. rent and rate rebates), education (e.g. school milk and meals), health (e.g. wigs, spectacles, prescriptions and dental services) and legal aid. (v) Family income supple-

---

1   *Ibid.*, p. 250.
2   For a fuller discussion of the poverty issue see A. B. Atkinson, *The Economics of Inequality*, Clarendon UP, 1975; A. B. Atkinson, *Poverty in Britain and the Reform of Social Security*, Cambridge UP, 1969; F. Field, *Poverty: The Facts*, Child Poverty Action Group, 1975; J. E. Meade, 'Poverty in the Welfare State', Oxford Economic Papers, November 1972; and A. R. Prest, 'The Negative Income Tax: Concepts and Problems', *British Tax Review*, Nov.–Dec. 1970. This section draws freely on these sources.

ment (FIS) aids very low wage earners with large families who claim the benefit. FIS is discussed in section II.9.

It was originally hoped that the National Insurance system as proposed by Beveridge would provide a level of benefits equal at least to the official poverty line, and that supplementary benefits (then called national assistance) would wither away expect as a last resort for the few people who fell through the National Insurance net. This hope has not been realized. The number of people receiving supplementary benefit (table 5.8) doubled between 1951 and 1971 although it fell modestly in the first half of the 1970s. The data in table 5.8 refer only to recipients of supplementary benefits. If we include dependants in 1975 some 4½ million people had their income and welfare determined wholly or partially by their supplementary benefit allowance. There are three main reasons for the large number of people receiving supplementary benefit. First, some National Insurance benefits have fallen progressively behind the official poverty line. (The fall in supplementary benefit recipients between 1971 and 1974 reflects in part the uprating of national insurance pension benefits in July 1974). Second, there is probably a decreasing reluctance to apply for supplementary benefit as memories of the old inter-war means test fade. Third, the absolute number of elderly has increased. It should be remembered that the figures in table 5.8 refer to benefit recipients at a point in time, i.e. they are stock data. During the course of 1974 many more than 2.68 million people received supplementary benefit at some time: the annual flow of recipients is greater than the stock because, for example, in the course of a year some single parents with dependent children will marry, some unemployed will find jobs and some pensioners will die.

TABLE 5.8

Numbers on Supplementary Benefit (000s)

	Total	Pensioners	Unemployed	Sick and disabled	Single-parent families
1951	1462	1055	66	119	41
1971	2909	1984	387	305	213
1974	2681	1844	303	162	248

Source: F. Field, *Poverty: The Facts,* table 1.2.

Criticisms: The current system has been criticized on a number of grounds, although some of the criticisms are contradictory. First, the growth in the numbers receiving supplementary benefits demonstrates that some groups are not adequately catered for by the other anti-poverty measures. The main groups under such a heading are (i) the chronic sick and disabled, (ii) the long term unemployed and (iii) fatherless families.

Whilst the earnings related sickness scheme aids those who become sick or disabled while they were working and insured it does not help the long term sick and disabled such as housewives who are not covered by the national insurance scheme, although the latter are eligible for an Attendance Allowance (discussed below).

Unemployment benefits include, since 1966, an earnings related supplement to the flat rate benefit; this supplement is, however, only paid for the first six months of unemployment. When unemployment rises rapidly (as it did in 1975) this is partially because more individuals register as unemployed but mainly due to the increased duration of unemployment, and the increasing duration causes a larger number of (especially older) workers to lose their earnings related supplement. Further, higher overall levels of unemployment imply that many individuals may have more than one bout of unemployment in a year and may thus exhaust their National Insurance flat rate unemployment benefit.

Fatherless families may have no income sources other than supplementary benefit. This group of benefit recipients has grown substantially recently. In 1966, 184,000 single mothers were dependent on supplementary benefits for their living while by 1972, 289,000 single women, with 538,000 dependents, received such benefits. The improvement of children's benefits in such cases in April 1976, in part response to the investigations of the Finer Committee,[1] may reduce the need for single parent families to resort to supplementary benefits.

The second criticism of the current arrangements is that, despite a battery of measures to alleviate poverty, a substantial number of people still exist below the poverty line defined by the supplementary benefit level. Some 1.2m families or 2m people lived below the official poverty line in November 1972.[2] There are two main reasons for this. First, many people, especially pensioners, while eligible for supplementary benefit do not claim it. Second, many individuals are poor despite working: their weekly earnings are below the official poverty line. The Family Income Supplement (discussed in the next section) was introduced in 1971 to mitigate poverty associated with low earnings.

The third criticism concerns the income related (i.e. means-tested) nature of many benefits. The core of the problem is whether benefits should be related to income or whether the National Insurance system should be designed to insure that everyone has a tolerable minimum income, with the tax system taking back some benefits (e.g. family allowances) from those who do not need them. The criticism has a number of strands. (i) Benefits which are related to income are traditionally unpopular and discourage a full take-up. Many of those eligible for supplementary benefits do not claim; the take up rate of rent and rate rebates and the FIS appears only to be around 50% of those eligible. One recently introduced non-income related benefit, the Attendance Allowance for the sick and disabled who need constant or partial supervision, appears to have a take-up rate of around 75%. (ii) The system involves considerable administrative costs, both direct, and indirect, such as social workers. (iii) It may result in absurd marginal tax rates for those with low incomes. This is known as the poverty trap: as the earned income of the family rises it loses not only monetary supplementation such as FIS but also benefits in kind such as free school meals or prescriptions. In August 1974 the DHSS estimated 50,000 poor families were subject to a marginal tax rate of over 100% and 150,000 would lose around 76p for each £1 increase in earnings. A typical family faced marginal tax rates of over 100% in much of the range of weekly earnings £26 to £34 in July 1975.[3] Given the government's belief that high marginal tax rates discourage proper work effort this situation is clearly anomalous.

---

1 Finer Committee, *Report of the Committee on One Parent Families,* HMSO, 1974.
2 These figures were provided by DHSS and cited in F. Field, *Poverty: The Facts,* table I.11.
3 CSO, *Social Trends,* No. 6, 1975, p. 115.

The final criticism concerns the benefits in kind. These distort the price system, the consumer paying less than the cost of providing the service (e.g. 'free' school meals or milk). Critics argue that individuals should be assured of some minimum money income and then left to spend it as they wish, with the purchases priced according to cost. This raises much wider issues than poverty relief and will not be pursued here.

Reform of National Insurance: The National Insurance scheme is currently being reconstituted, mainly to change the pension provision.[1] The division of employee contributions into flat rate and earnings related components was abandoned in April 1975. The new contributions are entirely earnings related. On earnings levels up to approximately one and a half times male manual workers' weekly earnings, employees pay (from April 1976), 5.75% of their pay in social security contributions (unless they earn under a specified minimum − £15 in April 1976) and employers contribute 7.5%. Thus after April 1976 workers earnings over £15 will pay 5.75% of their pay up to £95 per week into social security. These contributions include components to finance National Health services, Redundancy Fund and Unemployment and Sickness Insurance, as well as Old Age Pensions. Currently married women are able to opt out of most of the social security payments if they wish. However, when the new scheme comes fully into force in 1978 they will no longer be able to do so.

The benefit side is also changed. Unemployment and sickness benefit will contain, as now, flat rate and earnings related components. From 1978 the earnings related social security contribution will also buy an earnings related pension. The changes over the years in contributions for flat rate and earnings related benefits are as follows:

Type of benefit	Before 1961	Contribution basis 1961-75	1975-8	After 1978
Flat rate pension	NI stamp	NI stamp	ERSS	ERSS
ER pension	None	ER contribution	None	ERSS (but able to opt out)

Note: ER: earnings related. SS: Social Security.

Provided an employer runs an approved occupational pension scheme he may opt out of the earnings related component of the post 1978 state pension scheme and his contributions, and those of his employees, will be reduced accordingly. To be able to opt out the employer's scheme must be at least as good as the state earnings related scheme. Both the flat rate and earnings related pension benefits will be indexed (the former to earnings if more favourable, the latter to the price index). There are two other important features. First, contributions are collected via the PAYE system rather than by the stamped card method. Second, there are

---

1 For a thorough evaluation of the reform see N. Barr, 'Labour's Pension Plan − A Lost Opportunity?', *British Tax Review*, Nos. 2 and 3, 1975. Helpful conversations with Nick Barr on this and other social security matters are gratefully acknowledged.

annual reviews to determine the uprating of benefits and the earnings band over which contributions are to be paid.

Alternatives:[1] There have been three main sets of suggestions concerning the direction in which the present system might be reformed. They have a superficial similarity, in that under each scheme individuals will be guaranteed a minimum income at around supplementary benefit level and the need for supplementary benefits will be substantially reduced. In fact, however, the schemes are very different.

The first suggestion is for a 'new Beveridge Plan'. Under the original Beveridge proposals it was proposed that social insurance should guarantee everyone a minimum standard of living. This subsistence income was to be provided as a right, without a means test; the part played by national assistance was to be virtually phased out. In the postwar period, however, National Insurance benefits, especially pensions and family allowances, have nearly always been below the prescribed minima laid down by national assistance (now supplementary benefits). The suggestion is therefore to implement fully the original Beveridge proposals. One of the stated aims of the new pension scheme (discussed above) is to ensure pension benefits of sufficient size to virtually eliminate the need for pensioners to turn to supplementary benefits to augment their income. Advocates of this universalistic approach to curing poverty generally qualify it by suggesting that the benefits from raising social security payments can, via clawback, be directed towards those with lower incomes. However, many short term benefits (e.g. unemployment benefits) are not taxable and therefore could not be clawed back.

This policy would obviously be successful in raising the incomes of non-employed disadvantaged individuals. It does not involve high marginal tax rates and is therefore less likely to have disincentive effects on savings and working harder (or being mobile). Further it would not involve any major administrative problems. It has two disadvantages. First, it would be costly. However, this is not a substantive argument because it is merely another way of stating the seriousness of the poverty problem. Second, the problem of the employed with low incomes remains, and is unlikely to be generally helped by minimum wage legislation which is the policy most frequently advocated to raise earnings by the back-to-Beveridge protagonists.

The second scheme for reform, the Social Dividend, is the boldest. Under this scheme a non-taxable flat rate sum would be paid weekly to every individual irrespective of income. This would be accompanied by a proportional personal income tax. All other elements of the social security system (insurance contributions and benefits, supplementary benefits and family allowances) would be abolished. This system has the advantage that the benefit paid is insensitive to income. Work incentives may nevertheless be impaired because it is generally agreed that the proportional tax rate would have to be at least 50%. The scheme also has the administrative drawback of extending income tax to everyone, however small his income.

---

1 See F. Field, *Poverty: The Facts,* Child Poverty Action Group, 1975, for the general case for the 'back to Beveridge' proposals. See A. Cristopher *et. al., Policy for Poverty,* Research Monograph 20, IEA 1970 for the general case for a negative income tax. See J. Meade, 'Poverty in the Welfare State', *Oxford Economic Papers,* November 1972, for the case for the Social Dividend Scheme.

The third alternative, which has many variants, is the negative income tax. This scheme involves a minimum income guarantee and a break-even income. If an individual is employed and earns between the minimum and the break-even income his earnings are supplemented (by the negative income tax); beyond the break-even income he pays positive income tax. The FIS is thus a prototype NIT. This scheme could be all-embracing, covering the whole range of government welfare programmes, or could be oriented towards particular problems such as poverty caused by large families. The essential problem with this scheme is that a choice must be made between high marginal rates of negative income tax and low minimum levels of payment. For example, from 1976 the point at which individuals start paying income tax is £735. If the NIT is operated with a rate of 50% this means that 50p is payable to an individual for every £1 by which his income is less than £735. Thus the basic minimum payment is only £367. If this basic minimum is too low the tax rate could be raised to 75% giving a minimum of £551. Such a high marginal tax rate is likely to have disincentive effects on labour supply. Further problems with the NIT, which could be overcome with time and ingenuity, are (i) that the unit to which it applies, the individual, the family or the household, must be determined; (ii) that the NIT must be on a weekly basis, but (positive) income tax has always been assessed yearly; (iii) that people not in employment have to claim the NIT; (iv) that assets may be difficult to incorporate into the NIT scheme.

II.9   Low Pay[1]

We saw above that low pay is one part of the poverty problem. Industries which rank at the bottom of the earnings structure tend to be characterized by high proportions of small plants, of women workers, of unskilled workers and of falling demand for labour. It is also clear that low paid workers are heavily represented in the service sector. If we define those earning less than £30 per week in April 1974 as low paid, one half of all low paid manual workers are employed in the five main service sectors (distributive trades; insurance, banking and finance; professional and scientific services; miscellaneous services; public administration). Yet these industries only account for about one-fifth of male manual employment. Similarly two-thirds of low paid females (defined as those earning under £17 per week in April, 1974) are employed in the service sector.

Low pay is also related to age and skill. Teenagers, workers in their early twenties and workers over fifty are disproportionately represented. Older and unskilled workers not only tend to have relatively low earnings, but also to suffer higher rates of unemployment. Unemployment rates referring specifically to unskilled workers are at least three times the national average unemployment rate. The annual earnings differential between them and other workers is therefore greater than apparent from a comparison of the earnings of those in work.

Two important features of the structure of the low pay problem are worth noting. First, if the low paid are described as those in the lowest tenth of the distribution of manual earnings, we observe considerable movement across the boundary of this lowest tenth: of those people in the lowest tenth in April 1970

---

1   For a general survey of the problem of low pay see NBPI, *General Problems of Low Pay,* Report No. 169, Cmnd. 4648, 1971 and F. Field (ed.), *Low Pay,* Arrow 1973.

less than half were in the lowest tenth in each of the two succeeding years.[1] Second, low pay must be seen as part of a general problem of labour market disadvantages in that it is associated with a high incidence of job instability, ill-health and lack of fringe benefits. The low paid worker is more vulnerable to the interruption of earnings power, cannot save for old age or emergencies, and can only borrow at very high interest rates such as through HP. Thus low pay is an important element in the cycle of poverty.

In Britain we approach the problem of low pay in two main ways. First, the FIS is a form of negative income tax. Second, the wages councils provide a form of minimum wage legislation.

FIS was introduced in August 1971 to help mitigate poverty caused by low pay. When family income falls short of a prescribed level, from July 1976 £39 per week for a one-child family plus £4.50 for each additional child, the family is paid a benefit equal to one half of the difference between its total gross income and the prescribed level (with a maximum supplement of £8.50 for a one-child family and £11 if there are six children in the family). This is a potentially powerful policy to raise the welfare of the low paid. Its main drawback is that individuals have to claim their income-related supplement and it is estimated that only half of the 160,000 families (containing half a million children) have claimed their rights.

An oft-cited cure for low pay is a national minimum wage. Elements of a minimum wage policy exist via the wages councils which set minimum rates in certain industries. Direct state intervention in fixing minimum wages first occurred in 1909 with the Trade Boards Act. In 1945 trade boards were renamed wages councils. There are forty seven wages councils. They are generally believed to be ineffective in helping low paid workers and are thought to inhibit the development of voluntary collective bargaining arrangements.[2]

A national minimum wage (assuming it is set above the existing wage for low paid workers) will raise the money earnings of those who remain employed, but will cause some unemployment.[3] Recall that the old and unskilled, the people the minimum wage is designed to help most, already have the highest unemployment rates. It may also give only a temporary boost to the low paid. Overseas evidence suggests that the original wage differentials are quickly restored. Proponents of minimum wage legislation also argue that it raises the productivity of labour. So it will if capital is substituted for labour, but this is an inefficient substitution and unemployment will also result. It is sometimes said, however, that the minimum wage legislation will have a 'shock effect' and thereby raise productivity without any loss in employment. This is unlikely to be widespread in that it implies that firms currently have a careless attitude towards profits. Further, many of the low-paying industries are competitive and are therefore unlikely to need a national minimum wage as a spur to efficiency. Thus 'no false hopes should be attached to

---

1   *DEG,* April 1973. The great fluctuations in individuals' pay from year to year occur throughout the earnings distribution. This implies that there is less inequality in career earnings than there is in annual earnings.
2   NBPI, *op. cit.,* para. 124.
3   See E. G. West, 'Britain's Evolving Minimum Wage Policy: An Economic Assessment', *Moorgate and Wall Street,* Autumn 1969, for a full discussion of the theory behind this statement and a summary of US evidence.

a national minimum wage . . . our main conclusion therefore has to be that there is no single remedy for low pay'.[1]

This suggests that provision of more training facilities, better information about wages and opportunities both locally and nationally, inducements to labour mobility, wage subsidies, and running the economy with lower, more evenly distributed unemployment levels, are likely to be more effective solutions to the problem of low pay than is a national minimum wage.

III   WAGE INFLATION AND PAY POLICY

In the mid 1960s economists thought that they understood the operation of the aggregate labour market rather well. The work of Phillips suggested that a trade-off existed between the rate of wage inflation and the level of unemployment: it was believed that the Phillips curve provided a menu of choice for policy makers – a little less unemployment could be traded for a little more wage inflation.[2] This apparently tidy system (if indeed it ever existed) has, alas, been rudely shattered. It will be seen from table 5.9 that hourly earnings changes in the 1970s have always been in two digits despite unemployment levels which are high by post-war standards.

TABLE 5.9

Unemployment and Wage Inflation, 1955-75

	% Change in hourly earnings	% Unemployment males, GB
1955-60 (average p.a.)	6.2	1.6
1961-9 (average p.a.)	6.7	2.3
1970	16.0	3.4
1971	13.7	4.5
1972	14.6	4.9
1973	13.6	3.5
1974	21.9	3.5
1975	31.9	5.2

Source: DEG, January 1976, Tables 105, 125, 126.

Three of the central issues concerning wage inflation are examined here. First, we discuss the debate between those who believe that the cause of inflation is trade union power and those who see inflation as essentially a monetary phenomenon. Second, the labour market is not one market but consists of many separate labour markets by occupation, local area, industry and so on. The process of wage inflation cannot be fully understood unless some attention is given to these dis-aggregated labour markets. Third, successive governments have resorted to an incomes policy of one form or another in an attempt to moderate the pace of wage inflation. These pay policies are analyzed and evaluated.

---

1 NBPI, *op. cit.,* paras. 124 and 125.
2 A. W. Phillips, 'The Relation between Unemployment and the Rate of Change of Money Wage Rates in the UK', *EC,* XXV, November 1958, pp. 283-99. For a much fuller treatment of the theoretical justification of the Phillips Curve see R. G. Lipsey, 'The Relationship between Unemployment and the Rate of Change of Wage Rates in the UK, 1862-1957: a further Analysis', *EC,* XXIX, February 1960. For alternative rationales for the relationship the advanced reader may wish to consult E. Phelps (ed.), *Microeconomic Foundations of Inflation and Employment Theory,* Norton, 1970.

III.1 Union Power versus the Money Supply Hypothesis[1]

Although it has been demonstrated that unions influence the *relative wage structure* (cf. section IV) this does not necessarily imply that unions are central to the process of wage *inflation*. We seek to understand whether unions influence money wage inflation independently of excess demand; this is perhaps the most fundamental issue in the current debate on inflation. If unions are at the heart of the inflationary process then policies to inhibit their power over money wage changes, such as some form of pay policy or revised industrial relations legislation, are central to the control of inflation. (This is not to deny that inflation could be moderated by reducing aggregate demand sufficiently.) Alternatively, if unions are passive agents in the process, the authorities must look to other measures such as the control of the money supply to limit inflation.

The seminal study on the role of unions in the inflationary process is that of Hines[2], who set out an index of trade union pushfulness ΔT (= $T_t - T_{t-1}$, where T_t denotes the proportion of the labour force unionized, or union density, in year t). Hines' thesis was that ΔT is a measure of union activity which manifests itself simultaneously in both increased union membership and density and in pressure on money wage rates. He tested this hypothesis with aggregate data from 1893-1961 and found, broadly, that through time excess demand for labour had become less important as a cause of inflation and that in the post war period wage pushfulness was a key factor in the explanation of inflation. The importance of unions in industry level wage adjustment was confirmed in a subsequent article.[3]

Given the controversial nature of this topic and the originality of Hines' contribution it is not surprising that Hines' work has been subjected to careful scrutiny. The most wide ranging critique is that of Purdy and Zis[4] who examine Hines' theory, data, estimation technique and interpretation.

Their main criticism is that Hines presents no theoretical underpinning for the proposition that militancy (ΔT) shows simultaneously in increased membership and in upward pressure on wage rates: 'There is a presumption in his theory that unions aim to drive up their members' real wages by exerting pressure on money wages; that unions aim to extend the organized proportion of the labour force lying within their jurisdiction and that the rate at which they succeed in carrying out this latter objective is a major determinant of their success in pursuing the former.' (p. 296). However, none of this comes out of a formal model of union behaviour or a discussion of what unions do when conflicting objectives, e.g., higher wages associated with lower employment, occur. Even more important, theoretically, is that the pushfulness view pays little attention to the employer. Hines argues

---

1 For an extremely thorough survey of the literature on the inflationary process see D. Laidler and M. Parkin, 'Inflation – A Survey', *EJ*, vol. 85, no. 340, December 1975. For an exposition of the cost-push view see P. Wiles, 'Cost Inflation and the State of Economic Theory', *EJ*, vol. 83, no. 330, 1973. For illuminating, though less technical discussions see the articles by Parkin, Hicks,and Kahn in *LBR*, July 1975, October 1975 and January 1976, respectively.

2 A. Hines, 'Trade Unions and Wage Inflation in the UK 1893-1961', *Review of Economic Studies*, Vol. 31, pp. 221-51, 1964.

3 A. Hines, 'Wage Inflation in the UK 1948-62: A Disaggregated Study', *EJ*, Vol. 79, pp. 66-89, 1969.

4 D. Purdy and A. Zis, 'Trade Unions and Wage Inflation in the UK', in M. Parkin (ed.), *Proceedings of 1973 AUTE Conference*, Longman, 1973.

that, through time, employer resistance is of less consequence because of the wage round and because of administered prices. While this may be true it is still likely, *a priori,* that the secular reduction in employer resistance will have some cyclical variability superimposed on it − in the motor industry, for example, employer resistance is related to the demand for cars, indeed there is evidence that employers *initiate* strikes when demand is slack − and this should be discussed in the wage adjustment model.

A second criticism of the union pushfulness model is that it is not clear what ΔT measures: it is defined as a measure of militancy but the contribution of unions to the process of inflation may depend more on their strength than on their militancy. This distinction is slippery but not trivial. If unions are strong they may get large money wage increases with a small show of militancy (indeed, if they operate a closed shop ΔT, the militancy measure used by Hines, is by definition zero, see below). Further many labour historians (Phelps Brown,[1] Ross[2]) believe unions were more powerful (militant?) in forestalling and minimizing money wage cuts in the interwar period than they are in obtaining wage increases − in the words of Phelps Brown unions are stronger when they act as the anvil rather than the hammer.

Two semi-statistical problems concern (i) simultaneity between union density and wage changes and (ii) the fact that union density may not be independent of excess demand. The proportion of the labour force unionized is a function of the costs of organization, as measured by factors such as number of workers per plant, the benefits of membership and simply whether the union member can afford his dues. It is well known[3] that over long periods union membership is positively related to economic activity; for example, union membership fell steadily between 1926 and 1933 and rose steadily during the mid and late 1930s. It seems likely therefore that the level of union membership depends in part on money wage changes and on the level of excess demand.

Purdy and Zis point to data problems within the union pushfulness model. One such problem is that until recently there has been little variability in ΔT in the post war period. More important, where a closed shop exists the basis for using ΔT as a measure of militancy is unclear because union membership will only rise or fall as employment in the closed shop sectors rises or falls. Purdy and Zis quote evidence from McCarthy[4], who estimated that 3.75 million workers were employed in closed shop establishments and a further 1.35 million were in open shops within trades where the closed shop practice predominated, and which were therefore quasi-closed shops enforced by informal sanctions. In all 22% of manual workers were covered by closed shop arrangements and these constituted 49% of manual trade unionists. It is clear therefore that in large numbers of plants increased union activity is unlikely to be reflected in ΔT because the employees are already completely organized.

Finally, Purdy and Zis found that when they re-estimated the union pushfulness model to take account of their various criticisms, the impact of ΔT on wage changes,

1   E. H. Phelps Brown, *Pay and Profit,* Manchester University Press, 1968.
2   A. Ross, 'Changing Pattern of Industrial Conflict', in *Proceedings of Twelfth Annual Meeting of Industrial Relations Research Association,* edited by G. Somers, 1959.
3   E. Hobsbawm, *Labouring Men: Studies in the History of Labour,* Weidenfeld and Nicolson, 1964.
4   W. McCarthy, *The Closed Shop in Britain,* Blackwell, Oxford, 1964.

although still positive, was much reduced. This is confirmed by Wilkinson and Burkitt[1]. who used carefully constructed data on unionization by industry and found that ΔT is significantly associated with wage changes in only one industry, textiles, out of the eleven they studied.

The statistical studies discussed above have neither confirmed nor rejected the central place of unions in the inflationary process and, in consequence, the debate concerning the underlying causes of inflation continues unabated. It is generally agreed that a correlation exists between the growth in the money supply and the rate of inflation and that this correlation is stronger in the long run than in the short run. What is in dispute is whether inflation is caused by excessive growth in the money supply or whether union power or some other social force causes money wages to rise which in turn induces the authorities to expand the money supply in order that unemployment does not result. Those who hold the former view see the cure for inflation in a deceleration in the rate at which money is created whilst those who believe that unions are the key tend to favour a pay policy to reduce inflation.

The clarity of the dispute has, unfortunately, been blurred recently by ambiguous statements by the protagonists. In particular the monetarists have recently stated:[2]

> 'If the increase of union wages induces the authorities to expand the money supply either to finance public expenditure designed to reduce any concomitant unemployment or to finance the deficits of nationalized industries then such action will indeed be inflationary. It is simply not possible for the trade unions to be so powerful as to cause prices to rise generally unless there is concomitant increase in the money supply.'

This view is rather more moderate than the traditional monetarist view. It allows that trade unions may have some power to cause prices to rise providing the government manages its monetary flows to accommodate the wage set by the unions. This is very similar to the hypothesis advanced some twenty years ago by Hicks,[3] who argued that Britain was on a 'labour standard': whatever the wage set by collective bargaining the government managed the economy to ensure full employment — in effect the labour standard had replaced the gold standard for purposes of internal economic management.

The particular reason why the quoted statement blurs the debate is that many observers would interpret such a sequence of events as evidence in favour of cost-push inflation; for example this is the view of Branson,[4] who argues that such a pattern of events is evidence that the government is validating what is essentially a cost-push inflation via its aggregate demand policy. Similarly Phelps Brown, who is a firm believer in modifying the system of collective bargaining because of a shift in the balance of power towards trade unions,[5] believes that the sequence

1 R. Wilkinson and B. Burkitt, 'Wage Determination and Trade Unions', *Scottish Journal of Political Economy*, Vol. XX, No. 2, June, 1973.

2 Economic Radicals, *Letter to the Prime Minister*, 1974.

3 J. R. Hicks, 'Economic Foundations of Wages Policy', *EJ*, 1955.

4 W. Branson, *Macroeconomic Theory and Policy*, Harper and Row. New York. p. 326, 1972.

5 E. H. Phelps Brown, *Collective Bargaining Reconsidered*, Stamp Memorial Lecture, University of London, Athlone Press, 1971.

described by the monetarists is precisely that which has existed in the last thirty years; he sees the key feature of the postwar period as the 'soft market environment' — if employers made wage settlements that raised unit wage costs, governments would not in the event deny them the flow of monetary demand to keep their capacity fully occupied at the new wage level of costs. In such a setting resistance by any one group of employers to a wage settlement of the prevailing size came to be seen as futile and needless.[1]

It is clear that some sharply defined tests are necessary to distinguish the two views. This is not just because such tests will satisfy intellectual curiosity, but rather that the correct directions for macro-policy hinge on determining whether unions are, in part, responsible for cost and price rises. The monetarists recently proposed such a test. The Economic Radicals (1974, Table 1) suggested an examination of labour's share in national income. They calculated that wages and salaries (net of income tax and employees' National Insurance contributions) fell as a proportion of national income from 58.4% in 1948-50 to 55.7% in 1970-2 and inferred from this evidence that the power of unions is therefore illusory. Such a conclusion is too hasty on a number of grounds. First, on a theoretical plane, movements in labour's share in national income depend on the elasticity of substitution between labour and other factors as well as wages, and this was ignored in their analysis. Second, if we wish to draw conclusions about the power of unions over the distribution of national income and their responsibility for rising costs and prices we should, *a priori,* examine the share of wages and salaries prior to deductions for income tax and National Insurance contributions: in this case labour's share *rose* from 65% in 1948 to over 68% in 1972. Third, given the secularly increasing importance of the public sector we should not be surprised that *post tax* wages fall as a proportion of national incomes. Finally, the share of pre-tax profits in national income and the rate of return on capital have dropped dramatically recently. In an extremely thorough article Burgess and Webb[2] show that whichever method is used for the calculation, profits have declined markedly as a proportion of national income in the last two decades. For example, the calculation which shows the *smallest* decline in pre-tax profits (non nationalized companies gross trading profits less stock appreciation as a percent of GDP) shows that share falling from 14.4% in 1950 to 10.3% in 1972 — a reduction of over one quarter in the share of GDP going to profits in the post war period. Presumably this is evidence, on the monetarists' own ground rules, that unions *are* powerful — indeed it has been seen by some commentators[3] as hailing the demise of British capitalism.[4]

One way of getting a clearer understanding of the part played by unions in the inflationary process is to turn to microeconomic analysis. For example if it could be demonstrated that unionized sectors received large wage settlements in times of

---

1 E. H. Phelps Brown, *The Economic Consequences of Collective Bargaining,* Minutes of Evidence 38, *Royal Commission on Trade Unions and Employers Associations,* HMSO, 1967, para. 12.

2 G. Burgess and A. Webb, 'The Profits of British Industry', *Lloyds Bank Review,* No. 112, April, 1974.

3 A. Glyn and R. Sutcliffe, *British Capitalism, Workers and the Profits Squeeze,* Penguin, 1972.

4 For a very careful recent analysis of profits see J. Flemming *et. al.* 'Trends in company profitability', *BEQB,* March 1976.

heavy unemployment or severe deceleration in the rate of growth of the money supply and that such settlements were followed, with a lag, by the non-union sectors, this would suggest that unions are not irrelevant.

Some progress has been made recently towards a sensible synthesis of the demand and supply side views. For example both Tobin[1] and Hicks[2] have developed similar models which emphasize that the labour market is not one market but is composed of many markets by industry, occupation, area, etc. If one market is in disequilibrium with excess demand for labour, wages will be pulled up in that market and this wage rise will in turn, via either equity or labour supply considerations, feed into the other markets: inflation is initiated by excess demand factors and transmitted by the institutional arrangements and social pressures prevailing in the labour market. Hicks states that such social pressures 'may take the form of strikes, but that may not be necessary. Any arbitrator will agree that a rise in wages is "fair". And it will be clear to employers that they must raise wages for the sake of "good industrial relations" '. This certainly seems precisely the sequence of events which has occurred in many public sector pay settlements in the last few years.

This multisector view makes clear that there is force in both the monetarist and the social force views of the inflationary process. The various markets which make up 'the labour market' tend to have at any point in time different levels of excess demand. Those with large positive excess demand experience large money wage increases (the monetarist element) whilst those with excess supply do not, as in the distant past, experience money wage cuts. An active employment policy which aims for full employment 'on average' implies that some markets will always be experiencing excess demand and the wage increases in such markets spill over into the other markets via social pressures such as arbitrators' conceptions of equity or union power (the cost-push element).

The literature which examines wage inflation by disaggregating the various components of the labour market is not large and it is too soon to say whether the *a priori* plausible hypotheses of Hicks and Tobin are acceptable. This literature is discussed next.

III.2   Dissaggregated Analyses of the Wage Inflation Process

Regional: Regional labour markets have received more attention than other narrowly defined labour markets in part because of economists' long interest in regional policy. Regional wage differentials have been remarkably stable despite persistent differences in the regional unemployment rates. This fact leads, as Mackay and Hart[3] point out, to two interesting, interrelated, lines of investigation. First, what is it that holds the regional wage structure together in view of the regions' different labour market experience? Second, if a given national unemployment rate were to be associated with less dispersion in regional unemployment

1   J. Tobin, 'Inflation and Unemployment', *American Economic Review,* Vol. LXII, No. 1, March 1972, pp. 1-18.
2   Sir J. Hicks, *The Crisis in Keynesian Economics,* Blackwell, 1974.
3   D. Mackay and R. Hart, 'Wage Inflation and the Regional Wage Structure', in M. Parkin (ed.), *Contemporary Issues in Economics,* Proceedings of the 1973 AUTE Conference, Longman, 1974.

would the rate of wage inflation be lower? Thirlwall,[1] Metcalf[2] and Archibald[3] have each demonstrated that one important factor in preserving the regional wage structure is national wage bargaining.

A study which analyzed in detail the institutional structure of the engineering industry labour market (Lerner and Marquand[4]) found that local bargaining resulting in earnings increases substantially in excess of the nationally negotiated wage rates occurs initially in regions experiencing an excess demand for labour, and that these higher earnings spread out over the other regions via the mechanism of the shop stewards combine committees. Mackay and Hart,[5] in a careful study, provide econometric support for this hypothesis using data provided by the Engineering Employers Federation disaggregated to the level of the town. Although the mechanism by which similar earnings increases get spread out around the country is complicated, 'for London itself there is a very significant relationship between earnings changes and excess demand pressure, which may be transferred to other markets whose own earnings changes show little association with local excess demand pressure ... [further it is] possible that earnings changes in local labour markets exhibit strong associations with wage leaders in their more immediate vicinity'.

Whilst this institutional and econometric evidence relates only to engineering and does not necessarily hold for other sectors (cf. Lerner, Cable and Gupta[6]) it prompts the question: if, for a given national unemployment rate, unemployment rates were more evenly distributed spatially would the aggregate rate of money wage inflation be lower?

There are two reasons, *a priori*, why the dispersion in sectoral unemployment and inflation might be positively related. First, if each sector has similar non-linear Phillips curves (or, under certain circumstances, linear curves with different locations) the macro Phillips curve will lie above the micro curves. This is known as the aggregation hypothesis. Second, if the low unemployment sector is the wage leader macro inflation is largely determined by its unemployment rate and not the economy unemployment rate. The aggregation hypothesis has been much studied, although the data show quite plainly that the sectoral Phillips curves are not identical but that those for the high unemployment sectors, which have similar wage increases to the low unemployment sectors, lie above those for the low unemployment sectors. It seems likely therefore, that if dispersion in sectoral unemployment is positively associated with inflation this is because of spillovers rather than aggregation.

The possible link between lower dispersion in spatial unemployment and a lower inflation rate was responsible, in part, for the regional policy of the mid 1960s which,

---

1   A Thirlwall, 'Regional Phillips Curves', *Bulletin of Oxford Institute of Economics and Statistics*, Vol. XXXII, February, 1970, pp. 19-32.

2   D. Metcalf, 'Determinants of Earnings Changes: A Regional Analysis for the UK 1960-68', *International Economic Review*, Vol. XII, June 1971, pp. 273-82.

3   C. Archibald, 'Analysis of Regional Economic Policy', in B. Corry and M. Peston (eds.), *Essays in Honour of Lord Robbins*, Weidenfeld and Nicolson, 1972.

4   S. Lerner and J. Marquand (1963), 'Regional Variations in Earnings, Demand for Labour and Shop Stewards Combine Committees in the British Engineering Industry', *Manchester School*, Vol. XXXI, 1963.

5   D. Mackay and R. Hart, 'Wage Inflation and the Phillips Relationship', *Manchester School*, June 1974.

6   S. Lerner, J. Cable and S. Gupta, *Workshop Wage Determination*, Pergamon, 1969.

for example, limited office building in the South East and subsidized employment with the regional employment premium in the high unemployment areas. A number of studies have investigated this link by including the dispersion of regional unemployment rates as an explanatory variable in models of macro wage-adjustment. The results, unfortunately, are inconclusive. A sample of the empirical work shows that Archibald[1] and Thomas and Stoney[2] (1972) both find a significant positive association between the dispersion of regional unemployment and the rate of money wage inflation but Mackay and Hart (1974) do not, although they believe that there exists an underlying relationship between the dispersion of spatial unemployment and wage inflation but that this relationship is masked because the absolute dispersion and the average level of unemployment are themselves positively correlated.

Industry: A number of studies exist on the interrelationships amongst industrial wage movements. Kaldor[3] initiated a model in which the engine room of the inflationary process is the rate of increase in labour productivity in the production sector. In this model, firms in the production sector can afford to pay relatively large annual wage increases without their unit labour costs rising much because of the secular rise in their workers' productivity (this rise in productivity being caused, in general, by better organization and a higher capital: labour ratio rather than greater intensity of effort on the part of the operatives). Subsequently the wage increases gained by employees in the high productivity growth sector spillover to the service sectors causing a large rise in their unit labour costs. Thus at macro level the percentage increment to money wages is at least as large as the percentage increase in labour productivity in the production sector, which in turn, is substantially in excess of the percentage growth in aggregate real national income. The underlying mechanism has been confirmed both by Aubrey Jones[4] and by other Cambridge writers. For example Turner and Jackson[5] demonstrate that the model fits the facts about productivity increases and earnings increases in Britain. More recently Eatwell, Llewellyn and Tarling[6] provided an ingenious test of the hypothesis using international data. They examined the growth in earnings and the growth in output per man in the industries within the manufacturing sector in fifteen countries over the period 1953-67. Within each country it was found that earnings increases were much more similar than labour productivity increases. Further, the *average* rise in earnings in a country over the period approximated closely to the labour productivity increase of the three industries with the *fastest* growth of labour productivity rather than to the average increase in labour productivity across all the industries. One problem with this

1 C. Archibald, 'The Phillips Curve and the Distribution of Unemployment', *American Economic Review,* Vol. LIX, May 1969, pp. 124-34.
2 R. L. Thomas and P. Stoney, 'Unemployment Dispersion as a Determinant of Wage Inflation in the UK 1925-66', *Manchester School,* June 1971, Vol. 39, pp. 83-111.
3 N. Kaldor, 'Economic Growth and the Problem of Inflation', *Economica,* 1959.
4 A. Jones, *The New Inflation: The Politics and Prices and Incomes,* Penguin, 1972.
5 H. A. Turner and D. Jackson, 'On the Determination of the General Wage Level – A World Analysis, or "Unlimited Labour Forever" ', *Economic Journal,* Vol. 80, 1970, pp. 827-49.
6 J. Eatwell, J. Llewellyn and R. Tarling, 'Money Wage Inflation in Industrial Countries', *Review of Economic Studies,* 1975.

explanation of inflation is that it does not spell out how the wage settlement gained in the high productivity growth sector also gets paid to the employees in the other sectors; we shall return to this problem below. Further, other evidence differs as to which are the leading and lagging sectors. Sargan[1] found that the transport and scientific sectors appeared to lead the inflationary process, neither of which are production industries. Dicks-Mireaux[2] believes that the export and import competing industries have been the wage leaders in the recent inflation as a result of their profitability caused by the 1967 devaluation of sterling. Again, neither of these latter writers discusses the process by which the wage settlements in the leading industries are transmitted nationally.

III.3   Incomes Policy[3]

Background: On a number of occasions in the postwar period, the UK has attempted to deal with wage and price inflation via an incomes policy. If an incomes policy succeeds in keeping aggregate wage increases in line with aggregate productivity increases, unit labour costs remain stable and this is consistent with stable prices. Substantial price inflation is generally unacceptable to a government. There are two reasons for this. First, if other countries are inflating less rapidly it causes balance of payments problems. This is particularly important in an open economy like the UK. Second, unanticipated inflation reduces the purchasing power of those on fixed incomes, such as pensioners and landlords. Traditionally, monetary policy and fiscal policy have been the instruments used to attempt to control inflation; their use in this context causes an increase in unemployment (see chapter 1). In an attempt to circumvent the increase in unemployment, policy-makers have turned to two other methods to check inflation. First, so-called manpower policies, designed to improve the efficient functioning of the labour market. Such policies include, for example retraining unemployed workers, movement grants, and financial help while searching for a new job. Second, they have turned to incomes policies.

The rationale for an incomes policy is to keep wage increases more in line with productivity increases. It attempts to affect the way the parties to the wage bargain respond to supply and demand conditions in the labour market. An incomes policy may also be introduced in an attempt to rupture inflationary expectations. As inflation becomes anticipated labour tends to incorporate an inflationary hedge in its wage demands: this necessarily creates the inflation that labour is trying to avoid. If, via an incomes policy, the hedging elements in wage demands can be collectively eliminated, labour costs will not rise so fast and price inflation will slow down.

The different types of incomes policy experienced over the last ten years are summarized in table 5.10.

The pay policy in operation between July 1975 and July 1976 was extremely

---

1   J. D. Sargan, 'A Study of Wages and Prices in the UK 1949-69', in H. G. Johnson and A. Nobay (eds.), *The Current Inflation,* Macmillan, 1971.

2   L. Dicks-Mireaux, 'International Factors', in H. G. Johnson and A. Nobay (eds.), *The Current Inflation,* Macmillan, 1971.

3   Two volumes which contain a mass of material on incomes policy and inflation are F. Blackaby (ed.), *An Incomes Policy for Britain,* Heinemann, 1972, and M. Parkin and M. Sumner (eds.), *Incomes Policy and Inflation,* Manchester U.P., 1972.

TABLE 5.10

Types of Incomes Policy, UK, 1965-76

	Time Span	Format	Target % per annum
1	April 1965 – March 1966	Voluntary year	3.5
2	April 1966 – July 1966	Voluntary under plan	3.5
3	August 1966 – December 1966	Freeze, statutory	0.0
4	January 1967 – June 1967	'Severe restraint'	1.0
5	July 1967 – March 1968	'Nil norm'	3.0
6	April 1968 – March 1969	Ceiling (first year)	3.5
7	April 1969 – March 1970	Ceiling (second year)	3.5
8	January 1970 – December 1970	'Range'	3.5 (av.)
9	June 1970 – December 1970	No norm, confrontation	10.0 ?
10	January 1971 – June 1971	Formal dissolution NBPI March 1971 Precedence given to passage of Industrial Relations Act.	
11	July 1971 – July 1972	'De-escalation', Voluntary price undertaking 5%.	$n-1\%$
12	July 1972 – October 1972	Confrontation deepening. Temporary renewal, price pledge.	$n-1\%$
13	October 1972	Government envisages 'absolute' norm of £2.50 per week	–
14	November 1972 – January 1973	Wage and price freeze; statutory following negotiation breakdown	0.0(6 months)
15	January 1973 – April 1973	'Phase 1' announced; extension of 90 day freeze	0.0(6 months)
16	April 1973 – September 1973	'Phase II' £1 + 4% 7.3% on average. Price stability rules. Statutory. Pay Board and Price Commission	–
17	September 1973 – October 1973	Government – union deadlock over consultative document. Stage III.	
18	November 1973 – Autumn 1974	'Phase III' Statutory. Threshold. Restriction gateways: anomalies subject to flexibility wages, 'unsocial' hours, efficiency schemes, etc.	7.5 min. 10.0 max.
19	Autumn 1974 – Summer 1975	Social Contract Voluntary Restraint	?
20	July 1975 – July 1976	£6 per week. Voluntary. £0 for those earning over £8,500 p.a.	10.0

Source: J. Corina 'Incomes Policy: Retrospect and Prospect', Institute of Manpower Studies (IMS), *Monitor,* vol. 2, no. 4, February 1974 (updated).

simple: each person earning under £8,500 p.a. was entitled to a maximum pay increase of £6 per week, (plus any step due on an incremental payscale). Those earning over £8,500 were entitled to no pay increases. The pay policy was introduced when it became apparent that the Social Contract, an understanding that unions would moderate pay demands in return for speedy implementation of particular social and industrial policies by the Labour administration, was not causing the rate of wage-inflation to be reduced. The £6 per week limit was voluntary but could have become compulsory if evidence of evasion had become widespread.

Recent Innovations: The pay policies in operation since 1973 have included two extremely important innovations. First, they have favoured flat rate wage increases

(e.g. £6 per week) rather than percentage increases (e.g. 10% p.a.) and have sometimes prohibited those earning over a specified amount from receiving any pay
increase. Second, the policy in operation in 1973-4 incorporated a form of
indexation of pay to prices. Threshold payments of £0.4 per week for each
percentage point increase in the cost of living index greater than six percent
starting from a base of 100 in October 1973 was permitted. The first such payments
were made in April 1974. When the scheme ended in October 1974 those covered
were receiving £4.40 per week in threshold payments because the index had risen
by 17 points. It is not entirely clear why indexation was originally introduced.
It seems likely, however, that some people believed that indexation, by itself,
would be a panacea for inflation. This is nonsense. The indexation of wage
movements to price changes merely moderates certain unpalatable side effects
of deflationary fiscal or monetary policy: indeed indexation coupled with
expansionary fiscal or monetary policy speeds up the inflationary process
because wages rise automatically in line with prices rather than only rising after
wage negotiations. The flat rate wage increases and threshold payments may be
expected to compress the wage structure. The evidence on this is presented below.

Procedures and Problems:[1] (1) *The norm for the economy.* It is necessary to
decide the maximum permissible increase in the total wage bill. A norm increase
in wages equal to the expected increase in aggregate productivity is consistent
both with stable prices and an unchanged distribution of national income between
pay and profits.[2] It will be seen from table 5.10 that the macro-norm for wage
increases over the last four years has been well in excess of the increase in overall
labour productivity. Incomes policies now attempt only to moderate inflation,
not to eliminate it.

(2) *The norm for individual bargains.* Once the norm has been decided it must
be translated into individual decisions. There are two ways (broadly) that this may
be achieved. First, workers in an individual firm or industry may have a wage
increase equal to the productivity increase in that firm or industry. A moment's
reflection will show what a silly policy this is. Musicians, night club hostesses,
teachers, nurses and policemen, who cannot increase their productivity, would
never get a wage increase whilst workers in manufacturing industry would get
a substantial increase in earnings each year. Not only would such a policy be
inequitable but it would be inefficient and doomed to failure.[3]

---

1 See F. Blackaby, 'Incomes Policies and Inflation', *NIER*, vol. 58, November 1971,
   pp. 34-53, for a fuller discussion of the problems of establishing and carrying through
   an incomes policy.
2 Let national income equal 100 units, 80 going to wages and 20 to profits. Now let
   national income and wages both rise by 10%. In the new situation national income equals
   110, wages equal 88 and profits equal 22. Profits equal one-fifth, and wages equal four-
   fifths, of national income in both cases.
3 A full discussion of the distortions caused by such a policy is contained in J. R. Crossley,
   'Wage Structure and the Future of the Incomes Policy', *SJPE*, June 1968; and H. Turner
   and D. Jackson, 'On the Stability of Wage Differences and Productivity-based Wage Policies:
   An International Analysis', *BJIR*, vol. VII, no. 1, March 1969. There is abundant evidence
   that relative wage changes by industry have not been associated with corresponding
   changes in labour productivity by industry. See for example OECD, *Wages and Labour
   Markets*, 1965; and J. R. Crossley, 'Collective Bargaining, Wage Structure and the Labour
   Market in the UK', in E. M. Hugh-Jones (ed.), *Wage Structure in Theory and Practice*
   (North-Holland, 1966).

The alternative criterion for individual bargains is for all workers (subject to the exceptions discussed below) to get approximately the norm increases in wages. In these circumstances high productivity industries will be expected to reduce their prices (if in the car industry productivity is rising at 7% but wages are rising at only 3% the car industry would be expected to lower its prices by 4%) and service industries, which cannot offset the higher wages by higher productivity, to increase their prices to cover the increase in unit labour costs. The recent UK policy adopted this latter more sensible approach.

(3) *The institutions.* The institutional arrangements of incomes policies have varied over time and between countries. The Pay Board (1973-4) was established by law; key wage setters had to give advanced notice of proposed wage increases to it. Thus it was a quasi-governmental body, the arbiter of the national interest. Our policy was different from that in Holland and Sweden. The former had a tripartite policy which brought together the unions, employers and government to determine national wage increases. The latter involves unions and employers, but not the government.

(4) *Multiplicity of bargains.* A problem in implementing an incomes policy arises from the multiplicity of the number of bargains and the complexity of many of the settlements. Blackaby describes this problem thus (1971, p. 43): 'The policy-maker is faced with the difficulty that wage bargains are struck all the year round, after varying intervals, and often for unspecified periods in the future. There is the further difficulty that settlements are often so complex that it may be difficult to discover what they mean in incomes policy terms – that is as an annual percentage increase. Then there is the immense number of individual bargains'. It has recently been estimated[1] that there are over 7,000 collective agreements negotiated annually. Although the great majority of the public sector employees are covered by national agreements, in the private sector there are over 5,700 settlements which only cover between one hundred and nine hundred and ninety-nine employees each – a total of only 1.87 million employees. These local settlements are especially prevalent in metal manufacture, engineering and vehicles and in financial and professional services. The problem of the multiplicity of bargains would not be so serious if it were obvious that there were certain 'key' bargains. The evidence (see section III.2) hints that certain regions or industries may lead the wage adjustment process, but the institutional and econometric evidence is still too scanty for any firm conclusions to be drawn.

(5) *The exceptions allowed.* The 1965-70 incomes policy permitted wage increases greater than the norm on four grounds: where there was a serious labour shortage in a particular industry, occupation or region; where the wages of a particular group of workers were 'seriously out of line' with their traditional place in the wage structure; for low paid workers; and for productivity deals. The more recent 1973-4 policy added new exceptions such as unsocial hours. The problem with exceptions is that whilst they may be necessary to give flexibility to an incomes policy they also afford a method for powerful groups to circumvent the spirit of the incomes policy.

Effectiveness of Incomes Policy: The effectiveness of an incomes policy may be judged in terms of benefits and costs. An incomes policy is bound to impose some costs on the economy in the form of a loss of allocative efficiency – it

---

1 *Incomes Data Study*, No. 90, January 1975.

distorts the price mechanism. Therefore it seems reasonable to require that an incomes policy provides some compensatory benefits: that it slows down the rate of wage and price inflation below what it would have been had no policy existed.

The accumulated evidence on the effect on wage inflation of incomes policies as they have been applied in the UK suggests very strongly that they have been ineffective. Earnings increases are reduced below what they would otherwise have been whilst the policy is in operation but as soon as it is dismantled earnings increases become greater than they would have been had no such policy ever existed.

For example a Department of Employment Working Party[1] estimated that over the years 1965, 1966 and 1967 earnings rose about 4% less than they otherwise would have done without a policy whilst in 1968 and 1969 earnings rose 4% more than they would have done had there never been a policy. The total impact of the policy was nil. This raises the question: why are incomes policies taken off? Presumably the answer is that, at least as they have been applied in the past in the UK, they become politically or economically unsustainable after a while.

This is precisely the conclusion reached in an extremely thorough study of the effect of incomes policies over the whole postwar period. The authors summarize all the recent literature and conclude 'incomes policy apparently has little effect either on the wage determination process or on the average rate of wage inflation'.[2]

An alternative method of examining the impact of pay policy is to study the dispersion in the wage structure. The evidence indicates that pay policies immediately moderate cost-push tendencies causing the structure of hourly earnings to narrow but that over time the industrial earnings structure tends to widen again as the pay policy is relaxed. It is also particularly interesting that the dispersion of the industrial earnings structure is positively related to unemployment and negatively related to inflation. This suggests that wages in the union sector are less sensitive to both unemployment and inflation than are wages in the non-union sector.

An incomes policy also distorts the allocative function of the price system. A freeze on wage rates can be overcome by higher bonuses or more overtime; or by a reduction in the standard working week whilst hours actually worked remain constant; or by having fewer men employed but each one working longer hours; or by job reclassification (up-grading). A freeze on the earnings of each individual would inhibit labour mobility and hence productivity growth, and it would discriminate against the young who are still climbing the promotional and productivity ladder. Once the policy is no longer a freeze it can more easily be overcome and it still introduces distortions. For example, one recent suggestion[3] is for a punitive tax to be levied on employers who grant wage increases in excess of the incomes policy norm. Job reclassification, bonus payments and reduced hours of work could all overcome this type of policy.

We have no measure of the loss of output which results from the inefficient use of resources caused by the incomes policy. However, evidence on the allocative inefficiencies of unions, monopolies and tariffs suggests that the resulting output

---

1 DE, *Prices and Earnings in 1951-69*, HMSO, 1971, para. 57.
2 M. Parkin *et al.*, 'The Impact of Incomes Policy on the Rate of Wage Change', in M. Parkin and M. Sumner (eds.), *op. cit.*, ch. 1.
3 S. Weintraub, 'An Incomes Policy to stop Inflation', *LBR*, No. 99, January 1971 and Liberal Party, *Election Manifesto*, 1974.

loss is very small compared to the loss of output from not using resources at all (unemployment).

Thus although the evidence so far suggests that incomes policies impose costs (in the form of allocative inefficiency) and provide no compensating benefits (in the form of a reduced rate of wage inflation) it is probably true that *if* we could get an incomes policy which reduced wage inflation for a given level of unemployment (i.e. shift the Phillips curve to the left) it would be worthwhile having such a policy: the losses due to the resulting allocative inefficiency would probably be small relative to the gains from lower unemployment.

IV   TRADE UNIONS AND INDUSTRIAL RELATIONS
IV.1   Trade Unions

At the end of 1974 there were estimated to be 11,755,000 trade union members in the UK.[1] This implies that about half the nation's employees (in employment plus unemployed) were trade union members, a significant expansion from the corresponding figure of 42% for 1964. If one compares trade union membership with the number of employees in employment one sees a rise for males from 54.5% in 1964 to 62.8% in 1974 and a rise for females from 27.0% in 1964 to 34.8% in 1974.

The number of unions is still tending to fall, down from 641 in 1964 to 491 in 1974, in spite of a small increase in 1973 that was probably the result of the 1971 Industrial Relations Act. Nevertheless in 1974 there were still seventy-seven trade unions with less than a hundred members.

In addition to those in formal trade unions many workers belong to other associations that engage in collective negotiations and bargaining, for example, many individual business concerns have what are sometimes called 'company unions'. Other workers are in industries that have Wages Councils, public bodies that are designed to reproduce many of the features of collective bargaining where trade union growth is inherently difficult.

In 1973 the New Earnings Survey for the first time gave disaggregated estimates of the number of workers covered by various types of collective agreement.[2] There is was suggested that 17% of full-time male workers and 28% of full-time female workers were not party to a collective agreement. For both sexes the service sectors, particularly the distributive trades and personal services, were heavily characterized by individual negotiation and in the manufacturing sector, clothing and footwear had relatively little collective bargaining.

Formal unionization is particularly extensive among male workers, manual workers, semi-skilled and skilled workers and workers in the manufacturing and public sectors. There are no absolutely reliable figures, but one recent study[3] suggests that membership by industry varies from 100% of workers in coal mining and the railways to around 20-25% in food and drink and clothing.

Unionization is much more limited in newer industries and in the expanding white collar trades. Even where unions have been involved in the latter sectors they have traditionally differed from those in the blue collar sectors in their aims,

1   *DEG*, November 1975, pp. 1118–19.
2   *New Earnings Survey*, 1973, pp. 176-83.
3   J. Pencavel, 'Relative Wages and Trade Unions in the UK', *EC*, May 1974.

attitudes and militancy. Recently, however, the extent of white collar organization
has been growing, as has more aggresive union behaviour.[1]

Economists tend to analyse unions by their impact on resource allocation and
wages. Other observers might argue that what is more important about unions is
their impact on work rules, consultation procedures, worker representation and
so on.[2] Even if the latter view is true, the effect of unions on wage levels and
structures is still an interesting problem.

The conventional view is that unions will be most effective (i.e. will secure
for their members large wage gains at only a small cost of reduced employment
opportunities) where two conditions hold: (1) when the demand for labour
is wage inelastic; (2) when the costs and difficulties of organization are low.
Following Marshall, the demand for labour is seen to be less wage elastic: (a) the
lower is the price elasticity of demand for the labour's output, (b) the more modest
are the technical possibilities of substitution between labour and other factors,
(c) the less available are substitute factors and (d) the lower is the proportion in
total costs of labour costs. On these grounds it is often asserted that 'craft' unions,
i.e. unions of selected artisans like printers or boiler-makers, will be more successful
in securing large wage increases for their members than will 'industrial' or 'general'
unions.[3]

The costs of successful organization are less frequently analysed but they are
highly influential in determining union strength. It is usually said that such costs
are low when the workforce in question is (a) stable and so not subject to high rates
of quits or lay-offs, (b) concentrated among relatively few employers, (c) concentrated geographically and (d) possessed of certain attitudes, sometimes labelled
'class consciousness'.

So much for a sketch of the principles of effective unionization. For Britain,
empirical work which tests these principles and investigates the actual impact of
unions on wages is still very much in its infancy.

One strand of work has concentrated on the share of national income going
to labour as a whole. Underlying this work is the view that over the years, as
union membership became more numerous, one might expect more of the national
income to have gone to labour and less to other factors. In fact, it is very difficult
to see any such relation. Labour's share has not been completely static but until
the 1960s it did seem to be broadly constant in the long run except for increases
during the two world wars.[4] In the last ten to fifteen years it seems to have been
rising again[5] but neither this recent development nor the earlier patterns seem to
be linked to changes in union membership. The same is true for other countries,
notably the USA.

The usual interpretation of these results has been as follows. Given that unions
materially benefit their own members and that labour's total share in national
income is not related to total union membership, what must have happened is
that union members gained at the expense of those not in unions. The latter, the

---

1   G. S. Bain, *The Growth of White-Collar Unionism,* Oxford, 1970.
2   See W. J. McCarthy (ed.), *Trade Unions,* Penguin, 1972.
3   For some valuable qualifications to this view, see L. Ulman, 'Marshall and Friedman on
    Union Strength', *Review of Economics & Statistics,* November 1955.
4   E. H. Phelps Brown, *Pay & Profits,* Manchester University Press, 1968.
5   A. Glyn and R. Sutcliffe, *British Capitalism, Workers and the Profits Squeeze,* Penguin,
    1972.

unorganized, broadly consist partly of the relatively well to do and partly of many of the lowest paid workers. Which of these two sub-groups has been particularly affected is not established.

This discussion naturally leads on to a consideration of the effect of unions on the wages structure across industries or occupations. For Britain there has been very little empirical work here covering much of the economy.

One recent work[1] suggests that unions only have a perceptible impact on the wage structure where local bargaining supplements bargaining at the national level, as is common in the engineering trades for example. Another study[2] uses the data on collective agreements to suggest that in 'organized' labour markets wages are maybe 25% greater than in 'unorganized' markets, other things equal. These results are tentative and do not cover the whole labour force but they are none the less interesting.

IV.2 Strikes and Industrial Relations

In 1975 just under six million working days were lost through industrial disputes,[3] roughly two hours per year per member of the labour force. Put this way the phenomenon of strikes may seem less important than many newspaper headlines suggest. After 1967 the number of days lost rose from the 1-2 million per year it had been for some time up to nearly 24 million in 1972. Since then strike losses have tended to be smaller.

Strikes vary in incidence across different firms, industries and occupations. Thus, over the period 1966-73 mining lost on average 4,300 days per year per 1,000 employees; the next most strike prone sector was vehicles with 2,100 days, followed by shipbuilding with 1,820 days; in contrast the distributive trades lost seven days per year per 1,000 workers.[4] Another feature of strike behaviour is the strong inverse relation between plant size and days lost through strikes. For manufacturing plants employing more than 1,000 workers days lost averaged 2,050 per 1,000 workers over 1971-3 compared with fifteen days per 1,000 workers in plants employing between eleven and twenty-four workers.

More generally, strikes seem more likely when inflation is rising and when unemployment is low and less likely when recent wage changes are high. Comparing different industries, strikes are more likely in those industries with relatively few female workers, extensive payments-by-results systems, rapid technical change and slowly growing wages.

Strike activity is the most heavily publicised aspect of industrial relations but by no means the most important one. It arouses considerable public comment and often provides dramatic situations with great political significance but in so doing it tends to obscure other aspects of the relationships between employer and employee which make up industrial relations. For at least the last ten to fifteen years there has been much concern over the British 'system' of industrial relations, sparked off by two principal worries.

---

1 Pencavel, *op. cit.*

2 C. Mulvey, 'Collective Agreements and Relative Earnings in UK Manufacturing in 1973', *EC*, November 1976.

3 *DEG*, January 1976, pp. 26-7.

4 *DEG*, February 1976, pp. 115-23.

First, in many sectors the traditional industry-wide collective bargaining was becoming less important. It appeared that the sustained full employment in the postwar period had made the role of shop stewards and local negotiations much more important; in many manufacturing industries local agreements were mounted on the back of industrial agreements, causing substantial wage drift. Also the majority of strikes were unofficial. Second, the postwar period has also been marked by aggregate wage settlements substantially greater than productivity changes, leading to price inflation. It was felt that the relative strength of labour compared with employers had shifted unduly in favour of the former.

This concern, coupled with certain legal judgements particularly affecting the position of individuals, led to the establishment of a Royal Commission[1] to investigate the industrial relations system. This Commission virtually ignored the second problem, despite the fact that compatibility of collective bargaining with full employment and economic growth had by then become an open question.

The Royal Commission thought that the principal problem in industrial relations was that two systems — the formal and the informal — existed. It further believed that certain industries where the conflict between the two systems was very apparent, e.g., engineering, were industries whose bargains set a pattern for others. It saw the remedy in integrating the formal and informal systems and stressed the desirability of both plant bargaining and full employer recognition of unions. However, it strongly believed that the reform should be voluntary rather than imposed by law. It recommended the establishment of a Commission on Industrial Relations, a form of investigatory tribunal, to facilitate this voluntary reform. It believed implicitly that if reform could be achieved in a few key sectors this would percolate through the rest of the system. The report was not well received by independent observers who felt that it merely pushed people in the direction they were already going anyway, and that it did little to change the ground rules of the industrial relations system or to get at the problem of excessive wage inflation.

The report resulted in action from both Labour and Conservative Governments. Labour established a Commission on Industrial Relations whose functions the Conservatives subsequently altered; on returning to power in 1974, the Labour Government abolished the Commission. In 1969-70 the Labour Government proposed additional reforms but withdrew them in the face of strong union and backbench opposition. It was left to the Conservatives to legislate substantial reform but their Industrial Relations Act (1971) had a stormy history, arousing bitter hostility in the trade union leadership, before it was repealed in an early action by the Labour Government of 1974. That action, the Trade Union and Labour Relations Act, together with the associated Trade Union and Labour Relations (Amendment) Act (1976), in many ways restored the pre-1971 situation, but in some respects the position of trade unions was further strengthened. For example, under the controversial closed shop provisions, it will no longer be unfair for an employer to dismiss employees for refusing to join a union in those situations where employers and unions have agreed to a 100% union membership provision.

In addition to these measures, the present government has introduced the Employment Protection Act (1975) which in some respects encourages union

---

1 *Royal Commission on Trade Unions and Employers' Associations 1965-68* (Donovan Report), Cmnd. 3623, HMSO, 1968.

activity. Employers now must disclose certain information judged to be relevant to collective bargaining, consult with unions on the handling of redundancies and face more pressure to recognize independent trade unions when their employees wish to be represented. This legislation also gives powers to the new Advisory, Conciliation and Arbitration Service and extends the legal rights of individual employees, e.g. in maternity pay and leave provision. The position of unions has also been strengthened by the passing of the Health and Safety at Work Act (1975) and the Industry Act (1975). The latter gives worker participation in an embryonic form by encouraging Planning Agreements, i.e. agreements between individual employers, unions and the government relating to the operations of firms. Worker participation in its fullest form is, at the time of writing, being considered by the Bullock Commission.

REFERENCES AND FURTHER READING

B. McCormick and E. Owen Smith (eds), *The Labour Market,* Penguin, 1968.

Department of Employment, *British Labour Statistics: Historical Abstract 1886-1968,* HMSO, 1971.

Department of Employment, *New Earnings Survey, 1975,* HMSO, 1976.

D. Mackay et al., *Labour Markets Under Different Employment Conditions,* Allen and Unwin, 1971.

W. J. McCarthy (ed), *Trade Unions,* Penguin, 1972.

E. H. Phelps Brown, *The Growth of British Industrial Relations,* Macmillan, 1965.

E. Hobsbawm, *Labouring Men,* Weidenfeld and Nicolson, 1968.

R. Hyman, *Strikes,* Fontana, 1972.

A. B. Atkinson, *Economics of Inequality,* Clarendon Press, 1975.

TABLE A – 1
UK De Facto or Home Population,[1] 1960-75 (thousands)

	UNITED KINGDOM			ENGLAND AND WALES			WALES	SCOTLAND			NORTHERN IRELAND		
	Total	Males	Females	Total	Males	Females	Total	Total	Males	Females	Total	Males	Females
Census Figures													
1951	50,225	24,118	26,107	43,758	21,016	22,742	2,599	5,096	2,434	2,662	1,371	668	703
1961	52,709	25,481	27,228	46,105	22,304	23,801	2,644	5,179	2,483	2,697	1,425	694	731
1971	55,515	26,952	28,562	48,750	23,683	25,067	2,731	5,229	2,515	2,714	1,536	755	781
Sample Census													
1962[2]	53,788	26,044	27,745	47,136	22,841	24,295	2,663	5,168	2,479	2,689	1,485	724	761
Mid-Year Estimates[3]													
1960	52,372	25,271	27,102	45,775	22,097	23,678	2,629	5,178	2,482	2,696	1,420	692	728
1961	52,807	25,528	27,280	46,196	22,347	23,849	2,635	5,184	2,485	2,699	1,427	696	732
1962	53,274	25,809	27,465	46,640	22,614	24,026	2,651	5,198	2,495	2,703	1,437	700	737
1963	53,552	25,951	27,602	46,901	22,746	24,155	2,660	5,205	2,500	2,705	1,447	705	741
1964	53,885	26,134	27,751	47,219	22,922	24,297	2,671	5,209	2,501	2,707	1,458	711	747
1965	54,218	26,300	27,918	47,540	23,083	24,457	2,686	5,210	2,501	2,709	1,468	716	752
1966	54,500	26,424	28,076	47,824	23,209	24,615	2,694	5,201	2,496	2,704	1,476	719	757
1967	54,800	26,565	28,235	48,113	23,343	24,770	2,701	5,198	2,496	2,702	1,489	726	763
1968	55,049	26,698	28,351	48,346	23,467	24,879	2,706	5,200	2,498	2,702	1,503	733	770
1969	55,263	26,803	28,460	48,540	23,562	24,978	2,711	5,209	2,503	2,706	1,514	739	776
1970	55,421	26,880	28,542	48,680	23,626	25,054	2,717	5,214	2,507	2,707	1,527	747	781
1971	55,610	27,000	28,610	48,854	23,737	25,117	2,724	5,217	2,507	2,710	1,538	756	782
1972	55,793	27,106	28,687	49,038	23,841	25,198	2,735	5,210	2,503	2,707	1,545	762	783
1973	55,933	27,186	28,748	49,175	23,916	25,259	2,749	5,212	2,504	2,708	1,547	766	781
1974	55,965	27,214	28,750	49,201	23,940	25,261	2,759	5,217	2,508	2,709	1,547	766	781
1975	55,962	27,232	28,730	49,219	23,968	25,251	2,765	5,206	2,504	2,702	1,537	761	777

Sources: AAS, 1975, MDS, April 1976, *Population Trends*, 3, Spring 1976.

Notes: 1 The *de facto* or home population relates to people actually in the country (excluding members of HM forces serving overseas, while including commonwealth and foreign forces in the UK).

2 Except for Northern Ireland when a full census was taken, figures are based on the 10% sample census.

3 The figures for 1962 and later years are revised estimates based on the final results of the 1971 census.

TABLE A – 2
UK Gross Domestic Product, Expenditure (at 1970 prices) 1960-75 (£m)

Year	Consumers' Expenditure Durable Goods	Consumers' Expenditure Non-Durable Goods and Services	Public Authorities Current Expenditure	Gross Domestic Capital Formation Excluding Dwellings	Gross Domestic Capital Formation Dwellings	Value of Physical Increase in Stocks and Work in Progress	Exports of Goods and Services	Total Final Expenditure at Market Prices	Imports of Goods and Services	Adjustment to Factor Cost[1]	Gross Domestic Product at Factor Cost[3]
1960	1,677[1]	23,469	7,379	4,730	1,064[2]	767	7,021	46,132	−7,399	−6,104	32,652
1961	1,613[1]	24,121	7,647	5,219	1,142[2]	369	7,241	47,368	−7,346	−6,203	33,826
1962	1,693	24,586	7,889	5,197	1,177	12	7,358	47,872	−7,498	−6,209	34,161
1963	1,962	25,465	8,014	5,254	1,204	201	7,663	49,763	−7,769	−6,465	35,529
1964	2,141	26,189	8,138	6,038	1,503	936	7,991	52,936	−8,487	−6,771	37,678
1965	2,143	26,617	8,357	6,338	1,561	614	8,372	54,002	−8,571	−6,798	38,633
1966	2,106	27,195	8,595	6,488	1,604	412	8,701	55,101	−8,780	−6,918	39,403
1967	2,214	27,655	9,075	6,990	1,781	366	8,801	56,882	−9,370	−7,115	40,397
1968	2,369	28,229	9,103	7,309	1,866	503	9,818	59,197	−10,054	−7,278	41,865
1969	2,221	28,494	8,960	7,405	1,786	448	10,739	60,053	−10,358	−7,252	42,443
1970	2,401	29,071	9,095	7,737	1,643	425	11,275	61,647	−10,887	−7,533	43,227
1971	2,838	29,558	9,369	7,792	1,752	70	12,065	63,444	−11,413	−7,817	44,214
1972	3,376	30,968	9,716	7,883	1,871	−18	12,324	66,120	−12,732	−8,416	44,972
1973	3,595	32,299	10,118	8,251	1,757	1,064	13,737	70,821	−14,454	−8,973	47,394
1974	3,089	32,432	10,413	8,132	1,673	597	14,682	71,018	−14,484	−8,904	47,630
1975	2,954	32,459	10,760	7,994	1,766	−652	14,014	69,295	−13,659	−8,775	46,861

Sources: NIBB, 1964-1974, 1971; ET (Annual Supplement) 1975, ET, April 1976.

Notes: 1 Adjustment to factor cost represents taxes on expenditure less subsidies valued at constant rates.

2 Figures for 1960-61 have been converted to a 1970 base from the series at 1963 prices published in NIBB, 1971.

3 For years, 1960-62 the value of GDP differs from the sum of its components because the various items have been separately linked to the later series based on 1970 prices. See NIBB, 1964-74, p. 104. The extent of the adjustment between the sum of the main components and the estimate of GDP at factor cost is as follows (£m):−

	1960	1961	1962
	+48	+23	−44

TABLE A – 3
UK Personal Income, Expenditure and Saving 1960-75 (£m)

PERSONAL INCOME BEFORE TAX

Year	Wages and Salaries	Forces Pay	Employers Contribu- tions	Current Grants from Public Author- ities[1]	Other Personal Income	Total[2]	Transfers (net) and Taxes Paid Abroad	UK Taxes on Income (Payments)
	1	2	3	4	5	6	7	8
1960	13,735	393	1,046	1,569	4,360	21,103	−1	1,961
1961	14,855	385	1,167	1,708	4,693	22,808	−3	2,214
1962	15,640	401	1,265	1,881	4,882	24,069	−4	2,430
1963	16,395	419	1,381	2,128	5,227	25,550	23	2,480
1964	17,765	450	1,504	2,250	5,596	27,565	29	2,751
1965	19,115	467	1,714	2,596	6,165	30,057	27	3,297
1966	20,370	523	1,902	2,825	6,545	32,165	42	3,689
1967	21,140	524	2,054	3,189	6,922	33,829	64	4,069
1968	22,515	542	2,300	3,679	7,442	36,478	77	4,524
1969	24,110	539	2,433	3,937	8,047	39,066	71	5,139
1970	26,830	658	2,773	4,336	8,586	43,183	57	5,850
1971	29,685	758	3,057	4,784	9,501	47,790	35	6,424
1972	33,050	862	3,573	5,843	10,785	54,113	79	6,642
1973	37,970	928	4,284	6,403	12,886	62,471	115	7,807
1974	45,840	1,078	5,492	7,827	14,971	75,208	121	10,461
1975	58,915	1,296	7,593	10,160	6,971	94,935	122	15,265

Sources: *NIBB, 1964-1974; Economic Trends (Annual Supplement), 1975; ET,* April 1976.

Notes: 1 The figures exclude the net cost to public authorities of school meals, milk and welfare foods provided free or at subsidised prices, also expenditure on legal aid. These are now included in public authorities' current expenditure on goods and services.

2 Before providing for depreciation and stock appreciation.

3 Before providing for additions to tax reserves.

Column 6 = 1 + 2 + 3 + 4 + 5.

Column 10 = 6 − 7 − 8 − 9.

Column 13 = 14 − 11.

Column 15 = 10 − 14.

National Insurance and Health con- tributions	Total Personal Dispos- able Income[3]	CONSUMERS' EXPENDITURE					PERSONAL SAVINGS		
		Durable Goods		Other					
		Amount £m	as % of P.D.I.	Amount £m	Total		Amount £m	As % of P.D.I.	Year
9	10	11	12	13	14		15	16	
913	18,230	1,400	7.7	15,533	16,933		1,297	7.1	1960
1,072	19,525	1,351	6.9	16,484	17,835		1,690	8.7	1961
1,197	20,438	1,419	6.9	17,504	18,923		1,515	7.4	1962
1,303	21,744	1,588	7.3	18,530	20,118		1,626	7.5	1963
1,444	23,341	1,755	7.5	19,722	21,477		1,864	8.0	1964
1,685	25,048	1,785	7.1	21,079	22,864		2,184	8.7	1965
1,804	26,630	1,775	6.7	22,471	24,246		2,384	9.0	1966
1,909	27,787	1,909	6.9	23,538	25,447		2,340	8.4	1967
2,165	29,712	2,142	7.2	25,233	27,375		2,337	7.9	1968
2,244	31,612	2,083	6.6	26,950	29,033		2,579	8.2	1969
2,654	34,622	2,401	6.9	29,071	31,472		3,150	9.1	1970
2,835	38,496	3,060	7.9	32,033	35,093		3,403	8.8	1971
3,333	44,059	3,756	8.5	35,918	39,674		4,385	10.0	1972
3,930	50,619	4,176	8.2	40,909	45,085		5,534	10.9	1973
4,986	59,640	4,080	6.8	47,427	51,507		8.133	13.6	1974
6,810	72,738	4,874	6.7	57,775	62,649		10,089	13.9	1975

TABLE A – 4
Great Britain, Working Population, Unemployment, etc. 1960-75 (thousands)

Year	Total in Civil Employment[1]	Estimated Number of Employees[2]			Registered Unemployment (MONTHLY AVERAGES)[2] A	Unfilled Vacancies[3] B	Unemployment Rate[4]	
		Total	Males	Females			Total %	Males %
1960	23,711	22,333	14,413	7,920	345.8	313.8 —	1.5	1.7
1961	24,044	22,627	14,564	8,064	312.1	320.3 —	1.4	1.6
1962	24,232	22,944	14,757	8,187	431.9	213.7 —	1.9	2.2
1963	24,250	23,063	14,832	8,231	520.6	196.3 —	2.3	2.7
1964	24,527	23,209	14,851	8,358	372.2	317.2 —	1.6	1.9
1965	24,770	23,417	14,929	8,488	317.0	384.4 —	1.4	1.6
1966	24,914	23,554	14,903	8,651	330.9	370.9 —	1.4	1.7
1966	24,396	23,040	14,750	8,291	330.9	370.9 —	1.4	1.8
1967	24,036	22,813	14,592	8,221	521.0	249.7 —	2.3	2.9
1968	23,899	22,692	14,442	8,250	549.4	271.3 —	2.4	3.2
1969	23,931	22,631	14,306	8,325	543.8	284.8 —	2.4	3.2
1970	23,825	22,517	14,156	8,360	582.2	259.6 —	2.6	3.5
1971	23,490	22,335	14,013	8,322	751.7	176.1 —	3.4	4.5
1972	23,485	22,415	13,966	8,450	835.0	189.3 —	3.7	5.0
1973	24,066	22,727	13,939	8,789	587.7	397.7 —	2.6	3.5
1974	24,161	22,812	13,803	9,008	585.2	298.8 94.6	2.6	3.6
1975	24,002	22,966	13,858	9,108	935.7	147.1 32.5	4.1	5.4

Sources: British Labour Statistics: *Historical Abstract 1886-1968; AAS 1975, 1973, 1971; MDS*, March 1975, December 1975, April 1976; *DEG*, May 1976.

Notes: 1 This column consists of total estimated employees plus employers and self employed persons less unemployed. It excludes members of HM Forces.

2 For years 1960 to 1966 based on Insurance Card count. From 1966 to 1975 (below line) based on Census of Employment. The figures include registered unemployed but exclude employers and self employed. Part-time workers are counted as equivalent to whole-time workers.

3 For 1960 to 1973 column A relates to total vacancies. For 1974 and 1975 column A relates to vacancies notified to employment offices and column B to vacancies notified to careers offices. Columns A and B should not be added because of duplication in the series. All figures are monthly averages and cannot be compared directly with the series based on June each year. Figures for 1974 are averages of 11 months.

4 The unemployment rate is obtained by dividing the relevant monthly average unemployment figure by the relevant total employees (including unemployed) for the June of that year.

TABLE A – 5

UK Money Supply, Domestic Credit Expansion and Public Sector Borrowing Requirements (£m), 1960-75

Year	Money Supply (M_3)[1]	Change in Money Supply (M_3)[2]	External Financing of Public Sector	Other Bank Transactions	Domestic Credit Expansion[4]	Net Private Residents Lending to Public Sector[3]	Other Bank Liabilities	Bank Lending to Private Sector	Public Sector Borrowing Requirements[5]
	1	2	3	4	5	6	7	8	9
1960	10,077	182	-119	322	385	1,082	260	695	710
1961	10,339	262	117	134	513	510	73	258	704
1962	10,614	275	-330	330	275	831	283	513	546
1963	11,516	765	103	234	1,102	594	116	736	842
1964	12,155	653	656	254	1,563	504	175	999	989
1965	13,083	938	96	111	1,145	486	193	508	1,205
1966	13,555	479	413	-178	714	262	-141	52	961
1967	15,003	1,345	502	-45	1,802	665	-16	634	1,862
1968	16,092	1,152	1,111	-262	2,001	-13	-246	725	1,279
1969	16,596	503	-594	-57	-148	355	-133	597	-466
1970	18,175	1,586	-1,353	808	1,041	101	963	1,315	-18
1971	20,541	2,366	-2,670	1,445	1,141	2,102	1,429	1,856	1,371
1972	26,245	5,299	1,564	15	6,878	1,005	604	6,434	2,038
1973	33,478	7,232	-108	1,490	8,614	1,984	1,896	6,828	4,176
1974	37,698	4,221	1,490	1,929	7,640	3,456	1,860	4,671	6,356
1975	40,543	2,871	714	1,306	4,891	5,546	1,564	231	10,464

Sources: *Bank of England Statistical Abstract No. 1 1970, No. 2, 1975; Financial Statistics,* May 1976, February 1976, 1975, 1974, 1973, 1972; *Economic Trends (Annual Supplement),*1975; *Supplement to BEQB,* September 1969.

Notes: 1 M_3 is a wide definition of the money supply that includes currency in circulation with the public sector and resident private sector deposits on current and deposit account with all banks, the National Giro and discount houses, less items in transit. Totals given in column 1 are estimates of the amount outstanding at the end of each year.

2 Figures relates to the sums of quarterly changes in M_3 (unadjusted as given in *Financial Statistics*). Because of slight differences in statistical coverage the annual change in M_3 in column 2 may not be identical with the first difference in M_3 as derived from column 1.

3 The public sector is defined as the central government, local authorities and public corporations.

4 Column 5 = 2 + 3 + 4.

5 Column 9 = 2 + 3 + 6 + 7 − 8.

TABLE A – 6

UK Public Sector: Current Account 1959-74 (£m)

	1959	1960	1961	1962	1963
RECEIPTS					
TAXES ON INCOME	2,747	2,713	3,066	3,447	3,379
TAXES ON EXPENDITURE:					
Central Government	2,486	2,620	2,796	2,963	3,013
Local Authorities[1]	714	771	831	916	1,014
NATIONAL INSURANCE & HEALTH					
CONTRIBUTIONS	897	913	1,072	1,197	1,303
GROSS TRADING SURPLUS					
Central Government & Local Authorities	164	179	96	84	92
Public Corporations	391	534	639	745	840
RENT	398	442	491	528	556
INTEREST & DIVIDENDS ETC.					
Central Government	88	70	88	96	92
Local Authorities	34	37	40	48	52
Public Corporations	36	44	48	49	35
TOTAL	7,955	8,323	9,167	10,073	10,376
EXPENDITURE					
Current Expenditure on Goods & Services[2]	4,001	4,252	4,579	4,916	5,176
Subsidies	369	487	586	608	569
Current Grants to Persons	1,555	1,569	1,708	1,881	2,128
Current Grants Paid Abroad	82	94	118	121	132
TOTAL CURRENT EXPENDITURE					
EXCLUDING DEBT INTEREST	6,007	6,402	6,991	7,526	8,005
Debt Interest					
Central Government	774	857	893	874	930
Local Authorities	139	164	211	240	269
Public Corporations	151	144	153	143	87
TOTAL CURRENT EXPENDITURE	7,071	7,567	8,248	8,783	9,291
CURRENT SURPLUS[3]	884	756	919	1,290	1,085
TOTAL	7,955	8,323	9,167	10,073	10,376

Sources: NIBB, 1970, 1971, 1972, 1973, 1963-1973, 1964-1974.
Notes: 1 Rates.
      2 Excluding current expenditure on goods and services on operating accounts of public corporations and other public enterprises.
      3 Before providing for depreciation and stock appreciation and additions to tax and interest reserves.

1964	1965	1966	1967	1968	1969	1970	1971	1972	1973	1974
3,522	4,021	4,419	5,083	5,633	6,335	7,410	7,970	8,118	9,110	12,131
3,341	3,734	4,053	4,537	5,270	6,122	6,609	6,722	6,906	7,467	8,360
1,096	1,228	1,373	1,467	1,548	1,667	1,824	2,087	2,377	2,617	2,991
1,444	1,685	1,804	1,909	2,165	2,244	2,654	2,835	3,333	3,930	4,986
104	112	106	110	132	153	151	175	144	136	119
924	988	1,042	1,132	1,363	1,451	1,447	1,520	1,679	2,059	2,426
604	677	751	817	917	1,055	1,190	1,272	1,389	1,660	1,948
94	115	117	119	92	104	130	173	228	162	283
59	70	84	92	96	103	109	118	129	179	272
39	48	55	57	79	95	104	102	107	222	275
11,227	12,678	13,805	15,323	17,295	19,329	21,628	22,974	24,410	27,542	33,791
5,505	6,041	6,572	7,272	7,727	8,088	9,095	10,353	11,776	13,340	16,641
516	574	572	815	910	855	900	936	1,175	1,526	2,944
2,250	2,596	2,825	3,189	3,679	3,937	4,336	4,784	5,843	6,403	7,850
163	177	180	188	179	177	176	205	208	360	321
8,434	9,388	10,149	11,464	12,495	13,057	14,507	16,278	19,002	21,629	27,756
937	968	1,036	1,105	1,240	1,280	1,298	1,384	1,599	1,801	2,117
320	380	429	468	554	649	728	705	717	901	1,209
97	108	88	138	113	120	119	124	122	244	406
9,788	10,844	11,702	13,175	14,402	15,106	16,652	18,491	21,440	24,575	31,488
1,439	1,834	2,103	2,148	2,893	4,223	4,976	4,483	2,970	2,967	2,303
11,227	12,678	13,805	15,323	17,295	19,329	21,628	22,974	24,410	27,542	33,791

TABLE A – 7

UK Balance of Payments 1960-75 (£m)

CURRENT ACCOUNT

	Visible Trade			Invisibles			
Year	Exports (f.o.b.)	Imports[2] (f.o.b.)	Visible Balance	Government Services and Transfers (net)	Private Services and Transfers (net)	Interest Profits and Dividends (net)	Invisible Balance
	1	2	3	4	5	6	7
1960	3,737	4,138	−401	−282	205	233	156
1961	3,903	4,043	−140	−332	240	254	162
1962	4,003	4,103	−100	−360	254	334	228
1963	4,295	4,375	−80	−382	195	398	211
1964	4,521	5,021	−500	−432	184	393	145
1965	4,848	5,071	−223	−447	208	435	196
1966	5,203	5,269	−66	−470	250	387	167
1967	5,139	5,693	−554	−463	340	379	256
1968	6,282	6,949	−667	−466	528	335	397
1969	7,075	7,232	−157	−467	585	499	617
1970	7,907	7,932	−25	−485	688	557	760
1971	8,810	8,530	280	−527	794	511	778
1972	9,141	9,843	−702	−564	819	578	833
1973	11,772	14,104	−2,332	−798	898	1,390	1,490
1974	15,895	21,109	−5,264	−880	1,166	1,328	1,614
1975	18,772	21,972	−3,200	−997	1,223	1,272	1,498

Sources: *United Kingdom Balance of Payments, 1971, 1972, 1973, 1963-1973, 1964-1974;*
ET, March 1976.

Notes: 1 For items relating to capital flows a + sign means an increase in liabilities or a
decrease in assets, whilst a − sign means an increase in assets or a decrease in
liabilities.

2 Including payments for US Military Aircraft and Missiles.

3 Figures for 1967 and 1968 include EEA losses on forwards.

4 For most years the total of 'official financing' is the negative of the 'total currency
flow' with the sign of 'official financing' interpreted as in note 1. The two items
differ to the extent of gold subscriptions to the IMF and allocations of SDR's.

INVESTMENT AND OTHER CAPITAL FLOWS[1]

Current Balance	Official Long-Term Capital	Overseas long-term Investment in UK Private and Public Sectors	UK Private Long-Term Investment Overseas	Other Capital Flows, Mainly Short-Term	Total Investment and Other Capital Flows	Balancing Item	Total Currency Flow[3]	Official Financing[4]
8	9	10	11	12	13	14	15	16
−245	−103	228	−322	483	286	284	325	−293
22	−45	420	−313	−378	−316	−45	−339	339
128	−107	243	−242	103	−3	67	192	−192
131	−105	270	−320	56	−99	−90	−58	58
−355	−116	158	−399	56	−301	−39	−695	695
−27	−85	226	−368	−99	−326	—	−353	353
101	−81	299	−303	−493	−578	−70	−547	591
−298	−59	414	−456	−394	−495	227	−671	671
−270	17	583	−727	−628	−755	−134	−1,410	1,410
460	−99	673	−679	−4	−109	392	743	−743
735	−204	828	−789	735	570	−18	1,287	−1,420
1,058	−273	1,231	−834	1,770	1,894	276	3,228	−3,353
131	−255	865	−1,409	87	−712	−684	−1,265	1,141
−842	−252	1,939	−1,863	1,083	907	204	210	−210
−3,650	−275	2,950	−1,130	1,252	2,797	363	−565	565
−1,702	−251	1,862	−1,937	−84	−410	1,020	−1,092	1,092

TABLE A – 8

UK Reserves, External Liabilities in Sterling and Related Figures, 1960-75 (end period) £m

| Year | Gold Convertible Currency and SDRs | Total | Overseas Sterling Holdings (net) 1960-2 and External Liabilities 1962-75[1] | | | | | British Government Stocks Held by CMI[2,3] | Exchange Reserves in Sterling[4] | IMF Holdings of Sterling |
| | | | International Organizations Excluding IMF | All Countries | | Sterling Area Countries[5] | | | | |
				CMI[2]	Other	CMI[2]	Other			
1960	1,154	3,910	27	2,528	1,355	2,029	449	–	–	522
1961	1,185	3,608	62	2,537	1,009	2,097	534	–	–	896
1962	1,002	3,589	88	2,431	1,070	2,056	619	–	–	517
1962	1,002	2,819	86	1,182	1,551	766	823	1,044	2,312	517
1963	949	3,084	101	1,321	1,662	911	874	1,018	2,440	552
1964	827	3,053	104	1,245	1,704	894	931	1,087	2,436	881
1965	1,073	3,001	98	1,147	1,756	868	985	1,073	2,318	1,377
1966	1,107	2,951	109	1,158	1,684	849	1,030	1,037	2,304	1,538
1967	1,123	2,705	89	1,028	1,588	783	1,002	985	2,102	1,439
1968	1,009	2,419	105	854	1,460	712	984	961	1,920	1,965
1969	1,053	2,443	94	942	1,407	842	936	1,283	2,319	1,950
1970	1,178	2,839	96	1,070	1,673	968	1,111	1,381	2,547	1,929
1971	2,526	4,206	101	1,723	2,382	1,442	1,480	1,416	3,240	1,374
1972	2,167	4,337	139	1,907	2,291	1,718	1,319	1,572	3,618	1,132
1973	2,237	4,417	182	1,951	2,284	1,492	971	1,556	3,689	1,189
1974	2,345	6,081	237	3,344	2,500	–	–	1,053	4,634	1,143
1975	1,875	6,189	266	2,694	3,229	–	–	1,121	4,081	1,089

Sources: *UK Balance of Payments, 1966, 1972, 1973, 1964-74; ET,* March 1976.

Notes:

1 The series 'overseas sterling holdings' was discontinued in 1962 and replaced by a new series 'external liabilities and claims in sterling'. The latter series was revised in 1971 to become 'external banking and money market liabilities in sterling' which is the series shown above for 1962-75. For changes in definitions and coverage see *Pink Books,* especially *1964* and *1971.* From 1962 to 1975 the column for 'British Government Stocks' should be added to the column headed 'Total' to give the grand total of liabilities in sterling. There is a series break at 1973 in columns marked with a bar.

2 CMI = Central Monetary Institutions.

3 For this column only CMI includes International Organizations (excluding the IMF). Holdings of International Organizations are relatively small. See *Pink Books* for details.

4 'Exchange Reserves in Sterling' is the sum of 'British Government Stocks' and external liabilities to CMI's. It excludes any sterling counterpart of official short- and medium- term borrowing.

5 After 1973 the 'Sterling Area' Classification is abandoned in the sources from which this Table is derived. For 1973 Ireland is excluded from the Sterling Area. The new area analysis is too detailed for inclusion here and reference should be made to the *Pink Book* and *ET* for information.

TABLE A – 9

UK External Trade, 1960-75

Year	Value of the External Trade of UK (£m)				Volume Index Numbers 1970 = 100[4]				Unit Value Index Numbers 1970 = 100[4]				Terms of Trade[6]
	Imports (c.i.f.)[1]		Exports (f.o.b.)[2],[3]		Imports		Exports		Imports		Exports		
	Total	Manufac-tures	Total	Manufac-tures	Total (weight=1000)	Manufac-tures (weight=506)	Total (weight=1000)	Manufac-tures (weight=844)	Total (weight=1000)	Manufac-tures (weight=506)	Total (weight=1000)	Manufac-tures (weight=844)	
1960	4,655	1,522	3,789	3,104	66	47	63[5]	63[5]	79	73	74[5]	71[5]	93
1961	4,546	1,531	3,955	3,256	65	47	65	65	77	72	74	72	96
1962	4,628	1,556	4,062	3,336	67	49	66	66	77	71	74	72	96
1963	4,983	1,702	4,365	3,568	69	52	70	69	79	73	77	75	97
1964	5,696	2,161	4,565	3,773	77	63	72	72	81	75	78	76	96
1965	5,751	2,253	4,901	4,095	78	64	76	76	81	77	80	79	99
1966	5,949	2,471	5,255	4,390	79	68	78	78	82	79	83	82	101
1967	6,437	2,844	5,230	4,386	85	76	78	77	83	80	84	83	102
1968	7,897	3,772	6,434	5,413	94	89	88	88	93	92	91	90	98
1969	8,315	4,137	7,339	6,256	95	94	98	99	96	95	94	93	98
1970	9,037	4,572	8,061	6,806	100	100	100	100	100	100	100	100	100
1971	9,821	5,003	9,181	7,825	105	110	109	110	105	101	106	105	101
1972	11,143	6,093	9,759	8,257	116	131	111	112	109	105	111	111	102
1973	15,852	8,909	12,505	10,455	133	159	127	128	138	127	126	124	91
1974	23,283	11,928	16,600	13,685	134	166	133	135	210	167	161	155	77
1975	24,163	12,805	19,929	16,464	124	155	130	130	236	189	198	193	84

Sources: *AAS, 1968 to 1975; TI,* 11 October 1973, 25 November 1975; *MDS,* April 1976.

Notes:
1 Import figures differ from those in Table A-7 because of the inclusion of charges for insurance and freight. Apart from this, both series will differ because of certain adjustments made for valuation and coverage. Further explanation is given in the *UK Balance of Payments 1964-74.*

2 Export figures do not contain any allowance for the under-recording of exports, and differ from figures in Table A-7 on account of this and other coverage adjustments.

3 Export figures include re-exports which are no longer separately distinguished in the trade statistics.

4 Overseas Trade Statistics basis. Figures for 1960-62 kindly supplied by DTI.

5 Export indices for 1960 exclude re-exports.

6 Export unit value index expressed as a percentage of the import unit value index.

TABLE A – 10

Productivity in UK 1960-75: Index Numbers[1] 1970 = 100

Year	Output per Person Employed			Output per Man-Hour Worked
	Gross Domestic Product	Total Industrial Production	Manufacturing Industries	Manufacturing
1960[2]	78.3	73.3	74.1	70.1
1961[2]	78.9	73.3	73.4	70.1
1962	79.7	74.2	74.3	72.1
1963	82.2	77.6	78.2	75.9
1964	85.8	82.5	83.8	80.7
1965	87.5	84.1	85.4	83.3
1966	88.8	85.8	86.9	86.2
1967	91.7	89.2	90.0	89.9
1968	96.0	96.0	96.9	96.0
1969	97.8	98.3	99.3	99.1
1970	100.0	100.0	100.0	100.0
1971	103.4	103.6	102.9	105.0
1972	105.4	108.5	109.3	112.0
1973	109.3	115.0	117.7	118.3
1974	108.0	111.1	113.8	117.7
1975	107.8	109.3	111.7	116.0

Sources: *NIER,* February 1972, November 1973, May 1975, May 1976.

Notes: 1   Figures for 1960-3 may not be strictly comparable with figures for later years because of adjustment to the employment data from 1964 onwards.

        2   These figures were not available at the 1970 base and have been calculated from the same series based on 1963 = 100.

TABLE A – 11

UK Prices, 1960-75: Index Numbers 1970 = 100

Year	RETAIL PRICES	CONSUMER GOODS AND SERVICES							
		Total	Food	Drink and Tobacco	Housing (incl. rent and rates)	Durable Goods	Clothing	All Other Goods[1]	Services
1960[2]	67.2	67.4	73.2	63.8	53.8	83.8	78.7	66.0	62.3
1961[2]	69.5	69.4	74.3	66.7	56.4	84.1	79.9	68.6	64.8
1962	72.5	72.0	76.9	70.5	59.9	83.8	82.3	70.4	67.3
1963	73.9	73.4	78.2	71.4	64.1	80.9	83.5	72.2	69.2
1964	76.3	75.9	80.4	75.5	68.0	82.0	84.4	74.3	71.6
1965	80.0	79.5	83.2	82.8	72.5	83.3	86.5	78.1	74.8
1966	83.1	82.7	85.9	85.4	78.2	84.3	88.8	81.1	79.0
1967	85.2	85.2	87.6	86.6	82.1	86.2	90.1	83.4	82.9
1968	89.2	89.5	90.3	89.5	87.0	90.4	91.5	89.6	88.7
1969	94.0	94.5	95.3	96.2	92.4	93.8	95.0	94.8	93.9
1970	100.0	100.0	100.0	100.0	100.0	100.0	100.0	100.0	100.0
1971	109.4	108.3	109.4	104.2	110.1	107.8	106.7	108.0	110.1
1972	117.2	115.5	117.2	107.5	124.1	111.3	114.1	113.8	118.3
1973	128.0	125.6	131.9	110.6	142.1	116.2	124.9	119.9	131.4
1974	148.5	145.0	153.5	125.4	161.4	132.1	147.3	143.8	146.5
1975	184.4	176.9	188.4	158.2	187.9	165.0	168.3	180.7	177.0

Sources: ET (Annual Supplement) 1975;. NIER, April 1976 (Retail Prices only); NIER, February 1972, November 1973, May 1974, May 1976.

Notes: 1 Includes fuel and light.

2 Converted to 1970 base from earlier series based on 1963 = 100.

TABLE A – 12

Wages, Earnings and Salaries in UK, 1960-75: Index Numbers 1970 = 100

	ALL INDUSTRIES					
Year	Weekly rates of wages	Hourly rates of wages	Average weekly earnings	Average real weekly earnings[1]	Average salary earnings[2]	Average real salary earnings[1]
1960	61.3[3]	56.3[3]	53.2[3]	79.2	55.6	82.7
1961	63.9[3]	59.9[3]	56.4[3]	81.2	58.4	84.0
1962	66.2	62.7	58.5	80.7	61.8	85.2
1963	68.6	65.0	60.8	82.3	65.1	88.1
1964	71.5	68.4	65.1	85.3	68.7	90.0
1965	74.6	72.6	70.0	87.5	74.6	93.2
1966	78.0	77.4	74.5	89.7	77.9	93.7
1967	81.0	80.5	77.0	90.4	81.4	95.5
1968	86.4	86.1	83.2	93.3	86.6	97.1
1969	91.0	90.8	89.7	95.4	93.4	99.4
1970	100.0	100.0	100.0	100.0	100.0	100.0
1971	112.9	113.2	111.3	101.7	112.4	102.7
1972	127.9	128.4	125.1	106.7	125.4	107.0
1973	145.4	146.5	142.5	111.3	138.7	108.4
1974	173.1	174.7	167.5	112.8	156.8	105.6
1975	224.5	226.8	212.3	115.1	202.9	110.0

Sources: *NIER,* February 1972, November 1973, November 1975, February 1976, May 1976; *DEG,* December 1975, February 1976, April 1976.

Notes: 1   These are derived by deflating the indices for money earnings and salaries by the Retail Price Index from Table A – 11.

     2   This index is compiled annually, in October before 1970 and in April since 1970. All index numbers in the column are related to April 1970 = 100. The index for October 1970 on the same base is 105.9. For 1975 a new series refers to full-time adults, the 1974 index number on the new basis is 157.0.

    3   These figures were converted to a 1970 base from earlier figures based on 1963 = 100.

Index

Employment Protection Act, 1975, 269, 294
energy, EEC policy, 196
  UK consumption, 194–7
Engineering Employers Federation, 284
ENI, 200
Equal Opportunities Commission, 269
Equal Pay Act, 1970, 268, 269
Equity Bank (proposed), 233
equity share capital, 67
estate duty, 104, 251–2
estate returns, 250
euro-currency business, 81
Eurodollar market, 158, 160, 162
European Agricultural Guidance and
    Guarantee Fund (EAGGF), 193
European Atomic Energy Community
    (Euratom), 196, 197
European Coal and Steel Community (ECSC),
    174, 196, 207–8, 222
European Commission, 174, 196, 207, 218
European Court of Justice, 207, 218
European Economic Community (EEC),
  agricultural policies, 172, 173, 174,
    192–4
  competition and consumer protection,
    217–19
  effect on monetary and fiscal policies,
    112–13
  monetary union, 112–13, 174–5
  and nationalization, 206–8
  output growth, 190–1
  regional policies, 219, 226–7
  taxation and, 99, 102, 105–6
  trade concessions to USA, 180
  transport policy, 199
  UK investment in, 168, 169
  UK's membership of, 148, 171–5
  UK trade with, 129, 130, 137, 172
European Free Trade Area (EFTA), 129, 130,
    137, 146
European Investment Bank, 222, 226
European Monetary Cooperation Fund, 113
Evans, H. P., 32n
exchange control, 140, 141, 162
Exchange Control Act, 1947, 141, 169
Exchange Equalisation Account, 65, 93, 141,
    144
exchange market, framework of, 139–42
exchange rates,
  adjustment reforms, 178
  and balance of payments, 42, 55, 124–5,
    142–7, 153–60
  definition, 60n
  devaluation, 26
  effect on exports, 13
  fixed, 60, 106, 107, 142–5, 166
  floating, 57, 60, 153–60, 166–7, 181–3
  gold exchange standard, 176–8, 183–4
  and import prices, 42
  inflation and, 54
  influence on capital gains, 120

and long-term capital flow, 166–7
  managed floating, 181–3
  monetary and fiscal policies and, 60
  and short-term capital flow, 161
  speculation and, 155–6, 161
  system reform, 175–81
Exchequer, 66, 67
excise taxes, *see* customs and excise duties
expenditure, fluctuations in, 8–14
  and gross domestic product, 4, 5, 6, 7
  growth rate, 13
expenditure switching policies, 146, 148,
    160, 174
exports, 6, 23, 54, 307
  devaluation and, 148–52
  to the EEC, 129, 130, 137, 172
  fluctuations in, 13
  forecasting, 32
  and GDP, 116
  indirect tax rebates, 146
  and national income, 117
  to OPEC states, 159
  and par-value system, 142
  relative price of, 135
  to slow growing markets, 137
  trade structure, 129, 130–1
  UK's declining share of, 134–7
  value added tax and, 102
  volume and value of, 131–4
external accounts, structure of UK's, 118–24,
    141
external liabilities, 306

factor cost adjustment, 6, 23–4
Fair, D. E., 156n
Fair Trading Act, 1973, 208, 214, 215, 216
family allowances, 271
Family Income Supplement (FIS), 271–2,
    273, 276, 277
Farm Fund, 194
Farrell, M. J., 15n
Fearn, H. A., 173n
Federal Reserve System, 112
Ferranti, 233
Field, F., 271n, 273n, 275n, 276n
Finance Acts, 93
  1961, 93
  1971, 97
  1972, 220
  1974, 97
  1975, 104
finance houses, 81–3
Financial Statement and Budget Report, 32,
    35
Financial Times, 21
Finer Committee, 273 and n
firms,
  size, 229, 230–2
  structural reorganization, 231–2
  theories of behaviour, 186–8
  see also industry

profit maximization, 186, 187
and competition, 208, 209, 210
profits, and investment, 20, 21
Pryke, R., 202n
Psacharopoulos, G., 259n
Public Expenditure to 1979–80 (Cmnd. 6393),
1976, 54, 55
public sector debt ratio, 72, 73
public transport, 197–9
public utilities growth rate, 191
purchase tax, 30, 93, 102
Purdy, D., 279n
pyramid selling, 216

Radcliffe Committee, 108 and n
railways, 197–9, 207
employment, 243
Rajan, A. H., 137n
Ray, G. F., 136n, 137n
Reddaway, W. B., 166n, 263 and n
redundancy payments, 12
Rees, R. D., 264n
Regeneration of British Industry (Cmnd.
5710), 1974, 234
regional development grants, 99–100, 101,
227
Regional Development Rebate Fund, 226–7
regional employment premium (REP), 221,
222, 226, 227
regional policies, 219–27
EEC and, 219, 226–7
unemployment and, 219–20, 225, 283–4
Registrar of Restrictive Practices, 215
Renault, 200
Renton, G. A., 59n
Resale Practices Act, 1964, 214, 215
resale price maintenance, 215
Research and Development (R and D), 219,
227, 228–9, 234
reserve assets, accepting houses, 80
Bank of England, 67, 69–70
clearing banks, 76, 77–8
discount houses, 72
finance houses, 82
reserve ratio, uniform, 62, 64, 68, 70
reserves, 67, 68–70, 306
resident sterling, 141
Restrictive Practices Court, 215
restrictive trade practices, 208, 209–10,
214–15, 216–17, 218
Restrictive Trade Practices Acts, 1956 and
1968, 214, 215, 217
retail price index, 37, 38
Rhodes, J., 226n
Rhomberg, R., 133n
Richardson, H., 219n
Richardson, R., 245n, 264n
Riley, C. J., 32n
road transport, 197–9
Roberts, J., 239n
Robinson, D., 270 and n

Robinson, Joan, 33n, 35n
Rolls Royce, 200, 233
Rosendale, P. B., 150n
Ross, A., 280n
Routh, G., 261n
Rowley, C. K., 217n
Roy, A. D., 32n
Royal Commission on Distribution of Income
and Wealth, 250n, 252, 256, 260
Royal Commission on Trade Unions and
Employers' Associations, 1965–68, 294
rubber industry, 191

salaries, *see* wages
Sargan, J. D., 286 and n
Sargent Florence, P., 186n
Saving, T. R., 58n
savings, capital gains tax and, 98
personal, 85, 253, 298–9
ratio to personal disposable income, 15–16,
17, 41
Sawers, D., 210n, 229n
Sawyer, M., 264n
scale economies, 230–2
Schaus Memorandum, 199
Scherer, F. M., 228n, 229n, 231n
Schumpeter, J., 210n
Scotland, regional policies for, 221, 225
Scottish clearing banks, 64, 67, 68, 75n
Scottish Transport Group, 206
securities, government, 62, 66, 67, 72, 85, 87,
88, 92, 97
non-government, 67, 86, 87
Select Committee on Tax-Credit, 96
Select Committee on the Nationalized Indus-
tries, 205
Selective Employment Tax (SET), 102, 146,
221, 223
self employed, 238
seller concentration, in UK markets, 211–14
Sex Discrimination Act, 1975, 269
Shepherd, J. R., 24n, 32n
Shepherd, W. G., 213n
shipbuilding industry, 200, 219, 233
Shorey, J., 264n
sickness benefit, 3, 271, 272, 273, 274
sight deposits, 75
Silberston, Z. A., 230n
Simon, H. A., 187n, 231n
Sloan, B., 265n
Smith, Adam, 260
Smithsonian parities, 153, 180, 181
'snake in the tunnel' scheme, 175n
Social Contract, 287
Social Dividend, 275
Social Fund, 226
social service benefits, 3, 255–6, 271–4, 275
Somers, G., 280n
South Africa, 167
Soviet Union, 129